BEING JEWISH TODAY

BEING JEWISH TODAY

Confronting The Real Issues

Tony Bayfield

BLOOMSBURY CONTINUUM
LONDON · NEW YORK · OXFORD · NEW DELHI · SYDNEY

BLOOMSBURY CONTINUUM
Bloomsbury Publishing Plc
50 Bedford Square, London, WC1B 3DP, UK

BLOOMSBURY, BLOOMSBURY CONTINUUM and the Diana logo are trademarks of
Bloomsbury Publishing Plc

First published in Great Britain 2019

A catalogue record for this book is available from the British Library

Library of Congress Cataloguing-in-Publication data has been applied for

ISBN: HB: 978-1-4729-6208-9; EPDF: 978-1-4729-6206-5; EPUB: 978-1-4729-6209-6

2 4 6 8 10 9 7 5 3 1

Typeset by Newgen KnowledgeWorks Pvt. Ltd., Chennai, India
Printed and bound in Great Britain by CPI Group (UK) Ltd, Croydon CR0 4YY

To find out more about our authors and books visit www.bloomsbury.com
and sign up for our newsletters

This book and such loving insights as it contains
is dedicated to my wife
Linda (1947–2003),
whose memory is a perpetual blessing
to our faithful children
Lucy, Daniel and Miriam
and our extraordinary grandchildren
Francesca, Oliver, Zachary, Harry, Ben and Rafael

Contents

Preface: Our starting point: journeying through a
shared world   I

PART ONE — BEING BOTH JEW AND JEWISH
TODAY: YOU CAN'T IGNORE THE CONTEXT   5

1   The particular journey   7
Section one: The journey: less a rooted than a routed People   8
Section two: Characteristics of the journey   28

2   The shared context   39
Section one: Environment and terrain   39
Section two: The Jewish contribution   47
Section three: The environment today   54

PART TWO — BEING A JEW TODAY: IDENTITY
AND PEOPLEHOOD   71

3   Israel as People   73
Section one: Identity: inner and outer definitions of who is a Jew   75
Section two: Identity: women and the scandal of patriarchy   88
Section three: Identity: power and oppression within   93
Section four: Identity: the mistake of the *mamzer*   97
Section five: Identity: chosenness – still valid or objectionable
    in the light of modernity?   98
Section six: Identity: and secularity – People, culture but no God   101

4   Israel as Land   105
Section one: Clinging to the Land in the face of exile   107
Section two: Modern political Zionism and the end of exile   111

Section three: The untold story: Mizrahi Jews from Arab lands 122

Section four: Britain and independence 123

Section five: Five inalienable rights 128

PART THREE – JUDAISM TODAY: LIGHT AND
WEIGHT 135

5   Torah: Judaism's unique selling point 137

Section one: The *Sefer Torah* (Scroll) 137

Section two: Not one Torah but a Dual Torah 142

Section three: The Torah is itself interpretation 155

Section four: Dark texts and liberation 159

Section five: *Sefer Torah*, Dual Torah, Jewish teaching 163

6   Covenant theology: Halakhah, law 165

Section one: Covenant 165

Section two: *Mitzvot*: the terms of the Covenant 174

Section three: Halakhah 178

7   Covenant theology: Aggadah, ethics 195

Section one: Rabbinic ethics 195

Section two: Prophetic ethics 205

Section three: Catastrophe and crisis 212

Section four: A post-modern Jewish ethics 217

PART FOUR – JEWISH FAITH TODAY: GOD,
SUFFERING AND SILENCE 227

8   Fragments after the devastation 229

Section one: Before deciding 230

Section two: At Leo Baeck College 232

Section three: Through dialogue to the heart of darkness 240

Section four: The German tradition 253

9   My God, my God – what kind of God are you? 259

Section one: A challenging tradition 259

Section two: What can we say about God? 265

Section three: Reasoning about God 274

Section four: Experiencing God 282

10 Life beyond death: Individual survival and messianic hope 289
    Section one: Individual survival   289
    Section two: Jewish survival, messianism and the goal of the journey 299

    Glossary   313
    Jewish thinkers contributing to this book   319
    Notes   327
    Acknowledgements   351
    Index   353

Preface
Our starting point: journeying through a shared world

Many prefaces are throat-clearing, polite formalities readily disregarded. What follows is brief but, I believe, essential to understanding the nature and purpose of this book.

I can't pinpoint its beginning though I started writing seven years ago and there have been several versions and drafts. It hasn't been a process of obsessive revision (though I'm prone to that!) but one of evolution, development.

This isn't a series of contemporaneous, stand-alone essays but, rather, it reflects my journey from hesitant beginning to provisional conclusion. There are signposts – some explicit, some via endnotes referring you forward. But I hope you'll read along with me and, when you reach the end, find I've provided material addressing many of your questions, even if that material leads you forward in a different direction.

Being Jewish Today is full of protest and challenge. It makes a virtue of uncertainty, yet is driven by two deep convictions.

First, the days when theology purported to explain or interpret revealed truths – principles of faith – are long gone. That's not how any branch of thought works today. We think for ourselves, we hypothesize and, one would hope, test our ideas with humility against the distilled wisdom time has given to tradition. But our own reasoning and experience, though highly personal, is our starting point; we go forward from there.

The second conviction is as crucial as the first. Wherever we live today – London or Glasgow, Moscow or New York, Rome or Istanbul, Jerusalem or Tel Aviv – we're born into, educated within, work in, live and breathe the modern or post-modern Western world. It's what I share with every reader – Jew, Christian, Muslim, Humanist or Secularist alike.[1] We may be the bearers of widely divergent traditions; we may walk different terrain – but we share the same environment.[2] Many of the questions we ask about our world will be the same – though the answers we offer will be particular to each of us. That's why this book gives an account of *both* the journey of a particular British Jew *and* the journeys of millions of women and men through today's perplexing and challenging world. It's not an autobiography but there are a few carefully selected episodes from my life which, I hope, will resonate.

Let me add that I've employed gender-neutral language throughout, including when speaking of God. This occasionally leads to inelegant phrases but elegance is far less important than the principle.

Although the nineteenth-century poet Matthew Arnold is out of fashion today, one stanza from his poem 'Dover Beach' was a major stimulus at the beginning of this project:

> The Sea of Faith
> Was once, too, at the full, and round earth's shore
> Lay like the folds of a bright girdle furled.
> But now I only hear
> Its melancholy, long, withdrawing roar,
> Retreating, to the breath
> Of the night-wind, down the vast edges drear
> And naked shingles of the world.

Jewish communities in Britain today don't give much thought to matters of belief, metaphysics, theology. They have other concerns. Identity and peoplehood, authority and authenticity, and – above all – just plain survival (demographic as well as physical) concentrate collective minds. Perversely, this is one of the few characteristics all sections of Jewry share, right across the assimilationist–separatist spectrum. It may well be understandable but it's horribly reminiscent of King Canute.

Matthew Arnold's 'receding tide of faith' is recognizable in most parts of the Western world today, particularly Protestant northern Europe; this book is a response. It will disturb and antagonize some but that's not my purpose. However, I've long held the view that treating myths of great profundity as children's stories infantilizes faith. Regarding dogma as unchallengeable, and writing out of faith those who question it, infantilizes 'believers'. Those who continue to assert that God abrogates the laws of nature – and pray for such to happen – not only defy reality but set up expectations doomed to failure. All who justify the unethical in the name of God betray the God in whom they claim to believe.

It may be that what Arnold heard receding was inevitable, even necessary, but people of faith who refuse to see the cheerless shingles are in denial of how life is. Since we all share the shingles, let's go down to the water's edge and explore exactly what has and has not receded.

PART ONE

Being Both Jew and Jewish Today: You Can't Ignore the Context

Rabbi Hanina, the Prefect of the Priests, said: 'Pray for the welfare of the government; for, were it not for the fear of it, we would have swallowed each other alive.'

(PIRKEI AVOT 3.2)

Jews always pose a question to the cultures in which they live. They work too hard, they talk too much, and they don't quite fit. People want fake security – they want the world to stand still. But Jews are restless like the world, and move on, shaking the bureaucracies and official structures, the dominions and thrones, a disturbing element in the life of the world.[1]

(RABBI LIONEL BLUE)

I

The particular journey

Some Jews today give a false impression of Judaism by opting for stasis, misrepresenting a dynamic tradition out of fear of the modern world. When it comes to Jews and Judaism, journey isn't a cliché; it's vital to understanding both. Journey is decisive in Jewish history *and* Jewish thought; our physical reality *and* our spiritual reality. Jewish history affects Jewish theology and theology has an impact on history. Both define who and how Jews are today. What follows is not a history refresher course but an account of who Jews are and what Judaism has become.

The Story as Autobiography

Historian Simon Schama entitles the first volume of his account of Jewish history *The Story of the Jews*.[1] 'Story' doesn't belittle its veracity but emphasizes the importance of the historical narrative to the individual Jew – 'my story'. Schama begins in an unusual and personal place, opening the first volume with the Elephantine Jewish community in 475 BCE. Elephantine Island in the Nile, on the border with Nubia, housed a frontier community servicing a garrison of which Jews were part. These were Jews integrated with the Egyptian garrison and local community, living both as part of wider society and 'at the edge'. Each Jew will tell the Jewish story in their own way, stressing what's important to them, providing nuances that tell you how they see the Jewish present and future as well as the Jewish past.

My starting point is different and more conventional, but I share with Schama a passionate sense that the Jewish story is my story. When Israeli novelist Amos Oz wrote *A Tale of Love and Darkness*,[2] critics queried whether it was autobiography because Oz pays so much attention to his family in Europe in the nineteenth century. Our autobiography doesn't begin with our birth. All eight of my great-grandparents were either born or brought up within a mile of each other in the East End of London, although their parents had come from near and far across the Western world. While never having lived – except as an undergraduate – further than twenty miles from Marble Arch, I identify with 'journey' as integral both to Jewish identity and Judaism. It's the collective experience of all *toldot*, generations (the closest biblical Hebrew word to history), thereby carrying deep, shared psychological and emotional resonances. There's a hallowed phrase *shalshelet hakabbalah*, the chain of tradition: I regard my linkage as both an ambiguous privilege and a demanding responsibility; others feel indifferent, fearful or unnecessarily shackled – all understandable responses but sad . . .

I agree.

Don't worry, this is just a rhetorical device for asking whether there's a metaphysical dimension to my last sentence.

SECTION ONE
THE JOURNEY: LESS A ROOTED
THAN A ROUTED[3] PEOPLE

THE FIRST STAGE

The first 11 chapters of the book of Genesis – those frequently dismissed reworkings of still more ancient myths – provide a fundamental statement of the universal background to Jewish particularity. We are a negligible part of humanity but our story is still part of the shared story. It all begins with a single family.

Abraham and Sarah are told: *Lekh l'khah*, leave your home, follow God and become a blessing.[4] The meaning is clarified in a *mashal*, a Rabbinic parable:

> What did Abraham resemble? A phial of perfume closed by a tight-fitting lid and lying in a corner so that its fragrance did not escape. As soon as it was picked up, however, the perfume was spread. Likewise, the Holy One Blessed be God said to Abraham: 'Travel from place to place and your name [the values you carry with you] will become important to the world.'[5]

The journey is continued by Isaac and Rebekah, Jacob, Rachel and Leah, each of whose lives is made up of many journeys. Thanks to Joseph the journey survives famine and resettlement in Egypt. Then comes slavery and, centuries later, liberation led by Moses. If Genesis is criss-crossed by individual journeys, the four books that follow it are an account of a collective journey.

Chapter 33 of Numbers meticulously records journey and encampment, journey and encampment, on through the wilderness. The eleventh-century French commentator Rabbi Shlomo Yitzhaki, known by his acronym Rashi, goes straight to the point. As we'll explore shortly, Moses instructs the Israelites trapped between the pursuing Egyptians at their back and the sea in front of them: '*Vayisa'u*, go forward.'[6] All Hebrew words derive from a three-letter 'root' – the root of *vayisa'u* is *nun-samech-ayin*, which provides the usual word for breaking camp. Rashi starts with the form of the root in Exodus 40.38 – *mas'eihem*, most obviously understood as 'their breaking camp', 'their journeying on'. But Rashi explains it here (by reference to usage in Genesis) as 'their encampments, the places where they paused', making the point that the same root is shared by journey and encampment: 'Because from the place of encampment they always set out again on a new journey, therefore all the different stages of their journeys – including the places where they camped – are called *masa'ot*.'[7] Even pitching tents becomes part of the journey.

The historical status of this first phase is much disputed. Fundamentalist Jews insist on its absolute historicity; at another extreme – but also for ideological reasons – are those who insist it's all invention. We'll examine this further in Chapter 5 when considering the nature of Torah. But for me, whatever the 'status' of the text, it has a profound meta-historical significance, shaping both people and faith. Fleeing from Sodom and Gomorrah, Lot's unnamed wife defies the imperative not to look back and is turned into a pillar of salt.[8] We remember the past – disregard would be sheer folly – but we don't look back.

A Paradigm Shift

The American Jewish philosopher of science Thomas Kuhn observed that the development of science takes place through periods of relatively stable growth punctuated by episodes of revolutionary upheaval. He coined the term 'paradigm shift'[9] to describe transformative episodes which, though strongly connected to the past, change the direction of travel, are linked to the old but herald the new. Kuhn provides an enlightening way of seeing the Jewish journey. Whatever the historical status of the narrative recounted by the Torah, it clearly and dramatically undergoes a paradigm shift between the end of Deuteronomy and the beginning of the book of Joshua, between the journey through the wilderness and settlement of the Promised Land.

On crossing the Jordan, a new chapter opens for the Jewish people, bringing the challenges of land and self-governance: relations with others – external and internal, political and religious. Above all, it demands a transformation of the goal of Judaism. Up to now, Moses has led his people towards a vision of the Promised Land, not just a land flowing with milk and honey but the endpoint of the journey. The reality turns out to be both milk and honey, drought and wormwood. It's a land with other inhabitants, presenting new challenges not just physical but ethical, religious. Without denying the importance of the Land to Judaism,[10] it doesn't turn out to be Shangri-la.

THE SECOND STAGE

At the beginning of the first millennium BCE, Israel emerged as a minor power on the international stage – settled on the land-bridge between Egypt and Mesopotamia. The first flirtation with Great

Power politics saw short-lived glory under David and Solomon but ended in disaster. On Solomon's death the country split into a Northern Kingdom of Israel and a Southern Kingdom of Judah. Two centuries later: 'The Assyrian came down like the wolf on the fold'[11] and ten of the twelve tribes – the Kingdom of Israel – vanished from history if not from legend: the ten tribes of the Northern Kingdom assimilated into Near Eastern history.

Judah's cultural environment, with its fertility religion, posed a threat to Jewish identity; the voracious nature of international politics, conquest and empire-building proved an even greater challenge. Nevertheless, Judah staggered on, keeping the people and its faith intact, maintaining Solomon's Temple in Jerusalem, continuing the journey begun by Abraham and Sarah. Then Babylon, Assyria's successor as superpower, struck at the beginning of the sixth century BCE.

The destruction of the First (Solomon's) Temple in 586 BCE and the subsequent deportations became formative in ways other than those one might have expected. Less than 250 years earlier, the destruction of the Northern Kingdom had proved conclusive – Israelite religion had not taken sufficient hold for the identity of the population to survive. But the same was not true this time. It's both paradigmatic and heroic that the Jews deported to Babylon longed to return – 'By the rivers of Babylon there we sat. Yes, we wept as we remembered Zion'[12] – and retained their faith and identity over several generations in enforced exile, *galut*. Paradoxically, it may well be that the seeds of the ability to survive not just in exile but in diaspora, *golah*, were also sown in Babylon. 'How could we sing God's song in a strange land!'[13] We learned. Jeremiah, who'd previously warned of the allure of Canaanite fertility cults, wrote to the Jews in exile in Babylon:

> Build houses and live in them, plant gardens and eat their fruit. Take wives and have sons and daughters; take wives for your sons and give your daughters in marriage so they can have sons and daughters. Multiply there and do not decrease. Seek the wellbeing of the city to which I have exiled you and pray to God on its behalf; for in its welfare you will find welfare.[14]

But, wherever you are, never forget who you are and why you are.

Three Festivals of Pilgrimage

The extent to which journeying is imprinted on Judaism is graphically illustrated by the rhythm of the Jewish year. We have a group of three major festivals, now referred to as the *Shalosh R'galim*, the Three Foot or Pilgrim Festivals, because, in Second Temple times, Jews from all places of Jewish settlement journeyed to Jerusalem to make offerings at the Temple.

Pesach / Passover

All three festivals have roots in the Canaanite calendar. The origins of Pesach lie, according to anthropologists, in the nomadic springtime celebration of the birth of lambs. The book of Exodus absorbs the festival into Judaism as a commemoration of the exodus from Egypt[15] – hence its meaning as a celebration of liberation and freedom from oppression. Told and retold at each *Seder*, the story has become both part of Jewish autobiography and universally paradigmatic. It's freighted with the urgency expressed by Franz Kafka – an archetypal Jew of modern times – in his parable *My Destination*: 'Away from here, away from here.'[16]

This tone of insistence – on motion over direction – is captured in Rabbinic Literature. In an evocative scene in the book of Exodus, Moses and the Children of Israel have reached the apparently unpassable waters of the Reed Sea;[17] they hear the sound of Pharaoh's chariots coming to stop them and return them to slavery. In the early centuries of the Common Era, the Rabbis offered a vivid insight, visualizing the dramatic scene for themselves. The people say: 'Let's go back. Slavery in Egypt is better than death at the hands of the Egyptians.' Moses holds his ground and calls on God. The Rabbis then hear God responding to Moses: 'There's a time for a long prayer and there's a time for a short prayer. Now's the time for a very short prayer. Tell them "*Vayisa'u*. Go forward."'[18]

Rabbinic reflection on the crisis by the Reed Sea goes further. The Talmud records Rabbi Meir[19] imagining the tribes squabbling over who would have the honour of being first into the sea. However Rabbi Judah,[20] the realist, says to Rabbi Meir: That's not what happened at all; each tribe was unwilling to be first to enter the sea – until Nakhshon son of Amminadav[21] waded in.

Only when he was fully committed – up to his soul, suggests the midrash – did the waters part.[22] What we're hearing is a second-century reading of a much older text. But that doesn't diminish the insight: nearly two thousand years ago, Jews were immersed in the historical narrative, finding in it reflections of contemporary experience. We're in mortal danger. Go forward. As my grandson Oliver explained to me – repeating the same exegetical process – you have to stop talking and act. You have to take the plunge. Get in up to your neck because that's the very nature of our story and our relationship to the Divine. The beginning of the collective journey, the journey of a people, is riveted to the Jewish consciousness and it's the essence of Pesach.

Shavuot / Pentecost

The second of this trio of festivals is Shavuot. The Hebrew word means 'weeks', the festival falling seven weeks after Pesach. Shavuot marks the point where the journey out of Egypt ceases to be liberation from, 'away from here, away from here', and becomes 'freedom to', a journey with direction and purpose. Once the Canaanite wheat harvest, Shavuot re-enacts the encounter between the Children of Israel and God. Exploring what precisely happened at Sinai and the meaning of revelation is the subject of Chapter 5; but nothing can or should detract from that encounter as the foundational episode in the narrative of the Jewish people and of Judaism. It is both what the Jewish people left Egypt for and what provides inexhaustible fuel for the demanding and exhausting journey we're still on.

Yet even Sinai was 'only' a staging post. The Torah continues the journey, telling us that the symbolic fruits of the brief encounter – the two tablets of stone – were placed in the Ark of the Covenant and carried forward with the people. We don't stay where we are; we take what we can of Sinai with us.

Sukkot / Tabernacles

And so to the last of the three 'Foot' festivals – Sukkot. Pesach, as we've seen, evolved from spring lambs through the Exodus from Egypt to liberation as central to theology; Shavuot begins with the wheat harvest, becomes the giving of Torah at Sinai, and affirms the possibility of human encounter with the Divine. Sukkot is the autumn harvest festival. Today, it's taken on some of the rich colour of Christian harvest festivals, but has always been more ambivalent. It nods in gratitude to that which has been safely gathered in. But, just beneath the surface, is a sense of impermanence, fragility and anxiety about the season to come. The dominant symbol of Sukkot is the *sukkah* (hut), a flimsy structure thinly covered with greenery but open to the sky. It's possible that the *sukkah* has its origins in temporary booths put up in the fields of Canaan while the harvest was gathered. At Sukkot, these are transformed into symbolic expression of the wandering in the wilderness; the *sukkah* is the tent endlessly pitched but endlessly moved on.

Judaism has been shaped by a calendar in which three narrative festivals retell the story of leaving Egypt, pausing at Sinai and journeying towards the Promised Land. The journey of the Children of Israel, the collective journey told in Exodus, Leviticus, Numbers and Deuteronomy, is just as insistent a theme as the individual journeys of the patriarchs and matriarchs in Genesis. Its dual physical and metaphysical reality is encapsulated in the image of 12 tribes, each an entity but marching together, following a cloud of smoke by day and a pillar of fire by night, carrying their portable sanctuary and the Ark of the Covenant forward into the unknown. The individual and collective journeys are, above all, paradigmatic, setting a pattern for both the narrative of the Jewish people and their religion, Judaism – into the Land and far beyond.

The Journey through the Land and Prophetic Challenge[23]

Dominating the phase of the journey from the eighth century BCE to around 500 BCE is the emergence of a further formative dimension to the people and its faith – the Prophets and their books. The Hebrew for prophet is *navi*, plural *n'vi'im*. Referring at first to wandering, ecstatic groups, it was also applied to several individuals, most notably Nathan[24] and Elijah.[25] Prophetic Literature consists of three major literary works – Isaiah, Jeremiah and Ezekiel – and twelve shorter works beginning with Hosea and ending with Malachi. As you would expect of ancient literature – written down after the utterances were spoken – there are formidable problems of authorship, dating and textual transmission. The 15 voices are not a choir and don't sing in unison – though there's a considerable degree of harmony in addressing a number of specific and timeless issues.

A succession of empires tramped over the Israel/Judah land bridge – Mesopotamia seeking to attack Egypt and Egyptians eyeing expansion into Mesopotamia. Survival was an ever-present shadow yet society continued to develop. There were cities in which commerce flourished; villages and countryside where agriculture predominated. What provided distinctiveness and gave meaning to the identity of the population is what biblical scholars refer to as the monotheistic cult of YHWH and Jewish theologians call Judaism.[26] It alone can explain the endurance of the People.

The Literary Prophets are astonishing individuals who feel compelled to leave their occupation – be it fig-cultivator or priest – and challenge their society, at whatever personal cost and with little chance of winning approval or popularity: they have to say what they have to say.

First, the ruling elite played international politics – making alliances with one or other of the Great Powers in order to maintain its own hold on power and national independence. Such alliances are roundly condemned by the Prophets of the day. 'They'll be of no help; only God can guarantee national sovereignty,' they say. For them, God acts in history and the Great Powers are seen by the Prophets as instruments of divine disapproval, punishing Israel for disloyalty and infidelity – a deeply troubling view to be confronted in Chapter 8.

Second, the Prophets expose the inequalities that disfigure society within Israel and Judah,[27] repeatedly pointing to the treatment of the disadvantaged – the poor, the widow and the orphan. More important even than maintaining the cult is the compassionate treatment of the vulnerable, which leads to equally pointed observations about the treatment meted out to 'the stranger' – the non-Jew, the resident alien, the immigrant – living within this society. As we'll see in Chapter 7, the Prophets are concerned, above all else, with social and economic justice – an ethics as necessary to Judaism in the post-modern world as the view of God acting in history is problematic.

Finally, they address the purpose and goal of their religious culture. For the Prophets, the Promised Land towards which their ancestors had journeyed through the wilderness gives way to an End of Days – in this life – in which all social and economic injustices will be righted and threats to Israel's existence extinguished. The Prophets are also key to the final chapter of this book.

In Judah and Babylon

The people and its faith saw off the challenge of Babylon by discovering that both could, if compelled, endure in exile. Then Babylon itself fell. The Persian, Cyrus, took the view that his empire was less likely to be challenged from the inside if he allowed the conquered peoples within its midst a measure of identity and independence. That aided our story by permitting the return – of those who wished – to Jerusalem. Judah was reborn and, as we'll see in Chapter 5, with it that which gives the Jewish story its unique quality and significance.

But exile for some became Diaspora, which then continued to expand and develop. It wasn't, however, easy and straightforward. In his letter to the exiles in Babylon,[28] Jeremiah had told them to make the best of it, and the best of it was of decidedly uneven quality. Schama's account of the Elephantine community on the Nile is a case in point – it flourished for several centuries but finally fell victim to local jealousies and rivalries. The insecurity of diaspora experience is not just a constant of Jewish history; it's also imprinted on Judaism.

The cycle of the Jewish year – Rosh Hashanah, New Year and Yom Kippur, Day of Atonement as well as Sukkot, Pesach and Shavuot – is established in the Torah itself. The Jews in the Persian Diaspora contributed a further festival to the calendar, rooted/routed in the Jewish journey. *K'tuvim* – the collection of books forming the third part of the Tanakh, Hebrew Bible – includes the book of Esther. Probably dating from the third century BCE, the tale of Queen Esther is a historical novella with an overriding political purpose and message. Set in Shushan/Susa, capital of the Persian Empire, south-east of Assyrian Nineveh and east of Babylonian Babylon, it addresses the consequences of a minority wishing to retain a distinctive identity, laying them open to exploitation by demagogues. If you live within any empire, religious or secular, that offers little scope for stubbornly held alternative beliefs – beware but don't give up.

Here's another archetypal theme, far from exclusive to Jews, which speaks with great immediacy to the twenty-first century. The book of Esther – in defiant hope rather than gritty realism – ends with the enemy, Haman, exposed and vanquished. We Jews triumph: our survival is celebrated by the festival of Purim, which, many centuries ago, took on the spirit of carnival. Laugh in the face of adversity; the reality is too painful for tears.

Conflict with Greece: Learning from Hellenistic Culture

In the years following Alexander the Great, the division of the Greek Empire between Seleucus in Damascus and Ptolemy in Egypt once again enmeshed the Jews of Judah in the politics and alliances of survival against which the Prophets had railed centuries earlier. It's a complex and murky story confused as much as clarified by the two books of Maccabees, part of the Apocrypha. A second minor festival, Hanukkah, emerged, celebrating the successful resistance of Judah the Maccabee to Damascus. The subsequent Hasmonean dynasty restored Judean independence but – fatally – combined both royal and priestly leadership.

Judaism and Hellenism are often represented as opposites – Jerusalem versus Athens – but that's not the same as saying that Jews and Greeks couldn't coexist and learn from each other. The Jewish philosopher Philo of Alexandria, who synthesized Platonic and Prophetic ideas, is a well-known example. Greek words entered Rabbinic vocabulary. The Hebrew Bible was translated into Greek, known as the Septuagint – reflecting a tradition that it was the work of 70 Jewish scholars. It was incontrovertibly of advantage to a Jewish Diaspora that spoke its own form of Greek rather than Aramaic or Hebrew. The Septuagint penetrated the Greco-Roman world and greatly influenced the writing of the New Testament.

From the late second century BCE on, the division and fragmentation of the fragile Jewish State is already taking place. Accommodation or opposition – first with Greece, then Rome – set Jew against Jew. By the time the third stage of the journey begins, the seeds of disintegration and chaos out of which it emerged have not only been sown but are bearing the bitterest of fruit.

THE THIRD STAGE

The Journey into Exile

A second paradigm shift takes place more than a millennium after the first, after the closing of the Hebrew canon and before the Christian Scriptures are written down. From the middle of the second century BCE, Judah, Jewish life and Judaism are in turmoil as ruthless Roman occupation follows the steamroller of Hellenization. Amid this physical turmoil, many Jewish parties, sects, beliefs and philosophies clamour for attention. For obvious reasons, it's one of the most researched and therefore disputed periods in Western history! What we can be sure of is that, of the many groups and ideologies, only two have survived. One is Christianity, the other Rabbinic Judaism. Like siblings, they emerge from the same womb – the same people, place and time. Though hopelessly dysfunctional from the outset, siblings we were and siblings we remain.

Our focus is on the emergence of the Jewish sibling, Rabbinic Judaism. The Rabbis – the word rabbi means 'my master' (in the sense of 'school-master') and refers not to priests but to teachers – now assumed authority. They devoted their lives to a relentless interrogation of the Torah text in order to determine how that which came from a former age, couched in the language of an earlier agrarian society, could be applied and provide meaning and purpose amid the turmoil of the Greco-Roman world. In modest buildings that provided space for communal meeting, prayer and – above all – study, the Rabbis developed their 'Dual Torah'.[29] Through debate and discussion, and despite – or, rather, because of – frequent disagreement, the Judaism to which all Jews today are heir emerged.

During the three hundred years from the Maccabees to the mid-second century CE – a period of foundation-shaking bloodshed, destruction and expulsion – the four pillars of biblical Judaism were toppled. The (Second) Temple, the holiest of places, in Jerusalem was destroyed; with it went the authority and leadership of the Priests; the sacrificial system ended; the Land ceased to be the place where most Jews lived. Thanks to the Rabbis, these four pillars were replaced – the Temple by places of study, prayer and meeting not confined to one holy location; the authority of the Priests by that of the Rabbis, scholar-teachers; a rhythm of prayer recalled the regimen of Temple sacrifices; and the Rabbis responded to the involuntary loss of Land by creating a portable Judaism – an all-embracing body of faith and practice, derived from asking pointed questions of the Torah, embodying the spiritual perceptions and ethics that give meaning and purpose to Jewish life.

The Rabbis were intoxicated by the many layers of meaning to be found in the Torah. Their constant probing, enquiring, challenging, yielded an incomparably rich body of literature that adds life and depth to the Torah text. It also reveals much about the authors and their understanding of contemporary Jewish life. There will be many examples of their midrash – commentary, exegesis, enquiry, interrogation – throughout this book. From them, we learn an immense amount about how they understood the catastrophe of their times and its relation to the journey – still ongoing.

As Rome encroached further on Jewish space, the conflicting parties within the population grew more vociferous. In 66 BCE, rebellion broke out resulting in the siege and destruction, four years later, of the Second Temple by Emperor Titus. Further rebellions followed, in 115 CE – in the Diaspora around the Mediterranean – and in 132 CE, again in Judea, against Hadrian. A process of expulsion began and, although communities persisted in Judea and Galilee, the Romans saw to it that Jerusalem became Aelia Capitolina, a new Roman city, free of troublesome and rebellious Jews – at least for a while.[30]

The Third Sibling

One of the places Jews populated over the following centuries was the Arabian Peninsula down to what is now Yemen. Jews had almost certainly made lives there well before the expulsion by Rome. Now, existing diaspora communities were joined by exiles. Muhammad was midwife to Islam within a world in which Jews and Judaism were noticeably present. By the late fourth century, the Kingdom of Himyar, today's Yemen, had converted to Judaism. In Muhammad's day, Yathrib, later Mecca, contained a sizeable Jewish population. Not just Judaism and Christianity but Judaism and Islam are the

Children of Abraham; we are siblings – the term can be used of children with only one parent in common.[31] Judaism and Christianity are the children of Abraham and Sarah; Islam is the child of Abraham and Hagar. At birth, we reacted to each other with the same non-comprehension and, on the part of Christianity and Islam, the same sense of rejection. From the beginning, Christians couldn't understand why most Jews rejected their claim to be narrators of the climactic episode in the story of Judaism. Likewise, Muhammad was shocked and angered at rejection by those who he had been confident would be allies. Unexamined, frequently exploited feelings of rejection have poisoned our shared environment to an extent that even today appears irreversible.

Babylon

From the destruction of the Second Temple onwards, a series of Diaspora communities became, in turn, dominant in the development of Judaism. From the third century, for some eight hundred years, Babylon (the original Diaspora community) played that focal role – one can't overstate the importance of Babylon to the journey. It was in the Rabbinic Academies of Babylon that the Babylonian Talmud was compiled – beginning around 450 CE. In subsequent centuries, the Ge'onim, the Heads of the Academies in Sura and Pumbedita, were pivotal to the post-Talmudic development of Jewish thought and practice. It was also from Babylon that many Jewish merchants and traders set out, contributing to economic life throughout the region and far beyond.

Spain

At the end of the millennium, the focus of the Jewish journey moved to Spain. Islam never granted Jews equality: Jews were recognized as 'related' but given the status of *dhimmi*, defined by a raft of humiliating regulations that came with a swingeing poll tax, the *jaliya*. In practice, the situation varied from tolerable to intolerable according to the regime. Islam in Spain is characterized by periods of rich cultural expansiveness disrupted by waves of puritanical zeal – Almohads and Almoravids emanating from the mountains of North Africa. During the relatively good times there was a genuine cultural interaction in which Jewish thought grappled with Islamic learning – itself a major transmitter of Greek thought – to produce philosophy and theology of the type we recognize as such today.

The Christian re-conquest was, in the end, a disaster for the Jews of Spain. Judeo-phobia was cynically fanned; policies that led to isolation, torture and death were ruthlessly pursued, with shocking numbers of Jewish families lost to the Jewish world by unwanted conversion – the only alternative available. The malicious cruelty of the Inquisition continues to be a terrible indictment of the Catholic Church, its influence enduring.

Although surviving Sephardi Jews (the Hebrew name for Spain is *Sepharad*) resettled round the Mediterranean and in Holland, the focus of the story now moves north and is taken up by the Ashkenazim, from the Hebrew name for Germany, *Ashkenaz*. However, the expulsion from Spain had already been matched by the expulsion of Jews from Western Europe, eastwards.

In the early Middle Ages, Christian society had a fluidity that left Jewry, although classed along with women in terms of social status, able to participate in the wider culture. The First Crusade in 1096 sounded a warning – though not mandated by Church leaders, attacks on Jewish communities in the path of the Crusaders were widespread – and the legislation of the Fourth Lateran Council of 1215 signalled a policy of visual identification in order to separate and protect the body of Christianity from 'the Christ-killers'. The closing in of the Christian world against its Jewish minority heralds centuries of exclusion and isolation. There is an impulse, manifested by the leadership of the Church as distinct from its rank and file, to preserve this 'sinful' people for the Second Coming (echoed by today's fundamentalist Christian Zionists, resurgent in the USA). But the perpetuation of the notion of Jews as sinful, as both the rejecters and killers of Christ, brought rabid hostility rather than protection. It's worth noting that, after the expulsion from Spain in 1492, many Jews, Ashkenazim as well as Sephardim, migrated from Christendom into the Ottoman Empire where their *dhimmi* status – insulting and indecent though it was – was preferable to the Inquisition and bloody massacres.[32] By segregating Jewry, the Christian West added a further dimension to the tragedy: it greatly limited the Jewish contribution to Western civilization during the thirteenth to eighteenth centuries. And vice versa.

Eastern Europe

The repeated expulsion of Jews, particularly from Germany in 1348, saw the growth of Jewish communities from the Baltic right across what is now Poland and Russia. From the ending of the 'Golden Age' of Jewish life in Spain under Muslim rule, the lead community of Jewry is to be found in Eastern Europe, where Jews settled not out of choice but of necessity – there were few other accessible towns and lands that would tolerate us.[33]

Small communities formed and grew, separate, self-sufficient but participating in the wider economy. In the sixteenth century the Kingdom of Poland and the Grand Duchy of Lithuania united to form what became known as the Polish–Lithuanian Commonwealth. Here Jews achieved an unprecedented degree of autonomy and self-governance. The portable Judaism begun by the Rabbis of the first millennium of the Common Era governed almost every aspect of life. Codified into law – criminal and commercial as well as family and ritual – it supported a rich cultural intensity but one largely cut off from the mainstream of European thought and life.

Both inside the Commonwealth and beyond its borders, Jews played a liminal role – not part of the mainstream, occupying a vulnerable, outsiders' position. The clearest and bloodiest illustration is provided by events of the mid-seventeenth century. A Cossack revolt against Polish domination of the Ukraine led to the Chmielnicki massacres in which tens of thousands of Jews were murdered. It reflected a pattern already long established: autonomy and toleration by the ruling classes was paid for by compulsory assumption of the role of middle-man – tax collector, supervisor of feudal estates. Under pressure – or out of expediency – the ruling class would withdraw their protection. Hatred for Jews, who'd been interposed over the peasants, spilled out – the image of bailiff merging with the image of Christ-killer, making us ripe for further demonization. The Chmielnicki Revolt eventually subsided but violence against Jews continued. For many communities, extreme poverty and privation became endemic.

The Jewish world offered three religious and intellectual responses over the following two centuries. First, several flirtations with messianism, with followers of Shabbetai Zvi and Jacob Frank forming not insubstantial sects. Second, the rise of an uncompromising scholasticism, at its finest and most typical in the *yeshivot*, rabbinic academies of Lithuania. The *Mitnagdim*, as these rabbis came later to be known, adopted an austere and severe attitude to Jewish practice, engaging in highly intellectual, rigorous and detailed study – *pilpul* – of the Talmud, its commentaries and super-commentaries. For many outside the Lithuanian *yeshivot*, the rabbis appeared to have retreated into ivory towers, distancing themselves from the ordinary Jew and a hostile world. The third response, Hasidism, was a populist, revivalist movement for the masses, which turned people inwards in pursuit of desperately needed joy and spiritual consolation.

These various trends of the seventeenth and eighteenth centuries represent a Jewish response largely oblivious of the wider world of eighteenth-century European thought. Both in Eastern and Western Europe, Jewish communities had become ghettoized physically, socially and intellectually. Until the late 1700s, European Jewry was largely unable to interact with the wider culture of which it had been a founder member. The change that took place at the beginning of the nineteenth century was as dramatic as it was bewildering.

For the Jews of Eastern Europe there was no easing of pain and suffering. Indeed, the great-power struggles of eighteenth-century Eastern Europe delivered the Jews of the Polish–Lithuanian Commonwealth into the hands of Imperial Russia. Oppressive confinement in the Pale of Settlement, established by Catherine the Great in 1791, became murderously intolerable in the closing decades of the nineteenth century. At this point, it's vital to the narrative of journey to highlight just how many Eastern European Jews joined earlier settlers who'd made the immense journey – both physical and psychological – from the 'old country' to the New World. In America, Jews experienced liberation from oppression and achieved full rights as citizens, with fewer of the ambiguities of the fourth stage of the journey in Central and Western Europe.

THE FOURTH STAGE

Entering the Modern World

Intellectual history terms the eighteenth century the Age of Enlightenment. It's characterized by an emphasis on reason and analysis, the individual and the 'brotherhood of man'. The Enlightenment brought hitherto unimaginable benefits to Jews in Francophone and German-speaking Europe. The French Revolution, with its slogan *liberté, égalité, fraternité*, freed French Jewry from its medieval ghettos – but in a way peculiar to France. Jews became equal citizens but their Jewishness and Judaism was strictly a private matter – at large, *citoyen*; only at home, *Juif*. This separation may well be the reason why the engagement between the Jews of France and their compatriots, between Judaism and French culture, didn't stimulate the creativity that emerged in the extensive area ruled by the States of Germany and the Austro-Hungarian Empire.

The impact of modern Western culture and its collapse into the obscenity of the Death Camps is inescapable and all-pervasive. Here I want to highlight two readings, two ways of telling the story that today underpin world Jewry's double vision. Vienna-born Israeli historian Amos Elon expresses what is, I believe, the majority reading. *The Pity of it All*[34] is pointedly subtitled *A Portrait of Jews in Germany 1743–1933*. Despite being less than 1 per cent of the population, Jews from Moses Mendelssohn onwards contributed a disproportionate amount to European culture without ever, Elon argues, achieving acceptance as Germans or Austrians. That some Jews thought otherwise was a fatal error that compounded the catastrophe and represents a mistake that must never be repeated.

There is an alternative reading. Australian Jewish academic Ned Curthoys deploys a phrase with a long history, 'elective affinity' – meaning here the engagement of German Jewry with wider society with the intention of contributing to it and recognizing that, in the process, it too will be changed. This he terms the liberal Jewish tradition: 'An energetic worldview which seeks to accommodate the vitality and evolving nature of Jewish life in diaspora by emphasizing that in preserving the ethical kernel of genuine monotheism, Jews have an exemplary role to play in world history.'[35] Does the pity of it all, the catastrophic outcome of it all, render Diaspora in the twenty-first century an obtuse, perverse option, doomed yet again to disaster – or does Jewish tradition insist that some Jews must continue to try? It's a question that provokes high levels of anxiety and much invective, not least between Israeli and American Jewish leaders.

The gradual emergence of the Jews of Western and Central Europe into the dazzling light of modernity elicited many responses. Some simply abandoned the journey – if not for themselves, then for their children. Others converted to Christianity, usually to accelerate social and professional progress. Biographies of the great contributors to the cultural symbiosis often reveal the ambiguity of their families towards emancipation. Just as some plants flower most prolifically when put under pressure, the German Jewish flowering, one senses, took place 'at the edge' – on the margins of the community, not on its more stable centre ground. Nineteenth-century Germany also witnessed the birth of Jewish denominations, the equivalent of what had taken place within Christianity less than a century earlier.[36] 'Reform', 'Liberal', 'Orthodox' all originate in nineteenth-century Germany – as does 'Secular' Judaism. In German-speaking Europe, the narrative takes on many accents.

The Enlightenment first took hold among German, French and American Jews, arriving later in the Jewish heartland of Eastern Europe – though not as late as some might lead you to suppose. My mother's family – the Mann family – came from Przemysl, a small town in Galicia, close to the Austro-Hungarian Empire's border with Russia. Here the traditional, enclosed world of Eastern Europe met the ripples of Haskalah, Enlightenment moving out from Berlin and Breslau, Vienna and Frankfurt. A Reform synagogue was opened in nearby Lemberg (Lviv) in 1840; it was there that the most violent internal conflicts occurred.

Przemysl was smaller and more conservative than Lemberg. Yet even here the effects of the Haskalah were felt. My great-grandfather's brother was a *mashgiakh* (supervising butcher) and *sh'liakh tsibur* (prayer leader) in Przemysl. His sons were traditionally educated yet, for reasons now sadly irretrievable, he had two of them tutored in secular subjects. One, Yitzhak, gained a doctorate in Vienna, settled in Jerusalem, edited with unrivalled punctiliousness the early Hebrew publications of the Jewish National Fund and translated Marx and Marcuse into Hebrew! The other, Jacob, studied at London's Jews' College and London University before taking his meticulous skills in Genizah research to Hebrew Union College in Cincinnati. When the two boys left Galicia for careers in the 'enlightened' Jewish world, their father was dismissed as *sh'liakh tsibur* because his children had engaged in *treif-possul*, unkosher-forbidden studies.

The Haskalah penetrated more slowly and less evenly in Eastern Europe; many largely unaffected communities remained. Until the Shoah (Holocaust) destroyed almost everything and changed absolutely everything.

The Goldene Medina

Jewish settlement of the Americas goes back to the sixteenth century – first Sephardi, then Ashkenazi – but the first half of the nineteenth century saw a surge in Western European Jewish immigration to North America. This large-scale journeying from the Old World to the New was of incalculable importance not just to Jews but to Judaism. Embracing a society wedded to 'rugged individualism' and religious liberty – rather than Christianity or Islam – gave American Jewry a confident, individualistic, pioneering character not swamped by late nineteenth-century Eastern European immigration that so coloured British Jewry. If that conjures up a picture of the American Jewish journey as a wagon train headed for the frontier loaded with barrels of dill pickles and ambition, don't dismiss it. Indeed, America's 'Wild West' narrative includes Tombstone lawman Wyatt Earp, whose common-law wife – of 43 years – Josephine 'Sadie' Marcus, was a nice Jewish girl, born in New York in 1860 to a Prussian Jewish immigrant family, who'd moved west and later drew a veil over her early career as an 'actress and dancer'.

From the early twentieth century, American Jewry became the lead community, able to contribute decisively to Jewish survival and continuity after the destruction of European Jewry. In many respects America is different from all other countries that have been home to Diaspora Jews – symbolized by the words on the Statue of Liberty: 'Give me your tired, your poor, your huddled masses yearning to breathe free'. They're by Emma Lazarus, an American Jewish poet and economic justice activist. It's a staggering statistic that, today, more than 80 per cent of world Jewry lives either in North America or Israel. But reflection on the journey will supply the explanation.

THE FIFTH STAGE

On the Far Side of the Abyss

As a young man I saw myself as continuing the fourth stage of the journey. Only later was I forced to confront two incontrovertible facts I'd contrived to evade.

First, the Shoah represents an abyss. That which had existed prior to 1933 had been destroyed. Britain was never occupied, British Jewry never rounded up and murdered, but being unaffected was an illusion – or delusion.

Second, it wasn't just Jewish life that had been irrevocably changed. From 1914 onwards, the Western world experienced traumatic upheaval; the 20 years from the election of Adolf Hitler in 1933 to the death of Josef Stalin in 1953 changed the entire Western world forever. Defining modern and post-modern is for the next chapter – the terms we use are unimportant; what matters is the difference.

My mentor and rabbinic role-model, Dow Marmur, was born in Polish Silesia. Aged four, he fled with his family before the advancing Nazis and later sold soap on the streets of Fergana in Uzbekistan to support his parents and himself. After the war Marmur went to school in Sweden and then to Leo Baeck College to study for the rabbinate. After 20 years of working as a congregational rabbi in London, he was lured to Toronto by the incongruously named Holy Blossom Temple. Finally, he and his wife settled in Israel. He's the embodiment of recent Jewish history and that lends considerable authenticity to what he teaches.

In a pioneering study, *The Star of Return*,[37] Marmur argues that, for Jews, the old paradigm ended with the Shoah and a new one began with the foundation of the State of Israel in 1948. The observation is far-reaching: the Shoah marks the end of Jewish engagement with modernity and Israel represents the opening of a new way of being. It's a reading of the Jewish narrative wholly/holy in keeping with the wider process of disintegration that began with the First World War. For Jews and non-Jews alike, a further paradigm shift has taken place; the world is not what it once was.

SECTION TWO
CHARACTERISTICS OF THE JOURNEY

My account of the Jewish journey suggests that four seismic upheavals occurred on the way: after the journey to the Promised Land and at the beginning of the journey through the Promised Land; between the loss of Land and the development of a worldwide Diaspora; between separation from modernity and engagement with modernity; and between the collapse of the modern Western world and the emergence of the environment we experience today. All four result in traumatic paradigm shifts for both Jews and Judaism. They also each yield a characteristic, a quality, which defines my personal theology.

One: Provisionality

Provisionality is a brash and ugly neologism but the right noun to signify the state of being provisional. 'Paradigm shift' began life as a description of scientific advance and my sense of provisionality draws on scientific parallels. Albert Einstein (and later Stephen Hawking) dreamed of an elegant theorem that would account for everything but eventually came to see not only that he had failed to realize his dream but that the dream was unattainable.[38] However, while our search for '[scientific] understanding will never come to an end',[39] it will undergo periods of stable development and the occasional seismic upheaval. Einstein, like Newton before him, brought about seismic change but the quest, the journey continues; provisional doesn't mean temporary, it points to an innate quality of human knowledge – whether knowledge of science or knowledge of religion.

That's precisely why the end of the Torah and the beginning of the settlement of Canaan represent a paradigm shift. The Torah documents the first stage of the Jewish journey, its emergence into history. The Land that faces the Israelites across the Jordan in the last chapter of Deuteronomy, Canaan, is apparently the Promised Land, the Land of Moses' vision and Israel's dreams, a land flowing with milk and honey, the end of the journey. But it turns out not to be so and that realization precipitates a radical re-visioning.

It's not just that the reality of Canaan wasn't the Torah's 'Promised Land'; it changed the very nature of the journey. The Children of Israel were compelled to recognize that an understanding of the journey as completed, fulfilled, realized by crossing the Jordan had been provisional, the best available at the time. Arrival in Canaan, however, heralded a new stage in the journey and a new understanding (though connected to the old) of its purpose and end-point. The journey to and arrival in Canaan – both physical events – offer a fresh realization: the goals of the religious journey will require reassessment and modification. The truths of religion – like the truths of science – are not immutable but subject to new understandings. They're provisional – not in the sense of having little worth, always on the verge of being superseded, but, as Einstein acknowledged, not the final word.

This realization has pressing implications for where we find ourselves today. How do we tackle the inevitably unfamiliar, post-twentieth-century road forward? What's the end to which we're now heading? Such questions are in no way incompatible with respect for the past; they recognize the demands for adaptation and change that the journey makes on both Jews and Judaism. That's how it is: both physically and spiritually, we walk or – as with Jacob/Israel – limp[40] towards a goal, looking for a glimpse of 'God's' back,[41] trying to make out where 'God' has been. Is it just a semantic accident that vision and provisional are connected?

Quotation marks round God, rabbi?

For now.

Two: Liminality

Provisionality emerged in the paradigm shift from crossing the wilderness to settling in the Land. Liminality, the second characteristic, stems from expulsion and exile. The Latin word *limen*, a threshold, is recognizable in 'subliminal': that which is below the threshold of consciousness. Less familiar, liminality is a term first used in anthropology to refer to individuals or groups who've become detached from their clan and find themselves at a point where they have to make a decision whether to join another or form an independent clan of their own. The critical point at which they find themselves is a dangerous no-man's land between alternative thresholds.

The concept has been taken up in both psychological and religious literature. First to apply it to Judaism has been American liturgist Lawrence Hoffman, who uses the concept of liminality to understand the ritual of *Havdalah*. Hoffman shows that the *Havdalah* ceremony, at the end of Shabbat, is designed to signal a liminal state, the threshold between the specialness of Shabbat, which has just ended, and the ordinariness of the rest of the week, which has not yet begun.[42]

Liminality is ritualized in a different way in the autumn festival of Sukkot. Sukkot is the Jewish Janus festival. Janus, the Roman god of the doorway, the threshold, the *limen*, looked both ways: Sukkot marks a brief seven-day interlude, a time of liminality. We look back to the rich harvest of the summer – *sukkot* (huts) decorated with fruit, flowers and invitations to hospitality, but also forward to the late autumn and winter with the absence of fruit to harvest and climatic conditions from which no *sukkah* could shelter us. At Sukkot we live in a liminal period, a period between two seasons, two states of being.

It's now not difficult to see how liminality relates to the journey of the Jewish people, particularly the long phase following the destruction of the Temple when we were thrust into exile. What I find so interesting is the anthropological observation that one cannot sustain a permanent state of liminality: a choice has to be made, either to throw in one's lot with a new community or set up as a separate community in one's own right. From the expulsions from Judea in the first and second centuries right up to the present, that dilemma can be observed again and again. Jews have had to choose repeatedly between integrating into the wider community – always providing we were allowed to do so – or maintaining ourselves as a separate group within the countries to which our journeys have taken us. How to live as a distinctive religious minority within lands, principally but not exclusively Christian and Muslim, is a dominant theme of the journey and remains critical amid the secular imperialism of today. The feeling of liminality – of living in a dangerous place, on the threshold – has become part of the Jewish psyche to an almost overwhelming extent. It has much to do with the ambiguous welcome Jews received in the lands of our journeying. It also reflects an inner sense of being caught between the anger-provoking pain of exile and the seductive pleasure of diaspora.

Liminality can be both disabling and enabling. Today's remnant communities in continental Europe are irrevocably scarred by an acute sense of danger realized in continuing persecution and, ultimately, the Shoah. In Britain, too, the psychological damage is deep; many Jews continue to see themselves as victims, fed by the apparent ineradicability of anti-Semitism and by the form of anti-Semitism that manifests as anti-Israel polemic.[43] It disables many Jews from playing the role in society Jewish tradition demands. If this strikes you as hyperbole, consider the vast amount of resource – in terms of personnel and money – that goes into the protection of Jewish buildings, every synagogue included, and the psychological effect of training Jewish children how to behave in the event of an attack.

In the United States, however, where Jews have lived the American Dream for several centuries and are distanced from the Shoah, we can see the creative dimension to liminality reasserting itself to a far greater extent. Living between separation and assimilation, we have an active and valuable role to play in society for which the American theologian Eugene Borowitz coined the phrase 'creative maladjustment'. We can, should and – in America – do, bring our particular perspective, see what the majority may overlook, add the voice of critical co-citizen, while, at the same time, throwing in our lot with those with whom we share home and land – Pittsburgh shooting notwithstanding.[44]

Lacanian analyst Philip Boxer helped me develop my thinking about universally applicable concepts of 'otherness', 'diasporic' and 'living at the edge'. Boxer wrote to me:

Living in diaspora involves working with the otherness of the other ... Difference, disagreement and conflict are essential to growth. The key lies not in avoiding difference but in how it's managed, openly and creatively ... To do so, to work where different systems of meaning meet, is to live at the edge, a place both creative and risky.

To stay with liminality is both terrifying and rewarding; it's a function of that overwhelming sense of constant journeying and recalls Rashi's commentary that even the encampment is part of the journey.

Three: The Paradoxical

In emerging from the ghetto we moved from a closed world of our own into a modern one that belonged to others, thereby facing conflicting sets of truths and different systems of meaning. The encounter highlights the significance of paradox in Jewish history and thought. By this I mean apparently conflicting truths containing or pointing to a common underlying truth.

Paradox illuminates both Jewish identity and Jewish faith. Jewish identity – to be explored in Chapter 3 – is built on a series of paradoxes. We knew from the very beginning of the journey that we would never be a numerous people and yet were confident of survival 'not by power nor by might but by the spirit'.[45] The promise of becoming as numerous as the stars in heaven and the grains of sand on the seashore was made to Abraham;[46] it's been fulfilled through our siblings, Christianity and Islam, with whom we struggle endlessly. We defined ourselves as a people and a nation yet that peoplehood was always open – Ruth the Moabite was the great-grandmother of King David. Jewish tradition not only welcomes converts but insists, once someone becomes a convert, they're no different from any other Jew and are equally part of the journey stretching back to Sinai.[47] We've always felt a sense of chosenness and specialness but not of superiority, acknowledging that the reward for our specialness is more likely to be humiliation than glory.[48] We insist on the importance of our particularity but argue it's only through the particular that the universal can be realized.

We regard Torah as a gift to us, our inheritance, but deduce from its revelation in the wilderness that we may not claim it as our own exclusive property.[49]

We insist God is beyond human imagination and unknowable yet have produced an ocean of literature devoted to an anthropomorphic, passible (emotion-displaying) Being, the scrutiny of Whom has been a constant feature of Jewish God-talk.[50] We've long struggled with a good God and our own suffering.[51] With Job, we recognize the injustice but have refused to give up, insisting God is both good and just.[52] At the very heart of Judaism is free will: 'See I have set before you life and death, blessing and curse. Choose life and then you and your children will live.'[53] Yet we also say 'All is foreseen'.[54] We've experienced everything that could make a people despair of both human beings and God. Yet we refuse to give up on either and insist life offers meaning and hope.[55]

As Kafka wrote: 'The true way leads along a tight-rope, which is not stretched aloft but just above the ground.' And then adds: 'It seems designed more to trip one than to be walked along.'[56] Such is the Jewish journey.

Four: Uncertainty

In the four decades between the outbreak of the First World War and the death of Stalin, the modern Western world disintegrated. The catastrophe is both intensified and exemplified by the Shoah. The world as we knew it was irrevocably changed and with it went confidence in human progress and faith in the inexorable march of modern Western culture.

The Shoah shattered not just the physical Jewish world, not just the body of Jewry, but Judaism. The Jewish journey is now walked limping on both legs, amid a hail of fragments, in a swirling fog. The return to the Land and rebirth of the Jewish State has done little to diminish uncertainty about the future of the Jewish people. A sense of insecurity dominates Jewish life, particularly outside North America, to the point of obsession. Some can see no point in continuing a journey that apparently leads nowhere. Others retreat into a Judaism that seeks to revivify old certainties, which, unlike Ezekiel's dry bones,[57] cannot live again.

Uncertainty has two meanings – one that conveys wavering, hesitancy, woolliness, and one recognizing not being sure, not being clear, grasping that the simple is all too often simplistic and accepting complexity as endemic in the post-modern world. We Jews have no option but to live with uncertainty in both meanings of the word, overcome our understandable hesitancy and continue the journey – unclear about what the future holds.

But there is also this: Israeli-American economist Daniel Kahneman in *Thinking, Fast and Slow* demonstrates the extent to which people consistently overestimate how much they understand about the world and underestimate the prevalence of chance.[58] Certainty is humanity's greatest and most self-indulgent illusion. As columnist Janan Ganesh wrote immediately after the 2018 Pittsburgh Synagogue shooting:

> The underlying problem in modern politics … is an excess of intellectual certitude. The basis of democracy – of civilisation – is doubt. A person who is reasonably confident their ideological programme is correct is unlikely to harm anyone to advance that programme. A person who is absolutely certain might.[59]

Uncertainty is the midwife of humility, and all traditions, religious and secular, need a good dose of that.

Not long after my wife Linda died, I went to a meeting with a prominent rabbi. He greeted me by wishing me 'long life' – a traditional formula – then added, 'Some people are so important to God that he calls them to be with him. It only appears to you that it's much too soon.' Standing on the fog-shrouded terrain of the post-modern world amid the rain of fragments of our former theological world, silence is infinitely preferable to blasphemous platitudes or dogmatic clichés.

Don't you think I'd prefer his unwavering faith than your agonized unbelief, Rabbi Bayfield?

No. Anyway, I thought this was a literary device, not a conversation.

Pluralism

Finally, a characteristic that's a hallmark of all five stages in the Jewish journey. I don't want to claim it as a feature exclusive to Judaism, only to say that it's always present, indispensable for negotiating each paradigm shift. I've labelled it pluralism; how I use the term will become clear.

Let's start with Torah. There can be no question about the importance of *Asseret Hadibrot*, the Ten Commandments. There are, of course, two versions – one in Exodus and one in Deuteronomy – which aren't identical. When Judaism embraced both as the word of God, it wasn't fudging the issue or ducking questions of textual transmission but saying something about human 'hearing' and perception – and about God.

The implications are explored by Rabbinic Judaism in a text that should be required reading for every person interested in the claims of faith:

Rabbi Abba said in the name of Samuel: For three years there was a dispute between Bet Shammai and Bet Hillel, the former claiming, 'The halakhah (law) is in agreement with our view' and the latter claiming, 'The halakhah is in agreement with our view.' Then a *bat kol* (heavenly voice) announced '*Elu va'elu*, these and these are both the words of the living God but the halakhah is in agreement with the ruling of Bet Hillel.' Since, however, 'both are the words of the Living God', what was it that entitled Bet Hillel to have the halakhah fixed according to their ruling? Because they were kindly and modest, they studied their own rulings and those of Bet Shammai, and were even so humble as to mention the actions of Bet Shammai before their own.[60]

An astonishing text for its time. Or any other time.

First, the context of the text – which is Talmudic, from Tractate Eruvin. It's quoted in the name of the third-century Babylonian Rabbi Mar Samuel. He, along with his colleague Rav, was the most respected of the first generation of Babylonian teachers whose teachings – the G'mara – form the bulk of the Babylonian Talmud.

The passage cites a debate between the Schools of Shammai and Hillel: Shammai and Hillel were founding authorities of the Oral Torah, living in the late first century BCE during the turbulent, formative period of Rabbinic Judaism. So we have a figure of great authority, Samuel, utilizing the most authoritative source available to him. By any criterion, this is a heavyweight text.

And now the text itself: it's unusual, not that there's a dispute or a disagreement, but that we're not told what the disagreement is about. Rabbinic reasoning overwhelmingly favours working from the specific to the general rather than the other way round; but here, we're not given a specific. Why? Because to do so might detract from the principle – allowing the principle to be distinguished or restricted to the specific instance. The redactors of the Talmud are drawing on Hillel, Shammai and Samuel to make an observation of immense theological importance – *elu va'elu divrei elohim hayyim*, two conflicting arguments can both be right; two opinions may both reflect God's Truth in equal measure.

Although not given the facts on which the Schools of Shammai and Hillel disagreed, we are told that the subject was halakhic, not aggadic: matters of behaviour, practice, require a definitive decision in a way that matters of belief do not. So our text is pressing home its teaching: though this is an issue (undisclosed) that requires a decision (halakhic) and cannot be left, the decision cannot be made on the basis of which argument is the better, truer – both are 'the words of the Living God'. The ruling is then made on the grounds that the behaviour of the School of Hillel was more generous, respectful and humble – what you argue is important but how you argue it is also important. Not just, I would argue, as a nod to politeness but because the way you argue your case reflects your ethics and integrity.

What an astounding teaching, placed quite deliberately at the heart of a religious tradition founded on intellectual debate, discussion and disagreement. It isn't a statement of 'anything goes', an endorsement of that fatuous contemporary cop-out 'everybody's entitled to their opinion'; it isn't endorsing an inability to discriminate, tell right from wrong or have no opinion on matters of importance. The text is insisting on something that should halt us in our tracks and make us re-think. Two contradictory opinions can both be true – can both be the words of the Living God. And, if two complementary or conflicting truths are both the words of the Living God, then God God's Self is not simple but complex; God is still One but in a unifying rather than a unitary way.

A text related to but not simply a variant of *elu va'elu* is to be found in the Tosefta:

> Perhaps a man might imagine: 'Since the House of Shammai declares something unclean and the House of Hillel declares it clean; this one prohibits and that one permits' – he might then ask, 'why should I continue to learn Torah?'[61]

In other words, if there are two authoritative but contradictory opinions within our tradition, how can I ever know, ever learn, ever have certainty? The text continues:

> All the words have been given by a single Shepherd. One God created them, one Provider gave them ... So make yourself a heart of many rooms. Bring into it the words of the House of Shammai and the words of the House of Hillel, the words of those who declare unclean and the words of those who declare clean.

In the Jerusalem Talmud there's an observation attributed to a teacher of the third century, Rabbi Yannai: 'Had the Torah been given as one cut [with one final position in all matters without the possibility of divergent opinions] we [subsequent generations] couldn't stand on our own feet [by adding our voices to the enquiry and debate].'[62]

These two comments reinforce the radicality of the position: you're going to have to cope with 'many rooms' – this understanding of God and Truth will be uncomfortable, creating uncertainty, but that's how it is to be human in relation to the Divine. Don't complain; rejoice in being allowed to stand on your own two feet and contribute to the never-ending debate.

To be a Jew is to accept the provisionality of all thought – not least religious thought – embrace paradox, limp anxiously on through the fog of uncertainty and the clamorous challenge of conflicting truths, and live at the edge – socially, culturally and theologically liminal.

Really! And would you say you've lived up to your own, exacting standards? Is that how you, Rabbi Bayfield, have conducted your journey?

No. Of course not. You're right – nothing is more seductive than one's own rhetoric. That hurts, really hurts.

2

The shared context

SECTION ONE
ENVIRONMENT AND TERRAIN

Having spent a chapter looking at how I got to here, I want to devote this chapter to 'here'. What's the context in which I as me and I as your fellow human being live out – and make decisions about how to live out – my life? What is it like being Jewish today - and, more generally, being human - in that shared context?

Let me reiterate two fundamental points. First, I can only start with myself, my own particularity, and work outwards from there, choosing aspects of the personal that experience has taught me will resonate. Second, whatever the context is, it's a shared context: a world into which we're all born, educated, work, live and breathe; a world common to women and men of many faiths and none.

The 'Third Presence'

From the beginning of my rabbinic career, I went – with earnest regularity – to meetings of the Assembly of British Reform Rabbis. We covered a wide range of subjects including contemporary practice, matters of communal and public policy, our relationship with other rabbinic bodies and professional matters. We also discussed liturgy – but not theology. This didn't seem odd – or evasive – but I was aware that something was missing and that's what prompted my decades of Jewish–Christian (and Muslim) dialogue. In carefully constructed, long-lasting groups, ostensibly devoted to the theology

39

of the relationship between the three Abrahamic faiths, I took my first serious steps in trying to clarify what it was I believed.

It was an Orthodox rabbi of the old school – with attitudes formed in less embattled times – Rabbi Norman Solomon, who opened my eyes to the overriding importance of the context essential not just to this chapter but to this book. My aptly named colleague wrote:

> The members of our dialogue group came together on the pretext of participating in a bilateral dialogue. There were two sets of us, a set of Jews and a set of Christians, so the dialogue was bilateral. Or was it?
>
> The first circumstance that might have alerted us to the presence of an invisible guest was that we were all speaking English, our common native tongue, mediating our Hebrew and Greek traditions through another culture (for language is the articulation of culture). It was this shared culture that made the dialogue possible. But it did not – could not – provide a neutral medium. Rather, it was the 'third presence' in the dialogue, a presence whose profound influence was so all-pervasive it was in danger of not being noticed.
>
> Three cultures met – Christian, Jewish and a third, in which all of us Jews and Christians live and find our identity, mediated through the English language. This third was the culture of modernity, or of enlightenment.[1]

Solomon identified the un-evadable presence of a third dialogue partner – for some, more gate-crasher than welcome guest: modernity. And it's not just the context for interfaith dialogue; it's the context within which we all live our lives.

The Modern Western World

There's a broad consensus that the Middle Ages came to an end in Europe towards the end of the fifteenth century. The sixteenth century heralds the emergence of what Thomas Kuhn has enabled us to identify as a new cultural paradigm, best illustrated for me by the cosmologists Copernicus, Kepler and Galileo. By demonstrating that the earth moves round the sun, they were deemed by the Church to have challenged Truth as revealed in the Scriptures – an ecclesiastical ruling bringing religion into conflict with science and reason. Up to that point, reason had played a major role in Western theology – the great teachers of the Church had utilized Greek philosophy to bring an understanding of God derived largely from the Hebrew Scriptures to a world that thought in Hellenistic categories. As the trenchant Catholic theologian Hans Küng points out, under pressure Galileo recanted but the Church wouldn't compromise or countenance an accommodation.[2] By insisting that revealed religion (the texts of the Old and New Testaments) trumped science, the Church opposed both science and reason – a conflict that has proved an unnecessary but defining characteristic of modern Western culture, the environment in which, regardless of our particularity, we all think and breathe.

Amos Elon, as we saw, began his portrait of Jews in Germany in 1743. It was the year in which 14-year-old Moses Mendelssohn left Dessau, a small town in Eastern Germany, and made his way to Frederick the Great's Berlin. Mendelssohn is regarded as the founder of the Jewish Enlightenment. More than anyone, he initiated the process of trying to balance fidelity to Judaism with living within contemporary society. He wasn't, denominationally, a Reform Jew, nor the founder of Reform Judaism – though in the circle of the strictly Orthodox he was regarded as threatening and dangerous.

What defines the new environment ushered in by the sixteenth century? What is this 'modernity' or 'modern Western world', the context for us all, which the Jews of Germany and France were finally permitted to enter en masse at the end of the eighteenth century? I found the beginnings of an answer in a forthright book by British-born, Harvard-based historian Niall Ferguson – *Civilization: The West and the Rest*.[3] Though I was bothered by the absence of any 'post-colonial theory' critique, it took me on the first stage of my quest.

Empire of the West

Civilization sets out to explain what 'led to the conquest and colonization of so much of the rest of the world' by the West. What,

Ferguson asks, began in 1500, spread across half the globe and is now in rapid, terminal decline? What 'were the six killer applications – the killer apps – that allowed a minority of mankind originating on the western edge of Eurasia to dominate the world for the better part of 500 years?'[4]

Ferguson acknowledges it wasn't just the 'strength' of the West but the 'weakness' of the 'opposition' – China, India, Africa, the indigenous populations of the Americas – that played a part. But he sets out his 'six killer apps' with conviction: capitalist competition, science, the rule of law/private property rights, medicine, the creation of a consumer society, and the Protestant work ethic.

I came to the end of the book stimulated but dissatisfied. It was encouraging that Ferguson began, as I proposed to do, at 1500. I was impressed and inspired by his geographical scope: modern Western civilization – though it began in Western Europe – embraces the whole of Europe including the former Soviet Union, North America and the Near East. The inclusion of the Islamic world is imperative, recognizing its far-reaching cultural contribution – and the cut-throat competition between the three Western faiths over 1,300 years.

So why the dissatisfaction? Ferguson explains why Western civilization has been so successful over the last five hundred years but doesn't address the complex web of ideas and values that go hand-in-mailed-fist with an account of the mechanisms of imperial success. My interest is the broad 'theology' that both drives and emerges out of the strategy-driven six-point 'creed'. Ferguson describes the instruments by which a civilization attained and maintained political and economic power on the ground. We need to get to grips with the culture that those on the ground breathed.

Christianity and its Offspring, Secularity

Though all three Abrahamic faiths have played a role in the formation of modern Western culture, Christianity was dominant in the rise of modern Western civilization. So let's now turn to a work of contemporary Christian scholarship for a perspective taking us on from Ferguson. Canadian Professor of Philosophy Charles Taylor published his voluminous study *A Secular Age* in 2007.[5] Taylor is a

Catholic and a sense of what's been lost as much as gained pervades the book. His focus is so narrow that Jews, the Jewish contribution through the Hebrew Bible – and the Jewish catastrophe of the twentieth century – get scarcely a mention. But what he does tell us is extremely helpful – not least his dominant theme that Christianity is complicit in the emergence of secularity.

In 1500, says Taylor, it was almost impossible not to believe in God. The significant events of the natural order were acts of God: the sun shone, the rain fell, plagues raged – this was God acting in the cosmos in a purposeful, meaningful way. God was also 'implicated in society' – in the social hierarchy, in the economic life of the medieval guilds, in the rhythm of the year and its festivals. You couldn't avoid God. Indeed, society was utterly dependent upon God, since individual, sinful acts had implications for everyone – storm or plague were punishments affecting every member of society. Taylor describes an 'enchanted world' filled with spirits, demons and moral forces 'out there', regularly encountered and experienced. His phrase 'moral forces' describes how the ethical was externalized, seen as a facet of God's will. It was then self-evident that good would triumph in the end. What took place after 1500 was a process of disenchantment and internalization, what Taylor describes as the replacement of the 'porous self'– which the external, enchanted world could penetrate – by the 'buffered self' for whom there is only an inner world of thought and experience.[6]

It's a persuasive analysis illustrating a theology I recognize, at the same time one that greatly challenges me. In Taylor's enchanted world, God is not just outside of the individual, in the world but constantly intervening; the suffering inflicted on people by the natural world is divine punishment.

The process of dismantling this pre-modern, medieval understanding of the world is embodied in the Reformation. The Reformation, writes Taylor, regarded the enchanted world in which the Church had existed as derogating from the might of God – it hid it, undermined it. So rich in magic was the medieval Church – the healing power of relics, the efficacy of formulaic prayers and rituals, interventions brought about by pilgrimages and saints – that it both obscured and qualified the exclusive power of God. Says Taylor, 'the magic was discredited by the magician'.[7] For the new elite of the Reformation, medieval religion needed to be replaced, in both church and state spheres, by a regime ordered, rational and disciplined; by the middle of the seventeenth century, Christianity had been transformed. God was now the Creator of an ordered, rational universe; religion disciplined and ordered society; faith had become an internal matter –of the mind and heart.

Over the next century – again among the intellectual elite – the process of excluding God gathered pace. What Taylor terms 'Providential Deism' became dominant. God still existed but God's sphere of operation was reduced to the beginning and end of life; God created the world and God will be the Judge at the end of both life and the world. The secular *coup de grâce* was delivered in the mid-nineteenth century: evolution dispelled the need for a Creator God; scepticism about anything other than this world undermined the concepts of Judgement and Afterlife. So, by the middle of the Victorian period, restriction of life to the immanent, the conviction that human existence is about human flourishing and nothing more, was firmly established – at least in intellectual circles.

Taylor's treatment of the twentieth century is decidedly problematic. He accepts the trauma of the First World War and its position as a watershed, the start of a paradigm shift – using the poetry of Ezra Pound (given Pound's support for Hitler and Mussolini, a curious choice) to sum up the despair, loss and cynicism:

> There died a myriad,
> And the best, amongst them,
> For an old bitch gone in the teeth,
> For a botched civilization.[8]

He then moves rapidly on to the revival of spirituality outside the churches today, ignoring the Second World War and the Shoah.

The story of the modern Western world looks so different through Jewish eyes. I'm reminded of how important the perspective of the outsider, the one at home yet not at home, the faithfully maladjusted, can be. Historian Ferguson and philosopher Taylor nevertheless provide differing points of view, enabling us not only to see the wood but also to identify a number of trees for further study. In fact, we've now reached the point where we can define the environment through which we've all been journeying.

Six Working Definitions

Modern

The modern world dawned around 1500. Ferguson begins with Vasco da Gama's epic voyages and the establishment of Portuguese trade routes with the East. The Portuguese were the first of a series of European powers who together built the modern Western world and extended its reach to an area far greater than any previous 'empire'. Taylor takes the same start date – identifying it with the collapse of the medieval world view and the Reformation. I still favour starting with the mindless rejection of Galileo.

Western

The Western world is essentially European in origin with a culture rooted deeply in the soil of classical Greece and Rome, still Christian or post-Christian in character. It includes both Western and Eastern Europe – Brussels and Moscow – and the Middle East, where its three Abrahamic faiths were born. Some in the Middle East – Jews as well as Muslims – will kick against this but it's where Judaism, Christianity and Islam all stem from and continue to contribute, albeit dysfunctionally, to the culture that dominates so much of the globe today. The West also includes those lands colonized by Europeans who wiped out the indigenous population and their cultures – North America, Australia and New Zealand. Whether a Jew lives in Manchester or Los Angeles, St Petersburg or Cairo, Toronto or Sydney, Jerusalem or Tel Aviv, she or he lives within the Western world. As do the Christian, Muslim (and, today Buddhist, Sikh and Hindu), Humanist and Secularist residents of those same cities. Such is the extent of the West.

Civilization and culture

Ferguson uses the word civilization geopolitically – to refer to those areas over which a state or group of states exercises power and control – military, governmental and economic. A civilization is then defined by what is instrumental to that power and control. I've elected to use the term culture to go beyond Ferguson's economics and science to include, for example, religion, philosophy and the arts – all those ways in which a civilization expresses its values and its search for meaning.

Terrain and environment

Writing about the birth and growth of Western civilization, Ferguson concentrates by turn on Portugal, Holland, Spain, France, Britain and Germany – where modern Western civilization and culture began and developed. Each of those countries has its own terrain with particular characteristics. Portugal's position, on the Atlantic, made it easy to sail down the West Coast of Africa, round the Cape of Good Hope and into the Indian Ocean at a time when the existing spice routes were controlled by the Ottomans and Venetians. Britain's natural resources of coal and iron fuelled industrial revolution.

American society, Charles Taylor argues, was bequeathed by its founding fathers a different understanding of the role of religion from that in Europe. America, early on, saw itself as integrating different elements. *E Pluribus Unum* (Out of Many, One) referred to the different States but soon applied to 'denominations' – at first Protestants but, in the course of the twentieth century, coming to include Catholics and Jews: 'A way that Americans can understand their fitting together in society although of different faiths, is through these faiths themselves being seen as in this consensual relation to the common civil religion. Go to the church of your choice, but go.'[9]

Taylor makes the point that American society is horizontal – all men (*sic*) are created equal under God, a notion reflecting the Deist outlook of Washington and Jefferson. British society, by contrast, has retained a noticeable degree of the vertical with an established Church and a monarch who is Head of that Church. The differences are ones of terrain, weathered by history. The environment – which includes the changing nature of Christianity and its relationship to the secular – is the same across both terrains.

Terrain is important to the Jewish story – the horizontal features of America have ensured a different relationship to religion there from the more vertical terrain of Western Europe; Israel is terrain *sui generis*. But environment is broader, more all-pervasive – that into which we're all born and educated; within which we live and breathe all day, every day. It's the environment through which we journey. For the purpose of this book, *civilization* equates to an agglomeration of terrains; *culture* equals environment.

SECTION TWO
THE JEWISH CONTRIBUTION

Judaism and Western Culture before 1500

The Jewish contribution to the formation of Western culture looks – through my eyes – to be consistently under-acknowledged. The following are examples of what I mean.

Rabbi Hugo Gryn served West London Synagogue at Marble Arch for several decades. In common with most congregational rabbis, one of his duties was to show school parties round the sanctuary. Gryn would open the ark with its *Sifrei Torah*, scrolls, hand children copies of the *Siddur*, Prayer Book, and take them through the service. On one occasion, reaching the third blessing of the *Amidah*, with its quotation from Isaiah: 'Holy, Holy, Holy is the God of the heavenly hosts',[10] one student remarked: 'Wow. I'd never realized how much you Jews have taken from Christian prayers before.' The story may have been embellished in the telling but reflects the wry Jewish response to what we perceive as a Christian-centred view of the world and religion.

The year 2011 marked the four-hundredth anniversary of the printing of the King James Bible – a momentous event in the development not just of the Anglican Church but of the English language. The BBC commissioned a television series and book from Melvyn Bragg, fine novelist and veteran expounder of Western culture in the media. I watched the programmes with growing anxiety. Bragg argued convincingly that the King James Bible not only influenced the language of the English-speaking world but also prompted and moulded many of the humanist values of modern Western culture. What I didn't hear Bragg say was that the linguistic and ethical impact came not just from the New Testament but also from the much more extensive Hebrew Bible – I'd even have settled for 'Old Testament'. This went completely unacknowledged. Buying the book, I found there were only four references to Judaism in 350 pages assessing the impact of this translation of the Bible into English.[11]

An educational slogan of recent decades has been 'Remember Jesus was a Jew', popularly taken to mean that because the founder of Christianity was Jewish, 'Christians must be nice to Jews'. The sentiment is fine but the inference should be different. Jesus was – to say the least – a major Jewish teacher with a passionate bias towards the poor and outcasts of society, his teachings firmly rooted in Torah and Prophetic Literature. The causes he takes up arise from his distinctive understandings of the demands of Torah; the texts he cites – such as 'Love your neighbour'[12] – are from the Hebrew Bible. In a society in turmoil, with many parties and groupings, Jesus most resembles the Pharisees with whom he's presented as being in conflict. Rabbinic Judaism and Christianity come from the same stock. Each carried with it the same foundational literature – known to one as the Hebrew Bible and to the other as the Old Testament. 'Old' may be offensively supersessionist – 'Your covenant is now void; we're the favoured ones now' – but the great Jewish teacher and his Hebrew Bible travelled on with the New Testament and developing Christianity. To imply that what entered the modern Western world in 1500 was only a self-sufficient Christianity is obstinately wrong.

Judaism and Western Culture from 1800 to 1945

From the beginning of the thirteenth century, European Jewry became increasingly isolated – separated by dress, disadvantaged socially and commercially by law, in some cases confined to a ghettoized existence from the sixteenth century on. This had the effect of severely limiting interaction between Jewish culture and the culture beyond. It was as if Jewry had been put in a bottle, corked and then regularly shaken. Only external change – the political and cultural factors that brought about and are embodied in the American and French Revolutions – enabled Moses Mendelssohn to travel from Dessau to Berlin and herald the uncorking of the bottle. What happened over the following two centuries is extraordinary – wonderful and horrific – symbolic of modernity and its crucifying contradictions. Let me offer two recently observed echoes.

A convent was established hard up against the perimeter of Auschwitz. In the mid-1980s a large cross was erected in the grounds, visible from inside the extermination camp. The late Sir Sigmund Sternberg, a refugee from Budapest, was at the time the unofficial 'Foreign Minister' of British Jewry. For Jews throughout the world, a cross overshadowing, and thereby laying claim to Auschwitz was unbearable. Many had intervened but Sir Sigmund's initiative led to a meeting in 1989 with the Polish Primate Cardinal Glemp at the home of the Polish Ambassador to Britain, which Sir Sigmund invited me to join. Negotiations for the removal of the cross, the transfer of the nuns and the establishment of an interfaith centre were well advanced. Cardinal Glemp – previously publicly opposed to any concessions – was now on the verge of a volte-face. Towards the end of the evening, Sternberg was anxious to go public. At just after 10 p.m., he asked the Cardinal to sign the statement so that it could be faxed to *The Times* by their 10.30 p.m. deadline. To which Glemp replied: 'What's the hurry? You Jews own the Press – you can tell them to wait.'

More recently, my granddaughter Chessy, studying Verdi's *Requiem* for A-Level music, discovered that the Jewish orchestra in Terezin had played Verdi at least sixteen times – more than any other piece of music. In a late-night text, she asked me why Jews in a death camp would choose a Christian requiem. I replied that these were Jews steeped in modern Western culture who, with little if any Jewish equivalent, found the music appropriate to their circumstances. More importantly, they were Jews who were not willing to allow Hitler to eradicate them from the culture to which they'd contributed and were fully part. It was a defiant refusal to go 'like lambs to the slaughter', a prime example of spiritual resistance.

Some months later, I went to hear Chessy singing *St Matthew' Passion* with the Bach Choir at the Royal Festival Hall – in English. It's the most exquisite music, a pinnacle of our Western musical tradition, and yet the text, Matthew's Gospel, is arguably the most polemic with regard to Jewish complicity in the death of Jesus. At the end I exploded at my family: 'Why is it that at the very heart of Western culture we're portrayed as the personification of evil?'

Eternal ambiguity? Infernal paradox? Inescapable role?

Jews Uncorked

In Britain, at least, Jews are hesitant to voice the full extent of the Jewish contribution to contemporary life (beyond bagels and bar mitzvahs), aware that it could reinforce a murderous stereotype still influencing attitudes throughout the world – where there were, are, and even where there never have been Jews. Nevertheless, the uncorking brought a contribution to Western civilization and culture I feel compelled to confront explicitly. Here's a passage from Ferguson, which, for me, stood out like a sore thumb:

> The Jewish role in western intellectual life in the twentieth century – especially in the United States – was indeed disproportionate, *suggesting a genetic as much as a cultural advantage.* Accounting for around 0.2 per cent of the world's population and 2 per cent of the American population, Jews won 22 per cent of all Nobel Prizes, 20 per cent of all Fields Medals for mathematics and 67 per cent of the John Clarke Bates Medals for economists under the age of forty. Jews also won 38 per cent of the Oscars for Best Director, 20 per cent of the Pulitzer Prizes for non-fiction and 13 per cent of Grammy Lifetime Achievement Awards.[13] [My emphasis]

That tells me why I've included this section. I want to acknowledge I'm part of this extraordinary story, that being Jewish is compelling enough for me to want us and it to continue. But I also want to refute all notions of superiority, including genetic advantage with its overtones of racial superiority; I need to understand for myself how this contribution to modern Western culture came about. We'll start in Hollywood.

The role of immigrant Jews in the creation and development of Hollywood – as with the Broadway musical and American song-writing – is legendary. Back in the 1920s, Los Angeles was riddled with anti-Semitism. Jews couldn't join country clubs, send their children to private schools, and – shades of Black Americans in the

Deep South – restaurants even carried notices saying: 'No Jews served here'. Presumably not even on rye! Commercial banking, real estate and heavy industry were also no-go areas. The film industry, however, was new, on the creative limen; relatively few others were involved – no one could say that Jews weren't wanted. There we have the first factor in explaining Jewish achievement. Jews simply behaved in typical immigrant fashion. Excluded from the bastions of the traditional economy, they took up a place on the margins and worked creatively – a stance noticeable even today.

You can see several psychological and economic factors at work. California's Jews had gone doubly west – first from Eastern Europe and then from the east to the west coast. Here was a new frontier; a land of opportunity; they saw wealth and prosperity all around them, wanted some of it and set about getting it. They were able to overcome obstacles, which, unlike in the Pale of Settlement, were those of social prejudice, not repressive Tsarist measures backed by organized violence. Some worked all hours doing whatever it took to acquire the wealth and power to force their way into the clubs, schools and restaurants from which they were excluded. Others were prepared to work just as hard to be able to say, 'You know what you can do with your clubs, schools and restaurants; we'll build our own. We're just as good as you, if not better.'

The Jewish drive to succeed – not just in Hollywood but all over the modern Western world – has to do with grabbing opportunities with both hands after centuries of exclusion, coupled with a determination to demonstrate that we're at least the equals of our detractors. If you denigrate and confine a people for centuries and then allow them out of the ghetto and the *shtetl*; if you let people emigrate from repressive societies into societies of opportunity; if you uncork the bottle, it isn't surprising they seize the opportunity with great enthusiasm. Yet it can't just be that – the nature and extent of the contribution are not so easily explained.

But if it's not simply classic immigrant behaviour, does that take us back to Ferguson's 'a genetic as much as a cultural advantage'? I cringe. Having been victims of Teutonic theories of blood and condemned as *untermenschen*, being labelled *übermenschen* feels just as bad and even more dangerous. However, I can't simply shut my eyes in denial but need to examine the genetic theory.

In 2012 American Jewish geneticist Harry Ostrer published a study of Jews and genetics.[14] To help with its technicalities, I turned to Professor Sir Michael Marmot, one of the world's leading experts on the social determinants of health, familiar with medical statistics. Marmot's conclusion was that Ostrer had come to no clear conclusion; contemporary complexity reigns! Genetic analysis does reveal a clustering in specific Jewish populations that explains the prevalence of Tay Sachs disease[15] among Ashkenazi Jews. But there's no particular Jewish genetic profile; our profiles overlap with those of the populations where Jews have lived or live. Ostrer, explained Marmot, found nothing to indicate significant variations in IQ: nature and nurture, selection (given the pressures Jews have been under during the centuries, perhaps the more resourceful survived and passed on that predisposition), education and circumstances are all factors.[16]

Let's go back 2,000 years to the formation of Rabbinic Judaism, which favoured the brightest, those with aptitude for the intellectual process of developing post-biblical, post-Second Temple Judaism. It selected men who could make a contribution to developing the reasoning, formulation and application of the ideas. Rabbinic Judaism was created and developed by people who asked difficult and challenging questions, wanting nothing better than to struggle with the answers; it was built from debate among those drawn to the process.

For the next 1,800 years, prestige within the Jewish world didn't go to the tallest, most athletic or even the most economically astute. It went to the intellectual leaders, the rabbis – regardless of their social and occupational background. This is what large numbers of Jews aspired to for their children. And, as you might expect, the relatively wealthy, the more economically successful, often wanted nothing better than to marry off their daughter to a rabbi! One can over-generalize but it's reasonable to argue that Judaism favoured intellectuality and intellectual leadership – even over piety, selflessness, humility, a taste for the mystical or a vocation for celibacy. That constant favouring of learning and challenging was, generation after generation, transmitted through communal and family values. Nearly two millennia of giving preference, prizes and status to these skills has much to do with the outpouring of broader intellectual activity among Jews in the nineteenth and twentieth centuries.

We therefore have a number of factors accounting for the substantial Jewish contribution to Western culture – among which are: the effect of being released from physical and intellectual ghettos; the outsiders' perspective and determination to prove themselves; the very nature of Rabbinic Judaism, favouring the intellect as a constant in an ever-changing environment.

But Jews shouldn't be smug. The bottle of champagne was uncorked at the beginning of the nineteenth century (much later in Eastern Europe) and out it sprayed into society. We all know what happens to champagne once opened – what sprays out dries up; what's left in the bottle goes flat. The champagne Jews – from Mahler to Rothko; from Durkheim to Bohr; from Chomsky to Derrida – didn't, as a rule, hand on their Jewishness to the next generation. Before the First World War such Jews tended to define themselves and be defined against the Jewish community; in more recent years the majority have lived their lives outside organized religion and traditional beliefs. The established community has often maintained ambivalent feelings and done little to rescue their descendants and reattach them to the Jewish community.

Moreover, rabbis have now given up their intellectual role in favour, on the 'conservative right' of the community, of devotion to an obsessive-compulsive concern with ritual minutiae and the politics of piety; and, on the 'liberal left', with pastoral and clerical duties, building 'warm', inclusive communities. In a society suspicious of intellectuality, unlike France for instance, British Jewry prefers a culture of folk nostalgia to one of critical reading and thinking; much contemporary Judaism, like much contemporary Christianity and Islam, has failed to address the most pressing problems of today – the theological, ethical and practical concerns about why life is as it is and how, as a result, it should be lived. These were the *raison d'être* of classical Rabbinic Judaism; alarmingly, they aren't the meaning and purpose of Judaism today.

No mention of Me, I notice, Dr Bayfield.

Exactly.

SECTION THREE
THE ENVIRONMENT TODAY

On the Far Side of the Abyss

Between 1933, the year that saw Hitler democratically elected, and 1953, the death of Stalin, the Western world plunged into the Abyss. A paradigm shift had been signalled by the destructive tremors of the First World War, heralding radical change – notably the crumbling of the power of Britain's ruling elite, the shift from aristocracy to meritocracy, and the emancipation of women – all of which, though accompanied by un-anaesthetized labour pains, have been hugely beneficial. But, in the process, so much that had underpinned modernity gave way and the glorious city that was modern Western culture toppled into the Abyss. And with it, Jews and Judaism.

It's at this point we encounter contested terminology – what lies on our side of the Abyss I call 'post-modern'. The terminology hardly matters to me, but that there has been a collapse, a paradigm shift, is something on which I'll not concede an inch. You simply cannot tell a Jew that there hasn't been an earthquake – of human creation – off the Richter scale. If you're a Christian or a Humanist and cannot see the perplexing features and daunting challenge of the new landscape we share, a visit to an ophthalmic surgeon is long overdue.

The *Kulturschock* and the Post-modern Western World

Born in 1946, educated at a Romford grammar school, I read Law at Cambridge intending to become a solicitor. At that time, I'd no sense of the paradigm shift; on the contrary, my perception was of continuity. In my final year, I was much taken by an optional criminology course – studying the sociological and psychological determinants of crime based on scientific research. I applied to do doctoral research at the Cambridge Institute for Criminology – founded ironically (I knew not at the time) by a Jewish refugee, Leon Radzinowicz. In the end, however, I went to the Leo Baeck College – from criminology to rabbinics being an imperceptible step! Walking into that small precarious college in the early autumn of 1968, as a full-of-myself graduate, I was blissfully unaware of the paradigm shift. That proved to be the backdrop to a culture shock or, rather, *Kulturschock*, that took me decades to grasp.

The College had been founded only a few years earlier as successor to the Hochschule für die Wissenschaft des Judentums (rabbinic seminary) in Berlin. Its 'father', Rabbi Werner van der Zyl, Senior Rabbi of West London Synagogue, was himself from Germany – born and trained there. Its teaching staff were all survivors. I was no longer at Magdalene College, Cambridge, no longer in the rationalist, post-religious environment of a late twentieth-century English law faculty. In fact I wasn't in England's green and pleasant land at all, but in the displaced persons camp of the most despised and rejected of peoples[17] – German Jewry.

Dr Ellen Littmann, refugee from Heidelberg and Berlin, used to slap my desk and enquire (I can hear the accent even now)· 'Vy haf you not prepared, Mr Bayley?' She never did get my name right. 'You're so Inglish, Mr Bayley,' she would say. Surprisingly, I managed to refrain from saying, 'And you're so German, Dr Littmann', which would have hurt her enormously. I never appreciated the privilege and pathos of the experience, sitting at the feet of half a dozen surviving fragments of an intensely rich and productive chapter in Jewish history, utterly, brutally destroyed. Such was my insecurity and immaturity.

The recognition explicit in those last six words, I owe to another German-speaking refugee, Sigmund Freud, who had died a few miles away 30 years earlier but was as present at the Leo Baeck College as its surviving teachers. Psychoanalytic theory has moved on since Freud first enabled people to listen to themselves and explore their suppressed fears and anxieties. But self-consciousness and self-awareness are the most important tools for liberating ourselves from hubris, so often the source of damaging behaviour and perverted 'religion'.

People can be sidetracked by Freud's supposed hostility to religion. Freud was a Viennese Jew of his time and, as the distinguished psychoanalyst Adam Phillips points out, driven to give a voice to those who find their circumstances oppressive and life 'impossible to adapt to'.[18] The God Freud had encountered was an all-powerful, coercive figure, clearly antithetical to Freud's mission. But for me, it's not a question of either/or. The God of this book is compatible with psychoanalytic theory precisely because psychoanalysis offers liberation from the tyranny of beliefs and actions that lack of self-awareness causes.

I asked my mentor Professor Bill Fulford, specialist in the philosophy of psychiatry, for his assessment of Freud. He said Freud turned what had previously been the province of novelists and poets into a science; Freud's early papers, he added, are masterpieces of scientific method, far ahead of their times. Much critique and development has taken place subsequently in psychoanalysis and psychotherapy, but Freud's establishment of consciousness and the subconscious as objects for scientific study was and remains pivotal. We strive to be honest about what motivates us; we acknowledge ourselves as the subject, but not the prisoner, of our drives. My approach to Judaism and its beliefs would have been inconceivable before Freud.

My theology teacher at Leo Baeck College was Rabbi Dr Ignaz Maybaum, a last link in the chain of modern German Jewish philosopher–theologians that began with Hermann Cohen, included Franz Rosenzweig and Martin Buber, and ended with Leo Baeck, after whom the College was named. Maybaum, a disciple of Rosenzweig, had been installed as the first rabbi of Edgware and District Reform Synagogue. It wasn't a marriage made in heaven – the Jews of suburban Edgware wanted reformed rules of practice, not a final, defiant gesture from the German Jewish theological tradition. But it was one of my life's most memorable and formative experiences, sitting in the front room of Ignaz Maybaum's 1930s Edgware semi-detached house, with continental cake and proper coffee, listening to him try to formulate what I now realize was a theological account of his own journey. Maybaum became part of my heart and mind. But his theology was eccentric, out of time and place. Culturally, he remained in Germany and his responses to the Shoah couldn't possibly work for those who lived beyond Germany and far beyond 1945.[19]

Dr Littmann was absolutely right. I'm 'so Inglish'. How could I be otherwise? My parents chose to integrate into British society and had me educated in English institutions. I respond emotionally to Elgar and Vaughan Williams, Donne and Wilfred Owen. The English language means everything to me – just as 'Mr Buber, he says zis so vunderfully in zer Cherman' meant everything to brave, displaced Ellen Littmann whom I teased too much and empathized with too little. Raised and educated in post-war England, enveloped by British society, I brought to Ignaz Maybaum's theology classes a range of questions that weren't his and were therefore at odds with his answers. The Leo Baeck College, staffed by people with journeys very different in time, terrain and environment from my own, didn't address my questions. How could they? The task of dealing with the unimaginable and incomprehensible collapse of their world, the modern Western world, was overwhelming. I'd been born – as all Jews – a survivor, but beyond the Abyss, in a post-modern world; the encounter was a *Kulturschock* for me – and, of course, for them.

Still no mention of Me? Have you written Me off along with your Kulturschock?

I often think I'd like to but You don't exactly make that easy for me, do You? Anyway, we haven't discussed Your existence yet.

The Post-modern Landscape

Modernity is, in many ways, closed to us – a foreign country where they thought and did things differently. Yet being past at least lends a measure of detached clarity. The present is so filled with swirling, undifferentiated experiences – an endless staccato of events, unremitting change – that it's almost impossible to tell the important from the trivial and the lasting from today's news headlines. But we have to try.

Four areas dominate our contemporary landscape – communications, economics, science and technology, and, in a very different way, philosophy. Let me outline each, because to go into more detail would lose me – and you – in the un-clarity of the present. Between them, they characterize the post-modern world, the environment with which we and our traditions interact, and represent the most daunting challenge.

Back in the 1970s, we were warned by 'Futurologists' – led by Alvin Toffler[20] – of the exponential rate of change already under way. It would become increasingly bewildering and disorientating, they predicted; how right they were. The focus of much of their work was technology but, half a century later, it's the dawning of the Digital Age, the revolution in communications, that is the most immediate, pervasive and invasive example.

Communications

Professionally, pastorally and personally I'm overwhelmed by information – with access to more material than I can absorb let alone think about critically; bombarded by different selections and interpretations of the 'facts'. There are so many complex trees that knowing where I am in the wood is disturbingly difficult. Yet throughout this wood is information that provides a better basis for theologizing and practising than any rabbi of a previous generation was blessed with. How do I discriminate?

We're given more access to what's going on all over the globe than at any previous time in human history. We can watch a British surgeon helping a Syrian doctor perform life-saving operations in a hospital turned hell-hole; we're repeatedly shown sword and famine murdering and impoverishing across the globe. But someone is selecting what we see: who and what should we believe?

Unsettling, unnerving questions arise: since I live in a world so interconnected by news and social media, has everyone become my neighbour? Is the relationship between me and my physical neighbours the same as the relationship with the Syrian doctor and his patient's family? Do I owe them the same obligations? Does a single ethic cover my relationship to all humanity near or far? How should I respond?

We're experiencing societal change as important and more immediate than the invention of printing. Rich beyond measure in information, 'globally connected' and able to make our voices and opinions heard in ways previous generations could not conceive – we're also open to manipulation as never before. Unknown others can access our personal particulars; uninvited others can make contact with, 'target' us for commercial, political or sexual purposes.

I'm suspicious of social media – my instinct has always been to decry the virtual as opposed to the real (the very language is loaded). Deborah Blausten, a rabbinic student and specialist in education and technology, has made me aware that my scepticism is, in part, a generational response – one generation (mine) reading the socialization behaviour of another incorrectly. Along with Jewish and Christian colleagues, I've expressed concern that being able to connect virtually the world over with people with similar interests – religious, educational, environmental – threatens the local, rendering it dull and parochial. Blausten points out that the internet can be used to facilitate the local and make action more effective than it's ever been.

Truth itself is at the heart of this paradox. It's at our fingertips as never before, but such is the sophistication of contemporary communications that both the visual and oral can be faked. Unscrupulous politicians not only deny the truth by dismissing it as 'fake news' but create fake news themselves. Children in schools are taught strategies for discriminating but their elders repeatedly fall victim to what they want to hear.

In short, the e-revolution can enlarge our horizons, facilitate connectedness, provide undreamed of access to the plight of others, give a voice to the voiceless and downtrodden – but it can also be used to fill time with emptiness, provide dubious role models and manipulate our deepest anxieties and fears. To all those bent on flouting or subverting such shared values as post-modern Western society can agree, cyberspace offers endless opportunity.

A cost–benefit analysis of the e-revolution is only possible with hindsight and almost certainly futile. But questions about responsibility and control cry out as loudly as Abel's blood. Who now is our sibling's keeper? Where lies control? Yet, in the end, the medium is not the message. Raising the alarm is important but using it as an excuse for lack of collaborative religious and ethical response would be the worst possible form of evasion. We desperately need regulation but equally desperately have to agree the values determining that regulation.

Economics

A few years ago, listening to BBC Radio 4's *Today* programme while mentally preparing for the day ahead, the radio and my thoughts collided. The item was one of those interminable examinations of the 'unanticipated' consequences of government policy – the government had decided to limit entry visas to 100,000 potential immigrants a year, including prospective university students. A spokesperson for the Higher Education 'industry' protested this was having a disastrous effect on applications from the Indian subcontinent where, said the spokesperson, they think our universities are 'no longer open for business'. Three thoughts struck me in rapid succession. First, Higher Education is now an industry, part of the economy like widget manufacturing or financial services; second, the justification offered for opposing the policy was a business one – including students in the quota was detrimental in market terms. Third, the language used labelled people as either producers (the teachers) or consumers (the students).

Judaism has rarely advocated retreat from the material world – theologically or physically – but has sought a balance, far from evident in wider society today. The post-modern Western world is increasingly polarized between those arguing for unbridled free-market capitalism and others demanding that power move from those who control wealth to those who control the State. Whatever else, the arguments are dominated by economics, which moulds the lives and hopes of the entire population.

One of the Futurologists predicting exponential change was a British academic, Tom Stonier.[21] In the early 1980s, he argued that robots would take over both manufacturing and routine work, leaving the majority of us free to concentrate on health, education and care – fields in which human beings, Stonier believed, are indispensable. Although we can already see the effects of robotics, more drastic change lies ahead. Yet even thus far, we've largely ignored the consequences for those displaced and Stonier's optimism about how the majority would be occupied has proved a hollow prophecy. More than three decades on, a contemporary Futurologist, Yuval Noah Harari, predicts Artificial Intelligence will make *Homo sapiens* entirely obsolete.[22] At the very least, it will be our greatest challenge to ensure that AI benefits humanity economically and, more importantly, culturally and doesn't enslave us or lead to our extinction.

Science and technology
As far as post-modern Western culture is concerned, the war between science and religion – which opened with the battle over cosmology – has been won by science. Religion is either in retreat or denial, its metaphysics largely discarded in daily thought and life.

Science is indisputably exciting because it reveals the awesome complexity of the physical world and we have justifiable faith in its methodology: we hypothesize, we test and we demonstrate. Stephen Hawking, however, was explicit that in so doing we reveal 'the mind of God'.[23] The fact that the Big Bang, the awe-inspiring laws of nature and the fuzzy indeterminacy of quantum particles are compatible with my kind of religion is of little interest to the majority. Several hundred years of fighting a war over mistaken territory scarcely encourages the victors and the weary to return to the battlefield.

At least two areas of science — when taken to reductionist extremes — are not only problematic for religion but disturbing for humanism. Evolutionary biologists have continued the work of Darwin and many, following Crick and Watson's revelations about DNA, claim God is no longer necessary — evolution is a seamless process from the Big Bang to today, requiring no intervention by a Creator. This work has been compounded by some in the field of neuroscience who view the human brain as a pre-programmed, genetically determined organ that is 'all there is' — just chemical activity you can observe on an fMRI scanner. 'Hard-wired' has entered everyday speech as a scientific parallel to the dehumanizing use of economic terms to describe us as commodities.

I've no problem with the claim of the evolutionary biologists that you don't find God inside the process — of course you don't — but it doesn't follow that they've thereby vanquished God with this observation. The neuromaniacs — as neuroscientist Raymond Tallis[24] calls them — have rushed even further down the reductionist cul-de-sac, making the same arrogant and obtuse mistake. They reduce the world — about which science hypothesizes and which it demonstrates — to a single dimension. They persist in shouting ever louder that it's all there is; proclaiming the sure and certain faith that there is no metaphysical world, no dimension that science cannot access. The Canadian psychologist Stephen Pinker tells us that, thanks to science and reason, the world is making progress. In an important sense it is — most in the Western world would prefer to live now than in any previous generation. Yet 'getting steadily better' isn't most people's impression — because, intuitively, we don't measure progress by the achievements of technology alone.[25]

It's clear to many that technology has the potential both to fulfil our dreams and to bring about our worst nightmares. Two things are less clear. First, technology has no inherent ethicality – which ought to be self-evident but doesn't appear to be so. The Four Horsemen of the New Atheism[26] insist that science offers the best source of values by which to live. But nuclear power, for instance, is a tool, not a value – available for good and evil, for human flourishing or withering, for the life or death of the planet.

Second – more widely recognized and disputed – can technology be managed? If it's impossible to stop people letting the genie out of the bottle, can the genie be controlled once it's out? This isn't simply a case of some doctors somewhere exploiting gene editing for commercial gain, but a basic issue of power and responsibility – if the technology of robots, for instance, is to be controlled, with whom does the power and authority lie to decide what controls to impose? As we'll see in Chapter 7, such matters demand to be widely debated in the 'Public Square'. But the 'Public Square' is under occupation and I fear discussion will be overtaken by *fait accompli* and we'll be thrust into a world we've chosen not to choose.

German-born Jewish philosopher Hans Jonas will feature at several important points in this book. Jonas's understanding of the paradigm shift, exemplified by the Abyss, is that humanity now has the capability to destroy itself (using nuclear weapons) and the globe (by causing environmental catastrophe). A prophet of the modern Western world, as early as the 1970s Jonas was calling for a new global ethics.[27]

Scientific reductionism reaches the zenith (or nadir) of its challenge in the insistence that the human being is a one-dimensional animal – an animal like all others with none of the distinguishing features we've always felt we've had and that many of us still, intuitively, know we have. Such a conclusion leads to the bleakest possible view of existence, encapsulated in the work of the philosopher John Gray and his crushing manifesto *Straw Dogs*.[28]

Gray claims life is 'a fluke … a lucky throw in the cosmic lottery'.[29] Human beings are animals, highly inventive but predatory and destructive, not just 'exceptionally rapacious primates'[30] but 'a result of blind evolutionary drift'.[31] Gray reduces us to 'assemblies of genes interacting at random with each other and their shifting environments'.[32] 'Humanity' does not exist, he writes. 'There are only humans, driven by conflicting needs and illusions, and subject to every kind of infirmity of will and judgement.'[33] 'Humans cannot be other than irrational';[34] 'morality is a sickness peculiar to humans',[35] 'an ugly superstition'.[36] He concludes that progress is an illusion, 'our natural condition'.[37]

It's reductionism to a point beyond *absurdum*, denying all meaning, all hope. Yet, Gray's insistence that human beings are nothing more than rapacious and particularly unpleasant animals is a marked characteristic of a major thrust of intellectual and cultural life on this side of the Abyss. Though his prime targets are Christians, Humanists and Utopians, each one of us is collateral damage: all genetically determined, incapable of rational thought, with only an illusion of ethics.

Gray has recently been supplanted in secular intellectual acclaim by Israeli authority on 'World History', Yuval Noah Harari. In his first book *Sapiens*,[38] Harari identifies the 'Cognitive Revolution' – new ways of thinking and communicating – that enabled *Homo sapiens* to see off contemporary and future rivals. With Israeli biblical awareness he calls this 'the Tree of Knowledge mutation'[39] and a matter of pure chance. He then goes on to say that the 'Cognitive Revolution' led to our unique facility: 'only sapiens can talk about entire kinds of entities that they have never seen, touched or smelled'. He continues:

> Legends, myths, gods and religions appeared for the first time with the Cognitive Revolution. Many animals and human species could previously say, 'Careful! A lion!' Thanks to the Cognitive Revolution, *Homo sapiens* acquired the ability to say, 'The lion is the guardian spirit of our tribe.' *This ability to speak about fictions is the most unique feature of Sapiens language*.[40] (My emphasis)

The success of our species is attributable to our ability to imagine collectively and create fantasies that have no connection to reality. So the spring of Harari's 'Cognitive Revolution' dries up in the hoary empiricist insistence that only that which is directly accessible to sense perception exists. Neither in *Sapiens*, *Homo Deus*[41] nor *21 Lessons for the 21st Century*[42] – all spectacular bestsellers – does Harari even entertain the idea that reality may extend beyond the world of sense perception and our stories may point to a larger reality, perceptions of which only the language of myth and metaphor enables us to articulate.

Harari – who, as we've seen, is also a Futurologist – suggests that *Homo sapiens* will, in the relatively near future (through the creation of cyborgs, a direct two-way brain–computer interface and the re-creation of a human brain inside a computer), enable life to 'suddenly break out into the vastness of the inorganic realm'.[43] The most likely outcome of what is a second Cognitive Revolution is that *Homo sapiens* will not only make itself redundant but become extinct. Harari first dismantles our intimations of meaning; he then goes on to eliminate any hope for a future.

Hugo Gryn was 14 years old when he found himself, with his father, in a concentration camp, grotesquely called *Lieberose* – Lovely Rose. He recalled his father's words: 'You and I have seen that it is possible to live up to three weeks without food. We once lived almost three days without water; but you cannot live properly for three minutes without hope!'[44] The observation makes sense psychologically; but it wasn't intended as a psychological observation. Or as a placebo.

In the post-modern world, science reveals an undeniable and awesome dimension of existence. But is it the only dimension? Never was the question more acute nor the faith-crushing affirmative answer a given for so many.

Philosophy
Philosophy is a feature of the post-modern landscape in a different way – by its withdrawal into linguistics and logic, by what it no longer addresses. In a survey of the Western philosophical tradition, Bryan Magee makes the point that more than a century ago philosophy and theology parted company; twentieth-century philosophy is the province of academics attempting 'to understand the human condition in a universe no longer seen as created by God, or as having meaning and purpose of its own'.[45] The career of arguably the greatest Jewish philosopher of the twentieth century, Franz Rosenzweig, is illustrative. Rosenzweig was an outstanding young Hegelian philosopher with a glittering career in front of him when he chose to leave the cloisters of academia to work among the

lived lives of the German Jewish community. He rejected theology as intellectual theory and replaced it with reasoned experience.

As Keith Ward – a philosopher who became Regius Professor of Divinity at Oxford – observes: whether a philosopher in Britain today has a faith or not isn't regarded as relevant to the philosophy they do.[46] That doesn't mean philosophy since the Second World War is of no interest to Jewish theologians. A fascinating example is Postmodernism, which originated in Paris and the decades immediately after the Second World War. Oxford Professor of English Christopher Butler spells out Postmodernism's world view:

> The world, its social systems, human identity even, are not *givens*, somehow guaranteed by a language which corresponds to reality, but are *constructed by us* in language, in ways that can never be justified by the claim that this is the way such things 'really are'[47]

This is very unsettling – particularly to a tradition in which language is its USP.[48] But it can also be liberating by throwing us back on the realization – even revelation – of the questioning nature of every text. The philosopher who drove the Postmodernist movement was Algerian-born French Jew Jacques Derrida, liminal in many aspects of his background. Derrida was a remarkable figure whose life and work reward exploration – not least his increasing discomfort with Soviet Communism, so strongly defended by many of his colleagues in the Parisian intellectual elite of his day. But here, what's most relevant in Derrida – his methodology is known as deconstruction – is explained by a Christian contemporary of his, the French theologian Paul Ricoeur: 'Deconstruction is a way of uncovering the questions behind the answers of a text or tradition.' The text, the tradition, is never closed; what appears to be an answer is, in fact, a deeper question. It's provisional; we move on.

Equally important for our purposes is a non-Jewish intellectual with whom Derrida had frequent contact and exchange, the social theorist Michel Foucault. Foucault concentrated on 'the other' in society, his standard examples being homosexuals, women, the criminally insane, non-whites and prisoners.[49] He not only identifies such people as the victims of specific power structures within society but broadens the argument into the assertion that the discourse of our entire society has internalized subordinating norms. Foucault's exposure of the ubiquity of abuse of power is penetrating and sobering. The American Jewish philosopher Judith Butler provides a scarifying analysis of such abuses in her studies of gender, which, as we'll see in the next chapter, have far-reaching implications for the contemporary Jewish community, its patriarchal inheritance and structures.

It's important, finally, to mention fundamentalism here. Although it doesn't merit the term philosophy, fundamentalism describes a phenomenon common not just to the three Abrahamic faiths but also to the religions of the Indian subcontinent. At one extreme of each tradition are those so threatened by the post-modern Western world that they renounce its ideas, reasserting past dogmas in simplistic terms, insisting on false certainties. Not only do they long for a past world that never actually existed, they invade the political realm, seeking power to impose their views on others, often by incomprehensible violence. Religious fundamentalists are 'the sirens of total corruption of the soul';[50] theirs is the vilest feature of the post-modern environment.

I haven't attempted a comprehensive definition of the contemporary environment but I've identified a number of strands that both liberate and challenge us. That ambiguity is a striking feature of post-modern Western culture, expressing itself in complexity and uncertainty, raising those 'qualities' to the category of intellectual and theological imperative. Responding, exploring where they lead, is what the rest of this book is about. But first . . .

How Does it Feel to be a Jew in Britain Today?

I'm setting myself up for a fall with this section – how I view the community inevitably reflects my role in it over the last 45 years. Nevertheless, it's an exercise worth attempting because it connects the context with the theology that follows.

My overriding perception is of a community riddled by fear and anxiety: at the internal threats of diminishing numbers and a crisis of meaning beyond identity; and the external threats of never-ending anti-Semitism, the rise of populism and the consequences for democracy all over the Western world.

The Jewish community in Britain is far smaller than most people realize – at most 300,000. We give the impression of huddling together for mutual protection, which is not untrue but is also about the 'critical mass' necessary for communal life – worship, education, social and cultural activity. In 1950, the Jewish community was Britain's largest religious minority, equal to the sum of all the others put together. Today, we've fallen out of the 'top four', which does little for self-esteem – and the ability to engage, so localized are we.

The leadership of the British Jewish community regards Jews as an endangered species, in 2018 declaring anti-Semitism in the Labour Party to be an 'existential threat'.[51] Though the French Jewish community has a markedly different history – uninterrupted since the eleventh century, horribly damaged by the Nazis and their French collaborators, now considerably larger than in Britain as a result of immigration from North Africa – it shares the sense of existential threat, described by philosopher and film-maker Bernard-Henri Lévy as 'growing indifference to the killing of Jews'.[52]

There's no doubt the external threat – from indigenous anti-Semitic groups and outside terrorists – is uppermost in the communal mind. You can see it whenever you go to a Jewish communal building: security is visibly present both at high-profile institutions and suburban synagogues. Advocated by the police and admired by government, it also reinforces a long-established mind-set. All three Abrahamic faiths are prone to collective mental disorders – in the case of Jews and Judaism, paranoia. But as that sardonic observer of Jews and humanity, Woody Allen, said of us, quoting Joseph Heller's *Catch-22*: 'just because I'm paranoid, doesn't mean you're not out to get me'. The relationship between Jewish fears and *St Matthew' Passion* is a question Jewry poses to wider society – which it is manifestly unwilling to address.

I find it both interesting and thought-provoking that much of the British establishment today seems more aware of anti-Semitism and more determined that it has no place in British society than ever before – without wishing to probe its historic complicity. There's evidence that British Jews are not only part of the mainstream, part of the establishment, but have been widely accepted. Which offers the community a historic choice. Shaken by the recent Labour Party revelations, it can regard the change cynically or as a temporary blip and remain beleaguered. It can welcome the change and keep its head down, glad that, for once, there are larger, more visible groups of 'others'. Or it can accept the change but continue to see itself as at the edge, identifying with and supporting those who remain outsiders, knowing the heart of the immigrant because we were once immigrants in the land of Britain. In reality, all three choices will be supported – never mind the post-modern environment, we are, by virtue of our culture of disagreement, unable to speak with one voice. Thank God!

If British Jewry is anxious about its physical survival, it's also beset by an identity crisis. We were once clear about who we were and what we were for: but the environment in which British Jews live today has changed that irrevocably. All sections of the Jewish community are aware of the post-modern challenges to Torah and to God – even if a small but influential section continues to live and dress as if they were in pre-modern Eastern Europe. I'd identify two broad responses.

There are those who would make Jewish identity and Jewish observance identical: halakhah, the regime of Jewish practice, will preserve the Jews. If you want a graphic example, look no further than the recent disinterment of an old halakhic device, the *eruv*. Shabbat is observed by this section of the community with ever-increasing stringency – restrictions on carrying or pushing buggies outside the home on Shabbat can turn the house into a coop for young families. By erecting a system of poles and wires round residential streets, the 'home' is extended into what otherwise would be 'public domain' where carrying and buggy pushing are forbidden. Do Jewish, they say, and make sure your children do Jewish; I observe, therefore I am.

Other parts of the community emphasize community itself – you may be dubious about what Judaism means beyond affiliation but join a community, support it and find your Jewish identity in acts of identifying and belonging. Such communities focus on rites of passage, responsibilities towards other members of the community, and place a very high value on enabling members to feel at home – even if that means tempering the development of services and ritual with an appeal to fragments of practice and melodies half remembered from synagogues not attended in the past. Join community and make sure your children feel part of community. I belong, therefore I am.

Ritual and community are the talismans of the day, the response to widespread confusion over identity. 'Yes, we do want to survive, not least to defy all who wish us ill and all demographic predictions.' But for what? I'm tempted to write, 'now read on' – but first we need to look at a third characteristic of today's British Jewish community.

In common with some other religious communities, we're beset by issues of authority. These conflicts have, in part, to do with the particular history of the British Jewish community – the leadership of nineteenth-century Jewry was elevated to a quasi-established status. What later became the United Synagogue was seen as the equivalent of the Church of England, and the Chief Rabbi as the Archbishop of Canterbury. This establishment has long been under threat from those to its 'right' and those to its 'left', and, like all establishments, is loath to relinquish power. As we'll see in the next chapter, the struggle over authority most obviously manifests itself in the area of Jewish status – the right to determine who is a Jew – in reality a battle over who is a rabbi.

Conflicts of authority have also become conflicts over authenticity and there are those who would deny whether what is to come in this book is an authentic account of Judaism. After several decades at the forefront of battles over authority, I find myself curiously unbothered by the politics of authenticity – others, by finding what I write helpful (or not), will decide my authenticity.

For over seven hundred years, Jewish tradition has organized its understanding of itself by deploying a trio of headings – God, Torah and Israel. The Zohar, a late thirteenth-century mystical commentary on the Torah written in Spain, would appear to be the source. The Zohar says: 'There are three levels, linked with one another: the Holy One, blessed be He, the Torah and Israel.'[53] 'God' refers to metaphysical beliefs; 'Torah' to Jewish teaching, Judaism; and 'Israel' to both People and Land. Everything about the Jewish journey today tells me that, although the three headings are as useful as ever, the order needs to be reversed.

I move from first to last in your thinking, rabbi?

Identity is where Jews start today. Now read on.

PART TWO

Being a Jew Today: Identity and Peoplehood

Do not cut yourself off from the community.

(PIRKEI AVOT 2.5)

Few things have done more harm than the belief on the part of individuals and groups (or tribes or states or nations or churches) that he or she or they are in *sole* possession of the truth ... It is a terrible and dangerous arrogance to believe that you alone are right: have a magical eye which sees *the* truth; & that others cannot be right if they disagree. This makes one certain that there is *one* goal ... & that it is worth any amount of suffering (particularly on the part of other people) if only the goal is attained – 'through an ocean of blood to the Kingdom of Love' ... said Robespierre: & Hitler, Lenin, Stalin, & I dare say, leaders in the religious wars of Christian v Moslem or Catholics v. Protestants sincerely believed this: the belief that there is one & only one true answer to the central questions which have agonized mankind & that one has it oneself – or one's Leader has it – was responsible for the oceans of blood: But no Kingdom of Love sprang from it – or could ...[1]

(ISAIAH BERLIN)

3

Israel as People

Creating and building community was how I saw my role as a congregational rabbi in Surrey. We – the voluntary leadership and I – concentrated on contacting other Jews in the area, persuading them 'to join',[1] drawing them into community.

The wind of modern and post-modern individualism blows hard and is particularly threatening to Judaism. We were determined to reach out to people who retained any sense of Jewish identity and find a point of engagement – be it persuading a qualified referee to take charge of the religion school football team or allowing a former East African chess champion to trounce the rabbi by distracting him with challenging theological questions. This was around the time that American sociologists were deploying the phrase 'sovereign self' to describe the dominant view that we are autonomous individuals, primarily responsible to and for ourselves. If they became members of the synagogue, we stood a chance of chipping away at the sovereign self, prompting previously detached and semi-detached Jews to accept a degree of responsibility for the community. With hindsight, we wanted these Jews on the verge of assimilation to acknowledge those who'd preceded them and handed on to them their Jewish identity – and recognize the significance of each personal decision for the Jewish future.

It wasn't a case of all or nothing – you must do this or believe that – but finding an aspect of being Jewish meaningful to each person. While Jonathan Sacks correctly contrasts 'the sovereign self' with the 'situated self',[2] the latter term may be too static. We were and are journeying selves – we gave the synagogue the Hebrew name *m'vakshei haderekh*, seekers of the way. The task was one of opening hearts and minds to the worth of continuing the journey together.

You can tell a great deal from the people with whom I worked. Among them was a Welsh head teacher, a Hungarian Shoah survivor, a South African-born radiographer, the local barber, a car designer, the daughter of a famous band leader, our GP's wife, the solicitor next door, an accountant from Hampton Court and a music publisher who once employed Elton John as his office boy. We were reconnecting Jews, enabling them to find purpose in their Jewish identity – as we were ourselves.

Unfailingly supported by my smiling and hospitable wife, life proved richly rewarding. But something beyond the communal nagged away at me. As a rabbinic student, I'd been much taken by a particular figure who makes fleeting appearances in tractates of both Talmuds. Second-century Elisha ben Abuya is better known in Rabbinic Judaism as Akher, the Other, the Heretic.[3] The Jerusalem Talmud records the turning point in his life:

> Once, sitting in the Valley of Gineysar, he saw a man climb to the top of a palm tree on Shabbat, take the mother bird with the young [in breach of Deut. 22.7] and descend in safety. At the end of Shabbat, he saw another man climb to the top of the same palm tree, take the young but let the mother bird go free. As he descended, a snake bit him and he died.[4]

Elisha, in Rabbi Milton Steinberg's mid-twentieth-century literary account, rages: 'There is no Judge. There is no Judgement'[5] – bearing witness to the eternal yet agonizingly contemporary challenge to faith. What struck me was not only that Elisha ben Abuya, the Other, is an integral part of foundational Rabbinic Literature but also that there's a passage which records him as remaining in the House of Study itself – part of the Rabbinic debate – where he muttered continuously, subversive Greek texts dropping from his cloak when he got up to leave for the day.[6]

I vividly remember preaching a *Kol Nidrei* sermon about Akher – suggesting that the Other was part of us all – and looking up to the balcony of the hall where a member of the congregation of whom

I was particularly fond was sitting: dark, bearded, for all the world the Elisha ben Abuya of my imagining.

Knowledge and belief were no bar to membership of the Synagogue. The only questions around eligibility for membership were the formal ones, developed over the last 2,000 years in response to the demands of social policy and administrative necessity: who is a Jew?

SECTION ONE
IDENTITY: INNER AND OUTER
DEFINITIONS OF WHO IS A JEW

The Uniqueness of Jewish Identity: the Inner Definition

In using the term 'unique', I don't mean 'being superior' but rather 'having no parallel'. The British legal system, we've discovered recently to our cost, can't accommodate the uniqueness of Jewish identity and has applied a Catholic model instead.

Akiva School in Finchley, north-west London, was the first Progressive Jewish day school in the UK. Its ethos acknowledged the importance of offering children a firm grounding in their tradition but resisted being inward-looking, reaching out instead to other faiths through joint activities. Progressive Jewish day schools – there are now four in London – educate young Jews in the values of Judaism so that, later in life, they can – as Jews – work with others in building a fairer, more humane society. I played a part in advocating this departure from our previous position of opposing all 'sectarian' schools – and found myself involved in an unedifying but revealing episode about the nature of Jewish identity as well as the self-defeating internal politics of the British Jewish community.

Jewish schools have long been a feature of British Jewry. Well over a hundred years ago, the Jews' Free School in the East End of London played an important role in enabling children of Jewish immigrants to integrate into Britain while retaining their Jewish identity. In the second half of the twentieth century, mainstream Orthodoxy grasped the importance of Jewish schools to the maintenance of Jewish particularity in an open society and instituted what would prove to be a transformative programme of school-building both at primary and secondary level. That process included taking responsibility for the long-established Jews' Free School and supervising its moves, together with the Jewish population, first to Camden in inner north-west London, then to Kenton in the outer suburbs. All these schools, including JFS, were placed under the authority of the Office of the Chief Rabbi, the most prominent aspect of which emerged as ruling on Jewish status for the purpose of admission.

In 2007 a family, ironically more traditionally observant than many JFS families, challenged the ruling of the Office of the Chief Rabbi that their child was ineligible for admission because the child's mother had been converted under Reform auspices and was therefore not regarded as Jewish by the Office of the Chief Rabbi and the United Synagogue.

For me, the case was an unwanted distraction. We'd long known that the Orthodox authorities would exclude the children of Progressive converts. It was wounding and humiliating but the Reform Movement had grown and, with it, the leadership's self-belief and self-confidence. One reason for pursuing our own schools so assiduously was to avoid this blatant disrespect for our converts and our rabbis who'd supervised their conversions. More importantly, we wanted schools that would teach the full range of Jewish responses to contemporary life in an open, engaging and sensitive manner, not schools insistent that there's only one right way. At the time this particular family chose to challenge JFS, we'd just won a long political battle and were on the brink of opening the Jewish Community Secondary School (JCoSS) in North London – funded by the state. My objective was a constructive response to the political manoeuvrings of an insecure and threatened establishment, avoiding time-consuming and expensive battles. Unfortunately, I couldn't evade being drawn into the JFS case and was required to write a letter to the Treasury Solicitor providing background information necessary for the High Court hearing.

As so often, the legal battle turned on a particular point of law rather than on natural justice. The initial High Court hearing – it went to the Court of Appeal and then to the Supreme Court – established the battleground as the 1976 Race Relations Act: was the JFS Admissions Policy discriminatory and in breach of that Act? The Supreme Court ruled that it was – and that, in turn, adversely affected the admissions policies not only of schools under the auspices of the Chief Rabbi but of our own. We wanted JCoSS to be open to the children of all parents who wished them to identify as Jews; instead we had minimum observance requirements foisted on us all – Orthodox and Progressive alike. A parallel was drawn by the Court with Catholic schools, but Jewish identity and Catholic identity are different.

An acute dilemma presented itself when that official request for background information appeared in my in-tray. On the one hand, the discriminatory policy – in a state-funded school that had begun life for all the community – was outrageous. On the other hand, I was suspicious of the state and its legal system becoming involved in the community's internal battles and playing any part in defining 'who is a Jew'. In my letter to the Treasury Solicitor I said both – that the policy was strategically wrong, politically motivated, not in the interests of either the community or the family concerned, but that I was also very apprehensive of the Courts intervening or adjudicating, not least on grounds of racial discrimination.

I explained that Jews are a *people* formed at Sinai who make up a continuous chain composed of descendants and converts, of those born into the Jewish people and of those who choose to join the Jewish people. I added that when converts to Judaism become part of the chain, they're regarded as indistinguishable from those who are Jewish by descent, inheriting the history and culture and, at once, becoming part of it.

The term 'people' is crucial. The Hebrew word is *am*, with root meanings of being united, connected, related. The Jewish People is made up of smaller units, families, with strong ties to other families and to the larger unit, the people. But the ties are not blood ties, racial ties, ethnic ties. The Mishnah says that Sennacherib (a seventh-century BCE king of Assyria) confused all the races and since then there have been no pure races.[7] Jews come in all shapes, sizes and colours – at which point, a story. Ever journeying, Jewish merchants reached China during the Tang dynasty (seventh to ninth centuries). One Jewish community at least – in Kaifeng – survived into the twentieth century. It is said that a modern-day Jewish traveller reached Kaifeng and was directed to the synagogue; there he was greeted by a man of Chinese appearance and dress. The traveller was effusive, explaining he was a visiting Jew from the West. He was greeted with a cool, quizzical stare. 'Aren't you thrilled to see a fellow Jew?' he asked. After a pause, back came the reply: 'Funny, you don't look Jewish.'

In every generation, individuals have joined the Jewish journey, become links in the chain stretching back to Sinai. Indeed, Exodus tells us that even the slaves fleeing Egypt included '*erev rav*', a 'mixed multitude'.[8] When the Hungarian-born Jewish dissenter Arthur Koestler wrote a book claiming the Jews of Eastern Europe weren't descended from Ashkenazim moving east but from Khazars who'd converted to Judaism in large numbers in the eighth and ninth centuries CE, he was attempting to discredit the nineteenth-century killer virus that Jews and Judaism are a matter of 'blood' and race.[9]

Israeli philosopher Avishai Margalit recently published an investigation into the meaning of 'betrayal'.[10] As part of a detailed linguistic analysis, he deploys the notions of 'thick' and 'thin' relationships – 'thick' being those 'modeled on our relations with family and friends',[11] and he places the relationship between Jews in this category.

So now we have a definition of the Jew and of Jews: Jews are members of a people bound together by ties of family, history and culture, each individual a link in the chain stretching back through more than three millennia to Sinai – a definition sanctified early on, in a biblical passage so subtle that its conviction is easily overlooked. It comes at the beginning of the short but intensely moving book of Ruth:

'*Do not urge me to go back and desert you,*' Ruth answered [her mother-in-law Naomi]. The starting point is an intimate conversation between two widowed women about duty, not a public declaration by men about rules governing status. '*Where you go, I will go, and where you stay, I will stay.*' I'm joining you on your journey, becoming part of that journey. '*Your people shall be my people*' – I've become part of your family and therefore your people are mine. '*And your God my God.*' Ours is a religious journey with people and God as its enduring elements; your God becomes my God with the same intimacy as our relationship, Naomi. *Our God* – I neither want nor need to sound a note of triumph or superiority over anyone. '*Where you die, I will die, and there will I be buried.*' There's nothing conditional about my commitment; I'll remain faithful to you and your/our family and your/our people forever. *'I swear a solemn oath before the Eternal your God: nothing but death shall divide us.'* At the core of this commitment lies my fidelity to you, our family, our people, God – wherever we go.[12]

In Ruth's quiet, modest declaration of faithfulness lies a statement of the openness not only of the Jewish people but also of Judaism. Ruth remarries – a kinsman of Naomi's called Boaz – and bears a son, Oved. In one of the most remarkable sentences in the entire Hebrew Bible, the text concludes: 'He was the father of Jesse, the father of David.' David is King David, whose line will, according to tradition, eventually include the Messiah. Faithful Ruth provides Judaism with the definition of a Jew and her reward is the most significant genealogical line in the story of this People Israel.[13]

Being a Jew: Equally by Birth, by Choice

Judaism has always understood Jews to be a people with a particular role: to live out our understanding of God and God's demands in the context of humanity at large (remember Abraham as a phial of perfume). Christianity came to see itself as a mission to humanity worldwide. One is not superior to the other: the two faiths have distinct purposes and, therefore, different rules or boundary markers for acquiring and maintaining identity.

The acquisition of Jewish identity today is an important and revealing subject – important because it illustrates the all-pervasive conflict in the Jewish world over authority brought about by the encounter with modernity; revealing because it says so much about the nature of Jewish identity, the individual Israelite as a member of the People Israel.

From biblical days, Jewish identity has been acquired in one of two ways: by birth and by conversion. One is either born into the Jewish people or one chooses to become part of that people. Let's start with 'by birth'.

By birth
We've already seen that what's distinctive about Judaism is its inextricable connection to 'peoplehood' – the very word Judaism,

Yahadut, shares its derivation with *Y'hudah*, Judah, and *Y'hudi*, Jew. But we've also seen that 'people' is a carefully selected term; it doesn't denote race or ethnicity but a group bound together by ties of family, history and culture. That peoplehood has always been open – the canonization of the book of Ruth is an indication not just of openness but of a self-understanding existing from earliest times. If someone was born of Jewish parents – both members of this people – Jewish identity was automatic. That was no more and no less than a recognition of how families are. You don't apply to join a family when reaching the age of majority – that would run counter to the reality and logic of cultural transmission. Our family is our family; our people is our people. We reserve the right to opt out but having to opt in makes no sense.

From early on, the question arose as to identity when only one parent is Jewish. In pre-Rabbinic times, Jewish identity was determined by the father, but Rabbinic Judaism took a different view. What American historian Shaye J. D. Cohen calls 'the matrilineal principle' first appears in the Mishnah in the second century and comes 'like a bolt from the blue'.[14] Eighteen hundred or more years ago, Rabbinic Judaism decided that a Jew is someone with a Jewish mother (or someone converted to Judaism).

It's not surprising the early Rabbis needed to take a view – living in the Diaspora was becoming the norm rather than the exception. Since the Rabbis were men and patriarchy was to become more and more entrenched, it is surprising they decided Jewish status should be matrilineal. The standard explanation for this uncharacteristic lurch is that you can always be sure of who the mother of a child is but not always of the father (at least until the advent of DNA testing). Others point to the influence of Roman law – in cases of unequal status with regard to Roman citizenship, the status of the mother was the determining factor. Neither explanation is entirely convincing but, in any event, for 1,800 years, Jewish status has been passed down the maternal line.

This marker has been challenged in recent decades. But before looking at that, we need to explore the second part of Jewish formation: conversion, by adoption, by choice.

By choice

The founder Chair of my first congregation in Weybridge was a Welshman called Harry Cohen, head master of Finnart House School, the only Jewish Reform School in Britain – 'Reform' here indicating an institution to which boys in trouble with the law were sent for moral and behavioural reformation. The school had moved out to leafy Weybridge from its previous incarnation as Hayes Industrial School, one of whose graduates became world-renowned as Two Gun Cohen (no relation to Harry), personal bodyguard to Chinese revolutionary leader Sun Yat-sen. Jews lack *sitzfleisch* and turn up in the most unlikely places!

When I became rabbi of the North West Surrey Synagogue, only three of the 'inmates' of Finnart House were Jewish but it had a small synagogue in which our Erev Shabbat services were first held. We proudly proclaimed ourselves to be the world's only Reform *shul* in a Reform school. Harry was an educated, compassionate man, equally devoted to his vocation and his Jewish identity. But one, quite frequently repeated, remark used to pull me up short. I always took great pleasure in teaching the prospective converts within the community and supporting their enlistment. Whenever one was received into Judaism by the Reform Bet Din, rabbinic court in London, back in Weybridge, Harry would mutter: 'I can't understand why they would want a hump.' It was sobering testimony to just how many Jews of a particular generation regarded Jewish identity as something painful rather than joyful and were surprised that anyone should want to throw in their lot with the Jewish people. On reflection, the only surprise is that I should have been surprised.

To Recruit or Not to Recruit – that is the Question

American scholar Louis H. Feldman, who taught at New York's premier Orthodox academic institution Yeshiva University, published a commendably open-minded essay in *Christianity and Rabbinic Judaism*.[15] Feldman made it crystal clear that conversion to Judaism was a normative feature of Jewish life in the first century CE. He quotes Matthew 23.15: 'Woe to you, scribes and Pharisees, hypocrites! For you cross sea and land to make a single proselyte, and you make the new proselyte twice as much a child of Gehenna as yourselves.' It's hardly an appealing characterization of his fellow Jews but you get the proselytizing picture. Jews were a noticeable presence throughout much of the Mediterranean, including Rome; Philo's comment that Jews comprise half the human race is hyperbole but Jewish numbers reflected an active – and successful – policy of conversion. Oxford Professor Martin Goodman has offered a corrective, arguing we shouldn't be led astray by a Christian–Jewish polemic in which Christians missionized and implied that Jews did too. He suggests that Judaism saw itself in much the same way as Greek schools of philosophy – as confident, enthusiastically open to new adherents, but not convinced of the need to go out and missionize, take their truth, their 'good news' to the whole world.

Goodman writes:

> Before 100 CE Jews accepted as proselytes those gentiles who applied to join their number, but they did not feel impelled to encourage such conversions. Their liberalism was generally reinforced by a belief that God was not offended by non-Jews continuing to worship their ancestral deities, provided that such worship did not affect Jews.[16]

It's an attitude some non-Jews find hard to understand, but one that provides a model of conviction coupled with openness and tolerance that has much to commend it in a world still wedded to imposing one's own 'certainties' on others. A text relating to those older contemporaries of Jesus, Hillel and Shammai, is also illustrative:

> A heathen came to Shammai and said to him, 'Convert me on condition you teach me the whole Torah while I stand on one leg.' Shammai drove him away with a builder's measure he was holding. Then he went to Hillel, who made him a convert and said, 'What is hateful to you do not do to your fellow: that is the whole Torah; all the rest is commentary; go and learn.'[17]

In debates between Hillel and Shammai and their respective Schools, tradition follows Hillel, who represents leniency as opposed to stringency. What this passage tells us about conversion in the early Rabbinic period is that mainstream attitudes were generally relaxed, though not everyone felt the same way. Of equal importance, Ruth had brought with her an emphasis on peoplehood and God – 'Your people shall be my people and your God my God'. Now a third element has been introduced, that of learning: '*zil g'mor*', 'go and learn'. Learning becomes imperative for absorption into peoplehood, particularly landless peoplehood, and to participation in what was to become Rabbinic Judaism. There's no mention in this particular text of formal ritual – *t'vilah*, immersion in a *mikveh*, a ritual bath both for men and women and, prior to that, *milah*, circumcision, a men-only privilege – but they can be taken for granted; this particular text is not a statement of conversion ritual but of attitude.

Attitudes towards converts in early Rabbinic Literature are usually positive. An enthusiastic text asserts:

> Resh Lakish said: Dearer to God is the proselyte who has come of their own accord than all the crowd of Israelites who stood before Mount Sinai. For had the Israelites not witnessed the thunder, lightning, quaking mountain and blasting trumpets, they would not have accepted the Torah. But proselytes, who saw none of these things, nevertheless have come and surrendered themselves to the Holy One, blessed be God, and taken the yoke of heaven upon themselves – can anyone be dearer to God than they?[18]

However, external hostility led to a caution that came to define normative practice. A passage from the Talmud rules:

> The Rabbis teach: If a prospective convert approaches us these days we say to him: 'Why do you want to become a proselyte? Don't you know that Israel nowadays is harried, driven about, persecuted and harassed, and that sufferings befall us?' If he says, 'I know it and I'm not worthy,' we receive him at once.

The passage continues by adding an educational requirement – and a warning about the consequences of failures of observance. It then concludes:

> If he assents to all, we circumcise him immediately and, when he's healed, we send him to the *mikveh*, and two scholars stand by,

and tell him of some of the less demanding and some of the more demanding laws. When he's been immersed in the *mikveh*, he's regarded in all respects as a Jew.[19]

Over the centuries, not least in the face of medieval legislation forbidding Jews to make converts, caution and suspicion increased – wholly understandable but holy undesirable.

A sea change took place in response to the perceived threat posed by the Enlightenment.

Here's a further passage from the Talmud:

Rabbi Huna said: 'A proselyte below the age of bar mitzvah is immersed [in a *mikveh*, ritual bath] under the supervision of a Bet Din.' What is he [Rabbi Huna] telling us? It is an advantage for the infant [i.e., it's a good thing to be a Jew], and [the rule is that] one may act for a person in his absence [when it is] to his advantage. What you might have supposed is that an idolater would prefer a life without restraint [un-yoked by Jewish law], since it is an accepted principle that a slave definitely prefers a dissolute life. Therefore he [Rabbi Huna] is telling us this applies [only in the case] of an adult who has already tasted sin, but [in the case] of a minor, it's an advantage for him [to become a Jew].[20]

Harried or not, more cautious or not, the text says quite clearly that a court can convert an infant gentile. The rationale is that being Jewish is considered a benefit and one may confer a benefit upon a person without their knowledge and, therefore, as a baby. The ruling was codified in the sixteenth century in the *Shulkhan Arukh*.[21]

In the middle of the nineteenth century, a notorious halakhic dispute arose between two of the best-known Central European Orthodox authorities of the time – Rabbi Zvi Hirsch Kalischer and Rabbi Azriel Hildesheimer – over whether the child of a Jewish man and a non-Jewish woman could be converted as an infant. Rabbi Kalischer took the traditional, lenient line and said 'yes'; Rabbi Hildesheimer ruled that in the post-Enlightenment world a more stringent policy was required and prohibited conversion under such circumstances. Orthodoxy follows Rabbi Hildesheimer to this day and his embattled attitude dominates its approach to all conversion.[22]

Orthodox authorities in Britain and Israel also demand exacting standards of ritual observance – often requiring several years of residence in a strictly Orthodox environment – prior to conversion. The logic follows that of Rabbi Hildesheimer. Regardless of whether this is strategically sensible, what distresses me most as a progressive rabbi are the feelings of rejection and exclusion prompted in many sincere would-be converts.

Conversion and Gender Equality

Just as modernity brought about increased stringency, so increased stringency has been challenged by modernity. There's something in this of the fable of the wind and the sun, the sun being the widespread advance of egalitarianism. Thirty-five years ago, the American Jewish political philosopher Michael Walzer wrote:

> The aim of political egalitarianism is a society free from domination ... *equality*: no more bowing and scraping, fawning and toadying; no more fearful trembling; no more high-and-mightiness; no more masters, no more slaves. It is not a hope for the elimination of differences; we don't all have to be the same or have the same amounts of the same things. Men and women are one another's equal (for all important moral and political purposes) when no one possesses or controls the means of domination.[23]

If that's a fundamental truth and I believe it is – it must equally hold true for religion and religious community; a revelation of modernity, sobering that it didn't emerge through religion. 'I call heaven and earth to testify for me: whether Gentile or Jew, man or woman, male slave or female slave – only according to the deed done does the holy spirit rest upon any particular individual.'[24] This is a potentially inclusive text from a relatively late (ninth-century) compilation, *Seder Eliyahu*. Where it came from is unclear; sadly, the response it evinced is not.

Progressive Judaism, recognizing the force both of our own tradition of equality and justice and of the ethic driving wider social change, has responded. In theory, there are two options. We could insist Judaism is only transmitted if both parents are Jewish – but that would be a strategic disaster. Intermarriage, which proved a source of communal growth and enrichment in the early centuries of the Common Era, has, since the nineteenth century, become interwoven with the challenges of integration. It's been both an excuse for and cause of the erosion of Jewish numbers and communal decline. Finding the right partner in a society where the choice rests solely with the two people concerned is far from easy. In countries where Jews are a small and integrated minority, it's asking a lot of people to restrict their choice to someone Jewish. Anyway, why should they? Only because transmission of Jewish identity, culture and faith is statistically likely to be prejudiced by 'out-marriage'. A Jew and a non-Jew – living in a society broadly indifferent to religion, which even perceives religious identity to be problematic – will often take the line of least resistance and leave the choice to the children. Which isn't so much a deferred decision as decision by indecision – not to decide is to decide.

Moving Boundary Markers

Leading British Liberal Rabbi Andrew Goldstein points out that, from its inception at the beginning of the twentieth century, the British Liberal Movement was committed to the equal treatment of children with one Jewish parent, female or male. However, it was in post-Second World War United States, where rates of intermarriage were increasing inexorably, that the Central Conference of American Rabbis persuaded the American Reform Movement to adopt patrilineality – Jewish status passing to the child of a Jewish father when only the father is Jewish. Not to count in every Jew who wants to be counted in made no sense religiously or demographically: reason coupled with the wider spirit of egalitarianism prompted a strategic decision of the utmost importance.

My colleagues and I in the British Reform Movement struggled. Egalitarianism – treating all human beings with equal respect, acknowledging the equality of women and men, treating the children of Jewish women and men the same – is fully in keeping with our understanding of Jewish tradition and an invaluable revelation of modernity. But here it poses issues of social policy and strategy. First, do we require the children of a Jewish father (and non-Jewish mother) – if they're no longer to be treated as converts – to undertake some form of Jewish education so they can feel comfortable within the community and gain maximum benefit from their Jewish identity? And if we do, does equality demand we require the same of the child of a Jewish mother (and non-Jewish father) who has always been regarded as a Jew and never required to convert? Furthermore, adult 'converts' rarely have the experience that goes with being brought up within a practising Jewish family. Is it possible that, particularly in smaller, more isolated Jewish communities, a balance needs to be struck? Is it conceivable that where the boundary markers are best set – 'best' meaning in the interests of the community as a whole – might not be precisely where our fundamental principles and values dictate they should be? Over the last decade, British Reform, through the hallowed method of debate, discussion and much disagreement, has moved towards full equilineality.

Similar strategic issues occur with regard to the non-Jewish partners of Jewish members. Our liberal theology demands an empathetic, inclusivist approach – but are there public, confessional acts that should be the preserve of Jews? Should the non-Jewish parent at a bar or bat mitzvah be allowed to participate in the service and ceremony? Judaism has always understood marriage as the consecration of a relationship between two Jews, expressing a promise to establish a Jewish home: how then should we relate to the wedding of Jew and non-Jew – an inevitable feature of post-modern life? Orthodoxy is clear in its protective-restrictive response; liberal Jews (Reform and Liberal) agonize over what is best for the individual, best for the community – and where the balance lies. Theology and personal autonomy, Liberalism and pragmatism, strategy and tactics, are well-nigh impossible to disentangle.

Being a Jew: Wanting Out

Can a Jew cease to be a Jew, leave the Jewish people? Anti-Semites would insist 'no'; individual Jews today, 'yes'. As far as the Jewish community is concerned, it prefers to leave the door open whenever possible – it's only the active and whole-hearted adoption of another religion that's (usually) decisive. But consider this.

Oswald Rufeisen was a Jew from Poland who, during the Second World War, posed as a Pole of German extraction and smuggled arms to the Jewish underground. He was caught, imprisoned, escaped and took refuge with nuns, converting to Catholicism. He then left the convent to join the Jewish partisans and, after the War, became a Carmelite Brother. A little later, now known as Brother Daniel, he petitioned the Israeli authorities for the right to exercise the Law of Return, which gives all Jews an automatic right to settle in Israel. Notwithstanding his conversion to Catholicism, the Orthodox authorities at the time would have granted him the right since he was a Jew by birth – but the Israel Supreme Court took the opposite view and refused him. Ironically, he then petitioned, as non-Jews can, for the right to settle – which was granted. Brother Daniel lived out his life at the Carmelite convent in Haifa, the town where other members of his family already lived. Jews have been divided on the case ever since.

Such is the complex nature of Jewish identity and the extent to which the Jewish community perceives itself as under threat from assimilation into a culture dominated by secularity. For me, both principles and policy are of undeniable importance. But what is imperative is the meaning and purpose of identity. Without Jews, there can be no meaning and purpose to Jewish identity; but without meaning and purpose can Jewish identity be sustained and transmitted? Is being a Jew today and being Jewish today one and the same?

SECTION TWO
IDENTITY: WOMEN AND THE SCANDAL OF PATRIARCHY

The Precious Revelation of Modernity

Judaism has always been a patriarchal tradition. There were potential chinks of light in the Tanakh – the prominent parts played by Sarah, Rebekah, Rachel and Leah in Genesis; the inclusion of Deborah in the book of Judges; the pivotal roles of Ruth and Esther are all more than consequential. Nevertheless, patriarchy is rooted in the biblical narrative itself. Trail-blazing American Jewish scholar Judith Plaskow is unequivocal:

> Entry into the covenant at Sinai is the root experience of Judaism, the central event that established the Jewish people. Given the importance of this event, there can be no verse in the Torah more disturbing ... than Moses' warning to his people in Exodus 19:15, 'Be ready for the third day; do not go near a woman.' For here, at the very moment that the Jewish people stands at Sinai ready to receive the covenant – not now the covenant with individual patriarchs but with the people as a whole – at the very moment when Israel stands trembling waiting for God's presence to descend upon the mountain, Moses addresses the community only as men.[25]

Rabbinic Judaism, from its very beginnings, was a male construct with power and authority monopolized by an exclusively male rabbinate. Judaism – centred on words, on text – became a half-empty bookcase. The voices, understandings, insights of half the Jewish people were excluded from the interrogation and debate, the development of meaning and purpose that is the essence of Judaism. Judith Plaskow was not alone in asking whether it's even possible for Jewish women to engage with a tradition that has largely silenced them from the very beginning. A few, such as American feminist scholar Rita M. Gross, have turned instead to Buddhism – whether or not this is a less patriarchal tradition, it offers an alternative to Western theism.

Thankfully, Plaskow concluded redemption was possible, though – as ground-breaking British Rabbi Elli Tikvah Sarah points out – women will always find themselves standing on the shoulders of a patriarchal tradition. We can, concludes Plaskow, engage with Judaism, but radical change is required both to the way women are regarded 'as a class' and to the institutions that have developed 'around male norms'.[26]

Plaskow, therefore, insists on the need for Jewish communities to transform themselves so that 'subordinate' groups that 'require the individual to repress those aspects of themselves that are feared or despised no longer exist'. The Jewish people must be a people among whom differences are valued as necessary parts of the greater whole and every member feels equally empowered. For me, the argument is, once again, indisputable – theologically, ethically, rationally.

Similarly discomfiting is the work of another American scholar, Susannah Heschel. In an essay entitled *Feminism*, she exposes the core challenge with devastating clarity:

> The implications of the sexism in Judaism go to the heart of traditional Jewish beliefs concerning God, revelation, and Torah. For example, if the Torah holds women in positions of subservience or contempt, contradicting women's self-understanding, then, feminists conclude, either the God who has revealed the Torah is a malevolent deity or the Torah is not God's revelation but merely the projection of patriarchal society intent on preserving its status quo.[27]

The problem is not 'merely' one of changing practice both inside and outside the synagogue – it's not just a matter of ethics and social policy – but goes to the heart of Jewish theology. If the Torah commands discrimination against women, then what does that say about the authorship of Torah, its understanding of God – and of the God of Jewish tradition? Heschel takes this entire chapter beyond its apparently secular/humanist setting and places it in the religious context in which it belongs. I entirely agree with her and respond in Chapter 5 to the core issue she raises.

There's a strong argument that Lily Montagu – one of the founding figures of the Jewish Religious Union (precursor of Liberal Judaism), renowned social activist and advocate for the poor – paved the way for women in Britain by leading synagogue services. Liberal Judaism was always more committed to egalitarianism as a determining principle than Reform (it could only have been a British Reform synagogue that, in the 1930s, embraced mixed seating but reserved the first four rows for 'men with scruples'![28]). But it was the Leo Baeck College that, in 1975, with the acquiescence of both Movements, gave *s'mikhah* to Rabbi Jacqueline Tabick, Britain's first woman rabbi – only three years after the Hebrew Union College in Cincinnati ordained

Rabbi Sally Priesand.[29] Tabick was the courageous pathfinder – in a community numerically dominated by Orthodoxy – as was West London Synagogue, which employed her. Many of the women who followed Rabbi Tabick into the Reform and Liberal rabbinate told their individual stories – eloquently demonstrating what women have to teach about doing theology – in an innovatory book *Hear Our Voice*.[30] Women rabbis today are the equal of men in the two Progressive Movements – not least in numbers.

Further iconoclastic action was taken by Leo Baeck College less than two decades after Rabbi Tabick received *s'mikhah*. In the unflinching spirit of the Union of Liberal Rabbis in Germany – which had ordained the sadly neglected Regina Jonas despite the implosion of Jewish life all around – the College admitted two lesbian feminists, British-born and educated Elizabeth Sarah and Sheila Shulman from Brooklyn. The two women gained *s'mikhah* in 1989 and subsequently served in both the Reform and Liberal Movements. That this could have happened within any section of conservative British Jewry is, with hindsight, astonishing.

The active presence of Rabbis Elli Tikvah Sarah and the late Sheila Shulman didn't prove comfortable for many. Elli Sarah published the uncomfortably provocative *Trouble-Making Judaism* in 2012.[31] Sheila Shulman's book of sermons[32] is filled with challenges – political, social and theological – that characterized her revolutionary work with a same-sex community in London and her teaching of the next generation of students at Leo Baeck.

Over the last 20 years, Progressive women rabbis have come to head Leo Baeck College, lead the British Reform Movement, occupy senior rabbinic pulpits in the founding Synagogues of Reform (West London) and Liberal Judaism (Liberal Jewish Synagogue), take a seat in the House of Lords, and enjoy a prominent place in the leadership of British Jewry.

This section may well be the most important – for Jewish identity, teaching and theology – in the entire book: its influence is all-pervasive. It also demands a personal reflection that may well resonate with some of my generation. Breaking the shackles of patriarchy was essential and I'm proud of what we achieved – but I wasn't at the forefront. I was clear it was right but didn't see it as central to my work. Furthermore, I'd been brought up with the traditional attitude to men's working lives and used that as an excuse for not being available to share fully in the roles of homemaking and parenting. It's a reflection on how easy it is to miss what's truly important in the swirling fog of post-modernity; such is the pace of change today that we may well live to see the enormity of our misjudgements.

But one can learn, and I'm very aware of how much further we have to go to realize the full implications of equality. Nothing could illustrate this better than the work of American Jewish feminists over the last 25 years. Considerable scholarly groundwork has been laid by Rabbi Rachel Adler,[33] transforming ancient patriarchal ceremonies into modern, egalitarian ones 'based in Jewish law ... only lightly altered to create new resonances and meanings'.[34] A major contributor to the debate is American Rabbi Danya Ruttenberg, who deploys what Leo Baeck College Principal Rabbi Deborah Kahn-Harris calls a 'hermeneutic of curiosity' rather than one of suspicion.[35] In *Yentl's Revenge: The Next Wave of Jewish Feminism*,[36] Ruttenberg brings together voices exploring a range of subjects from male expectations regarding female body shape to transgender theory, from Ashkenazi dominance to gender and God, from the excluding male image of the Zionist to sexual abuse. In her acknowledgements, Ruttenberg thanks her collaborators for 'working to make Judaism a safer street to walk down at night': that speaks enlightening volumes.

Rabbi Ruttenberg's work showed me, as I was completing this book, that these were issues not just to invite readers to consider but for me to address personally. In formulating my chapter on Israel, I was – and still am – much influenced by *My Promised Land* by Israeli political commentator Ari Shavit. I'm not alone in regarding the book as the best account of liberal Zionism in the twenty-first century. Recently though, Shavit was exposed as an abuser of what he regarded as 'male privilege'. He's not been accused or convicted of criminal offences but has a history of behaving towards women in an inappropriate fashion, assuming they would welcome his attention. He's acknowledged his behaviour, regretted it and attempted to rehabilitate himself – but has lost his position with the newspaper *Ha'aretz* and and the respect of many, especially younger women, in Israeli society. I can now see that the book itself is written from the perspective of a male Ashkenazi Zionist with the limitations and flaws that implies. But it's an influential and important book. A wise friend advised me not to risk alienating millennial readers at a time of change and progress. But how do we respond to the many who behaved in a way we can see with hindsight was part of a hierarchy of unjustifiable and unacceptable male privilege? It's a question with many obvious contemporary parallels that I'd prefer to pose, rather than expunge Ari Shavit for reasons of expediency.

Many men, myself included, thought that by renouncing our patriarchal past and ensuring all our formal rights were reassigned on an equal basis, we would right past wrongs and end the matter. What a misjudgement; how much men and women still have to open their eyes to.

SECTION THREE
IDENTITY: POWER AND OPPRESSION WITHIN

Equality in Sexual Orientation: Gays and Lesbians

Unlike the Romans among whom they lived, the Rabbis did not tolerate homosexuality, although they didn't view it with quite the obsessional horror that some other cultures have displayed. The English term 'sodomy' is laden with disapproval and derives from the supposed behaviour of the residents of Sodom, one of the 'Cities of the Plain' in Genesis 19. A colourful Talmudic passage identifies marital abuse, legal corruption, flagrant injustice, mistreatment of the poor and cruelty to innocents as the sins of Sodom – not homosexuality.[37] Until well into the second half of the twentieth century, however, Jewish communities behaved towards homosexuals with all the self-righteous distaste and blatant discrimination of wider society.

In 1982, the British Reform Movement published *Jewish and Homosexual* by physician, counsellor and agony aunt Wendy Greengross. It carried my introduction:

Jewish tradition prohibits homosexual relations. That is a basic statement which cannot be denied. The Torah prohibits sodomy and Talmudic law extends the prohibition to associated, including lesbian acts … It is true that the *halakhah* does not seem to recognise a category of 'homosexual' as such but the mainstream of Jewish tradition, as it is generally understood, is unequivocal in its view of homosexuality as an 'unacceptable perversion'.

Occasionally a rabbi encounters an issue on which both reason and conscience place him [sic] at odds with contemporary understandings of mainstream Jewish tradition ... The condemnation of the homosexual seems to me to belong to another world – a world which had more rigid ideas of what is 'natural' ... Above all, it belongs to a world which dealt with its fear of that which is different by seeking to eradicate the object of the fear rather than by examining the nature of the fear itself.[38]

What I wrote then lacked full understanding and empathy – but it was a start.

Wendy Greengross and Berlin-born psychoanalyst Irene Bloomfield – demonstrating the influence of Freud – pioneered the teaching of Pastoral Care and Counselling at Leo Baeck College. Greengross insisted her rabbinic students reflect on our attitudes towards sexuality – demanding we examined why we felt towards people and situations as we did and not simply endorse gut feelings stemming from nature and nurture. Greengross and Bloomfield provided the spiritual insight for their students, a springboard for change that has become an enduring hallmark of progressive Judaism and, possibly, a model for other faith institutions in wider British society.

The Abuse of Power within Society and Community: LGBTQ+

The recognition of how abuse of power – oppression – has characterized relationships throughout modern Western society and culture is a revelation of Postmodernism. One of its pillars, Michel Foucault, was a substantial influence on arguably the most important American Jewish philosopher writing today, Judith Butler.

Butler's work is extremely challenging – intellectually, politically and Jewishly. In an essay entitled *Ethical Ambivalence*, Butler writes: 'I began my philosophical career within the context of a Jewish education, one that took the ethical dilemmas posed by the mass extermination of the Jews in World War II, including members of my own family, to set the scene for the thinking of ethicality as such.'[39] She lists the Jewish philosophers who've influenced her – Spinoza, Walter Benjamin and Hannah Arendt; Marxist Jewish thinkers of the Frankfurt School; Derrida, her Postmodernist mentor – along with Foucault.

Derrida's influence is evident when she describes her own writing as texts that establish the task of rethinking and reconfiguring the possible within political theorizing. She frames her texts as questions but the only answer she's prepared to offer is the withdrawal of the reassurance of definite answers. Butler abandons the anchorage of propositional thinking and advises us to follow the example of cows and learn 'the art of slow rumination'. She has helped me to see that not only are my 'texts' something for others to ruminate on but they are themselves the product of rumination. However strong the temptation to provide glib reassurance, we need to resist it because the old epistemological and theological anchors – back to uncertainty and complexity – have been swept away in the post-modern world.

Butler asks what it means to be human today, telling us we have to extend and expand our present categorization, as her collaborator Sarah Salih explains:

> so that subjects who do not conform to its hetero-normative, racialized imperatives need no longer suffer the violence of social exclusion. As part of this commitment, Butler continues to represent the rights of 'sexual minorities' … 'all kinds of people who for whatever reason are not immediately captured or legitimated by the available norms' – with the long-term goal of transforming the power structures which currently prescribe what counts as 'human'. This is a particularly pressing impetus, given that the norms by which 'humans' live are largely unavailable to groups such as gays, lesbians, transsexuals, 'racial minorities', and other others who are condemned to the social death of extra-normativity.[40]

At the heart of Butler's work are matters of gender – by working with women, gays, lesbians and people who are transgender, she identifies those whose humanity is compromised by the various ways in which society separates them out, categorizes them and sees them as not the norm. Butler's work asserts the imperative of according to each human being their true equality that categorization subverts. This reflects the key passage from Mishnah Sanhedrin (quoted in Chapter 7), which regards each human being as singular and equally precious in the eyes of God.[41] Her ethics, rooted in Jewish experience, expresses a profound understanding of the potential for violent dehumanization inherent in defining groups over against the norm.

Butler lays down a daunting challenge (which many find reasons to resist). The liberation both of women and of sexual minorities has and will continue to affect the shape and balance of Jewish families. But why should that be seen as a problem? What constitutes family has changed over time and place: family has proved to be not just a constituent of peoplehood but a flexible and evolving vehicle for expressing and transmitting Jewish values. It must continue to adjust to the needs of *all* Jews.

Professor Butler would be the first to acknowledge that questions of power and abuse of power go beyond gender. Indeed, she's had a far-reaching influence on wider challenges. A current sociological theory, 'Intersectionality', examines how interlocking systems of power have an impact on the most marginalized in society. It began by exploring the oppression of 'women of colour' and has developed into an analysis of class, ethnicity and culture, examining complex relationships in contemporary multicultural societies. We can no longer regard issues relating to Jews and Judaism as unitary; rather, they are matters that touch on class, culture and ethnicity. How we are perceived by marginalized and impoverished minorities of colour and how we respond to them, their quest for their rights to be vindicated and their needs met, must be understood with an awareness of the multiplicity of power structures that favour many of us over many of them.

Intersectionality has internal, synagogual implications as well. Foucault identified those confined in mental institutions as victims of social oppression; the analysis made by intersectionality compels us to recognize how power structures and concepts of 'normativity' relegate those with learning difficulties and those suffering from mental illnesses to the economic and social margins of society and community. Reversing their marginalization – enabling those previously excluded from bar and bat mitzvah to take their rightful place; asking not just what support we can offer to those facing mental health challenges but what part those who so wish can play in Jewish communal life – is an urgent and accessible task.[42]

Eradicating the abuse of power both within society and community is a *sine qua non* of justice. Israeli philosopher Avishai Margalit argues that the prevailing definition of justice advanced by the American secular philosopher John Rawls is insufficient. Margalit offers instead a compelling teaching from his own life lived liminally – amid Israel's conflicts – urging the building of 'decent societies', those 'whose institutions do not humiliate people'.[43] Long ago an unnamed rabbi recited a still older teaching: 'One who publicly humiliates their neighbour is as though they had shed blood.'[44]

SECTION FOUR
IDENTITY: THE MISTAKE OF THE *MAMZER*

One of my best-loved mentors was dissenting Anglican theologian and publisher Dr John Bowden.[45] John used to hurl verbal barbs at his colleagues about the untenability of Christian doctrines founded on mistakes. The *mamzer* is just such a Jewish mistake.

The word appears only once in Torah, in Deuteronomy 23.3. It's a difficult term to translate but the context is telling. The preceding verse reads: 'No one whose testicles are crushed or whose penis has been cut off shall be admitted into the congregation of God.' This is directed against eunuchs who played a part in the surrounding cults; the following verse says that no Ammonite or Moabite shall be admitted into the congregation of God. Whatever *mamzer* means, the context tells us that it's to do with excluding a pagan category from the Israelite community. Rabbinic Judaism, however, applied the term to the child of an adulterous or incestuous sexual act – using this interpretation to support and develop a separate legal category, *mamzerut*. A *mamzer* was only permitted to marry another *mamzer*.

Rabbi Louis Jacobs, founding figure of British Jewry's Masorti Movement, would point out that it hadn't been an insuperable problem in the *shtetlakh*, the predominantly Jewish villages of Eastern Europe. A couple where one was restricted by the status of *mamzerut* would travel to a village some way away and get married there, secure in the knowledge, said Jacobs, that rabbis don't make inquiries into status unless they have good reason to believe there might be a problem. This compassionate, common-sense approach, he pointed out, has given way both in Britain and Israel to probing questions prior to the centralized authorization of marriages, coupled with demands for documentation, which will expose the 'defect', held to continue for ten generations.[46]

It's not just a mistaken interpretation per se but an appalling injustice, an affront both to Judaism and God. I once asked an Orthodox rabbinic friend how he could collude with the injustice. 'Ah,' he said, 'it may appear to you to be an injustice but in the eyes of God it isn't and the divine intention will become clear in the fullness of time.' I can't accept such theology – and neither can Progressive Judaism.

SECTION FIVE
IDENTITY: CHOSENNESS – STILL VALID OR OBJECTIONABLE IN THE LIGHT OF MODERNITY?

'How odd of God to choose the Jews' is a familiar jibe by an otherwise unremembered British writer, William Ewer. American businessman Cecil Browne responded: 'But not so odd / As those who choose / A Jewish God / But spurn the Jews.' The notion of chosen people plays a much larger role in anti-Jewish sentiment than it does in Jewish self-understanding. The term 'chosen people' doesn't translate into biblical or Rabbinic Hebrew but 'chose' does in a number of familiar places such as *Kiddush*. The notion has its origins in Deuteronomy: 'It is not because you are the most numerous of peoples that God was drawn to you and chose you – indeed, you are the smallest of peoples: but it was because God loved you.'[47] The verse is quite clear: chosenness isn't about numbers or any other factor denoting group superiority; Israel isn't bigger, stronger, cleverer, more endearing – nor even more righteous. Even God's love is devoid of special privilege and comes without protective intervention. There's no dispensation for transgressions;

the reverse – the consequence of chosenness is obligation. 'You alone have I known [so intimately],' says Amos, 'therefore I will punish you for all your iniquities.'[48]

The prophecy of Isaiah makes explicit the purpose of chosenness. It's to be a light in a dark world, to establish justice, to build a righteous society and bring about a world of peace and mutual understanding. Chosenness is a task, a duty – to break the yokes of oppression; to give bread and shelter to the hungry and homeless; to turn swords into ploughshares – and to bear witness to these ethical imperatives even if the unwelcome price is suffering. But let me emphasize that feeling committed to those values is not reserved exclusively for Jews; to be passionate about justice is central to Judaism but not its copyright; what motivates Jews can and does motivate others.

Chosenness is important in post-biblical Jewish literature and thought – though not as important as one might have been led to think. Maimonides, the dominant figure in medieval Jewish theology, doesn't regard it as a matter of defining principle. As others understand it, chosenness is feeling significant and loved – as all children of a loving parent feel.

There are instances when those natural feelings do spill over into a sense of being favoured and having special merit or talent. Such a development is to be found in the writings of Judah Halevi, philosopher and poet of the late eleventh/early twelfth century. According to Halevi, in his book the *Kuzari*,[49] Jews have a special religious faculty, a unique soul, and are the beneficiaries of supernatural providence. There are also echoes in the kabbalistic claim that only the souls of Israel are from God, while the souls of others are base material or *k'lipot*, shells. Such claims were a means of making bearable, if not intelligible, the continued oppression of the Jewish people. The more Jews were excluded from society, the more we were tempted to emphasize our difference from the cruel gentile world. And feel an aggrieved, defiant sense of chosenness.

Today, unease with the concept of chosenness is widespread among Jews integrated in the modern Western world. It's a complex reaction, with roots not just in the 'How odd of God' jibe but in contemporary egalitarian attitudes. One Jewish response is to abandon the concept altogether. The much-respected American rabbi Harold Schulweis argued that the claim is an 'aristocratic conceit'[50] demeaning all other people. He wrote: 'Judaism ... now has an opportunity to make a major moral contribution to the world by pioneering the rejection of all religious claims to exclusive divine revelation, its own included.'[51] I share his objection to claims of exclusive divine revelation but that's not how I understand or, more accurately, experience chosenness.

Every public Torah reading is prefaced with a blessing: 'Blessed are You, our Living God, Sovereign of the universe, who chose us from all peoples to give us your Torah.' 'To give us' cries out to be read as 'by giving us'. Our chosenness lies in the fact of this tradition and our attitude to it. It isn't the only narrative and tradition; it most definitely isn't the one true religion.[52] But it's infinitely valuable and it's ours. We bless you God for choosing us by giving us this particular Torah from which debate and discussion flow endlessly – the historical starting point for a distinctive tradition, the source of an unending search for meaning and purpose. Chosenness is defined by the undeniable fact of our particular tradition. As French philosopher Bernard-Henri Lévy writes: 'By vocation and destination, but certainly not by situation.'[53]

Ignaz Maybaum, who inspired me to take theology seriously, wrote:

The Jewish people ... is a God-made people. In our nobility and in our shabbiness, in our cultural refinement and in our vulgarity, in our endurance and in our weakness, in our glory and in the shame of our de-humanisation in Auschwitz – we are the people of God ... We did not choose to be Jews, God has chosen us.[54]

'A God-made people'; 'the people of God'; not choosing but chosen. For me, too, there's something involuntary and inescapable about my very identity as a Jew. It could be late career self-justification or the needs of my particular personality, but I don't think so.

To what or Whom does it point then, rabbi?

You don't get it do You? If You exist, how come You chose us to be shamed by our dehumanization in Auschwitz? Why forsake us, abandon us and leave us to die?

SECTION SIX
IDENTITY: AND SECULARITY – PEOPLE,
CULTURE BUT NO GOD

Israeli historian Shmuel Feiner locates the roots of Secular Judaism in the second half of the eighteenth century. He argues that Moses Mendelssohn's great achievement was to frame the terms of the encounter between modern Western culture – with its powerful secularist dimension – and the mainstream of Judaism and the Jewish community. Though he maintained traditional beliefs, Feiner notes that even Mendelssohn had a 'narrow escape' on his journey to Jewish eminence in Berlin. Feiner quotes Mendelssohn himself:

> How near I once came to being completely ruined. My feet wandered from the blessed path of truth. Like hellish furies, cruel doubts about providence tortured me; indeed, I can confess, without skittishness, that they were doubts about the existence of God and the blessedness of virtue. At that point, I was prepared to give rein to all vile desires. I was in danger, like someone drunk, of reeling into the wretched abyss into which the slaves of vice slide ever more deeply with every passing hour.[55]

The language may have changed over 250 years, but not the nature of the challenge.

David Biale, American historian and secularist theoretician, observes: 'Many of the most avowed critics of religion, those we call secularists, could never escape the tradition they overturn.'[56] He cites Bialik, Scholem, Herzl and Freud – but then highlights the twentieth century as the time when secularism ceased to be the preserve of the intellectual elite and became a major feature of Jewish life.

The largest investment made by the Jewish community in Britain in recent years has been the establishment of a Jewish cultural/community centre, JW3, in a prominent position in north-west London. It's a major success in attracting Jews who choose to explore and enjoy aspects of their culture and thereby give further substance to their identity. Many are Jewish secularists; they aren't, however, defined by what Biale called the 'dialectic between modern rationalism and the Jewish tradition'[57] but are simply Jews connecting to community through what touches them. I recognize the strategy! But as a young rabbi in Surrey my ulterior motive had to do with synagogue and Judaism. Is the cultural attachment offered by Secular Judaism today – invaluable though it is – sufficient for the transmission of Jewish identity, a viable long-term strategy for the survival of the Jew and flourishing of the Jewish people? That's not, I hasten to add, a rhetorical question.

Who Am I? Who Are We?

A decade ago – perhaps as part of my first thoughts about this book – I started compiling a family tree. Who I am cannot be divorced from where I've come from. It came as a chilling surprise that, wherever I looked – my father's family from Amsterdam, my mother's family from Przemysl – I found mass extermination. We Jews are all the children of survivors. It's most apparent among the remnant communities of Europe and least obvious to American Jews: terrain matters but cannot deny environment.

In recent years my Leo Baeck College theology students have challenged me, insisting we aren't the children of survivors, the Shoah isn't prominently in the background and it's time the College stopped claiming to be the successor to the Hochschule and moved on. Sociologically, I'm sure they're right – they know themselves and their generation much better than I do. That only compounds the uncertainty about identity of the many and the anxiety of the older generation with leadership roles. Though what the younger generation will make of the recent prominence given to anti-Semitism by Britain's hard left and its resurgence as an instrument of hard-right politics in Austria, Hungary and Poland is difficult to predict.

Theologically, I believe they're mistaken. The destruction of the Second Temple cast its shadow over Rabbinic theology and halakhic strategy for centuries and entered the calendar on Tisha b'Av, the Fast of the ninth of Av. So too with what Maybaum named the Third Hurban (Destruction), which destroyed so many of the illusions of modern Western 'civilization'.

In Britain, the post-modern world tells us we're all multifaceted citizens of a democratic state. Multi-faceted is the key word: British by birth or not; English by cultural inheritance or inheritor of several cultural traditions; variously gendered; son or daughter; mother or father or not; student, employer, employee or unemployed; Mozart-lover, soccer supporter; Jew by birth or choice; Jew, Christian, Muslim, Hindu, Sikh, Buddhist, Humanist or Secularist; and so on. We each formulate our own list, which is flexible and changes during our lifetime – as do the facets we prioritize or feel are most important at any given time. Sometimes several facets conflict, rub against each other, and the results, though painful, can be clarifying and fruitful. Very often, we simply ignore what is of less importance to us in order to give priority to what matters most about our identity at the time.

Looking at Jewish identity in that socio-political light, we can readily understand not just the complexity but also the uncertainty and anxiety, which more than anything else is shared across the British Jewish community.

4

Israel as Land

Defining Ambiguity

My Promised Land: The Triumph and Tragedy of Israel[1] is an unsettlingly honest book by Israeli political commentator Ari Shavit. The subtitle points to a paradox: triumph is often the only alternative to tragedy yet comes at a high price both for the triumphed over and for the triumphant.

Both triumph and tragedy are explicit in Judaism's formative paradigm: Moses and Israel escaped slavery, pressed forward into the Reed Sea rather than surrender their freedom – and lived to sing in triumph on the far shore as the pursuing Egyptians drowned. It's the culpability of the Egyptians contrasted with the innocence of many of those triumphed over today that accentuates the contemporary tragedy. In a midrash acknowledging the breadth of the Rabbinic perspective, the ministering angels sing a song of triumph on behalf of Israel. God remonstrates: 'My creation, the Egyptians, are drowning and you want to sing?'[2] The same is true today.

[Divine eyebrows are raised.]

What disturbs me most about today's triumph and tragedy is its seeming unavoidability.

Judaism's Most Challenging Particularity

In 2017, I completed a five-year project with a group of leading Jewish and Christian thinkers that concentrated on building strong relationships of respect and trust between members of the group so that we could confront long-standing causes of theological conflict.[3] The work went well and we made encouraging progress together. The most challenging aspect of our discussions proved to be our particularities: the Jews had varying degrees of trouble getting their heads round incarnation while the Christians struggled most of all with accepting that Israel is as important to Judaism as it is to Jews. At one of our closing sessions a leading Catholic, Sister Teresa Brittain from the Sisters of Sion, observed that much of her work lies in educating Christians in new ways of understanding Jews and Judaism – how to walk side by side together. These days, she said, whatever billing is given to her talk, the only subject her Christian audience wants to discuss is Israel, its treatment of the Palestinians and its right to exist. The silence that followed this observation was painful and profound.

At the time, I found it as difficult to know what to say as did the rest of the group. Curiously, completing this book at a time of raging protest against the anti-Semitism of Britain's Labour Party under Jeremy Corbyn clarified for me Sister Teresa's observation. The narratives people tell about themselves may be comforting and inspiring – but are nevertheless flawed.

Becoming a Zionist

In early August 1969, we flew to Israel – an intense and timid 23-year-old and his new wife who'd never before left Ilford's children and grandchildren of East End Jewish immigrants for more than a fortnight. We found Jerusalem bewildering and foreign – its people curt, prickly, opinionated and assertive, in ways quite unlike Ilford, let alone Cambridge or the Hochschule at Marble Arch. My abiding memory is of lying in a single bed, fixed at right-angles to Linda's, in a student block, listening to shells exploding in the Judean hills. It was only two years after the Six Day War; an Australian Christian Zionist had just tried to set fire to Al-Aqsa Mosque to make way for the rebuilding of the Temple and the Second Coming.

We held hands at the back of Ulpan Ezion, did some cautious touring, never felt at ease – but weren't eager to leave. I couldn't have articulated it then but I'd begun to grasp that these people told the same story as me – in different accents but a shared story nevertheless. We were on the same journey, members of the same people. Which is why 'Israel as People' and 'Israel as Land' are twin chapters on identity. Many – Israelis and Diaspora Jews – leave it there. The exceptions are most obviously our religious fundamentalists – waving the Torah as a Divine Property Deed. But a determinedly liberal theologian needs to struggle with God, even in the place where God has been murdered more times than anywhere else on earth.

SECTION ONE
CLINGING TO THE LAND IN THE FACE OF EXILE

The second-century Hadrianic expulsions precipitated a shift in the centre of Jewish life to Babylon. But Simon Sebag Montefiore's biography of Jerusalem[4] is a revelation to all who think Jewish attachment to the Land ended until the even tenor of our absence was disrupted by European Zionists more than seventeen hundred years later. Not only did Jewish life continue in Galilee and along the Mediterranean coast, but the development of Rabbinic Judaism took place there as well as in Babylon. When anti-Jewish policy softened a little, Septimus Severus and his son Caracalla met with the leader of the remnant Jewish community, no less important a figure than Judah HaNasi, compiler of the first great book of Rabbinic Judaism – the Mishnah. Jews were then permitted to pray opposite the ruins of the Temple.

Sebag Montefiore records that when the Persians laid siege to Jerusalem, 20,000 Jews from Antioch and Tiberius joined them. For a brief spell – between 614 and 617 CE – Jerusalem was even placed under Jewish rule.[5] The city was then returned to Byzantine control and its Jews forced to retreat to Jericho. But they were soon back and witnessed the conquest of Jerusalem by an Arab dynasty.

We Jews welcomed the Umayyads after centuries of Byzantine repression. Omar's[6] interest in the Temple Mount understandably excited Jewish hopes – he not only told the Jews to maintain the Temple Mount but also allowed them to pray there with Muslims. He invited the leader of Tiberias's Jewish community and 70 Jewish families to return to Jerusalem, where they settled in the area south of the Temple Mount.[7]

Not long afterwards, 'Jews, many of them from Iran and Iraq [i.e. Babylon], settled in the Holy City, living [in the same area], retaining the privilege of praying on (and maintaining) the Temple Mount.'[8] But after nearly a century of freedom to pray there, a new Caliph, Omar II, banned Jewish worship – a prohibition maintained for the rest of Islamic rule.

In the tenth century, life under the Fatimids[9] became increasingly difficult and the Jewish community in Jerusalem grew more and more impoverished. New depths were plumbed under Caliph Hakim, an unbalanced despot who ordered Jews to wear wooden cow necklaces (to remind them of the Golden Calf) and bells to alert Muslims of their approach. Jews were instructed to choose between conversion and leaving the country. Yet somehow we clung on both in Jerusalem and in other cities of what had been known to the Romans and Byzantines as Palaestina. In 1099, the Crusaders arrived.

The Crusader Kings threatened the Jewish presence in Jerusalem more than at any time since Hadrian. They ransomed Muslims and Jews alike and even 'sold' the Jewish community's Hebrew manuscripts to Egyptian Jewry – where numbers of Jews fleeing Spain had found refuge. Among them was Maimonides, who became one of the Sultan's doctors. As a young man he'd escaped the Almohads and went on pilgrimage to Jerusalem:

> On 14 October, during Tishri, the month of the Jewish New Year and the Day of Atonement, a favourite season for pilgrimages to Jerusalem, Maimonides stood on the Mount of Olives with his brother and father. There he first set eyes on the mountain of the Jewish Temple, and ritually rent his garments … Maimonides grieved for the Temple: 'in ruins, its sanctity endures. He then entered the vicinity and prayed.'[10]

Under the Ottomans, the focus of Jewish life in Eretz Yisrael shifted to the town of Safed in the hills overlooking the Sea of Galilee. When Spanish and Portuguese Jewry were expelled from the Iberian Peninsula at the end of the fifteenth century, Jews – including a number of prominent rabbis – made the tortuous journey to Safed.

Among them were the Kabbalists Moses Cordovero and Isaac Luria, Joseph Caro, compiler of the *Shulkhan Arukh*, and Solomon Alkabetz, author of *L'kha Dodi*, a hymn still sung today by Jews of all denominations to welcome Shabbat. Under Ottoman rule, Safed became a global centre of Jewish learning as well as an important commercial hub.

Back in Jerusalem, its Jews, impoverished by Ottoman taxes, experienced a brief flicker of hope. Jewish history is punctuated by outbursts of messianic fervour, desperate attempts to 'force the end'. One of the best known involves Shabbetai Zvi, son of a poultry-dealer from Smyrna who, in 1648, declared himself to be the Messiah. The Jews of Jerusalem asked him to raise funds from the better-off Jews of Cairo. But not all Jerusalem Jewry was convinced. While his supporters round the Jewish world soon began packing bags for their journey to greet the Messiah in Jerusalem, Jerusalem Jewry doubted he'd turn out to be their financial saviour, let alone Messiah. Shabbetai and his new bride turned up in Istanbul and were promptly offered the choice of conversion to Islam or death. Shabbetai chose the decidedly un-messianic course of conversion; Jerusalem's Jews continued in faithful poverty and subjection.

Simon Sebag Montefiore takes us forward to the nineteenth century and the arrival of a young Englishman, a novelist and aspiring politician who rode into town as part of his grand Oriental tour. Benjamin Disraeli was entranced by the romance of it all – the Temple Mount, the impoverished Jews, and the Arabs to whom he referred as 'Jews on horseback'. Disraeli the rising politician reflected that 'restoring the Jews to their land, which could be bought from the Ottomans, was both just and feasible'.[11] Enter the British Empire, stage right.

Judaism and the Land

It's clear Jews consistently refused to let go of this Land. It was never just another place, or universalized in the way of Christianity. But it ceased to be the place where the majority of Jews lived – so it's legitimate to ask what relevance it continued to hold for Judaism.

The synagogue was – and remains – oriented towards the Land; Jews pray facing Jerusalem. The traditional Jewish regimen of worship consists of daily evening, morning and afternoon prayer. At the heart of each service is a series of blessings known as the *Amidah* – no less than three of which call for liberation and redemption (tenth), the rebuilding of Jerusalem (fourteenth), and the return of God's presence to Zion (seventeenth). The dominant feature of the Shabbat service is the Torah reading, each service reminding us '*Ki mi-Tzion tetzei Torah u'dvar Adonai mirushalayim*': Torah goes out from Zion and the word of God from Jerusalem.[12] The rhythm of the festivals – their timing and practice – reflects the seasons of the Land, not the seasons of Eastern Europe. Not only was the Mishnah compiled in the Land but Rabbinic development continued there in parallel with Babylon, producing the Yerushlami, Jerusalem Talmud. Halakhic tradition – developed in exile/diaspora – pays considerable attention to laws that apply only to those living in the Land and are specific to the Land. The *Seder*, the celebration of liberation on the first evening of Pesach, ends with the declaration 'Next year in Jerusalem'.

This is standard Zionist-Jewish apologetic – but that doesn't, *ipso facto*, invalidate it. It does, however, beg an important question: how significant was the Land to ordinary Jews by the rivers of fifth-century Babylon, in the cities of tenth-century Al-Andalus, and in the *shtetlakh* of fifteenth-century Lithuania? Rabbinic Judaism incorporated return to the Land into its messianic vision of the redemption of the Jewish people. For some it may well have become part of a distant Jewish eschatology, a vision of the End of Days. For others it was a dream, a folk romance far removed from the realities of daily life. Yet it was never simply theoretical eschatology or wistful dream. It's hard to believe that the injunction to plant trees on Tu BiSh'vat, the fifteenth of the month of *Sh'vat*, in the depths of the Polish winter or celebrating the harvest with Ruth in May didn't sound a note of spiritual maladjustment to Diaspora living. The American Jewish scholar Lawrence Fine underlines just how many Jews of the Middle Ages either visited Palestine during their lives or actually settled there permanently. He quotes philosopher-poet Judah Halevi – who in 1140 tried unsuccessfully to get there:

My heart is in the East, and I in the depths of the West.
My food has no taste. How can it be sweet?
How can I fulfil my pledges and my vows,
When Zion is in the power of Edom [Christianity], and I in the
fetters of Arabia [Islam]?
It will be nothing to me to leave all the goodness of Spain.
So rich will it be to see the dust of the ruined sanctuary.[13]

Fine concludes there was 'continuous and frequent' travel by ordinary Jews from the twelfth century onwards, despite the extreme dangers, usually out of simple piety.[14] What a palpable physical expression of 'memory, prayer and longing'.[15]

SECTION TWO
MODERN POLITICAL ZIONISM AND THE END OF EXILE

The Enlightenment brought many changes to European Jewry. Far from diminishing the place of the Land in Jewish hearts and minds, it prompted a Movement – Zionism – determined to transform prayer and yearning into reality. We can begin to understand this vital turn in the journey through the life and works of three representative philosopher-theologians of Zionism.

The earliest, Moses Hess, was born in Bonn in 1812, given a religious education by his grandfather and studied philosophy at a German university. A friend of Karl Marx, he became one of the early Jewish advocates of socialism. So many Eastern European Jews followed, becoming Marxist revolutionaries, that neither Zionism nor subsequent Jewish history can be understood without reference to Marx at this point.

Karl Marx was the son of German Jews who converted to Christianity. So great was Marx's hatred of religion that he remained a Jew! His political philosophy became a worldwide movement; in these days of capitalist domination we shouldn't ignore the fact that the West has given rise to two economic systems. Some argue that Marxism should be seen as a secular religion: without doubt it embodies an eschatology, but one brought about by human action.

For me, Marxism poses problems for three reasons. First, like Hegel and his Idea of History, Marx puts the process before the individual caught up in it. Second, it's utopian, offering a detailed guide to the world at the End of Days and how to get there.[16] And third, it doesn't appear to work – there are few instances in which Marxist ideals haven't crumbled in the face of the assumption of power by the revolutionary leadership. But Marxism/Leninism/Communism attracted huge numbers of Jews – not just because it promised to overthrow murderous Tsarist rule, but also because it carried with it unmistakable Prophetic resonances denouncing the tyrannical abuse of power and the redemption of the oppressed.

When I was growing up in the 1950s and 60s, these ideals and their resonances remained powerful for the Jews of Britain and America, determining the political allegiances of the majority. My father, who taught educationally disadvantaged teenagers on the Isle of Dogs, would often bring home a friend and colleague – a gangling East Ender called Bill Fishman. Fishman became one of Britain's foremost historians of the Jewish East End, introducing me to its radicals, socialists and anarchists.[17] Later, the policies of the Thatcher/Reagan era moved the centre of gravity somewhat to the right but the tradition of the Eastern European Jewish immigrants remains: my mother remembers her father Nathan Mann's 'set of large red Labour Party books' and watching him play cricket for his employer, the Anglo-Palestine Bank. Which takes us back to Moses Hess.

After much travel around Europe, Hess moved back to Germany where two phenomena of Jewish life came to preoccupy him – assimilation and anti-Semitism. Hess uses the word assimilation to describe the process of throwing off the constraints of ghetto life and thought and embracing modernity: at first diluting Jewish belief, learning and practice, then discarding it in order to enjoy the opportunities provided by German society. This, Hess was convinced, would cost Jews their culture yet gain nothing in return: anti-Semitism would ensure that Jews could never escape their identity; but the process of attempted assimilation would eradicate Jewish life and learning. In his book *Rome and Jerusalem*[18] Hess brought together his Marxism and analysis of anti-Semitism, viewing history as a series of race and class struggles that would end in inevitable disaster for European Jewry, and he proposed a Jewish socialist state in Palestine.

Hess highlights three elements of the emergent Zionist Movement. First, it's a reaction to anti-Semitism and the inability of Europe, despite many centuries of Jewish presence and participation, to permit its Jewish minority to live in freedom, equality and security. Second, Hess's thought reflects the rising tide of nationalism, the widespread demand for independent states. The third element is socialism as the vehicle of liberation and the quest for social and economic justice.

Hess also identified the twin compulsions of Zionism: the desire for 'normality' – a people with its own land like any other; and the quest for 'redemption' – through building a just and egalitarian society. It's that dual vision which leads me to suggest that for Hess and many others, the conventional distinction between secular and religious confuses rather than clarifies.

The second philosopher-theologian, Leon Pinsker, born in Russian-occupied Poland in 1821, came from a family who had already moved out of the closed world of religious orthodoxy but still gave him a strong sense of Jewish identity. One of the first Jews to be admitted to the University of Odessa, he became a physician. Pinsker first thought the 'Jewish problem' could be solved by integration but the wave of violence and pogroms, which set in train mass emigration of Jews from the Pale of Settlement, changed his views. He founded the movement known as *Hov'vei Tzion*, 'Lovers of Zion', and wrote an influential pamphlet *Auto-Emancipation*, translated into German, cementing the relationship with like-minded Central European Jews. In Pinsker we meet the dominating conviction that neither the spread of Haskalah among Eastern European Jewry, nor the adoption of socialism, would halt anti-Semitism. Jews were hated and demonized not because they were separate and different but simply because they were Jews.

The best-known of the trio, Theodor Herzl, was born in Budapest in 1860 but his family moved to Vienna, where he became a playwright and highly respected journalist on the *Neue Freie Presse*. He was working in Paris at the time of the trial of French Jewish army officer Alfred Dreyfus and witnessed his conviction for espionage on trumped-up charges. The conviction was later upheld despite cogent evidence that someone else was the spy – and the farcical process unleashed a torrent of violent anti-Semitism, in which the right, including the Catholic establishment, was at the fore. That horrifying experience brought Herzl to the same conclusion as Hess and Pinsker about the future of European Jewry. In his book *The Jewish State*, written in 1896, Herzl says:

> I consider the Jewish question … a national question … We are a people – one *people* … We have sincerely tried everywhere to merge with the national communities in which we live, seeking only to preserve the faith of our fathers. It is not permitted us. In vain are we loyal patriots, sometimes superloyal; in vain do we make the same sacrifices of life and property as our fellow citizens; in vain do we strive to enhance the fame of our native lands in the arts and sciences, or her wealth by trade and commerce. In our native lands where we have lived for centuries we are still decried as aliens, often by men whose ancestors had not yet come at a time when Jewish sighs had long been heard in the country. The majority decide who the 'alien' is.[19]

What had become terrifyingly obvious to Herzl was that Europe – Western, Central and Eastern alike – would never be free from anti-Semitism. Jews had tried repeatedly to integrate, as had his own parents, but would never find acceptance. The only solution lay in understanding this as a 'national question' – Jews are a nation like other nations and entitled to their own land. Though some were desperate enough to consider part of Argentina or Uganda, Herzl was soon clear that only Palestine – or rather, Eretz Yisrael, the *alt-neu* land – would do, because Israel had always been the national homeland of the Jewish people.

The statistics of violent exclusion bear him out. In 1880, there were between 11 and 12 million Jews in the world, 60 per cent of whom were living under a Tsarist regime actively seeking Jewish attrition. Though the major Zionist thinkers were from Eastern, Central and Western Europe, the *Halutzim*, early pioneers, were almost exclusively from the East – those most immediately under threat. The majority of those leaving Eastern Europe between 1881 and 1914 found safety in the United States but a minority, mostly young, sought an old/new way of living in Palestine.

Zionism wasn't a colonial exercise. But Ari Shavit's British grandfather Herbert Bentwich was, in one telling aspect, typical of those who'd taken the British Empire to North America, Australia and New Zealand. When he visited Palestine in 1897, he saw only *terra nullius* – a land without people. Therein lies the paradox, the inevitability that Shavit calls 'The Triumph and Tragedy of Israel'. There was no alternative to leaving Europe, as Herzl knew and history demonstrated; to choose Palestine as a refuge from Tsarist tyranny and violence was also commanded by history. But others were living there – it wasn't a country without people for a people without a country, as the slogan, coined by nineteenth-century Christian Zionists, insisted.

In the earliest days of Zionism, when the majority were escaping to America, only a handful of young visionaries, utopians, found their way to Palestine. These settlers came in two waves, known as the First and Second Aliyah. Some 25,000, mostly from Russia, arrived between 1880 and 1903, settling on land they bought from Arab and Turkish landlords. Between 1904 and 1914 the Second Aliyah brought a further 40,000 Jews, mostly from Russia, Galicia, Romania and Poland – many working as hired labourers. The first kibbutz – Degania – on the southern shore of Galilee was founded by young Jewish idealists bent not so much on a better life as on a new way of living, influenced as much by Tolstoy as by their Jewish tradition. Then came the First World War – striking Eastern European Jewry as Armageddon. Hard on its heels came the October Revolution – seen by some as the dawning of the Messianic Age – followed by post-revolutionary Civil War. Yet persecution grew worse and worse.

Shavit focuses on the newly formed Labour Brigade. In 1921, the first small group of young men and women, some not out of their teens, made a tented camp in the valley of Harod at the very heart of what was to become the State of Israel. They were all, to use Shavit's term, 'orphans', from a world in chaos. Those with parents alive would never see them again; they'd been severed from their religious tradition and brought precious little with them except the rudimentary dream of building a just, egalitarian society.

The land on which they pitched camp had been bought for them, with full legal compliance, from an absentee landlord. Above the valley were several villages where tenant farmers eked out a bare, 'traditional' living; the valley itself had long been a malaria-infested swamp. The group worked with a collaborative energy and determination that beggars belief. They organized themselves, drained the swamps, built a dairy, started a quarry and constructed a kibbutz, Ein Harod – turning the valley into a place of agricultural productivity as never before in its history. Some neighbouring Arabs drifted away but most stayed to observe; there were occasional skirmishes. The kibbutzniks didn't want conflict; some actively sought coexistence – but all regarded the valley as theirs. What grew over the next 20 years – mutual fear, increasing separation, violence – was tragic but seemingly inevitable.[20]

Shavit follows his account of Ein Harod with the story of nearby Lydda – a town with a cathedral and two mosques – which had prospered under British rule. The story ends in 1948, with the desperate picture of Lydda's Arab population expelled, a column marching away as Arab armies invade the Land. With searing honesty, Shavit details an atrocity committed by a rogue Jewish officer against the few who had stayed behind and hidden in one of the two mosques.[21] Tragedy, once again, was seemingly inevitable.

Zionism and Judaism

Up to this point, I've presented Zionism as a 'secular' movement. While predominantly correct, this doesn't tell the whole story. Abraham Isaac Kook was born in what is now Latvia and hailed as an *ilui*, a child prodigy exhibiting an exceptional talent for rabbinic learning. He studied at the Volozhin Yeshivah in Lithuania, taught and wrote, but, in 1904, moved to Ottoman Palestine as Rabbi in Jaffa, next to which the *alt-neu* city of Tel Aviv would be established five years later.

We've seen how leading Jewish figures of the Middle Ages – Judah Halevi and Maimonides, for example – not only longed for the Land and Jerusalem but also risked everything to travel there. The leaders of Lithuanian Orthodoxy had adopted a very different position. They were committed to the notion of *kibbutz galuyot*, the ingathering of the exiles, but affirmed it as an exclusively messianic ideal; the idea of physical return there and then, that was so exciting non-orthodox Jews, was resisted. Kook was unusual and courageous in arguing that re-establishing Davidic rule – which would herald the Messianic Age – wasn't necessary to asserting Jewish political sovereignty: an orthodox Jew could live in Israel, within a modern Jewish State, without making an eschatological claim. Kook understood that settling in Eretz Yisrael was a legitimate, necessary and urgent part of the journey – not an attempt to anticipate or force the End of Days.

Rav Kook became the unchallenged leader of Ashkenazi Judaism in Palestine and took unprecedented steps to build bridges between *dati*, 'the religious', and *hiloni*, 'the secular'. The following passage sheds a rare but shining light on the possibility of religious and secular coexistence within the Yishuv and today:

> For the building is constructed from various parts, and the truth of the light of the world will be built from various dimensions, from various approaches, for 'these and these are the words of the living God'[22] ... it is precisely the multiplicity of opinions which derive from variegated souls and backgrounds which enriches wisdom and brings about its enlargement. In the end all matters will be properly understood and it will be recognised that it was impossible for the structure of peace to be built without those trends which appeared to be in conflict.[23]

There's something positively post-modern in this recognition of complexity and the partial nature of the truths we so fervently advocate.

As important and more representative is Asher Ginsberg. Better known as Ahad Ha'am, One of the People, Ginsberg was born in 1856, in a small town near Kiev, to Hasidic parents. He rejected the constraints of Orthodox Judaism and with them the notion that *kibbutz galuyot* was an exclusively messianic ideal. Travelling to Palestine, he saw the early pioneers at work and argued for a dual approach that emphasized not only settling the Land but also making it 'a permanent and freely developing centre of our national culture, of our science and scholarship, our art and literature'.[24]

Ahad Ha'am's emphasis on Israel as the Land where a renaissance of Jewish culture would take place is an indispensable contribution to the thought of the pioneering period; his vision of a 'great cultural institution' was prophetic. In the same decade as Ein Harod was founded, so also was the Hebrew University in Jerusalem. Its first Board of Governors included Martin Buber, Albert Einstein and Sigmund Freud – figures who speak for themselves, in the same language.

Almost all the founding Chairs of the new University were occupied by world-class German Jewish scholars. Whatever their field, they shared a strong Zionist commitment and a determination to reinvent Jewish scholarship in a new form. A number of them – notably Gershom Scholem – play an important part in the later chapters of this book. They were idealists and visionaries, seeking 'normality' in the freedom to pursue scholarship without the restrictions and inhibitions European society placed on Jewish academics. All believed in the cultural importance of Judaism to the Zionist enterprise, their vision for society driven by deeply held Jewish values.

There were those among the secular founders of Ein Harod who saw their Arab neighbours only as a threat to the Zionist project, but philosopher Martin Buber – example *par excellence* – took a very different view. Buber argued that the two claims – Jewish and Arab – could not objectively be pitted against each other; a compromise leading to both peoples developing the Land together was essential, a sentiment shared by numbers of Jews. But, perhaps significantly, Buber stayed in Berlin longer than contemporaries like Scholem, only arriving in Jerusalem in 1939, by which time the hope he expressed was no longer realizable – if it ever had been.

Zionism and Britain

Early in the First World War, Britain became intensely interested in the Middle East. The Ottoman Turks were an ally of Germany, and in Mesopotamia – the land between the Tigris and the Euphrates, modern-day Iraq – was oil. During 1915/16, Britain and France, with the tacit assent of Russia, agreed on how the region should be divvied up between them. Britain's Empire would be increased by Palestine and Mesopotamia; French territory would include what is now Lebanon and Syria. At the same time, a land for the Jews was very much in the air – in Britain as well as on the Continent. Relatively large numbers of Jews had entered Britain between 1881 and 1905 – until the flow was stemmed by The Aliens Act, Britain's first immigration control measure.

It was known that the First World War was further exacerbating the suffering of the millions remaining in Russia, Poland, Galicia and Romania. In 1915, in the light of the expected imminent defeat of the Turks at the Dardanelles, Herbert Samuel[25] pressed for a British protectorate over Palestine, in the interests of future Jewish settlement. Other ministers had different views. Asquith wrote to a friend:

H Samuel has written an almost dithyrambic memorandum urging that in the carving up of the Turks' Asiatic dominions, we should take Palestine, into which the scattered Jews cd in time swarm back from all the quarters of the globe, and in due course obtain Home Rule. (What an attractive community!)

Curiously enough, the only other partisan of this proposal is Lloyd George, who, I need not say, does not care a damn for the Jews or their past or their future, but who thinks it would be an outrage to let the Christian Holy Places – Bethlehem, Mount of Olives, Jerusalem &c – pass into the possession or under the protectorate of 'Agnostic Atheistic France'! Isn't it singular that the same conclusions shd be capable of being come to by such different roads?[26]

Indeed! And notice Asquith's 'swarm back' and 'what an attractive community!'.

The Zionist figure who engaged the British Government at this point of opportunity was Russian-born Chaim Weizmann, a chemist and Senior Lecturer at Manchester University – three decades later to become Israel's first President. Weizmann pressed the case with such skill and determination that little more than two years later, British Foreign Secretary Arthur Balfour set about formalizing Britain's support for a Jewish State in a letter to its senior British Jewish proponent Lord Rothschild.[27]

The member of the Cabinet most fiercely opposed was Edwin Montagu – like Herbert Samuel, a Jew who'd joined the British establishment. He was driven by fears about what re-establishing

Israel would say about the nature of being Jewish and how British citizens of 'the Mosaic persuasion' would then be regarded. This wasn't his fear alone but was shared by both the Board of Deputies and the Anglo-Jewish Association, and had unforeseen consequences. The first draft of the Balfour Declaration referred to the establishment of Palestine – on either side of the Jordan – as the national home for the Jewish people; Montagu's implacable opposition played a part in the territorially much more modest – and contentious – outcome.[28]

On 2 November 1917, Balfour wrote to Lord Rothschild:

> His Majesty's Government view with favour the establishment in Palestine of a national home for the Jewish people, and will use their best endeavours to facilitate the achievement of this object, it being clearly understood that nothing shall be done which may prejudice the civil and religious rights of non-Jewish communities in Palestine or the rights and political status enjoyed by Jews in any other country.

Britain did indeed seize Palestine from the Ottomans and, on 11 December, General Allenby entered Jerusalem, the thirty-fourth time in the city's history it had been conquered.

Some Bargain!

A bargain was implicit in the Balfour Declaration: in return for support for the Zionist enterprise, Weizmann and Rothschild would encourage Russia and the United States to support British ambitions in the Middle East.[29] But almost immediately this useful, unthreatening perception of Jewry changed; Jews and Zionism became the focus for widespread international alarm. A private telegram sent to the Foreign Office on 12 October 1919 by the British Government's representative in Georgia, John Wardrop, is not untypical:

> I cannot too strongly insist ... that nearly all the present misery of world is due to Jewish intrigues. Your Lordship will understand what I mean in reference to Zachariah Ch. XII: [Jerusalem] is become a burdensome stone for all people, a cup of reeling, a pan

of fire amongst wood, a torch of fire among sheaves. In England and America as well as in this part of the world a diabolical plot is being carried out for the ruin and enslavement of Christendom.[30]

The Russian Revolution – not least the murder of the Russian royal family – shocked Western Europe and alarm bells rang far and wide. Jews and Bolsheviks became instantly synonymous; the Jew as personification of evil – so embedded in Western culture – surfaced yet again in polite society. Confronting it in *The Illustrated Sunday Herald* on 8 February 1920, British Secretary of State for War Winston Churchill declared: 'Some people like Jews and some do not but no thoughtful man can doubt the fact that they are beyond all question the most formidable and the most remarkable race which has ever appeared in the world.'[31]

Sir Martin Gilbert, Churchill's official biographer, provides a précis of *The Herald* article. The conflict between good and evil, Churchill wrote, 'nowhere reaches such intensity as in the Jewish race'. The Jews had evolved a system of ethics 'incomparably the most precious possession of mankind, worth in fact the fruits of all other wisdom and learning put together'. They had also produced Bolshevism, a system of morals and philosophy 'as malevolent as Christianity was benevolent'. Indeed, he continued, 'it would almost seem as if the gospel of Christ and the gospel of Antichrist were destined to originate among the same people; and that this mystic and mysterious race had been chosen for the supreme manifestations, both of the divine and the diabolical'.

Among the main sufferers from Jewish Bolshevism, Churchill continued, were millions of innocent Jews, 'helpless people' on whom the 'hordes of brigands' of Russia did not hesitate 'to gratify their lust for blood and for revenge'. As a result, one now saw in Russia 'the most brutal massacres' against Jews, and 'an eager response to anti-Semitism in its worst and foulest forms'. Zionism, wrote Churchill, offered the Jews 'a national idea of a commanding character'. Palestine would provide 'the Jewish race all over the world' with, as he put it:

A home and a centre of national life ... if, as may well happen, there should be created in our own lifetime by the banks of the Jordan a Jewish State under the protection of the British Crown which might comprise three or four millions of Jews, an event would have occurred in the history of the world which would, from every point of view, be beneficial, and would be especially in harmony with the truest interests of the British Empire.[32]

In 1923, the League of Nations formalized the British and French division of the Middle East, granting each a 'Mandate'. Both countries had set about drawing lines on maps and creating European nation states in areas without coherent boundaries and populations. Britain established the Hashemite Kingdom of Jordan on the east bank of the river and imported Abdullah, second son of the ruler of Hejaz in Western Saudi Arabia, as king. Britain also created modern Iraq with its tribalized mixture of Shiites, Sunnis and Kurds, while the French established Syria and later separated off Lebanon.

SECTION THREE
THE UNTOLD STORY: MIZRAHI JEWS FROM ARAB LANDS

In *In Ishmael's House: A History of Jews in Muslim Lands*,[33] Martin Gilbert describes the context in which Islam was born and highlights the sense of rejection caused by the refusal of the local Jewish population to follow Muhammad. He underlines the ambiguity of status and treatment of Jews – periods of mutual creativity and periods of savage violence. He also confirms the relative tolerance of the early Ottoman period as compared with Christendom at the same time.

The eighteenth and nineteenth centuries saw an inexorable decline in this tolerance. As the Ottoman Empire ceased to be expansive and successful, so conditions for Jews deteriorated. In 1840 in Damascus, a new and sinister feature entered the relationship. An Italian friar and his Muslim servant disappeared; local Christians accused the Jews of murdering the two men in order to use their blood at the *Seder*. Charges were then brought by the French Consul in Damascus, supported by the city's Egyptian Muslim Governor. Seven leaders of the Jewish community were arrested and tortured – two died; one accepted Islam to save his life. Sixty-three Jewish children were imprisoned and many Jewish homes destroyed in the search for the friar's body – before it emerged that he'd been killed by a Muslim. The Christian blood-libel had infected the Arab world.

In 1869 the situation deteriorated further when European anti-Semitic literature reached the Ottoman Empire and 'again and again during the second half of the century, violence disrupted the settled calm and creativity of Jewish life'.[34] So appalling and widespread did the violence become that sizeable numbers of Jews fled homes and communities in which they'd lived, through good times and bad, for centuries. Where did they go? To Palestine, their ancestral home. From places as far apart as the Yemen and Baghdad, Libya and Bukhara, Jews took whatever they could rescue from the destruction of their homes and lives and went to Jerusalem. Several decades *before* the arrival of the first Zionist pioneers from Russia, the Jewish population of Jerusalem had risen to 50 per cent and by 1890 Jews had been in the majority for more than thirty years.[35]

That comes as startling information to both Jews and Muslims who tell the story exclusively from the perspective of European Jewry and modern political Zionism. In fact, the return of Jews to Jerusalem from Arab lands – from Islamic countries – pre-dates the *Halutzim* from Eastern Europe. The Jewish return to our ancestral homeland isn't simply the flight of Eastern Europeans from persecution; it's a response to the inability of both Christians and Muslims to allow Jews to live as full and equal citizens within their lands.

Although exporting Christian anti-Semitism to mid-nineteenth-century Muslim countries points the finger of guilt at one sibling, at root both New Testament and Quranic views of Jews – and both Christian and Muslim resentment at their sibling's refusal to accept Christ and Muhammad – are facts from which none of us have been able to escape.

SECTION FOUR
BRITAIN AND INDEPENDENCE

Not Our Finest Hour
If we now return to the British Mandate and Palestine west of the Jordan, Britain quickly found the situation it had so assiduously sought difficult to manage. Violent Arab opposition to a Jewish State

grew – personified in the figure of a young Arab nationalist, Amin al-Husseini. Appointed by Britain as Grand Mufti of Jerusalem, al-Husseini was among the first to articulate ideological opposition to Zionism – going beyond fear of economic competition or political domination and formulating a Palestinian-Islamic nationalism.

Britain found it hard to keep the peace and maintain its own shifting national interests. Several attempts at partitioning the Land were made – notably by the Peel Commission in 1937 and Woodhead Commission in 1938. Some Jews, the Revisionists, were opposed to any partition but the majority were prepared to settle for what was now an exceedingly small area of Jewish self-rule. The Arabs rejected all such proposals.

The rise of Hitler and the outbreak of the Second World War further complicated matters for Britain. In the face of Rommel's successes in North Africa, protecting Iraq and its oil fields became the priority; Britain was also increasingly anxious not to antagonize the Muslims of India. Grand Mufti Al-Husseini embraced the Nazis, fled first to Iraq and then to Europe, where he was an active propagandist for the Axis powers.

The period from 1945 to 1948 is a moral nadir in British history. Britain turned away boat-loads of desperate Shoah survivors, interned them on Cyprus, and engaged in increasingly violent conflict with the Haganah, the official Jewish defence force, and with militant groups like Irgun. In 1947 we British declared our intention of giving up the Mandate and getting out of Palestine. The United Nations produced yet another partition plan and recognized, by a vote of 33 to 13 with 10 abstentions – of which Britain was one – the State of Israel; we Zionists declared independence. The British-/ French-created states of Jordan, Iraq, Syria and Lebanon – together with Egypt – invaded, bent on strangling the Jewish State at birth, occupying the areas designated as the Arab State of Palestine by the United Nations partition plan.

Declaration of the Establishment of the State of Israel

Modern Israel's founding declaration belies both decades of frustration and the mortal danger in which it was issued:

The State of Israel will be open to Jewish immigration and the ingathering of exiles. It will devote itself to developing the land for the good of all its inhabitants. It will rest upon foundations of liberty, justice and peace as envisioned by the prophets of Israel. It will maintain complete equality of social and political rights for all its citizens, without distinction of creed, race or sex. It will guarantee freedom of religion and conscience, of language, education and culture. It will safeguard the Holy Places of all religions. It will be loyal to the principles of the United Nations Charter.

Even amidst the violent attacks launched against us for months past, we call upon the sons of the Arab people dwelling in Israel to keep the peace and to play their part in building the State on the basis of full and equal citizenship and due representation in all its institutions, provisional and permanent.

We extend the hand of peace and good-neighbourliness to all the states around us and to their peoples, and we call upon them to co-operate in mutual helpfulness with the independent Jewish nation in its land. The State of Israel is prepared to make its contribution in a concerted effort for the advancement of the entire Middle East.

We call upon the Jewish people throughout the Diaspora to join forces with us in immigration and construction, and to be at our right hand in the great endeavour to fulfil the age-old longing for the redemption of Israel.[36]

There are those who argue these principles owe as much to the American Declaration of Independence as they do to Jewish values – as if that's a criticism. Yet it's beyond challenge that the sentiments are at least the equal of the founding principles of any state created over the last hundred years. It also reflects a determination to honour ambiguity – to be a Jewish State *and* a state for all its citizens. This is precisely why Israel's 2018 Nation State Act is a disturbing, retrograde step.

Israel's first Prime Minister David Ben-Gurion told the Peel Commission in 1936 that the aim of the Zionist Movement was 'to make the Jewish people master of its own destiny not subject to the will or mercy of others' but that it was no part of the Jewish aim 'to dominate anybody else'. The Arabs, he insisted, 'have a right not to be at the mercy of the Jews'.[37] Ben-Gurion accordingly developed the Hebrew term *mamlakhtiut* to describe a civic consciousness or public spiritedness grounded in the commitment of citizens to the State. Israel, he was clear, could only function as a modern democracy in which all parties and groups, religious and secular, Jews and Arabs, acknowledged each other's legitimacy and accommodated each other's interests.

Ben-Gurion later reflected that what was so remarkable about the Declaration was that it was signed by every group involved in the political process:

> From the Communists, who had forever fought against the Zionist enterprise as reactionary, bourgeois, chauvinistic, and counter revolutionary, to [Orthodox] Agudat Yisrael [founded in Europe in 1912 to oppose Zionism], which had perceived as apostasy any attempt to bring about the redemption of Israel through natural means . . .[38]

There are two facts of overriding importance. First, Israel brought together people from every conceivable background and political experience. What bound them together was their Jewish identity, their membership of the Jewish people. Second, in the face of reality, narrow political ideologies were set aside: those who didn't, in theory, believe in secular statehood, those who didn't want partition, those whose ideal was a bi-national state – all agreed to what has now become known as the 'two-state solution'.

The Triumph and the Tragedy

By the end of 1948, Zionism had fulfilled Moses Hess's twin objectives embodying Jewish hopes: Judaism could develop in a state of normality and seek redemption by building a just and egalitarian society in the Jewish people's own *alt-neu* Land. But it wasn't an endpoint – as Canaan hadn't proved to be the Promised Land more than three millennia earlier: it was a paradigm shift heralding a renewal of the journey with new possibilities and challenges. The last 70 years have raised issues of international importance and I wouldn't want to stand accused of evading difficult and painful matters.

The triumph of Israel lies in securing – at least temporarily – the future of the Jewish people. It's predicted that, before the middle of this century, more than half of world Jewry's 14 million will live in Israel. Moreover, it's far from being a relic of some distant past: Israel has taken its place among the nations of the modern Western world – a multi-party democracy. It has a genuinely independent legal system, guarding the rights of all citizens zealously, with a judiciary cognizant of the importance of human rights. From medicine to music, from agriculture to scientific and cutting-edge technological innovation, from literature to education, Israel is illustrative of the ambitions and achievements of the modern Western world.

But it's much more than that. It's the only place in the world that responds to the Jewish calendar, where the rhythm of life is that of Judaism, where the Jewish narrative holds primary place in schools, where the daily language is a constant reminder of Jewish teaching, and where debate, discussion and disagreement are as central to life as they have been for the last two millennia. Israel is the one place where, for better and for worse, we Jews can be wholly/holy ourselves. Despite legitimate and understandable existential fears – and the glaring shortcomings of typically twenty-first-century governments (nationalist, populist) – Israel is an enriching, sustaining and profoundly Jewish place to live, an encouragement to all, religious and secular, who would look with unprejudiced eyes.

The tragedy of Israel, more than the triumph, was sadly predictable. Israel isn't fully a state for all its people, nor has it found a way to live peaceably and collaboratively with its Palestinian neighbours. Wrong decisions have been made – Ari Shavit points to Ofra, the first fateful Jewish settlement on the West Bank.[39] But it's arguable that, left to their own devices, Israel and the Palestinians would, in the end, have settled for their two small states. As in the distant past, so in recent decades competing great powers have internationalized the local; Israel and the Palestinians have become proxies for the interests of others. Some in Europe and elsewhere see Israel as a tool of American imperialism, Goliath, not David. Arab countries see Israel as a European intrusion – even a Trojan Horse – into an Arab world still reeling from its inexplicable decline over 300 years and the disasters of British and French colonial policy. As a result of attacks from the outside, Israel has become an occupying power, a situation from which its government, indefensibly, no longer wishes to escape, one that is tragic not just for the occupied but for the soul of the occupier (more damaging even than the disastrous demographics).

There have been internal disasters too – arrogant Ashkenazi treatment of Mizrahi (from Arab lands) Jews, which left many as an underclass, fuelling resentment. And Israel – like almost all other democratic Western states – has suffered from a decline in statesmanship, the collapse of the middle ground and polarization. Like Christian and Muslim countries Israel has seen the rise of religious fundamentalism with its subversive attitudes to democracy. Many early Zionists – driven by necessity to seek normality – wanted nothing more: it's been achieved. Yet many always aspired to something more, and that yearning is still present, still able to move hearts and provide meaning and purpose. But existential fear and realpolitik determine votes, government and policy. In this respect, international norms triumph over – but don't eradicate – redemptive aspirations.

SECTION FIVE
FIVE INALIENABLE RIGHTS

The First Four

The rights that bind Jews to the Land should now be clear.

First, the *historic right*. After the suppression of Bar Kokhba's revolt by Hadrian, Judea was renamed Syria Palaestina and the majority of Jews were compelled to leave. This was a catastrophe, yet, against all odds, not only did Jews cling on and maintain a presence but the Land continued to shape Judaism. It's an indisputable claim, however inconvenient. But two peoples – Jews and Palestinians – now have valid claims to the Land. There's an illuminating midrash, the teaching of which should be irresistible but sadly isn't. Deuteronomy includes the injunction *tzedek, tzedek tirdof*: justice, justice shall you pursue.[40] Regarding no word in the Torah as superfluous, the Rabbis asked why 'justice' was repeated and answered – to teach us that no one is entitled to total justice, to affirm justice is not only divisible but compromise is always necessary.[41] Tragically, that truth hasn't been acknowledged by the fearful and doctrinaire on either side, and peace eludes both Israelis and Palestinians.

Second, the *pragmatic right*, resulting from we had 'no choice'. Both the Ashkenazi and Sephardi narratives demonstrate that Jewish survival depended on the establishment of the State of Israel. There was no alternative. Wherever we Jews lived we were under threat; demonization meant that rising tides of nationalism, fascism and totalitarianism made continued existence where we were untenable. Every single country placed quotas on Jewish immigration in the twentieth century. Indeed, Shavit makes the point – only obvious once it's been made – that as far as the Jews of Europe are concerned, Zionism, in one terrible respect, failed: it wasn't able to save the six million from annihilation.

The third, I'll call the *'moral' right*, using the term to indicate fairness. Neither Christian Europe nor Muslim Arabia was able to countenance Jews living in 'their' lands as full and equal citizens. Century after century of opportunity to realize both faiths' doctrinal commitment to tolerance and respect of others was disregarded. Given such a damming record, how is it possible to deny the 'moral' right of Jews to a land of our own? I can understand the objection of secularists who condemn all religion but such a critique doesn't entitle 'sovereign' individuals from denying their relatedness to the past and responsibility for it. Whether Britain is a Christian or post-Christian country, the legacy is the same.

Fourth – unarguable – is the *legal right*. Israel exists by virtue of a vote of the United Nations; there is no power to rescind such a right in international law. I would in no way wish to compare Israel with today's rogue states but no one denies their right to exist, still less the long litany of countries that have murdered or expelled their Jewish population.

The Fifth Right: a Theology of Zionism and Diaspora

As one would expect, there were those who greeted the re-establishment of Israel in its Land by hailing divine intervention.

Some argued it was compensation for the Shoah, others that God had ensured military victory. Repugnant though such views are, they highlight the perennial difficulty of reading the present – as well as one of the many blasphemous dimensions to religious fundamentalism. Rav Kook had insisted these were not messianic times; seeing the present as *hevlei hamashiakh,* the birth pangs of the Messiah, was wrong. That's the foundation for my understanding too.

A book that broke new ground, *Judaism and Modern Man,*[42] was published as long ago as the 1950s. Its author, Will Herberg, was born in Belarus, grew up in a secular Jewish family in Brooklyn, first identifying himself as a communist but then rejecting Marxism and becoming a rabbi.

Herberg argued that Jews exist on two levels: on a 'natural' level as individuals and citizens of our native lands – whether that land be America, Britain or the new State of Israel. But, collectively we also exist on a 'supernatural' level, as what he called 'a covenant folk'. All Jews, wrote Herberg, are living during 'the great parenthesis' – between the call of Abraham and the return to Zion as the Promised Land. During that parenthesis the task in the Land is to establish national life and seize the opportunity of building towards the community of Judaism's vision. In Diaspora the Jewish task is to be maladjusted, at odds with the flaws of the present, and so bear witness to God and God's values.

What I find so helpful about Herberg is that he not only sees the Jewish journey continuing both in the Land and in Diaspora but offers metaphysical meaning and purpose for this dual existence.

Herberg's thinking was at odds with many louder voices. Once again understandably, many in Israel wanted to eradicate all memory of the Diaspora, obliterate its humiliations and promote the image of the Jew as a proud and free citizen of their own land – normal, no one's suffering servant. There were also intellectual voices from Diaspora – notably that of literary critic and polymath George Steiner, who found the 'normal life' of Israeli citizens distasteful and opted for remaining exclusively 'the guest', living on sufferance and voicing that which others don't want to hear wherever in Diaspora they don't want to hear it. There were always those for whom national identity was the be all and end all of Jewish existence and they were joined by immigrants from the Soviet Empire with experience of nationalism but little of Judaism. Conversely, there are Diaspora figures – among them Judith Butler – who cannot abide the compromise of 1948 and continue to argue for a bi-national state.[43]

Forty years after Herberg, Dow Marmur published *The Star of Return*.[44] He begins by taking issue with the Polish-born American Jewish theologian Abraham Joshua Heschel and his 'architecture of time'. Judaism, argued Heschel in his book *The Sabbath*, is a religion not in space and the material things that fill it but in time; 'the Sabbaths are our great cathedrals'.[45] Marmur redresses the balance:

> Jewish geography is no less significant than Jewish history; there is Jewish space and … Jewish place, not just Jewish time; Jewish aspirations are not only about the world beyond but are also about an address on this earth; the heavenly Jerusalem and the earthly Jerusalem are contingent upon each other.[46]

Marmur's title and structure are modelled on Franz Rosenzweig's work *The Star of Redemption*.[47] He adopts Rosenzweig's two triangles, which form a *Magen David*, Star of David. Writing of the return to the Land of Israel, Marmur has, as the points of his first triangle, God, People and (the State of) Israel, with 'hope for a better life', 'the challenge of power' and 'righteousness in relationship to the Arab population' as those of his second.

Moving away from Rosenzweig's overriding universalism, Marmur reasserts a balancing particularism expressed in Land. He doesn't deny the Diaspora – for a decade Rabbi Marmur spent half the year in Jerusalem and half in Toronto – but teaches that Jewish covenant is rooted not solely in Jewish time but in Jewish place as well, a place with historical meanings, where past events are remembered, and one that provides continuity and identity across the generations. For Marmur, as for me, the physical, earthly Jerusalem, *Yerushulayim shel matah*, grounds the spiritual, heavenly Jerusalem, *Yerushulayim shel ma'alah*; each depends on the other.

Marmur contributes immeasurably to the theme of journey, now shaped by Israel present as well as Israel past. God made a covenant with the Jewish people at Sinai – with their descendants and with those who choose to join. From that moment on, a journey of meaning and purpose towards the Prophetic vision of the End of Days has continued, challenged both from within and without, often battered and sometimes severely damaged but never entirely halted. The journey has been through a number of paradigm shifts, the most recent being the re-establishment of the State of Israel. There's no simplistic or blasphemous connection between the last phase of the old paradigm and the beginning of the new – Israel isn't compensation for the Shoah; we remain at an unknowable distance from the End of Days and the realization of the messianic vision. But the journey – on which God continues to accompany us – now has two inextricably interconnected routes: we continue the journey in a new-old (or old-new) way, on the Land *and* in Diaspora.

Which takes us back to the beginning of this chapter, to Sister Teresa Brittain's acknowledgement of rank-and-file Christian antipathy towards Israel. It stems from a Christian narrative in which Jesus defied oppressive rule and took the side of the poor, the weak and the disenfranchised. It follows, therefore, that Christians today should be on the side of the poor and oppressed Palestinians and challenge illegitimate and oppressive rule – now no longer Roman but Israeli.

Islam, too, has a single – today largely unchallenged – narrative which defines the Middle East as Islamic and regards the Jewish State as Western colonization rather than the return of its closest Abrahamic sibling to the land where all three faiths were born.

Both narratives gravely distort reality. In an article in *The Times*, much-respected journalist Daniel Finkelstein identified yet a third narrative: that of today's Labour Party. 'Israel', he wrote, 'is a tiny country. It's the size of Wales. At one point you can cross the country on foot in less than two hours. But to Mr Corbyn and his allies it is a symbol of the one thing that they battle against more than any other: the evil of Western imperialism.'

'Zionism', Finkelstein continued, 'has, for them, ceased to be a description of the desire for a homeless refugee people to make a small state for themselves in their ancient homeland. Instead, it stands for an ideology of occupation and world domination. This translation of the practical project of Jews seeking security into a world conspiracy to spread imperialism is, by its nature, anti-Semitic.'[48]

Finkelstein is right: the virus of anti-Semitism is seemingly ineradicable, not least because of its ability to mutate. Whether the hard Left in Britain today is aware of the nature of its narrative or not, it is as disturbing as the current hard Right Christian and Muslim accounts of Israel. What makes them even worse is the collective denial that Israel is part of Jewish theology. This paves the way for the new lie: Israel is about Jews, not Judaism, and is, therefore, at best an unnecessary enterprise and, at worst, a racist one.

I can only repeat: *Judaism* has a geography as well as a history. That may be unpalatable – but the otherness of the other is so often unpalatable.

Is that a piece of neat, academic theology or the personal affirmation we've all been waiting for?

It's an affirmation that I need to unpack and explore – later.

Despite history, I still believe in Diaspora as well as Land. And my much-resisted inheritance from the Leo Baeck College won't go away: I'm wedded to the German *Liberale* tradition and elective affinity. Some years ago, I attended a lecture in Paris by the Jewish historian Diana Pinto. She savaged what she identified as the European Jewish sense of victimhood and retreat into exotic otherness (Haredi Jews lighting *hanukkiot* in public squares with politicians standing by), arguing that Jews should stop thinking of themselves as 'victims' and consider themselves 'as the full-fledged, integrated and positive actors they are across Europe'. Jews should balance concern for themselves with 'shared universal principles in the creation of an open, tolerant but value-laden space'. She concluded:

> Jews know what they need, in terms of cultural and religious spaces and respect for multiple identities, in order to be able to live as fulfilled citizens in their respective countries … The most important lesson for the future is that democracies can only exist and prosper if they contain citizens, not a collection of competing victims.[49]

Despite the re-emergence of anti-Semitism in France – and in the UK – what Pinto urged continues to be valid, perhaps even more so.

For much of my career I visited Israel annually – usually in support of the World Union for Progressive Judaism, the largest synagogue umbrella organization in the world. Numerically dominated by the American Reform community, it nevertheless has a vigorous, indigenous Israel Movement – determined to enlarge the ground between politically powerful right-wing religious fundamentalists and secularists long stripped of all respect for religion. Though twice prompted, I decided against making aliyah, settling in Israel. Perhaps it's the triumph of hope over experience but I believe in the *dual* journey.

Working with our fellow citizens in the building of a decent, just and compassionate society is central to my understanding of Judaism. As is demonstrating that the three Abrahamic faiths needn't be hopelessly dysfunctional and can work together for the benefit of humanity. It's vital, not just for Jews, that minorities can survive, maintain their distinctive culture and contribute to wider society rather than be absorbed into the morass of materialism and cynicism so widespread.

Tragically, it's not clear that Jews and Judaism are any safer today in Israel – implacably opposed by most Arab states; playing high-stakes games with superpowers – than they were when squeezed between assimilation and anti-Semitism in the Diaspora.

Ari Shavit ends *My Promised Land*:

> We take part daily in a phenomenal historical vision. We participate in an event far greater than ourselves. We are a ragtag cast in an epic motion picture whose plot we do not understand and cannot grasp. The script writer went mad. The director ran away. The producer went bankrupt. But we are still here, on this biblical set. The camera is still rolling. And as the camera pans out and pulls up, it sees us converging on this shore and clinging to this shore and living on this shore. Come what may.[50]

I'll go along with that. With one correction. The Director never runs away. The Director observes, wills us to cling on – to the Land and its purpose – but doesn't direct.

PART THREE

Judaism Today: Light and Weight

If a person fell and died, [the builders of the tower of Babel] paid no attention. If a single brick fell, they sat and wept saying: 'Woe upon us – when will another brick be brought up in its place?'

(PIRKEI DE RABBI ELIEZER 24)

I swore never to be silent whenever and wherever human beings endure suffering and humiliation. We must always take sides. Neutrality helps the oppressor, never the victim. Silence encourages the tormentor, never the tormented. Sometimes we must interfere. When human lives are endangered, when human dignity is in jeopardy, national borders and sensitivities become irrelevant. Wherever men or women are persecuted because of their race, religion or political views, that place must – at that moment – become the centre of the universe.[1]

(ELIE WIESEL, NOBEL PEACE PRIZE
ACCEPTANCE SPEECH)

5

Torah: Judaism's unique selling point

SECTION ONE
THE *SEFER TORAH* (SCROLL)

House of Torah

Designed and built at the same time, St Peter's in Rome and the
Blue Mosque in Istanbul are breath-taking, their openness to the
Transcendent awe-inspiring. As a Jew I'm envious: we've nothing
like them and, in some respects, the equivalence of synagogue,
church and mosque is false. Whether the synagogue has its origins in
Babylon or later in Judea, it was designed *not* to be the Temple but a
modest, multi-purpose building that can be constructed anywhere.
A meeting place (*bet k'nesset*), a place of worship (*bet t'fillah*) and,
above all, a place of study (*bet midrash*), the synagogue has retained
this smaller-scale functionality for two millennia.

There are a number of external reasons – the unsettled nature of
Jewish life, an often imposed insistence on not rivalling other places
of worship – but they're not key. In nineteenth-century western and
central Europe more impressive buildings emerged, reflecting greater
confidence and resource – if not coherence of style. That American
Jewry reverted to the term 'Temple' (following the German Reform
precedent), and has even employed architects of the stature of Frank
Lloyd Wright, exemplifies a change in the place of Jews in society.
But even here, we're rarely if ever talking of buildings at the vanguard
of architectural progress in the service of spaces reaching up to the
heavens.

Apart from orientation towards Jerusalem, only one feature makes a synagogue what it is – and that tells you what lies at the heart of Judaism. Even in today's utilitarian buildings, constructed down to the maximum budget the community can raise, you'll find the *aron hakodesh*, the ark – a cupboard (over which a *ner tamid*, a constant light, burns). Inside is a Torah scroll – or as many Torah scrolls as the community can afford – Genesis, Exodus, Leviticus, Numbers and Deuteronomy, meticulously written by a scribe on parchment in the manner prescribed by halakhah, Jewish law. It's Torah that makes the synagogue; the synagogue is the building that houses Torah.

Birth of Judaism's USP

Back to Simon Schama and *The Story of the Jews*.[1] The time is the middle of the fifth century BCE. Judah – the area surrounding Jerusalem – had fallen to the Babylonians (Solomon's Temple was destroyed around 586 BCE). Large numbers of Jews had been exiled to Babylon, particularly the leaders of the community – the royal family, priests, bureaucrats: only a motley remnant had remained. Seventy years later, the Babylonian Empire itself fell to the Persians; Cyrus, the Persian ruler, instigated a new policy with regard to the conquered peoples who made up his empire. He decreed the Jewish exiles could return – if they so chose. Zerubbabel, of the Davidic line, and Yeshua, the High Priest, were authorized to lead the Jewish returnees.

Some decades later, Nehemiah, living in Susa in today's Iran, cup-bearer to the new Persian king Artaxerxes, was appointed governor and went to inspect Jerusalem. The city was still in ruins and the rebuilding of the Temple had barely started. All this and what follows is recorded in the book of Nehemiah, written not long after the time it describes. The number of Jews in Jerusalem and the surrounding area is probably overstated but this, unequivocally, is history.

Nehemiah tells us that Ezra, priest and scribe, orchestrated a dramatic event. On the first day of the month of Tishri, Rosh Hashanah, the Jews of Jerusalem and the surrounding area, remnant and returnees, were assembled. Not, Schama stresses, near the Temple still undergoing rebuilding but by the Water Gate, as an event in its own right/rite. As the first eight verses of Nehemiah Chapter 8 tell us, beginning at first light the Torah was read to the people publicly, translated and explained as the reading proceeded.

The Torah stands alone; it's not surrounded by ceremony and prayer; engagement with the text of Torah is the totality of the event that Ezra (and Nehemiah) designed, the occasion at which the particularity of Judaism is first fully expressed. The core, the truly distinctive feature of Judaism, its USP, was confirmed on Rosh Hashanah in 445 BCE. Judaism isn't about sacred buildings – the rebuilding of the Temple notwithstanding – nor about monuments or solemn ceremonial. As Schama says, Jews have 'at their devotional centre a scroll of words':[2]

> The genius of the Israelite-Judahite priestly and scribal class was to sacralise movable writing, in standardised alphabetic Hebrew, as the exclusive carrier of [God's] law and historic vision for his people ... It was the obsession of the makers of Israelite book-religion to make the Torah ubiquitous, *inescapable*, not just established at some sacred site, but available in miniaturised forms on property and person. Instead of an image of a divine creature or person hung over a doorpost to repel demons, it was the Torah writing of the *mezuzah* that would keep Jews safe. Phylactery boxes, the *tefillin*, were made so that its words would even be bound on the head and arms of the observant as they prayed ... No part of life, no dwelling or body, was to be free of the scroll-book.[3]

Hebrew is particularly well suited to the purpose. 'Standardized alphabetic Hebrew' consists solely of consonants, its vocalization determined by grammar. Between the sixth and tenth centuries CE, scribe-scholars known as the Masoretes developed a system of vowels so that the vocalization of the Torah for public reading was fixed. But these do not appear in the scroll, leaving every word open for study – for alternative readings, commentary, midrash.

What, precisely, Ezra's Torah scroll contained isn't clear – we can be reasonably sure the content has changed little over the last 20 centuries but earlier is impossible to establish. Schama's point, however, is incontrovertible. Christian colleagues have even suggested that Torah plays the same role in Judaism as Christ (rather than the

Gospels) does in Christianity. Torah and interpretation have been the heart of Judaism for 2,500 years. But the modern Western world has thrown down a potentially fatal challenge – parried or ignored by many to this day – which a liberal theologian has to meet head-on.

Oh God, I know where this is leading.

I vividly remember the new building my parents' community built behind a Methodist church in a humdrum suburb of metropolitan Essex – functional, multi-purpose, and I can see the Ark, to which much thought had been given, as if it were yesterday. As a teenager, I proved adept at vocalizing the Hebrew of the Torah scroll and translating it phrase by phrase, basking in the approval given to my performances, blissfully unaware at the time of the questions Torah raised for Jews both then and, even more widely, today.

Long ago, Jewish tradition divided the five books of Moses into sections called *sidrot*. A section is read each Shabbat with the cycle beginning and ending on Simkhat Torah, the Rejoicing of Torah which rounds off the *embarass de richesses* of autumn festivals beginning with Rosh Hashanah. Simkhat Torah is celebrated by processing the Torah scrolls with much singing and dancing and even a little alcohol. Samuel Pepys records with bemusement a visit to 'the Synagogue' (a rented house in London) seven years after the Resettlement under Cromwell on Simkhat Torah in 1663:

> Their service all in a singing way, and in Hebrew. And anon their Laws that they take out of the press [ark] are carried by several men … round about the room, while such a service is singing. And in the end they had a prayer for the King, which they pronounced his name in Portugall; but the prayer, like the rest in Hebrew. But Lord! To see the disorder, laughing, sporting, and no attention, but confusion in all their service, more like brutes than people knowing the true God … Away thence with my mind strongly disturbed with them, by coach.[4]

The Shabbat morning service, barnacled by time, is now excessively long for most modern tastes. A lengthy liturgy leads eventually to the intended climax of the Torah service and the chanting, 'leyning', of the *sidra* (section of Torah for the week), often by a bar or bat mitzvah. Here modernity's challenge to the Torah is revealed weekly. For a start, there's very little of the uplifting prose one might hope for. Instead we listen to a mixture of ancient mythology, the stories of the patriarchs/matriarchs and then, following the Exodus and Sinai, legislation from a remote age including detailed instructions on how to make priestly vestments or treat skin diseases – not to mention censuses and genealogies. Of even greater impact, the Torah takes us into a world in which God not only speaks but intervenes, punishing the wicked and rewarding the righteous, a world few recognize as our own.

Of course, there are very many verses that have become part of the lifeblood of modern Western culture – not just linguistically but ethically and spiritually. But the way the encounter with Torah happens today seems guaranteed to underline remoteness more than presence, the unbelievable instead of the compelling. It's no small wonder that the phrase-by-phrase translation of my youth – an attempt by Reform to increase accessibility – has given way to resumption of the tradition of leyning in Hebrew. At least one can enjoy the melody (or lack of it depending on who's doing the leyning), but it can become a performance or just plain boring.

In recent decades, sitting in the body of the congregation as opposed to leading the service, I couldn't fail to notice the 'disconnect', the switching off. Many congregational rabbis are equally aware. Rabbi Jonathan Wittenberg, disciple of Louis Jacobs, is the much-admired leader of Britain's most innovative orthodox (Masorti) synagogue. He identifies with his congregants, the majority of Jews who ask:

> How can I relate to the different concepts, the apparently distant and different reality, of which the Torah speaks? How am I expected to make sense of the way in which in the Torah God simply stretches out an arm and intervenes in history when there is little sign of God's doing that today? How can one escape the conclusion that either the world, or God, or both are different now, and what impact does that have on the degree to which we find the Torah relevant to our own lives? ... Can we believe that meaning is to be discovered in those lengthy sections of the Torah which deal with rituals that have ceased to be kept for almost two

thousand years, such as the details of the Temple observances, and of the sacrifices in particular? How are we to find significance in material apparently so recondite, irrelevant and unappealing?[5]

There's a major *liturgical* issue about the way we deploy what Schama saw as 'reading that begs for argument, commentary, questioning, interruption and interpretation' as the inflexible, performance-driven climax to a long worship service.[6] But it's the underlying *theological* issue as to the nature of the text itself that is unavoidable – and Judaism doubled that challenge two thousand years ago.

Forgive me, Doctor of Divinity Bayfield, for stopping you in full flow, but do you find Me as remote, unbelievable, as you allege your fellow congregants do?

Absolutely. Many's the time I've concluded that it's all empty pantomime, redundant anthropology. But then You give me a sharp, discomfiting kick for which I'm not grateful but can't ignore – God knows I've tried. This is challenge, protest, not atheism.

SECTION TWO
NOT ONE TORAH BUT A DUAL TORAH

By Whose Authority?

There's a passage from the Talmud on which generations of Jewish children were once weaned:

Hillel used to earn a dinar a day, half of which he gave to the doorman at the *Bet Midrash* and half he used for the maintenance of his family. One day however he'd earned nothing and the doorman wouldn't let him in. So he climbed up and sat by the window on the roof to hear the words of the Living God from the mouths of Shemaiah and Avtalion. It was a winter Friday and snow fell. At dawn Shemaiah said to Avtalion, 'My brother, usually it's light; today it's dark. Perhaps it's very cloudy outside.' They looked up and saw the shape of a man against the window covered by three cubits of snow. They brushed off the snow, washed him, put ointment on him and put him by the fire, saying: 'He's worthy that the laws of Shabbat be set aside for his sake.'[7]

Here we are, in the very early stages of Rabbinic Judaism – before rabbis were called rabbis: the teachers are translating, interpreting and explaining Torah in the new context of the oppressive, unsettling Greco-Roman world. They're creating their own game-changing hermeneutics (rules for interpreting Torah); developing an unquenchable flow of exegesis (interpretation). They're forming the practical, ethical and spiritual fabric of portable Judaism, teachings that are memorized, repeated and passed on to the next generation. Once again neither sacred building nor solemn ceremony is important – only words, the words of Torah, explanation and interpretation; debate, discussion, disagreement, intellectual cut and thrust: Torah, Judaism's USP. But the creativity and brilliance begs a question – one of authority. Who empowered the Rabbis to open this new chapter in the journey of the Jewish people and the story of Judaism?

The title of one of the earliest books of Rabbinic Literature is Pirkei Avot, often translated as the Ethics of the Fathers. This rendering of the Hebrew word perek, 'chapter' (pirkei means 'chapters of'), is prompted by the contents of the book – a series of sayings by the leading figures of each generation who built Rabbinic Judaism over the three centuries up to 200 CE and the compilation of the Mishnah; almost all the quotations or sayings are homiletic with a strong ethical dimension. In many ways, Pirkei Avot is atypical of Mishnaic literature and has long served as a book for Jews to study on Shabbat afternoons. On the surface it's simple, wise and accessible – but its opening contains more than meets the eye.

Pirkei Avot begins: 'Moses received Torah from Sinai and handed it on to Joshua and Joshua to the Elders and the Elders to the Prophets and the Prophets handed it on to the Men of the Great Synagogue. They said three things . . .'[8] After detailing the 'three things', the Men of the Great Synagogue[9] hand it on to 'Shimon the Just, survivor of the Great Synagogue'[10] and he to the forebears of the Rabbis and the forebears of the Rabbis to the Rabbis themselves.

We're presented with the claim of an unbroken tradition that stretches back to Moses receiving Torah at Sinai. Here, at the very beginning of a popular collection of the best-loved sayings of classical Rabbinic Judaism, comes a statement both defining and ideological. Defining, because it tells us that Torah means the totality of what Moses received at Sinai; ideological, because it places the Rabbis and Rabbinic Judaism in direct line of descent from Moses, cutting out the Priests and the authority of those who administered the Temple and its rites. In just a few words, this apparently innocuous introduction to Pirkei Avot lays the foundation for a new theological definition of the term Torah and legitimizes the authority of the Rabbis as its sole interpreter.

We need to spell out the implications of those two interconnected points because they take us to the very heart of what Jews do or do not subscribe to today and raise the central issue of authority in modern and post-modern Jewish life and thought. Let's start with the definition. It's now become a given that Moses received Torah at Sinai – not just the two tablets on which the Ten Statements or Ten Commandments were written. From the outset, Rabbinic Judaism insisted that the entire Torah – from 'In the beginning ...'[11] to 'in the sight of all Israel'[12] – was 'received' (not written in an authorial sense) by Moses.

And that's not all. The Rabbis called this 'document' the *Torah she-bi'khtav*, the Written Torah. Moses, insisted Rabbinic doctrine, also received the *Torah she-b'al peh*, the Oral Torah, the entire body of interpretation (or at least the hermeneutics, the rules of interpretation) of which Mishnah and Talmud are foundation stones. Rabbinic Judaism, the tradition flowing from biblical Judaism and born alongside Christianity, rests upon a definition of Torah as being *dual* – both the Pentateuch, the five books of Moses, and the entire corpus of classical Rabbinic interpretation. This Rabbinic claim to exclusive, divinely sanctioned authority for interpreting Torah empowered the Rabbis and their successors.

Make no mistake, I'm full of unqualified admiration and gratitude. At a time when the authority of the Priests had been corrupted by infinitely more corrupt Roman rulers and was on the point of being destroyed along with the Temple, the Rabbis accepted responsibility and took control with a timely, Judaism-saving coup. Their programme of development through interpretation saved the Torah by giving new life to its theology and practice in the most innovatory and creative way. I've often asked myself whether the process was conscious or not: were the compilers of Pirkei Avot and the major teachers of the Mishnah aware they were imposing their authority and taking Judaism in a new direction? I suspect some were, but most were not – they were convinced by their own doctrine. In any event, their methodology was unique and their end product gave Judaism vitality and strength.

Rabbinic Judaism Holds Sway

The Rabbis became the uncontested leaders of the Jewish people and Rabbinic Judaism held sway. There were Karaites, a group who, it's thought, originated in Baghdad in the seventh to ninth centuries but who were rarely a threat numerically or theologically. They were as resolute in their commitment to the Written Torah as every other Jew but rejected the Oral Torah. The following text – from a tenth-century Rabbinic compilation – graphically illustrates the underlying assumptions on which Rabbinic Judaism is based:

> Once I was on a journey and came upon a man who attacked me as heretics do. He accepted the Written but not the Oral Law. He said: The Written Torah was given to us from Mount Sinai. The Oral Torah was not given to us from Mount Sinai.
>
> I said to him: But weren't both the Written and the Oral Torah spoken by God? Then what difference is there between the Written and the Oral Torah? To what can this be compared? To a king of flesh and blood who had two servants and loved them both with a perfect love. He gave them each a measure of wheat and a bundle of flax. The wise servant, what did he do? He took the flax and spun cloth. Then he took the wheat and made flour. The flour he cleansed, ground, kneaded and baked. He put it on the table and spread the cloth over it, leaving it until the king might return. The foolish servant did nothing at all. After some days, the king returned from a journey and came into his house and said to them: My sons, bring me what I gave you. One servant showed the wheaten bread on the table with a cloth spread over it.

The other servant showed the wheat still in the box with a bundle of flax on it. Alas for his shame, alas for his disgrace!

When the Holy One gave the Torah to Israel, God gave it only in the form of wheat for us to extract flour from it, and flax to make into a garment.[13]

In the Middle Ages it wasn't the doctrine of the Dual Torah but the insistence on divine authorship of every word of the Written Torah that caused surface ripples. Famously, the early twelfth-century Spanish philosopher and Bible commentator Abraham ibn Ezra queried the first verse of Deuteronomy: 'These are the words which Moses spoke to all Israel beyond the Jordan.' It was the phrase 'beyond the Jordan' that struck him. The expression only makes sense to someone writing in Canaan/the Promised Land, which Moses never entered; that appeared, in turn, to suggest that some parts of the Torah were written after Moses' death and not at Sinai. So unnerving an observation was this that Ibn Ezra felt he could only hint, commenting enigmatically:

If you understand the secret of the twelve, and of 'And Moses wrote', and of 'And the Canaanite was then in the land', and of 'In the mount where the Lord was seen', and of 'Behold his bedstead was a bedstead of iron', you will discover the truth.[14]

What did he mean? Let's follow Rabbi Louis Jacobs who, 800 years later, was to develop Ibn Ezra's hint into a broader understanding of the emergence of Torah within the context of human history. Jacobs writes:

The secret of the twelve probably refers to the last twelve verses of the Pentateuch (Deut. 34). These describe how Moses went up to die on the mountain and he did not come down again so that he could not have written this chapter. The words 'And Moses wrote' (Exod. 24.4; Num. 33.2; Deut. 31.9) suggest that someone other than Moses wrote the words 'And Moses wrote'. 'And the Canaanite was then in the land' (Gen. 12.6) suggests that they were no longer in the land when this was written, but in Moses' day they were still there. 'In the mount where the Lord is seen' (Gen.

22.14) is understood as referring to the Temple which had not yet been built in Moses' day. 'Behold, his bedstead was a bedstead of iron' (Deut. 3.11) speaks of the bedstead of the giant Og, king of Bashan, who was slain by Moses toward the end of the latter's life, while the words seem to imply that the bedstead was pointed out as an exhibit in the equivalent of the local museum long after Og had been dead.[15]

The doctrine that every word had been received by Moses and written down at Sinai or at later stages in Moses' life may have frayed a little at the edges in the twelfth century but not a great deal seems to have come from Ibn Ezra's enigmatic remarks. Perhaps because most rabbis were reluctant to risk cutting off the ideological branch of the tree on which they were sitting.

Spinoza: Iconoclast and Pariah

The ultimate challenge came early in the development of the modern Western world – from a genius so thoroughly rejected that even today's Progressive Jewish world largely ignores him.

Baruch Spinoza was born in Amsterdam in 1632, son of Portuguese Jews whose ancestors had formally converted to Christianity to save themselves from persecution, maintaining their Jewish identity and faith in secret. The Spinozas left Portugal in order to practise Judaism openly and, on finally reaching Amsterdam, found a Jewish community of similar descent. But more than a century of estrangement from Jewish communal life had created a gap between expectation and reality – both for the Spinozas and for the Amsterdam community.

Baruch grew up within the expansive, free-thinking environment of the Dutch Republic and, though Jewishly educated, found himself an outsider to the religious life of Amsterdam – a thoroughly liminal figure. He studied Latin and engaged with Descartes. In a very short period of time, Spinoza emerged as a dominating figure in early modern Western philosophy, employing the logic of Euclidean geometry, dismantling Cartesian dualism – reuniting mind and matter. He also reached the conclusion that the Torah was the work of human hands, reflecting human limitations, not coming directly, un-mediated from God.

Spinoza cut through the heart of seventeenth-century religious ideology and doctrine, charting the road ahead that so many would travel – and still do. His Jewish education had acquainted him with Ibn Ezra's hints as to the origins of Torah and may have played a part in his revolutionary claim. He was considered to have rejected the classical Rabbinic understanding of revelation, challenged the foundational doctrine of the Dual Torah, arousing consternation within the Jewish community. He also upset Amsterdam's Calvinists – likewise wedded to the authority of the Bible – and it's possible their outrage put pressure on the Jewish community to pronounce a ban of *herem*, excommunication, on Spinoza, aged only 24.

Spinoza continued to write, finally settling in The Hague where he worked as an innovative lens maker, dying at 45 of lung disease probably caused by the fine dust produced when grinding and polishing lenses. It's clear Spinoza's challenge to the Dual Torah and the Rabbinic understanding of Sinai were what the leaders of Judaism rejected and expelled – understandably so; it's less apparent why, several centuries later, he should still largely be disregarded by Progressive Jews. It's perhaps understandable that Chief Rabbi Jonathan Sacks could write: 'No one could follow Spinoza and remain a Jew.'[16] But even the distinguished Reform Jewish theologian Eugene Borowitz – following Hermann Cohen – is roundly critical, suggesting Spinoza's identification of God and nature produced 'an ethics that does not seek to transform the world but to adjust one's intellect to it'.[17] Yet Spinoza's posthumously published *Ethics* is a founding text of Humanism and he set out the case for freedom of speech a generation before Locke. Louis Jacobs himself was also lukewarm, recognizing Spinoza's contribution to historical criticism but alienated by his understanding of God.[18]

And there I believe lies the key to Progressive Jewish indifference. The contemporary debate runs as to whether or not Spinoza was an atheist. He would seem to be a pantheist – yet his identification of God with nature has, as Brian Magee points out, a religious quality to it that supports and explains Spinoza's fierce denial of atheism.[19] So why should we still treat him as a pariah? Spinoza refused to turn his back on his faith and remained, even after the *herem*, a Jew. In some ways he resembles people I address 350 years later on Yom Kippur: humanist, totally committed to Jewish identity and the ethics of Judaism, mindful of Judaism as a religion but profoundly aware of the religious abyss between themselves and the God Who dictated the Torah to Moses on Sinai; Who determines, annually according to the Yom Kippur liturgy, 'who will live and who will die'.

Spinoza challenged traditional understandings and dogma in a way that was necessary before Judaism could engage further and more creatively with both the Torah and the modern world. Our pariah treatment of him delayed that progress and left us behind the curve. The Synagogue has treated Spinoza in a manner reminiscent of the Church's rejection of Galileo; repentance and rehabilitation are called for.

Raising the Barricades: Samson Raphael Hirsch

The Enlightenment in Germany gave rise to historical criticism – the understanding that, whatever its origins, the Bible is a complex document, written down over a period of time and pieced together by human beings. The early 'reformers' in Germany embraced this view of Torah and were met with strong resistance by the 'traditionalists'. It was seen as incompatible with the Rabbinic doctrine of the Dual Torah and, therefore, a threat to the authority of those who wished to maintain Rabbinic Judaism unchanged, unresponsive to the Enlightenment.

In mid-century, among those who advanced the Orthodox position was Rabbi Samson Raphael Hirsch who, though he believed in Jews participating in wider society, felt obliged to pursue a policy of resistance to and separation from Reform over this issue. As the historian and President of Hebrew Union College Professor David Ellenson writes: 'Jewish tradition, for the Orthodox, was clear. Judaism rested upon the notion, as Hirsch phrased it, "that the Written Law and the Oral Law were equal, as both were revealed to us from the mouth of the Holy One, blessed be He".'[20]

From 1851 onwards, Hirsch was rabbi of the traditionalist section of the community in Frankfurt. His determination to reassert the unimpeachable authority of the Dual Torah finally prompted him to take a stand, detach from the rest of Frankfurt Jewry and form an independent 'Torah-true' community. He wrote an article entitled, with deliberate irony, *Judaism Up To Date*:

> Let us not deceive ourselves. The whole question is simply this. Is the statement 'And God spoke to Moses saying', with which all the laws of the Jewish Bible commence, true or not true? Do we really and truly believe that God, the Omnipotent and Holy, spoke thus to Moses? Do we speak the truth when in front of our brethren we lay our hand on the scroll containing these words and say that God has given us this Torah, that His Torah, the Torah of truth and with it of eternal life, is planted in our midst? If this is to be no mere lip-service, no mere rhetorical flourish, then we must keep and carry out this Torah without omission and without carping, in all circumstances and all times. This word of God must be our eternal rule superior to all human judgement, the rule to which all our actions must at all times conform; and instead of complaining that it is no longer suitable to the times, our only complaint must be that the times are no longer suitable to it.[21]

A new understanding of Torah, emerging following the Enlightenment, was rejected. Reform Judaism was deemed not to be Judaism at all; total separation from it became the order of the day. And so it was to remain.

Louis Jacobs: Orthodoxy's Own Challenge to Hirsch

A century later, one of Orthodox Judaism's own, Rabbi Dr Louis Jacobs, accepted the historical, human dimension to Torah. Graduate of a traditional yeshivah in Manchester, scholar of immense learning and otherwise unimpeachable orthodoxy, Jacobs concluded that reasoning about Torah necessitates accepting the fruits of historical criticism.[22] His appointment as Principal of Jews' College was revoked and he was cast out by Britain's Orthodox leadership. The 'Jacobs Affair' threw Britain's United Synagogue into turmoil, leading to a breakaway synagogue and, eventually, despite Jacobs's reluctance, to a new denomination, Masorti or 'Traditional' Judaism.

This passage from the book of the controversy, *We Have Reason to Believe*, summarizes Jacobs's stand:

> Revelation is an encounter between the divine and the human, so that there is a human as well as a divine factor in revelation. God revealing His Will not alone to men but *through* men … [our new knowledge prompts us to attribute more to the human than in the past] but this is a difference in degree, not in kind. [It does not affect] our reverence for the Bible and our loyalty to its teachings. God's Power is not lessened because He preferred to co-operate with His creatures in producing the Book of Books.
>
> [Swiss theologian] Emil Brunner asks us to think of a gramophone record. The voice we hear on the record is the voice we want to hear, it is the actual voice of the artist who delights us, but we hear it through the inevitable distortions of the record. We hear the authentic voice of God speaking to us through the pages of the Bible – we know that it is the voice of God because of the uniqueness of its message and the response it awakens in our higher nature – and its truth is in no way affected in that we can only hear that voice through the medium of human beings who, hearing it for the first time, endeavoured to record it for us.[23]

It's measured and reasonable but was understood by the leadership of the United Synagogue as challenging the authority of Rabbinic Judaism. Jacobs's use of historical criticism and preference for reason over dogma was roundly rejected; the United Synagogue maintained and still maintains precisely the position taken by Samson Raphael Hirsch.

Jonathan Sacks: *Torah min ha-Shamayim* and Hirsch Defended

The sturdiest contemporary defence of the Dual Torah comes from that most articulate and philosophically educated of all today's Orthodox rabbis, Lord Sacks. When he was appointed Chief Rabbi, Orthodoxy had long encapsulated its position in the phrase *Torah min ha-Shamayim*, Torah from Heaven. In 1995, Rabbi Sacks used his own house journal, *Le'ela*, in which to reprint parts of two chapters from a recent book, *Crisis and Covenant*,[24] to state his position.

The style is characteristic of Rabbi Sacks – historically rooted, intellectually sophisticated and elegantly phrased. He begins with a restatement of the issue – the challenge of historical criticism to the Rabbinic understanding of Torah:

> No challenge could be more fateful for Jewish destiny than an assault on the belief in what the sages called *Torah min hashamayim*, 'Torah from Heaven'. This, for Judaism was the greatest trauma of the Enlightenment. From Spinoza onwards, the Torah came to be seen by biblical scholars as a text to be analysed like any other, a human document, indeed a series of documents composed at different times and embodying different traditions, pieced together by a redactor ... no element of traditional Judaism could survive this order of biblical criticism. For if the Torah were indeed the work of human beings, its laws could not be divine commands, nor could its covenant carry certainty or authority. This was more than the shaking of the foundations. It was their destruction.[25]

That clarifies the concerns of Samson Raphael Hirsch and his contemporaries, against which they took their stand. If the *Torah she-bi'khtav* is seen to be a document written down by human beings over time and not something 'extra-historical', delivered in its entirety to Moses by God at Mount Sinai, then its traditional authority collapses. It would follow that the *Torah she-b'al peh* – developed on the basis that the *Torah she-bi'khtav* is literally God's word – loses the logic behind its hermeneutic as well as its exclusive claim to be the correct method for interpreting God's word. Rabbinic Judaism is thus exposed to a double – or dual – whammy.

Rabbi Sacks goes back to early Rabbinic Literature, to texts illustrating the significance of each letter and syllable of the Torah, and reaffirms them. He then turns to the early twentieth-century Orthodox response to historical criticism and cites at some length 'the great German Orthodox scholar Rabbi David Zvi Hoffmann', who accepted the traditional position but 'now took on secular criticism ... on its own ground'. This section of the essay concludes by affirming that the challenge presented by historical criticism was unprecedented:

> Despite the fierce philosophical disputes of the Middle Ages, this was the unshakeable ground on which all Jews stood. That ground was split asunder by the earthquake of the Enlightenment. Since then Orthodoxy alone has preserved the Torah of tradition into the twentieth century, while other groups have filtered its voice through independent and prior imperatives: ethics, autonomy, history or national culture … [undermining] its central, seminal authority as the constitutive document of a covenantal people. A relatively small part of modern Jewish theology has been devoted to the question of 'Torah from Heaven'. It is as if scholars have sensed that in confronting it they approach holy ground. For the fate of Torah in Jewish thought is little less than the axis on which the meaning of Jewish existence turns. At stake are the central terms of Jewish belief, textuality and history, interpretation and time, revelation and the covenant between God and a chosen people.[26]

In the second part of the essay Sacks embarks upon 'what *Torah min hashamayim*, "Torah from Heaven", meant for rabbinic tradition' and what is therefore at stake. Torah, argues Lord Sacks, is not only 'the constitution of the covenant between God and Israel' but came out of a 'breakthrough of the transcendent into the world of the senses'. It revealed 'God himself: for God is found not in nature but in words' immune from detached academic study. The Torah is extra-historical.

The essay ends, as it began, highlighting the encounter with modernity. Sacks observes that the nineteenth century posed a series of crises seeming to explode fundamental concepts into fragments: 'The depth of this drama cannot be overstated. To experience God, for Judaism, is not to see but to hear. The assault on the Word could not but be an assault on the Jewish God.'[27]

What becomes apparent is Sacks's technique of contrasting extremes. He opened by characterizing the opposition 'from Spinoza onwards' as biblical scholars who analysed the Torah as text 'like any other, a human document, indeed a series of documents composed at different times and embodying different traditions'. Now he explicitly equates modern culture with incompatible secularity and reflects: 'within a century, the culture which had reduced the book of the covenant to fragments had reduced a third of the people of the covenant to ashes'. That last statement is unworthy and doesn't, I'm sure, reflect Jonathan Sacks's own attitude to modern Western culture as a whole. It is, instead, an appeal to the siege mentality of those who've retreated back into the pre-Enlightenment ghetto.

Sacks employs an either/or argument: either you retain the traditional Rabbinic understanding of *Torah min ha-Shamayim* and tell the Enlightenment to go hang, or you side with secular, non-Jewish scholars who regard our Torah as just another piece of literature. He 'overlooks' two hundred years of Jewish thought based on an intermediate position, an alternative reading of the term *Torah min ha-Shamayim*, namely that the Torah is an interpretive document told, written and then pieced together by human beings but testifying to a time when our ancestors encountered God and later recorded that experience.

It should already be clear that 'Jewish belief, textuality and history, interpretation and time, revelation and the covenant' are not automatically lost by challenging the Hirsch/Sacks understanding of *Torah min ha-Shamayim*. Indeed, for many Jews it's only by challenging the unmediated, 'extra-historical' understanding of Torah that Jewish belief, revelation and covenant can be sustained. The choice offered by Rabbi Lord Sacks is dismissive of the culture in which we, including him, were educated, live and breathe. It ignores all views except those of nineteenth-century German Orthodoxy and hostile gentile secularity, refusing to acknowledge those faithful Jews who cannot accept that God would provide any group of human beings with a book that is 'extra-historical', untouched by human hands. Such views also provide inexhaustible ammunition for Jewish secular fundamentalists such as Californian member of the Four Horsemen, Sam Harris.[28]

To write out of Judaism those who say that this isn't what God does because this isn't Who God is betrays an understandable fear of the consequences but at the expense of fidelity to the determinedly progressive spirit of Judaism: *vayisa'u*, Go forward. To argue as though such people don't exist may be a successful polemic for a limited internal audience but the stance is politically defensive and theologically unreasonable as far as the vast majority of open-minded, thinking Jews are concerned.

SECTION THREE
THE TORAH IS ITSELF INTERPRETATION

A Moment of Metaphystory

Some years ago my younger daughter and her husband took a break on the shores of the modern-day Red Sea with a side-trip to Mount Sinai – this Mount Sinai being one of at least three mountains on the Sinai Peninsula identified as the scene of the biblical revelation. It's the one most people opt for today and has long been the Christian choice, with St Katherine's Monastery near the foot. Reaching the top, Miriam says she was 95 per cent sceptical and remained so, but the 5 per cent was very alive.

I'm more than 95 per cent agnostic about location, time and what precisely happened. It's interesting to learn there was an eruption on Santorini in the sixteenth century BCE, memories of which may provide a naturalistic backdrop to the plagues, the parting of the waters at the Reed Sea and the thunder and smoke of Sinai. But that's backstory to metaphor, neither confirming nor debunking the revelation itself. The Torah provides us with an account of the founding metaphystory of Judaism – the moment at which the Metaphysical and Jewish history touch for the first time. For a moment, a minute or an hour, God is present in a different way in human history than immediately before or immediately after; but there are only human beings to tell of that encounter and only human beings can later record it. Where precisely it happened, or when, or what we'd have experienced had we been there, is unknowable. Sinai was, is and always will be Judaism's most powerful and enduring metaphor without which there can be no Torah.

That, if I may say so, Rabbi Professor, is pathetic. You question the location; you question the time; and you dismiss the words as not Mine. With theists like you, who needs atheists!

That's not fair. And it's Your fault, a consequence of Your nature – You don't send physical proofs of Your existence whistling through outer space to one favoured group of people – or to anyone. It's not even that You're too elusive and light on your feet to be captured by faded love letters or written agreements signed by you as Yud-Heh-Vav-Heh – or any other Name. It's simply not Who You Are.

And yet you claim to exchange words with Me from time to time and now want people to believe this is a genuine conversation, not a clever rhetorical device?

[Long silence] Touché. But I don't take back what I've just said.

Let's press on, to the most spiritually disturbing episode in the Torah: the account of the Golden Calf in Exodus 32. Moses ascended Mount Sinai, received the two tablets of the Covenant and stayed with God for 40 days and 40 nights; when he came down, he found the Children of Israel dancing round a Golden Calf manufactured out of their own jewellery. That is truly shocking: the Children of Israel stood at the foot of the Mountain; there was a spectacular sound and light show with thunder, lightning, smoke and the Voice of God. The Voice of God! Less than six weeks later, not only do the people doubt whether Moses is coming back but they've begun to worship a god antithetical to the God of Sinai – mute, visible, indisputably their own creation.

What can we infer from this? The encounter with the Divine, revelation, the religious experience – even group experience – is fragile and evanescent; that which was so vivid melts faster than snow in the same wilderness. Human beings cannot recapture, relive what they experience – be it painful or pleasurable or profound; they can only remember *that* they experienced, *that* they felt. The experience of God is even more delicate and fleeting – 'Could it really have happened? No. I must be deluded. It's group hysteria.' Yet were it to be more permanent, it would become a spurious title deed; God is neither for owning nor ownable. But the collective account has been passed down to us and – despite the elusiveness of place and time, the nature of an experience that defies words and description other than metaphorical – the divine voice-prints are there in the Torah and in countless generations of commentary, discernible within the human words. Why should it be like that, so elusive and meta-rational? Because that's the nature of God and revelation.

The Rabbis of the classical period explored the revelation at Sinai, using all their faith-filled powers of religious imagination. The following text is quintessentially Rabbinic:

> Rabbi Abbahu said in the name of Rabbi Yohanan:
> When the Holy One, blessed be He, gave the Torah,
> No bird cried, no fowl flew, no ox bellowed, the
> angels did not fly, the seraphim did not say Holy,
> the sea did not stir, no human beings spoke,
> But the world was still and silent,
> And the Voice went forth: '*Ani / Adonai / Elohekha*
> I am / the Eternal / Your God' (Exod. 20.2).[29]

The Voice out of silence affirms the verbal content of revelation – identified both by historian Simon Schama and theologian Jonathan Sacks – but the main thrust of Rabbinic commentary suggests that what was heard by the people at Sinai was brief. Some commentators say they only heard the first three Hebrew words – hence the last line of the midrash.

Others understand it as an individual experience:

> Torah teaches: 'The voice of God is with power' (Ps. 29.4), not 'with His power' but with power, that is to say, according to the capacity of each individual … Rabbi Jose ben Hanina says, 'If you are doubtful about this, then think of the manna that descended with a taste varying according to the taste of each individual Israelite. The young men eat it as bread; the old as wafers made with honey; to the babies it tasted like rich breast milk; to the sick, it was like fine flour mingled with honey; while to the heathen, its taste was bitter and like coriander seed. Now if the manna, which

is all of one kind, became converted into so many kinds to suit the capacity of each individual, was it not even more possible for the Voice, which had power, to vary according to the capacity of each individual so that no harm should come to them?'[30]

What insight. We experience revelation (or not) according to who we are; the experience of God isn't uniform but fragmentary and shaped by our individuality. If that's true for those present at Sinai and who for a moment or a minute encountered God – yet had no frame of reference for the experience, tried to speak to each other about it and told their descendants – how much more must it have been true for those who didn't have that experience but continued to speak about it and for those who wrote it down, the redactors of the Torah, the people who wove the oral traditions together and first committed them to writing. I recently heard historians Bethany Hughes and Irving Finkel apply what they agreed was 'the tenacity of oral memory' to the Mesopotamian Gilgamesh epic, affirming its roots in the historical; so should we to the narrative that the redactors of the Torah recorded. That same Torah text was handed on to the Rabbis who wrote their commentaries and to us who read it in the light of modernity, historical criticism, fundamentalist dogmatism and the secularist/atheist assault.

Let me summarize: I'm not dismissing or downgrading the Torah text nor the infinite number of meanings generations have found and continue to find in it. But I am insisting that even the primary text is an interpretation of our ancestors' experience of God, not the experience itself. *The text of Torah is itself interpretation.*

The tradition of interpretation remains Judaism's unique selling point, well suited to the post-modern world of provisionality and plurality, complexity and uncertainty. As Professor of English Gabriel Josipovici writes:

We too long in our daily lives for an end to decisions, choices, uncertainty, talk. Yet we also know most of the time that life will not provide such an end, that we will always be enmeshed in uncertainty. It is quite extraordinary that a holy book should dramatise precisely this, rather than giving us the assurance we desire, but that is what the Hebrew Bible does.[31]

For me, the most intriguing contemporary expression of this approach is Jacques Derrida's insistence that we read in order to uncover the questions behind the answers of a text or tradition. What are the questions that lie behind the revelations of Torah? What questions do the claims of the biblical text yield? Rather than closing a discussion, interpretation opens up the way forward.

SECTION FOUR
DARK TEXTS AND LIBERATION

Insight into the Divine is not a Closed Shop

There are a number of well-known passages in the Torah that have disturbed as well as inspired commentators over two millennia – and that particularly trouble me.

Take, for example, the story of Pinchas who, in Numbers 25, takes the law into his own hands, summarily executes Zimri and Cozbi – an Israelite man and a Midianite woman who, as a cultic act, are having intercourse – and is rewarded by God with the honour and privilege of hereditary priesthood. Generation after generation of commentators have been troubled by this, distinguishing the case so that it shouldn't be used as a proof-text for zealotry – but few if any felt able to say that the biblical authors hadn't properly expressed the divine role in the episode.[32] The Pinchas narrative is what I regard as 'a dark text', and I feel liberated by being able to learn from the obvious concern and distinguishing analysis of previous commentators without being compelled to accept that God sanctions, justifies or rewards extrajudicial murder. God doesn't, and, thank God, I can say so! Similarly, I no longer feel obliged to accept that God would approve of Sarah's behaviour in expelling Hagar and Ishmael in Genesis 21. The texts are faithful records of authentic oral traditions but aren't infallible interpretations of God's intention or will. After centuries of textual exploration, we're still capable of further insight into the nature of the Divine.

For many, this an unnerving conclusion but, for me, it's liberating. Let's pursue it through two different episodes.

The Akedah (Binding of Isaac)[33]
The Akedah is a story that has caused me inner conflict for decades. On the one hand it's immensely rich and powerful, which justifies its choice for reading on Second Day Rosh Hashanah in a way that Genesis 21 – traditionally read on First Day Rosh Hashanah – no longer (for me at least) does. But it's always nagged away at me.

On an important level, the text is a trumpet blast against child sacrifice – Canaanites sacrificed the eldest child to the god Molokh. It's called in Jewish tradition the 'binding' (not the 'sacrifice') of Isaac and makes the clearest possible statement that God doesn't require us to sacrifice our children for God's sake. 'Parable of the Old Man and the Young', by First World War poet Wilfred Owen, adopts something of the same methodology as Rabbinic midrash and also its radicality of interpretation – God doesn't want human sacrifice and Owen brutally exposes our wilful disregard:

> … Behold,
> A ram, caught in a thicket by its horns;
> Offer the Ram of Pride instead of him.
>
> But the old man would not so, but slew his son,
> And half the seed of Europe, one by one.

Magnificent. But it doesn't address my most acute difficulty: what kind of God sets diabolical tests for Abraham to pass rather than question (as he'd always done before)? What kind of religious outlook sees preparedness to sacrifice one's own child as an admirable expression of belief? According to Kierkegaard, Abraham is a 'lonely knight of faith', representative of 'the teleological suspension of the ethical'.[34] It's my deepest conviction that God never suspends the ethical in Judaism and if God appears to do so, we have misunderstood God.

I'm encouraged in my challenge by three contemporary Jewish voices unencumbered by traditional rabbinic inhibitions: Woody Allen satirizes Abraham's unquestioning acceptance in a short prose piece, 'The Scrolls: Two'.[35] Nobel Laureate Bob Dylan (Robert Zimmerman) savages the murderous instruction in 'Highway 61 Revisited' and Leonard Cohen emphatically rejects the paradigm in his song 'The Story of Isaac'. To which I can only say 'Hallelujah!'

Deuteronomy 7.1–4
This passage is not only hideous but illustrates how even in the Torah, God can be traduced:

> When the Eternal our God brings you to the land that you are about to invade and occupy, and God dislodges many nations before you – the Hittites, Girgashites, Amorites, Canaanites, Perizzites, Hivites, and Jebusites, seven nations much larger than you – and the Eternal your God delivers them to you and you defeat them, you must doom them to destruction: grant them no terms and give them no quarter. You shall not intermarry with them: do not give your daughters to their sons or take their daughters for your sons. For they will turn your children away from Me to worship other gods, and God's anger will blaze forth against you and God will promptly wipe you out.

If you have any doubt what 'doom them to destruction' means, Chapter 20.16 makes it clear: 'you shall not leave a soul alive'. I've no difficulty with the fact of settlement in the Promised Land, nor with the paradigmatic nature of that period for Judaism; I recognize God's presence with my ancestors on that – and every other stage – of the journey. But I have an insuperable problem with the notion that God would not only urge the mass expulsion of the indigenous population but be party to their extermination. No God in whom I could believe would command such behaviour; indeed the concept of such a God is blasphemous.

Here, historical and literary criticism go a long way to easing the problem. Many modern Bible scholars regard the book of Deuteronomy as coming from a different source to the other four books; there may well be a connection between Deuteronomy and the book found by the priests during the reign of King Josiah, recorded in 2 Kings 22. It's possible that the traditions that make up Deuteronomy were redacted, edited and put in their final shape then or later. The fact that Deuteronomy may have begun to take its present form in the seventh century BCE, and has linguistic and cultural features of that period, doesn't mean it's a fraudulent document without genuine roots in the time it describes. But it could help to explain the apparently inexplicable and unacceptable.

Scholars have argued that archaeology suggests a gradual settlement rather than a quick, comprehensive military conquest. The evidence supports a measured 'infiltration', a process of spreading out and settling among the existing inhabitants of the Land, not a widespread smash-and-grab conquest with *shofar* blasts, circuits and walls-come-tumbling-down again and again. As the process of settlement developed, the Jewish presence acquired a physical coherence, stability and structure; but it wasn't without its problems. The other inhabitants of the Land had their own religion or religions and there's much evidence to suggest the biblical description of their practices is well founded – Canaanite cults that included, in Jeremiah's oft-repeated line, fertility rites and sacred prostitution 'on every high hill and under every leafy tree'. Unsurprisingly, this had attractions for some of the Jewish settlers and their descendants – an invisible God Who demands justice and ethical behaviour was less appealing, to men at least, than one offering fleshly inducements.

There's a persuasive scholarly theory suggesting that these verses in Deuteronomy, which rightly trouble so many of us today, are retrojections, glosses added to the original narrative long after the conquest or settlement of the Promised Land had taken place.[36] The redactors of Deuteronomy were saying that if only the Children of Israel had got rid of the troublesome neighbours when they first got there, we wouldn't be tearing our hair out now at intermarriage and defection to pagan cults. It's not a very edifying or ethical sentiment: even understood as retrojection, the text is acutely embarrassing, supplying cogent ammunition for selective quotation by proponents of the New Atheism. But it's a plausible explanation of a desperately dark theme in the Torah. It also gives rational, historical support to my conviction that God doesn't command the displacement and elimination of other peoples under any circumstances. Thank God, I say, for the Enlightenment and historical criticism.

[Slow, ironic applause] Let's suppose, Rabbi Bayfield that, in theory, there's some validity to your position. I'm going to play what you call devil's advocate. Have you considered it might be pure theological self-indulgence? You offer people the uncertainty of trying to sift My wheat from human chaff; you challenge a doctrine that's sustained the Jewish people for two millennia and replace it with a theory that requires more speculation than the would-be-faithful can bear. Let people stick with the 'implausible' rather than the 'reasonable' – the outcomes will be better. Let them stay with the old teachings and don't encourage them to make ethical and theological choices – all they'll do is suit themselves. You're fond of the word 'hubris'; this is your hubris working overtime.

You're right about the hubris ... but I still can't buy Your argument.

[Intake of breath through nose] Why not, rabbi?

SECTION FIVE
SEFER TORAH, DUAL TORAH, JEWISH TEACHING

Torah, then, is the scroll raised, read, translated and explained ever since Ezra.

It's also the Dual Torah of Rabbinic Judaism – the interrogation and debate of the Rabbis in Judea and Babylon, the codes of practice and philosophy of Muslim Spain, the mysticism of Safed, the *pilpul* of Lithuanian *yeshivot*, the stories of the Hasidim and the continuing engagement of the orthodox with Rabbinic Judaism and life today, in the Land and in Diaspora.

And it's the whole of Jewish teaching that began at Sinai – that which flows from the Ark of the Covenant and continues in the post-Enlightenment world. It's the theology and philosophy of

German Jewish scholars from Hermann Cohen onwards, and their later counterparts in Europe, the United States and Israel. It's the conflicting ideologies that Rav Kook saw as part of a whole and the agonized words of those who've struggled with God and God's justice and compassion ever since the Shoah. It's what we Jews carry with us as we journey on into the challenges, complexities and uncertainties of the twenty-first century.

Torah is the word of God mediated by us as we journey through a constantly changing environment. It's both imperious and evanescent. For Judaism, words are key and words are always open, yielding questions even though they masquerade as answers. Think of the language in which our tradition has been transmitted – the letters on the tablets of stone and on the Scroll, Hebrew letters, consonants without vowels, the very vocalization of which depends upon the human beings who vocalize them and allow them to speak. Torah is interpretation of interpretation. And of that there is no end.

6

Covenant theology: Halakhah, law

Acquaintances used to ask my late mother-in-law what her son-in-law did. With a sharp intake of breath she'd reply: 'He's-a-very-clever-boy-and-could-have-done-anything he wanted-but-he's-a-rabbi.' 'Oh', her questioner would respond, 'he must be very religious.' 'No,' Phyl would say, 'he's Reform.'

Most Jews in Britain or Israel would understand instantly what she meant. We're back with Rav Kook and the term *dati*, translated as religious but understood as traditionally observant. The more obsessively you observe *kashrut*, the dietary laws, the more tightly your Shabbat is restricted, the more *dati*, religious, you are. It makes me howl in frustration.

SECTION ONE
COVENANT

Judaism isn't a religion characterized by 'doctrines' that attempt to articulate God's nature. It's fuelled instead by broader religious insights that shape it. For me, the most significant is covenant – which takes us back to Torah.

Three Models of Covenant

Seventy years ago, American Lutheran scholar George Mendenhall undertook pioneering research into societies that shed light on the patriarchal period. He found that ancient Near Eastern rulers made various kinds of solemn, binding agreement or covenant – the Akkadian word is *biritu* – with their subjects or fellow rulers. One type of *biritu*, named by Mendenhall a promissory pact, presumed the inequality of the parties but nonetheless bound the ruler to the ruled unilaterally, out of imperial beneficence. In a second kind, the suzerainty treaty, the ruler bound his vassals to a comprehensive set of obligations, promising nothing in return except, implicitly, protection. There was a third form of *biritu*, the parity treaty in which mutual obligations were undertaken by two equal parties – between rulers, for instance.

The Akkadian word *biritu* gives us the Hebrew word *b'rit*, widely used in Torah and best known from *b'rit milah*, covenant of circumcision – circumcision being a physical sign of the covenant between Abraham and God. Arnold Eisen, now Chancellor of the Jewish Theological Seminary in New York, offered an original – and very helpful – view of covenant in an essay drawing on Mendenhall's research.[1] What Eisen reveals is the way the biblical authors drew on 'the political lexicon of the ancient Near East'[2] to derive startling metaphors for the relationship between Israel and God.

The first example of *b'rit* in the Torah is found early in Genesis. God says to Noah:

> For my part, I now establish my Covenant (*b'riti*) with you and your offspring to come and with every living thing that is with you – birds, cattle and every wild animal as well – all that have come out of the ark, every living thing on earth. I am establishing my covenant (*b'riti*) with you: never again shall all flesh be cut off by the waters of the flood and never again shall there be a flood to destroy the earth.[3]

Ancient political vocabulary has been reworked into daring and complex theology. The covenant between God and Noah is a *biritu* of the promissory kind: God, the Ruler, makes a promise and expects nothing from God's subject(s) in return except, by inference, trust and loyalty. It is fundamental that the first *b'rit*, the first covenant in the Torah, is made between God and Noah as the progenitor of all humanity (in its second, post-flood version). I can't emphasize strongly enough: the first covenant is between God and all humanity; all subsequent covenants must be understood as subordinate to that universal relationship.

The next example, also of a promissory covenant, comes eight chapters later – in very different circumstances:

> When Abram was ninety-nine years old, God appeared to Abram and said to him: 'I am El-Shaddai; walk before me and be blameless. I will set my covenant [*b'riti*] between me and you, and I will make you exceedingly numerous ... You shall no longer be called Abram, but your name shall be Abraham, for I will make you the father of a multitude of nations ... I will establish my covenant [*b'riti*] between me and you and your offspring to come as an everlasting covenant [*b'rit olam*] throughout the generations, to be God to you and to your offspring to come. I will give the land in which you have sojourned to you and your offspring to come, all the land of Canaan, as an everlasting possession. I will be their God ... Such shall be the covenant [*b'rit*] between Me and you and your offspring to follow which you shall keep. Let every male among you be circumcised.[4]

Once again, the explicit terms bind only God – circumcision is a sign of the covenant, not a requirement imposed on the human side. Eisen also cites the covenant with David in 2 Samuel 7: 'Like a lover, he [God] accepts the partner just as he is – David even in his sinfulness, the whole of humanity despite [its ethical imperfections]'.[5] You are My beloved; I'll treat you as My beloved – all I demand in return is faithfulness and trust. God is Patron, Benefactor, Lover.

But not so at Sinai. In the book of Exodus, the *biritu* model changes. Chapters 19 and 20 culminate in the Ten Commandments and constitute a different kind of covenant, a suzerainty treaty. Only if Israel obeys its Suzerain and complies with rigorous, detailed terms will it become 'a kingdom of priests and a holy nation'. Here the Ruler is demanding and uncompromising, asking a great deal and offering in return only presence and protection. That's the covenant made at Sinai – in Exodus.

By contrast, Eisen points out, the *biritu/b'rit* in Deuteronomy follows neither the promissory nor the suzerainty model. Instead, says Eisen:

> Deuteronomy's reiteration of the covenant follows the parity form precisely, adopting even the standard six-part structure: preamble, historical prologue, detailed stipulations, provision for deposit and/or reading of the text, invocation of divine witnesses (in this case, heaven and earth), and, finally, the recitation of blessings and curses.[6]

The two accounts of revelation at Sinai, in Exodus and Deuteronomy, differ theologically: in Deuteronomy the covenant between God and Israel is seen neither as an agreement between Lover and loved, nor as between Lord and subject, but as one between parties who are mutually dependent. In that succinct analysis, founded on Mendenhall's research, theologized by Eisen, we glimpse the richness and complexity of Who God may be.

In the Preface, I stressed that today, theology starts with the self. We work outwards, perhaps upwards, and won't all arrive at the same place. A sense of being in a particular kind of covenantal relationship is, for me, compelling; in trying to convey what this means, my hope is that you, reading the first part of this chapter, will find a reverberation or be prompted to explore what the metaphor might mean for you. Now let me reflect from a personal perspective.

*Promissory model: God is my Protector, the One Who loves me
and accepts me for who I am*
If this is so, then why is life so unloving for so many people? I recognize the disproportionate number of blessings heaped on me, yet I don't experience God in that way. Demanding, yes: loving, no. It's not a comfortable place to be, since it's not what Western culture teaches about God – not just Christianity but also admirable Jewish theologians such as the American-born Israeli Modern Orthodox Rabbi David Hartman. Hartman was a theologian for whom – like me – covenant is an indispensable theological concept. In his appropriately titled book, *A Living Covenant*,[7] Hartman's faith is

expressed by the promissory model – critically, angrily contrasted with the suzerainty model. God's love for the Jewish people is the dominant feature, inspiring love and gratitude in return. Central to Hartman's model of Jewish life is prayer: in prayer a Jew 'can live before God without being overwhelmed and terrified'[8] and go out from prayer to live a covenantal life by observing the terms of the covenant, the *mitzvot*, in a joyful rather than fearful way. It's both a bitter polemic in the context of Judaism in Israel today and particularly attractive as an expression of faith.

Suzerainty model: God is my Suzerain, the to-be-feared One Who makes innumerable demands to which I'm expected to submit
Franz Rosenzweig is said to have responded to a question about whether, after his return to Judaism, he was going to start putting on *t'fillin*, phylacteries, 'Not yet' – he wasn't ready to take on the entire panoply of traditional observance but acknowledged its authority. One of the first graduates of the Leo Baeck College, Rabbi Michael Leigh, advocated the same position for British Reform. I acknowledge the authority of covenant but not the terms of the suzerainty model; the residual guilt I felt when debating the matter with Rabbi Leigh has long gone, distancing me even further from a model that understands God as my feudal overlord. God is definitely demanding – constantly so. But I won't submit without challenge and debate, not just because of the influence of the post-modern world but out of fidelity to the argumentative tradition in which I've been brought up.[9] No one's beyond challenging and questioning, particularly God.

Parity model: God is my Partner Who needs me just as much as I need God
At first glance that's both irrational and absurd. God is, our liturgical poets declare, Great, Mighty and Awesome and we're nothing. Indeed, for Maimonides God is so Other we can only speak of God by saying what God is not. Yet Eisen writes of the God of Torah: '[The people] can rest confident that God will submit to the seeming indignity of human conversation. He will negotiate, with Abraham, over the destruction of Sodom, and agree, after the pleading of Moses, to pardon the transgressions of Israel.'[10] And he continues:

God, it seems, has no choice. This is the true daring of the covenant idea: God, who inscrutably commands Abraham to bind his son, no less inscrutably binds himself to his own children through cords of immutable obligation. A moral God who seeks a moral world, he has created humanity free to disobey.

That's an understanding of God rooted in Torah, conveyed by the parity model of covenant, which speaks, despite its apparent hubris (or perhaps because of it!), to me: God is the embodiment of the ethical and not only requires but needs human beings to behave ethically for both our S/sakes.

B'rit demonstrates – if it were needed – that complexity isn't the exclusive preserve of the post-modern period; covenant, in all its nuanced richness, is the canvas for my portrait of Judaism and frames the challenge of faith.

The Paradoxical Covenant: Compelled and Free

There's a passage in Tractate Shabbat in the Babylonian Talmud that further speaks with singular intensity and highlights the paradoxical nature of the covenantal relationship. The context is a discussion of the phrase 'be ready for the third day' in Exodus 19.15. The debate then moves on to verse 17: 'They took their places at the foot of [the Hebrew word is *takhat*, literally 'under'] the mountain': 'Rabbi Avdimi bar Hama bar Hasa said: This teaches that the Holy One, blessed be God, turned the mountain upside down over them like an [inverted] cask, and said to them, "If you accept the Torah, all well and good; if not, here will be your grave."'[11] The observation reflects the aggadic tradition that the Children of Israel weren't eager to accept the Torah because they knew how demanding the terms of the covenant were going to be. But what Rabbi Avdimi is saying is startling. The passage in the Talmud goes on:

R Akha ben Ya'akov said: That's a major claim of duress against the [validity of the acceptance of] Torah. Said Rabbah[12]: Nevertheless, they re-accepted it in the days of Ahasuerus, for it is written, [in

the book of Esther], '… and the Jews confirmed and accepted …'
They confirmed what they had already accepted [long before].

Rabbi Akha's immediate, alarmed interjection is of the utmost importance. Avdimi, Akha points out, claims the covenant was agreed only because God was annoyed by Israel's indecision and held Sinai over their heads. God threatened them with acceptance or death and surely, Akha says, if that were true it would invalidate the covenant – an agreement made under duress is void. Rabbah 'solves' the problem by saying that, much later, the covenant was voluntarily re-affirmed in the time of Esther (a thought-provoking source to quote from since it's the only book in the Tanakh that doesn't mention God).

The G'mara continues but Avdimi's observation isn't contradicted: Israel didn't accept the Torah freely and without pressure. Nor is this a 'rogue' text included for the sake of completeness. The Talmud was very carefully constructed: the redactors chose to include Avdimi's observation, have the objection voiced but allow it to stand. I'm by no means the first Jew to feel that God gives me little choice. The covenant isn't an entirely voluntary one; we aren't as autonomous as some modernists might like to think.

Shoah and the Breaking of the Covenant

Coping with the destruction of the Second Temple and enduring exile posed the severest theological – as well as political and behavioural challenge to emergent Rabbinic Judaism. The normative response was to see the trauma as punishment for breaking the terms of the covenant as a suzerainty treaty – 'u'mipnei hata'einu galinu mei-artzeinu': 'because of our sins we were exiled from our land'.[13] The cause of the catastrophe was readily identified as the internal violence and bloodshed, 'sin'at hi'nam', 'groundless hatred',[14] that had preceded it. Like other disasters, it was also seen by some as yissurim shel ahavah: trials of love.[15] But they weren't the only responses; there were, even then, those who challenged God and God's fidelity to the covenant.

Look at this text from the midrashic collection Lamentations Rabbah, commenting on the destruction of the First Temple in 586 BCE but reflecting the destruction of the Second in 70 CE:

> This is like a king who was enraged by his consort and drove her out of the palace. She went and waited behind a pillar. It happened the king was passing, saw her and said, 'You're acting impudently!' She replied, 'My Lord King, so it is seemly, right and proper for me to do, seeing no other woman except me has accepted you.' He retorted, 'It was I who disqualified all other women [from marriage with me] for your sake.' She said to him, 'If that's so, why did you enter such-and-such a side street, such-and-such a court and place; was it not on account of certain women who rejected you?' In similar manner the Holy One, blessed be He, spoke to Israel: 'You are acting impudently.' They replied: 'Lord of the Universe, so it is seemly, right and proper for us to do, seeing no other nation except us accepted Your Torah.' He retorted, 'It was I who disqualified all other nations [from accepting it] for your sake.' They said to Him, 'If that's so, why did You hawk Your Torah round the nations for them to reject?'[16]

Today, many Jews are likewise angry with God; God has again been 'unfaithful'. As in the years following the Second Destruction, so in the hideous shadow cast by the Third, some of us wait behind a pillar, preparing to say just what we think.

What was an exceptional challenge nearly two millennia ago has become more widespread since the Shoah. How can the covenant maintain its meaning after the darkness of our destruction and the inaction of our Lover, Sovereign and Partner?

Irving Greenberg, a courageous American rabbi, born into the New York Orthodox community, responded out of the Jewish tradition of challenge. In a 1982 essay Greenberg reasserted the covenant – but as voluntary. He begins with a scarifying account of the brutality inflicted on children in Auschwitz: 'Thrown directly into the burning pits to economize on gas',[17] while other children watched: 'Could there be a more total despair than that generated by the evil of children witnessing the murder of other children ... being absolutely aware that they face the identical fate

... there is now a Godforsakenness of Jewish children that is the final horror.'[18]

'Does not despair triumph over hope in such a moment?' writes Greenberg. 'Since there can be no covenant without the covenant people, is not the covenant shattered in this event?'[19]

He then quotes Elie Wiesel, spokesperson for the Survivors: 'The Jewish people entered into a covenant with God. We were to protect His Torah, and He in turn assumes responsibility for Israel's presence in the world ... Well, it seems, for the first time in history, this very covenant is broken.'[20]

Greenberg recalls the words of the Yiddish poet Jacob Glatstein:

> We received the Torah at Sinai
> And in Lublin we gave it back
> Dead men don't praise God
> The Torah was given to the living.[21]

By rights, Greenberg concludes, Jews should have rejected the covenant. Yet we haven't – in fact the majority of surviving Jews, theists and atheists, observant and non-observant, have chosen to validate it by continuing to identify as Jews. He asks:

> What then happened to the covenant? I submit that its authority was broken but the Jewish people, released from its obligations, chose voluntarily to take it on again. We are living in the age of the renewal of the covenant. God was no longer in a position to command, but the Jewish people was so in love with the dream of redemption that it volunteered to carry on its mission.[22]

I'm immensely moved by Greenberg and desperately hope his last sentence continues to hold good for sufficient numbers of Jews – however confused and uncertain about the meaning of our identity we are.

Similarly, American Reform Rabbi Eugene Borowitz, in his magnum opus *Renewing the Covenant*,[23] recognized the sociological reality of autonomy, voluntary commitment. But he then stressed that once a Jew chooses to opt into Jewish life, we take on, renew our covenantal obligations – to God, People, History, Hope and the Jewish self.[24]

As after the destruction of the Second Temple, so after the Shoah we've chosen to renew the covenant. But with whom/Whom?

SECTION TWO
MITZVOT: THE TERMS OF THE COVENANT

The concept of *mitzvah* is central both to Jewish theology and battles over authority. *Mitzvah* derives from a Hebrew root *tsadeh-vav-heh* and means a divine command expressed as an obligation or term of the covenant. Thus far all denominations are agreed, but no further.

Ten or Six Hundred and Thirteen?

The word 'commandment' suggests to English speakers the Ten Commandments – for which the Hebrew is *asseret ha-dibrot*, the ten words or statements, and not *asseret ha-mitzvot*. The phrase 'ten statements' is theologically as well as philologically significant: the opening 'I am the Eternal Your God Who brought you out of the land of Egypt' in Exodus 20 is a statement, not a commandment. Indeed, it's *the* statement of where the narrative of Israel begins and of the source on which it draws. So Judaism (unlike Christianity) begins the Ten Statements/Commandments with 'I am the Eternal Your God ...'; it's the first 'commandment' and 'You shall have no other gods but Me' is the second.

Mitzvot – commands, commandments, obligations – also derive from the covenant at Sinai. This passage from the Talmud was to prove unpredictably influential:

> Rabbi Simlai, preaching, said: Six hundred and thirteen *mitzvot* were communicated to Moses, 365 negative *mitzvot*, corresponding to the number of days in the solar year, and 248 positive *mitzvot*, corresponding to the number of bones in the body. Rabbi Hamnuna asked [rhetorically]: What's the proof text for this? It is 'Moses commanded us Torah' [Deut. 33.4]. The numerical value of Torah is 611 [Hebrew letters are also used as numbers] – plus the first two commandments which are not included because we

[the Children of Israel] heard them directly. Then David came and reduced them to eleven [eleven commands are found in Ps. 15] ... Then came Isaiah and reduced them to six [the reference is to Isa. 33.15–16] ... Then came Micah and reduced them to three, 'Do justice, love deeds of kindness and walk humbly with your God.' [Mic. 6.8]. Then Isaiah came again and reduced them to two, as it is said, 'Maintain justice and do what is right' [Isa. 56.1]. Then came Amos and reduced them to one, 'Seek Me and live' [Amos 5.4]. Or, alternatively, then came Habakkuk and reduced them to one, 'The righteous shall live by their faith' [Hab. 2.4].[25]

Rabbi Simlai lived during the second half of the third century – born in Babylon but spending much of his life teaching in Judea and Galilee. It's probable he didn't pluck the number 613 out of thin air, but we can be sure he didn't mean to be taken literally – there were far too many discussions and disagreements for such a precise number and, anyway, that was not his aim. Simlai is a noted aggadist, invariably focused on Jewish theology. The passage begins '*Darash Rabbi Simlai*, Rabbi Simlai aggadised, sermonized, preached': he's seeking to express the essence of Judaism in a single phrase or idea.

Despite the aggadic, homiletic nature of the passage, attempts began quite early to identify the *taryag* (613 in Hebrew letters, vocalized as a word) *mitzvot*. Simlai had already divided the *mitzvot* into 248 'positive' (what we must do) and 365 'negative' (what is forbidden). For some, that served as the organizing principle for their list; others tried to arrange the 613 under ten headings corresponding to each of the *asseret ha'dibrot*, the Ten Statements. It wasn't an easy task: there are more than 613 injunctions in the Torah that could be classified as commandments, obligations, *mitzvot*, and which to select was made difficult – I would say arbitrary – by the Procrustean bed unwittingly set up by Rabbi Simlai's homily.

In the end, Maimonides came up with a list – adopting Simlai's division – found in his book *Sefer HaMitzvot*. It wasn't the same as previous tries and there were subsequent, divergent attempts. But, as usual, Maimonides saw off the opposition and his is the list that people refer to – if they refer to one at all – dominating the entry for commandments in *Encyclopaedia Judaica*.[26] If I sound cynical it's because of the fevered and intensely irritating politicization of the *taryag mitzvot* – not all of which are observable today. Many of the *mitzvot* on the Maimonidean list relate to the Temple, Priests, sacrifices, donations to the Temple, idolatry and the Nazirites – none of which apply today. Number 38 on Maimonides' list, derived from Leviticus 21.13, says: 'The High Priest must marry only a virgin.' Where in today's society can you find a High Priest?

For Haredi Jews and for all Orthodox Jews engaged in the political battle against the 'non-orthodox', *mitzvah* means one of 613 commandments identified by Maimonides towards the end of the twelfth century. On this view, Rabbinic Judaism has made explicit what was implicit in the Torah given to Moses at Sinai – a once-and-for-all-list of 613 binding obligations, whether or not they're observable or applicable today.

But this isn't the only way of understanding the concept of *mitzvah*.

Covenant and *Mitzvot*

Here, Eisen's analysis of the three types of covenant becomes even more helpful: the type of covenant to which one relates determines one's understanding of *mitzvot*.

Suzerainty
Both Haredi and mainstream Orthodox Jews today maintain the suzerainty model of covenant as in Exodus. God has imposed an unprecedented burden of obligations – *ol*, the yoke of the *mitzvot* – on the Jewish people, and the consequences of breaking even one of them are severe. Jews with such an outlook erect higher and higher precautionary fences (called *s'yag latorah*): don't do 'a' lest it leads you to do 'b', and sin inadvertently.

Promissory
Hartman's Modern Orthodox model of covenant is of the promissory kind; we demonstrate our love for the God who loves us when we perform *mitzvot*, loving acts that mirror God's love and reflect gladly acknowledged obligations owed to others. As times pass, added Hartman, the environment changes and we encounter new situations; we respond – to what is a living as well as loving covenant – by paving the road ahead with new rabbinic interpretations of the *mitzvot*.

Parity

Greenberg's 'voluntary covenant' and Borowitz's 'renewed covenant' are powerful descriptions of the Jewish condition today. We choose whether to recognize our identity; we then opt in but the terms of our acceptance of what the past was sure God demanded is different in the present. The parity model best expresses my relationship with the Divine and therefore determines my understanding of its terms. Despite the past, we're bound together, not as equals but as vulnerable partners who, mysteriously, need each other to complete a shared task. *Mitzvot* are those actions that the shared task demands.

And what's that shared task, Rabbi Hutzpah?

As soon as I wrote that last sentence, I realized the full enormity of my presumption. Life contains many joys and I've had more than my fair share and still do. But it's also difficult and painful not just for me but for most. That's what stays with me, disturbs me, hurts me. The Schools of Hillel and Shammai once debated why You bothered creating human beings in the first place;[27] for once they agreed with each other – it would have been better had You not created us at all. I don't think I agree with that but I share their conclusion: since the world is as it is, since we are as we are and You are as You are, We/we both have to get on with it.

Get on with what?

[Long pause] It's an impossibly grandiose answer ... the redemption of humanity and the repair of the world. Isn't that what You need us to do or, if You're honest, to partner You in accomplishing?

Was that a grimace or a glimmer of a smile?

Redemption and repair through the performance of those innumerable *mitzvot* which, immeasurably small in themselves, nevertheless redeem humanity and repair the world.

I understand the *mitzvot* to be small, dutiful acts of goodness that redeem life from meaninglessness and repair our imperilled world. Are they commanded by God? Not in a literal way, as deeds noted down and points chalked up. But do I feel commanded, cajoled or threatened by the shadow of upturned Sinai if I'm neglectful? I do. Are they all derived from Torah? No. As David Hartman taught, the Torah couldn't envisage how the world has developed, and reading the present back into the past is self-deceiving: they're derived both from Torah as commentary and from commentary on Torah. They're not on the Maimonidean list then? Some are, some aren't – any list needs constant attention, provided by learning, debate and discussion. Are they only ethical – *bein adam lahavero*, between persons? Should we discard ritual obligations, *mitzvot bein adam laMakom*, between a person and God? Certainly not – human beings can't live by ethics alone. We need ritual, observance, practice (made gender-neutral) of the kind defined so lucidly and vividly by Rabbi Lionel Blue as the knots we tie in our handkerchief to remind us of our shared task and our difficult, enigmatic Partner Who, mysteriously, still needs us to uphold the covenant and perform *mitzvot*.

Where I've ended this exposition is illustrative of the theological world liberal theists like me inhabit: the sense of being obligated, commanded, is strong in innumerable specific situations. We need constant, informed debate but, contrary to what I once thought, listing those obligations divorced from particular circumstances isn't possible – or desirable. Lists frozen in time frustrate an ongoing, evolving partnership.

Which takes us to the third section of this chapter and current definitions of 'religious'.

SECTION THREE
HALAKHAH

Halakhah and Aggadah

Let's return to the formation of Rabbinic Judaism and enquiry into the meaning of the text of Torah. The Hebrew term translated 'enquiry' is midrash – the Talmud contains innumerable *midrashim* (plural), passages of enquiry. There are also separate collections of *midrashim*, some very extensive. Both in the Talmud and in the collections we can discern two different purposes. The first is to tease out and determine rules of practice – termed halakhic midrash, enquiry designed to produce halakhah, law. The second is to derive meaning, find ethical or spiritual teaching, talk about God – we call this aggadic midrash.

Today, the halakhic tradition dominates the aggadic – it's uppermost in the Jewish consciousness, apparent from the way many of today's Jews tell the Jewish story, summed up in my colleague Rabbi Colin Eimer's phrase 'a tale of pots and pans'. Earlier, I pointed out that Rabbi Simlai was an aggadist who, when referring to 613 *mitzvot*, was deploying a homiletic device to ask what constitutes the essence of Judaism. Yet, by the twelfth century, Simlai's homily had become prescription and Judaism was expressed in 613 *mitzvot*, 613 obligations. I look at classical Rabbinic Literature – Talmud and Midrash – and the aggadic, the theological, leaps out at me, but that's not the reflex of contemporary Orthodoxy and isn't how, in the main, British Jews today characterize Judaism, whatever their denomination.

Berlin-born Rabbi John Rayner grew up within the Liberal community in Britain and was without doubt the most influential thinker of the British Liberal Movement in the post-war period. He was also the most proficient halakhist not brought up and educated within the orthodox world to whom I've ever been exposed. In conversation, he told me several times that halakhic literature was Judaism's most precious resource: the more I've thought about it, the more I differ with my teacher in this one respect.

There's a passage from Abraham Joshua Heschel's book *God in Search of Man*, known to many British Reform Jews from its inclusion in the Study Anthology of the 1977 Reform *Siddur*:

Halakhah represents the strength to shape one's life according to a fixed pattern; it is a form-giving force. Agadah is the expression of man's ceaseless striving, which often defies all limitations. Halakhah is the rationalization and schematization of living; it defines, specifies, sets measure and limit, placing life into an exact system. Agadah deals with man's ineffable relations to God, to other men, and to the world. Halakhah deals with the law, agadah with the meaning of the law. Halakhah deals with subjects that can be expressed literally; agadah introduces us to a realm which lies beyond the range of expression. Halakhah teaches us how to perform common acts; agadah tells us how to participate in the eternal drama.

The interrelationship of halakhah and agadah is the very heart of Judaism. Halakhah without agadah is dead, agadah without halakhah is wild.[28]

What Heschel asserts is the *equal* importance of halakhah and aggadah, of practice and theology – balance. But there's no doubting the power of halakhah, an unparalleled creation arising out of a life-saving and life-enhancing enterprise. It matters very much what use we make of it today – but before we tackle that subject, let's remind ourselves of the vision and courage of the Rabbis and the all-embracing scope of halakhah with three examples from different legal areas.

The radicality of Halakhah: three examples

1. *Criminal law: capital punishment*
The Mishnah, compiled from repetition of oral teachings around the year 200 CE, includes a tractate entitled Sanhedrin.

The Sanhedrin (a Greek word) was the Supreme Court from the second century BCE on. Many will be familiar with the Sanhedrin from Matthew's Gospel, which describes Jesus' trial[29] – where the Head of the Sanhedrin is the High Priest. This will surprise those brought up on Rabbinic tradition, which tells us he was a non-priestly figure given the title Nasi or Prince (abolished as a title at the time of the second-century Hadrianic revolt but, unlike the Sanhedrin, later revived). Tractate Sanhedrin makes it clear that the Sanhedrin had exercised the death penalty: 'The court had power to inflict four kinds of death-penalty: stoning, burning, decapitation and strangulation.'[30] A body of scholarly opinion, following some hints from Tractate Sanhedrin, believes the Romans took away this power in 30 CE; in any event, the Sanhedrin ceased to exist with the fall of the Temple – ending any centralized Jewish legal authority.[31]

In another tractate, Makkot, we find the following: 'A sanhedrin which imposes the death penalty once in seven years is called murderous. Rabbi Eleazar ben Azariah says: Once in seventy years. Rabbi Tarfon and Rabbi Akiva say: If we were on a sanhedrin no-one would ever be put to death.'[32] Since the Sanhedrin had ceased to exist by the year 70 CE and the renowned Rabbis quoted in the passage lived in the second century CE, the discussion is obviously theoretical – though such discussions continued well into the Middle Ages.

What's so revealing – the reason I've chosen this particular aspect of Jewish criminal law – is that the teachers cited, giants of the formative period of halakhah, had serious questions about the Torah text itself. The Torah prescribes the death penalty for a wide range of individuals, not just murderers but adulterous women, men indulging in bestiality and rebellious sons. The Rabbis were self-evidently uncomfortable: capital punishment runs counter to the broader principle of the sanctity of human life; it conflicts with the teaching that God alone gives life and God alone takes life away. Despite their reverence for Torah, they refused to carry over the death penalty from an earlier time into their vision for how society should be.

What becomes apparent is the uniqueness of Rabbinic methodology: reading Torah through the lens of their own interpretation and thereby becoming part of a dynamic process; opposing unquestioning literalism; being driven by overarching values permitting the all-encompassing, portable way of life to develop and go forward. Halakhah enabled the Jew to proceed unshackled to the past, even if the chains of the past had been forged by the Torah itself.

2. Civil law: the Prosbol

The best place to start is with Deuteronomy 15, which deals with the seventh year – in which land must be allowed to lie fallow. Known as the *sh'mitah*, year of release, the text says:

> Every seventh year you shall practise remission of debts ... every creditor shall remit the debt for which he has a claim against his neighbour ... Beware lest you harbour base thoughts in your hearts [and disregard the obligation] ... There will never cease to be needy people in your land which is why I command you: open your hand to the poor and needy kinsfolk in your land.

In a simple agrarian society, not being able to farm would cause hardship for those working the land. The Torah acknowledges this by removing their burden of debt, insisting all outstanding loans be waived. But in the more economically sophisticated Greco-Roman world, those working the land were dependent on credit to see them through. The debt-remitting provision of the Torah, which had earlier enabled the poor to cope, now had the reverse effect. This is recognized in the Mishnah:

> The Sabbatical Year cancels any loan whether it is secured by a bond or not ... [However a loan secured by *Prosbol*] is not cancelled [by the Seventh Year]. This is one of the things that Hillel the Elder ordained. When he saw that people refrained from lending one another money [in the run-up to the Sabbatical Year] and transgressed what is written in the Torah: 'Beware lest you harbour base thoughts in your heart,' Hillel ordained the *Prosbol* ... This is the formula of the *Prosbol*: 'I affirm to you, Messrs X and Y, judges in such-and-such a place, that concerning any debt due to me, I may collect it any time I wish.' The judges sign below . . .[33]

Hillel, that student on the roof of a *bet midrash* in snowy Jerusalem, solved the problem with his *Prosbol* (another Greek word), a legal document that accompanied the loan and transferred it to the courts – because loans within the public domain were not subject to remission. As a result, everyone was a winner – the (wealthier) lender was protected from compulsory remission and the (poorer) borrower got the credit for which he was desperate.

The *Prosbol* is often described as a loophole or legal fiction – but that's to disparage a courageous halakhic development. It's also suggested the motivation was solely economic, required for the development of commercial life. The *Prosbol* was unquestionably beneficial economically but the motivation couldn't be more explicit. The Torah text is concerned with poverty and ameliorating the conditions of the poor. The Mishnah is equally explicit, referring to the Deuteronomic offence of harbouring base thoughts – that is, not lending for fear of remission. People were acting in an unacceptable way by withholding loans and the *Prosbol* removed the reason. Helping the poor, the driving force of the Torah text, is just as important to Hillel (who himself came from the rural poor).

Several leading Rabbis of the Talmudic period expressed worries over Hillel's *Prosbol*, implying that, given his seniority, they had no authority to abolish it – otherwise they would.[34] So troubled were they about the nullification of an express law in the Torah that, for them, it outweighed Hillel's perception that the intention of the Torah was being defeated and required assistance. Thankfully, the *Prosbol* survived, living on in halakhah. Once again, Rabbinic interpretation translated the purpose and meaning of Torah into and for changed times.

3. Law relating to religious observance: Shabbat

Tractate Shabbat in the Babylonian Talmud is a long and technical affair – each mishnah is subjected to detailed scrutiny and only gradually do the rules as to what's permitted and what's forbidden on Shabbat become clear. Tractate Shabbat runs to 157 double-sided pages; yet it's only when we reach page 150a that we find a mishnah beginning: 'A person must not hire labourers on Shabbat, nor instruct his neighbour to hire labourers on his behalf.' The G'mara asks: 'How does he differ from his neighbour?' – in other words, isn't it obvious that if he mustn't engage labourers on Shabbat, his neighbours can't do it for him? It then explores whether the mishnah means that he can't *ask* his neighbours on Shabbat. But the text goes on:

> Now, is speech forbidden? [Of course not] Surely Rabbi Chisda and Rabbi Hamnuna both said: Accounts in connection with religious actions may be calculated on Shabbat; and Rabbi Elazar said that one may arrange charitable grants for the poor on Shabbat. Rabbi Yokhanan said: One may transact business which has to do with saving life or with public health on Shabbat, and one may go to synagogue to discuss public affairs on Shabbat. Rabbi Yokhanan said: One may even go to theatres and circuses on Shabbat for such a purpose [i.e. you can go to a public meeting held in a large auditorium]. In the school of Manasseh it was said that one may talk about the future marriage of one's children on Shabbat, or about the children's education, or about teaching them

a craft, for the Torah forbids 'your business', but 'God's business' is permitted.[35]

In the midst of the technical process of teasing out the details of Shabbat observance – just as much a subject for halakhah as capital punishment or loans – a dazzling observation suddenly appears: what makes Shabbat Shabbat is that we spend six days doing *our* work and the seventh on *God's* work. What is God's work? Arranging for alms for the poor, saving life, public health, public affairs, the future marriage of one's children and their education. All are responsibilities we have towards our fellow human beings; God's work means fulfilling the terms of the parity covenant – dutiful acts that contribute to family, community and society. The halakhah serves the aggadah; the way we walk through life is determined by our theology.

The Decline of Halakhah as the Servant of the Overarching Vision

The *Prosbol*, the abolition of capital punishment, and Shabbat as a day for God's work are constituents of a volcanic eruption. Slowly, inevitably, the flow of molten lava cooled and solidified.

First, the 'way through life' became more and more introverted. Halakhah may have begun by being as concerned about maintaining Jewish distinctiveness as separation, but external hostility exacerbated tendencies towards self-absorption. Resisting hostility, staying alive and intact, became paramount for communal policy and this manifested itself in the halakhah. If we move forward many centuries from the beginnings of Rabbinic Judaism to its decline, the retreat of the Lithuanian Mitnagdim into their ivory study towers and the eruption of populism embodied in early Hasidism reflect rabbinic introversion. The impact of the originating, open context – over increasingly closed centuries – gradually but remorselessly drained away.

Second, halakhah lost its dynamism, its responsiveness, and became ever more rigid. Although there was no formal legislative body, the Mishnaic and Talmudic Rabbis gave themselves power to go beyond interpreting and to legislate. They could issue a '*takkanah*', a remedy or repair in order to revise rulings that no longer satisfied the requirements of the time or tackle a new situation, basing their response on a fresh interpretation of Torah. *Takkanot* are frequent in the Mishnaic period and continue – though in diminishing numbers – as far as the early eleventh century but, from then on, there's scarcely any legislative process to assist Jewish 'common law'.

Third, the sheer weight of the past stifled innovation and restricted room for manoeuvre. This was, at the very least, aided and abetted by the doctrine of *y'ridat hadorot*, diminution of the generations. A text from Tractate Shabbat puts it succinctly: 'Rabbi Zera said in the name of Raba bar Zimuna: if the earlier [scholars] were children of angels, we are children of men; if the earlier [scholars] were children of men, we are donkeys.'[36]

A process of codification began in the second half of the eighth century culminating in Maimonides' extensive and determinative *Mishneh Torah* (Repetition of the Torah). It had the effect of systematizing and clarifying but also increasing the authority of what future generations might wish to challenge.

There comes a point at which humility becomes failure of nerve. This failure was sealed, ironically, by the greatest possible boon to a word-focused tradition, the printing press. The *Shulkhan Arukh* (Table Prepared) is a sixteenth-century codification of Jewish law by Sephardi Rabbi Joseph Caro from Safed. It was printed – and widely circulated – with a balancing Ashkenazi commentary called the *Mappah*, Tablecloth.[37] Tradition insisted that no group could challenge the rulings of a previous group, unless there were precedents for disagreement from that time, and emphasized the diminution of the generations. How then could seventeenth- or eighteenth-century rabbis challenge their predecessors from whom they were separated by the publication of a widely available definitive code, the *Shulkhan Arukh* and *Mappah*?

Halakhah and the Enlightenment

We've already seen that the Enlightenment introduced a further factor to the decline of halakhic dynamism – the sense of threat that caused the volte-face over conversion of minors. To this we must now add communal politics, the bitter struggle over authority.

Several decades ago, I chaired a session for Jewish undergraduates led by John Rayner. He began with texts from the Mishnah and Talmud, unequivocal that the core of the daily service – the *Sh'ma* and the *Amidah* – can be said in the vernacular and, indeed, that it's preferable for those who don't understand Hebrew to recite them in a language they do understand. He took the students through a series of medieval codes to the *Shulkhan Arukh* and then to a nineteenth-century commentary on the *Shulkhan Arukh*:

> One may pray in any language … but as for an ignorant man who does not understand the Holy Tongue, although he could recite the *Tefillah* [*Amidah*] in the Holy Tongue, it is better he should pray in a language he understands, even when praying as an individual, so that he may pray with *kavvanah* [attention, concentration], than he should pray in the Holy Tongue without *kavvanah*. For prayer without *kavvanah* is nothing.[38]

The position could hardly be clearer. Finally, Rabbi Rayner turned to a passage published just before 1900:

> Know that the statement that the reading of the *Sh'ma* and the *Tefillah* [*Amidah*] may be recited in any language certainly applies only if the three paragraphs of the *Sh'ma* and all Eighteen Benedictions are translated perfectly into the other language, for otherwise it is not a recitation of the *Sh'ma* or the *Tefillah*. Consequently this law was operative only in the age of the *Mishnah* and the *G'mara*, when they understood the true nature of our language and were therefore able to translate it. But nowadays it is well known that we have a number of doubts about the exact meaning of some words … And therefore nowadays it is forbidden to recite the *Sh'ma* and the *Tefillah* and all the blessings in any language other than Hebrew. And so the world's greatest scholars have taught these past approximately eighty years; and that is the substance of the law.[39]

What was it that happened 'approximately eighty years' earlier, in 1818? What produced this total halakhic volte-face? asked Rabbi Rayner. The answer – which the students provided immediately – was the establishment of the first Reform Synagogue in Germany, with German translations as part of the service. Rayner concluded with two brief observations. First, in response to the emergency that Reform Judaism was perceived to be, halakhic change was possible after all. Second, even leaving aside the threat posed by Reform, the post-Enlightenment tendency is always towards the more restrictive, the more stringent.

Post-Enlightenment Choices

Given the journey, the role of halakhah, and the contemporary environment, it's not surprising that there are almost as many responses to Jewish practice as there are Jews – maybe more! It's helpful, however, to acknowledge five broad groupings:

1. 'Nothing has changed; it's business as usual.' This is, broadly, the Orthodox response: since the authority of Rabbinic Judaism holds good, so too does the Dual Torah. All contemporary tendencies towards restriction, fence-building, seemingly obsessive-compulsive behaviour, are justified by the need to protect the Jewish people and Judaism from the threats of the post-Enlightenment world.

2. 'We acknowledge human involvement and development in history but wish to retain the halakhic system – its hermeneutics as well its corpus of laws. We will, therefore, continue to develop traditional halakhah but in a way that is self-aware, takes account of the historical and recognizes our responsibilities to Jews today.' This, broadly speaking, is the approach of Modern Orthodox and Masorti Judaism.

3. 'We are no longer addressing theists in the traditional sense and recognize that many Jews no longer respond to the concept of a divine command. Let's retain the traditional system of *mitzvot* as the glue binding our Jewish civilization' [American Reconstructionist Movement] or, argue some in the American Conservative Movement, at least apply sociological and psychological insights enabling us to emphasize those aspects of practice that are most likely to appeal.[40]

4. 'We need to engage in a radical rebuilding of the halakhic edifice, restoring the ethical and spiritual to its determinative position as the *raison d'être* for the portable Judaism of the Rabbis.' Drawing on foundations laid by colleagues in the United States and Israel, no one articulated this more precisely than John Rayner, but it's not apparent any Movement within Judaism has taken the task on.

5. 'Halakhah as a system has been rendered inoperative and of little use by modernity with its emphasis on the supremacy of the individual/individual autonomy. Since many Jews today adopt this position de facto, we'll save what we can that still works but emphasize other areas of Judaism such as identity and community, and social justice.' This is the position of many non-Orthodox denominations worldwide.

None of them fits comfortably with the tenor of this book.

Responsible Autonomy

Twenty-five years ago, I published a monograph, *Sinai, Law and Responsible Autonomy*.[41] The subtitle *Reform Judaism and the Halakhic Tradition* tells you what it was about. We live in an age when the halakhic tradition understood as law doesn't work for many Jews; but the halakhic tradition is as particular, valuable and un-discardable as the aggadic tradition.

The difficulty of hermeneutics

We've seen the extent to which exegesis, interpretation, lay at the heart of the halakhic enterprise. The process was far from being a free-for-all but was governed by hermeneutics, rules of interpretation. The Oral Torah both included and was developed (or made explicit) by those rules of interpretation stamped with divine authority. That may well seem academic but will become clearer when we look at an example.

The methodology was based on the assumption that the Torah was literally from God and therefore every word, repetition, grammatical nuance and juxtaposition had significance. In Exodus

31 there's a description of the construction of the *mishkan*, the desert sanctuary, immediately followed by a passage dealing with Shabbat. The Rabbis deduced from the hermeneutic rule of proximity that the juxtaposition reflects divine intention: work – *m'lakhah* – forbidden on Shabbat should be defined by those acts involved in the building of the *mishkan*. They then identified 39 categories of work undertaken in the construction of the sanctuary and declared these activities to be work that may not be done on Shabbat. Such was the power of hermeneutic logic that, in time, the penetrating insight that 'our work is prohibited' but 'God's work is permitted' became obscured.

The various hermeneutic principles led to the disciplined, restrictive Shabbat observed by the Orthodox community today. Cars are not used, electricity is not switched on and off, and carrying in what is termed the public domain is prohibited – hence the use of those poles and wires to create an *eruv*, extending the private domain of the home (which according to the *Shulkhan Arukh* is the only place where carrying is unconditionally permitted) to a much larger area within which carrying is permitted.

All this has a compelling inner logic as long as the Rabbinic doctrine of the Dual Torah with the hermeneutics stamped by divine authority holds sway. But once this is challenged – as it has been by the Enlightenment – then, *pace* Samson Raphael Hirsch, it becomes vulnerable to penetrating questions. Does it express Shabbat as *oneg*, a delight? Does it meet the understanding of Shabbat expressed in that passage from Tractate Shabbat as a day for doing God's work? Surely, one asks, the issue is one of purpose. If abstaining from driving prevents one from skipping synagogue and going on a self-indulgent shopping spree, it's a valuable restriction. But if it prevents one driving across town on Shabbat afternoon to visit a housebound relative – let alone attending synagogue in the morning – it makes no sense. Hasn't the system undermined the purpose and rendered the wood invisible as well as impenetrable because of the trees?

The problems of authoritarianism and elitism
For many centuries, the Rabbis who developed the system were the outstanding minds of their generation; halakhah, like aggadah,

represents the distilled wisdom of Judaism and, for that reason, should never be discarded. But all the Rabbis were men, wielding power as well as authority. The halakhah they developed is, unarguably, mono-vocal and patriarchal – women were assigned religious roles determined by men. It was also, by definition, elitist; though there was scope for internal disagreement and decision by the majority among the Rabbis, the vast majority of Jews – ordinary men as well as women – were excluded from the process. Today, we reject discrimination against women, recognize that responsibility for the Jewish future rests with the whole of the Jewish people and acknowledge the ethical and practical importance of enabling people to be part of the process by which patterns of behaviour and practice are further developed. Developmental psychology has identified the shift from heteronomy to autonomy as a sign of greater maturity – internalized ethics are preferable to decisions made in deference to an outside authority. I regard a system in which people defer to rabbis, who in turn call upon the authority of Torah as interpreted by them alone, as infantilizing, and submission to such a system as ethically flawed.

The question of law itself

Jewish law developed in and for autonomous Jewish communities and embraced every aspect of life – criminal, civil, family and religious. For most Jews, large areas of that system were rendered redundant by the Enlightenment and the enfranchisement of Jews as citizens. Today, what's left of the halakhic system for the average Jew? Personal and communal observance; ethical behaviour; our spiritual lives, our relationship with God. How well suited is law to such areas? This is not an argument for reform or renewal; it goes to the very nature of religious law in our times. I find immeasurable help, guidance and discipline in halakhic literature as to how I engage with others and God. But it's guidance and personal support I need in actual situations; not broad-brush prescriptions and constraints.

When researching this book, I was much encouraged to discover that Judaism is far from alone in facing this challenge. Psychiatrist and philosopher Professor Bill Fulford resists the growing tendency to tackle matters of medical ethics by retreating into a rule book and ignoring the interplay of ethics with multifaceted, nuanced practice. For him the ethical can only be worked out through a process of engagement in specific situations involving doctors, patients, patients' families and their ethical traditions – he calls the approach 'values-based practice'.[42]

As Fulford argues so cogently in the area of medical ethics and treatment, values will conflict and what is right in any given situation is more subtle and personal than law – however compassionate and flexible – can deal with. More often than not, we have to weigh competing values and teachings and choose the better of two goods or the lesser of two evils. Halakhah isn't constituted in a manner that readily allows for shades of grey or individual choice. Personal observance is also – by definition – very personal. Quite often, I go to synagogue on Shabbat morning and have a pointed conversation with the difficult and demanding Being I take to be God. I come home, make *Kiddush*, have lunch – and then collapse into a chair with the crossword or go to football with my partner, son, daughter-in-law and three claret-and-blue grandchildren. In the last analysis, only I can determine whether that's, for me, part of *oneg Shabbat*, the delight of the Sabbath, or an evasion of God's work in favour of self-indulgence.

You could ask Me.

And I do – as You very well know. But all You do is ask me what I think!

A way forward for post-halakhic Judaism
My starting point is the individual Jew. She or he may think of themselves as 'sovereign selves', autonomous individuals; I recognize that many Jews, like many individuals in the post-modern Western world, see themselves as such. They may well acknowledge responsibilities – to family and society for instance – but also feel their first obligation is to themselves, expressed as 'you only live once'; 'personal fulfilment is paramount'; 'happiness is the most important thing'. I accept that fact as a psychological and sociological reality, but it's one at odds with Jewish theology, which demands we see ourselves as 'journeying selves', thinking, choosing individuals who

live in the context of family, community and society and need to respond Jewishly to our much changed environment. We have rights but also duties, and it's in discovering the appropriate balance that we live authentic Jewish lives.

We stand, as it were, not alone in an otherwise empty square but in a heavily populated conversation at the centre of a triangle. We bring a particular issue, articulate our initial thoughts and acknowledge what might be best for us. We then address each of the three sides of the triangle in turn.

The first side of the triangle is labelled '*Community*'. This is Israel as People. It's constituted by family and community, past, present and future. And also by society – for just as the individual Jew exists in the context of Jewish community, so Jewish community exists not just against the backdrop but within the context of wider society. What does 'community' have to say on this particular issue?

The second side is labelled '*Tradition*' – Torah in its broadest meaning as the entire body of Jewish tradition: halakhic and aggadic, philosophical and kabbalistic, medieval and post-Enlightenment. This side also acknowledges post-modern Western culture with which we engage and in which we live and breathe: new learning, new understandings both enlarging and threatening, supportive and seductive. What do the many voices of 'tradition' bring to the conversation?

The label on the third side is '*God*' – as in the God of Abraham, Isaac and Jacob, Sarah, Rebekah, Rachel and Leah; God as the embodiment of the ethical – compassionate justice. For Jewish theists and humanists alike, it's our sense of the ethical imperative, what our behaviour – current or intended – looks like if we step outside ourselves and expose that behaviour to an unwavering but empathetic gaze. It's also informed by faiths and ethical systems other than our own. 'Be honest: what's the right thing to do?'

This response to halakhah is, I believe, consonant with the theology of this book, acknowledging both Rabbinic and Prophetic tradition and the post-modern world. It recognizes the undiscardable importance of halakhic literature while accepting it can no longer be treated as law binding on all communities and individuals.

The collapse of the authority of the Dual Torah – coupled with contemporary understanding of the individual – has propelled us into a post-halakhic age, regardless of whether we feel liberated or alarmed or both. Autonomy is a sociological, psychological, political and philosophical category; the triangle of responsibility gives it an appropriate, balanced place in theology.

7

Covenant theology: Aggadah, ethics

The Jewish journey has produced two bodies of ethical literature – Rabbinic and Prophetic. They reflect different ages and environments but together offer complementary perspectives from which to question how we live as Jews and human beings today. Rabbinic ethics are commentary on Torah and the place we'll start.

SECTION ONE
RABBINIC ETHICS

Six Characteristics of Classical Rabbinic Ethics

Making any selection from the ocean of Rabbinic Literature will say as much about the selector as the content but I believe these six principles are representative and helpful to contemporary theists and humanists alike. They aren't exclusive to Judaism, only characteristic.

1. God is the embodiment of compassionate justice
The early myths of Genesis – Cain and Abel, Noah – understand God as neither fickle nor arbitrary but consistent in demanding justice: for the Rabbis, that's God's overriding quality. However, their daring anthropomorphizing of God, so out of keeping with theology today but with which I feel increasing empathy, makes for a rich subtlety.

The following parable is typical. Its starting point is Genesis 2.4: 'When Lord God made heaven and earth'. 'Lord' is used to translate the Tetragrammaton; 'God' translates *Elohim*, a frequent synonym. The midrash comments:

This may be compared to a king who had some empty glasses. The king said: 'If I pour hot water into them, they'll burst; if I use cold, they'll snap.' What then did the king do? He mixed hot and cold water and poured it into the glasses, which stayed unbroken. So, said the Holy One, blessed be God: 'If I create the world on the basis of compassion alone, its sins will be great; on the basis of justice alone, the world can't exist. Hence I'll create it on the basis of justice *and* compassion, in the hope it will then be viable!' Hence the expression, Lord God.[1]

Abraham's paradigmatic challenge to God over the fate of the innocent in Sodom and Gomorrah[2] is pressed home by the Rabbis:

Rabbi Levi commented: Shall not the Judge of all the earth act justly? (Gen. 18.25). If You want the world to endure, there can be no absolute justice; if You want absolute justice, the world can't endure. You insist on holding the cord by both ends, wanting both the world and absolute justice. Unless You forgo a little of the latter, the world can't endure.[3]

This same tension lies behind a startling question: what, ask the Rabbis, does God pray? They answer: 'God prays "May My compassion overcome My desire for strict justice."'[4] Though it's not self-evident that the internal wrestling match will always come down on the side of fallible humanity, the compassionate justice principle is a core conviction, the heart of Rabbinic ethics.

2. Each human being is unique, precious and equal
The second characteristic derives from a Mishnaic source, Tractate Sanhedrin,[5] referred to earlier when we explored capital punishment. Although the Sanhedrin had long ceased to exist, knowledge of its modus operandi was preserved; how the Sanhedrin had functioned was part of the Jewish narrative and of concern to the Rabbis. The Tractate moves steadily through the rules governing the Sanhedrin and its operation and, at the point at which our mishnah occurs, has reached capital cases and the admonition of witnesses. The judge must point out this is not like other cases where, if a mistake is made, restitution is possible:

In capital cases the witness is responsible for the blood of the person [who is wrongfully condemned] *and* the blood of their descendants [who would have been born had the person not been executed] to the end of the world. That's what we've learned from Cain who slew his brother, for it's not written blood but: 'The bloods [plural] of your brother' – his blood and the blood of his descendants ... Therefore just one person was created to teach that if any person has caused a single soul to perish, Scripture regards them as though they have caused a whole world to perish; and if any person saves a single soul, Scripture regards them as though they had saved a whole world.

This is remarkable – a sustained passage of theology emerging out of the prosaic historical record. Repeating it underlines the revelation: if someone is responsible for the death of another person, it's as if they've destroyed a whole world – for each human being exists within the context of family and descendants. That world has been wiped out. The story of Cain and Abel reminds us we're all siblings: you, the witness, hold the fate of your sibling – the defendant – in your hands. We are, each of us, worlds inseparable from other worlds. What's at stake is not just the destruction of a world but part of your world. The reverse, remember, is also true: save a life and you save a world, your world.

There could hardly be a more dramatic statement of the value of a human life than that. But the passage from Mishnah Sanhedrin is far from finished:

Again [one person was created] for the sake of peace among humanity, that none should say to their fellow: 'My father was greater than your father' ... Again [just one person was created] to proclaim the greatness of the Holy One; for human beings stamp out many coins with one mould and they're all like one another; but the King above the kings of kings, the Holy One, blessed is God, has stamped every person with the mould of the first Adam, yet not one of them is like their fellow. Therefore everyone must say, 'For my sake was the world created.'

Cain and Abel were the children of Adam – invoked for us to recognize that all human beings are descended from the same parent, so no one can say they're more important or of greater value because their parents were greater or more important than ours. Not only are we infinitely precious, we're all 'equal' – understood in religious, not economic terms. Coins stamped from a particular die are all the same and of equal monetary value; human beings are stamped from the same die yet are all different and infinitely valuable in non-monetary terms. Each of us bears the stamp of Adam, equal in our preciousness, respect-worthiness and responsibility for the other – that's why we're each obliged to say the world was created for us, celebrating our unique individuality and acknowledging our responsibility for a world filled with precious individuals like us.

The Mishnah then resumes the even tenor of its legal way and continues with the procedures of the Sanhedrin. The poetry is bound up with the prose, the aggadah with the halakhah, and each is dependent on the other – such is the nature of Judaism.

3. Imitatio Dei

Steeped in traditional texts, American Rabbi Byron Sherwin began a book on Jewish ethics[6] by citing a passage from the Yerushalmi: 'A human king issues a decree. The king may then choose to obey it or the king may choose to have only others obey it. Not so the Holy One. When God issues a decree, God is the first to obey it.'[7]

Sherwin then offers the intriguing observation that, although Torah forbids making an image of the Divine, God did not obey that commandment when creating human beings – God made an image of God: Genesis 1.26–27 tells us that the human creature alone is created in 'the image and likeness of God'. Sherwin concludes: 'As Rabbi Joshua ben Levi said, "A procession of angels pass before a human being wherever he or she goes, proclaiming: make way for the image of God."'[8] Our unique responsibilities follow.

The relationship between God and the ethics to be derived takes two forms. The first insists these values or characteristics are of the *essence* of God:

> Rabbi Akiva taught that not only have human beings been created in the divine image, but divine grace allows them to become aware of it: 'Beloved are human beings for they were created in the [divine] image. Even more beloved are they, because they can be

aware of having been created in the [divine] image. As it is written, "For in the image of God, God made human beings" (Gen. 9.6).'[9]

The second tells us that the ethics reflect God's *behaviour*. Rabbi Hama son of Hanina asks rhetorically: What is the meaning of 'You shall walk after the Eternal Your God'? (Deut. 13.5) and answers: 'Just as God clothes the naked, attends the sick, comforts the mourners and buries the dead, so you must do likewise.'[10] Just as God performs acts of kindness and decency, so must we.

It's worth reflecting that, whereas the Torah also describes God as acting angrily, jealously, the Rabbis exclude such behaviour from what we ought to copy.

4. Duties give rise to rights – not the other way round

All three forms of covenant emphasize obligation, duty – whether out of love, fear or mutual need. Leviticus 19 is typical, exemplary, listing duty after duty, obligation after obligation, *mitzvah* after *mitzvah*. In verses 9 and 10, for instance, landowners, when harvesting, mustn't reap the corners of the field or pick up the gleanings; when picking grapes in their vineyard, they shouldn't take small bunches or fallen fruit but leave them for the poor and the stranger.

The Torah imposes upon landowners a specific duty giving rise to a correlative right of the needy to glean in the owner's cornfield and gather grapes in their vineyard. The Hebrew word for what's often translated as charity is *ts'dakah*, from the root *tsadeh-dalet-kuf*, righteousness, justice. The root also gives rise to the verb *l'hatsdik*, to vindicate – in the Roman law sense of the word – to claim one's rights. The Torah is unequivocal: Jewish law starts with duties, obligations, *mitzvot*, which give rise to rights, not the other way round. Even a cursory glance at *Human Rights in Jewish Law* by Israel Supreme Court Justice Haim Cohn reveals a list of 26 human rights, all rooted in duties found in the Tanakh – in Torah and in Prophets.[11] The American Communitarian Movement, founded in the early 1990s by German-born Israeli-American Amitai Etzioni, reasserted duty to community in the face of the dominant political emphasis on rights.[12]

While recognizing Judaism's contribution is to emphasize duty, we should also acknowledge the prominent part played by Jewish jurists in the development of international human rights law – such as French Nobel Peace Prize Laureate René Cassin, who drafted the International Declaration of Human Rights in the wake of the Second World War. Which leads to the next characteristic.

5. Balance

There's a passage in Leviticus 25 that deals with the Jubilee Year. The text recognizes people may fall on hard times, lose their land and independence. Every 50 years, the situation was therefore rectified and the individual restored to their original independent status. Some biblical scholars question whether such legislation could ever have been implemented, suggesting it's an affirmation of an idealized past in which the Children of Israel had settled the land with each tribe and clan having their own holding. Whatever the historical status of the Jubilee Year, it illustrates social reality. No system, the Jubilee Year declares, can freeze a utopian equality; all systems create winners and losers – and require regular corrections to ensure extremes are prevented and balance restored.

Balance is an unusually important principle in Jewish ethics – not just with regard to social and economic life – as affirmed by Judah Halevi in a quite different context:

> The divine law does not impose asceticism upon us. Rather it prefers that we keep to the golden mean and give to every mental and physical faculty its appropriate share, without giving too much to one faculty and too little to another. Thus, someone who's inclined to lust decreases their thinking faculty; and on the other hand, someone who is inclined to abstinence decreases some other faculty. Fasting for a long period is no act of piety for someone whose appetites are weak, whose faculties are feeble and whose body is thin; instead they should pamper their body. Nor is decreasing your wealth an act of piety, if you happened to have earned it in a lawful way without trouble, and owning it does not keep you from studying and performing good deeds, especially if you have dependants and children and your desire is to spend money for the sake of God – better that such a person should amass wealth.[13]

This stress on a balanced approach to life is not a position much associated with religion but is characteristic of Rabbinic ethics.

A dictum appears in a number of places in the Talmud: *tafasta m'ruba lo tafasta*: if you try to grasp too much, you won't get hold of anything. It continues: *tafasta mu'at tafasta* – if you grasp a little, you will be able to hold on to it. The thrust of tradition is not so much to articulate a distant aspiration but to counsel against trying to bite off too much at one go; we should never lose sight of the ideal but move towards it in sensible, manageable steps. I suspect this is why a particular observation of the Viennese-born philosopher of science Karl Popper – another of those Jewish refugees from the Nazis who finally settled in Britain – so appeals to me. Popper, defender of the open society and democracy, urges us not to be obsessed with building the perfect school or hospital but to get on with building better schools and better hospitals.[14]

Second-century Rabbi Tarfon famously declared: '*lo alekha ha'm'lakhah lig'mor*', you don't have a duty to finish the work but neither are you exempt from making a start.[15] We're required to begin the journey but not expected to get there; we're obliged to recognize our responsibilities for a wide range of ethical situations in community and the wider world; we know we can't fulfil every need or resolve every situation of conflict but that doesn't mean we're freed from the duty to make a start with some needs, some situations – now. Balance is always required between the vision and the journey, the ideal and the achievable.

6. Free will
First, a midrash:

> 'God looked at every thing God had made and, behold, it was very good' (Gen.1.31).
> Rav Nahman said in the name of Rav Samuel:
> 'Behold, it was *very* good' – that is the inclination to evil.
> Is the inclination to evil good? That's astonishing!
> Were it not for the will to evil, men wouldn't build homes, or take wives, or have children, or engage in business.[16]

The Talmud adds:

> They said: This being an acceptable time, let's pray and ask for the opportunity to confront the inclination to evil.
> They prayed and the inclination to evil was handed over to them.
> The prophet said to them: Be clear, if you destroy this inclination the world will come to an end.
> They imprisoned it for three days.
> Then they searched for a new-laid egg all over the land of Israel. Not one could be found.[17]

It's hardly the stuff of Western philosophy or conventional ethical literature but it's graphic and razor sharp.

We are born, taught the Rabbis, with two drives, but the distinction between y*etzer tov*, inclination to good, and *yetzer ha'ra*, the inclination to evil, shouldn't be understood simplistically. The *yetzer ha'ra* isn't in itself evil but is the drive or passion from which so much creative and competitive action derives: the outcome determines whether it's been used for good or evil. Evil is what happens in the world as a result of misapplications of human drives; misapplications, as often as not, freely chosen.

A second text acknowledges the complexity lying behind those two words 'freely chosen':

> Rabbi Hanina bar Pappa explained: The name of the angel appointed over conception is Night. He takes the seed and lays it before the Holy One, blessed be God, and says: Master of the Universe, what is this seed to be – mighty or weak, wise or foolish, rich or poor? But he doesn't say 'wicked or righteous'. So it is according to Rabbi Hanina. For Rabbi Hanina said: Everything is in the hands of heaven, except the fear of heaven.[18]

A penetrating observation: physique, intellectual ability and economic standing are determined by genetics or sociology. Ethical behaviour is a matter of personal choice.

The criminology course I took in the late 1960s assumed criminal behaviour was either psychologically or sociologically determined. Contemporary Western philosophy has little to say about free will, yet secular philosophy is as vulnerable as Judaism to determinism. The challenge today comes from evolutionary biologists whose television programmes have influenced several generations by stressing the genetically determined nature of both animal and human behaviour. There are some neuroscientists who argue that most apparent choices are illusory, programmed by evolution.[19] If free will is the most important principle of Rabbinic ethics, it's also the principle most severely under challenge; a dispute not *l'shem Shamayim*, for the sake of Heaven, but in which Heaven's very existence is at stake; a dispute in which Jewish voices are engaged on both sides.

Steven Pinker is Professor of Psychology at Harvard, a Jew disparaging about his Reform Jewish upbringing in Canada. In *The Blank Slate*, Pinker argues that the Judeo-Christian view of children – as 'blank slates', just waiting to be inscribed by their upbringing, their nurture – is wrong.[20] Not acknowledging 'human nature' as it really is, argues Pinker, leads to so many of society's ills. He then advances a view of 'human nature' in which our genetic predisposition to gender-specific, selfish, violent behaviour is much more influential than our upbringing. It's hard to understand how classic Jewish texts about the limits to free will – and the influence of nature as well as nurture – have passed Pinker by; I can only conclude that religious fundamentalists have made secular fundamentalists of all too many articulate and original thinkers.

Contrast Pinker with American philosopher Thomas Nagel – a Jewish refugee from Belgrade. A professed atheist, he shows respect for religion, but much of his writing over 35 years has been directed at vindicating free will and moral choice on non-metaphysical grounds. Nagel argues it's extremely unlikely we'd have got from the Big Bang to now and from inert material to sophisticated, sentient human beings by the operation of physics, chemistry and natural selection alone.

Nagel challenges those neuroscientists who reduce all emotion to neural activity in the brain, observable under an fMRI scanner. Like dissenting British neuroscientist Raymond Tallis, he underscores the logical fallacy in saying our feelings of love or pain are identical to what happens in the brain when we experience them: the latter is a consequence of the former but they're not the same. Nagel contends that our mental state, our consciousness, our ability to think and reflect, is real; conscious experience can't be reduced to neural activity and is 'permeated, both in action and in cognition, with intentionality, the capacity of the mind to represent the world and its own aims'.[21]

Nagel doesn't reject Darwin and evolution; on the contrary, he expands evolutionary theory to include the development of consciousness and self-consciousness; to have evolved reflective human beings capable of forming 'true beliefs' about 'the right thing to do'. Our reasoned, ethical evaluations – which resemble 'physical truths, psychological truths, and arithmetical and geometrical truths' – have emerged through the process of evolution. These norms are as real as neural activity in the brain: 'Mathematics, science, *and ethics* are built on such norms [my emphasis]'.[22]

This is a crucial conclusion. It challenges the underlying empiricist assumption of the secular fundamentalists currently spearheaded by Yuval Noah Harari – the assumption or insistence that only that which can be demonstrated by sense perception is real, exists. No, says Nagel, our reasoned ethical truths, which have evolved as we have evolved, are equally well-founded. Jewish values or Humanism are far from being the fantasy or self-delusion of *Homo sapiens*.

Professor Sir Michael Marmot's[23] primary concern is the health of the impoverished. 'My privileged position in society,' he says, 'gives me much more scope for choice – in the ethical as well as economic spheres – than a man of similar age in the Sudan, always assuming he's still alive at my age to make choices; the extent to which you can exercise your personal choice is dependent on your circumstances. We want people to accept personal responsibility but we have to create conditions which enable people to take control of their lives.'[24]

Hence my repeated watchword to myself and you: judge yourself with more justice than compassion; judge others with more compassion than justice.

This is becoming ever more affirmatory of Me, Rabbi Bayfield.

It's affirmatory of the ethics we derive from You but not of You and Your behaviour. Be patient – isn't that supposed to be one of Your attributes?

SECTION TWO
PROPHETIC ETHICS

A Complementary but Related Source

Malachi is the last of the Prophetic books. It ends with what American biblical scholar Andrew E. Hill describes as two seals – verses 22 and 23 – which place the authority of the Torah of Moses and the authority of the Prophetic books side by side.[25]

It occurred to me to ask how often Rabbinic Literature uses Prophetic Literature as proof texts: the answer is relatively infrequently. The Rabbis saw themselves as interpreters of Torah and that served as their primary inheritance. It wasn't until the nineteenth century that Reform Jews, initially in Germany, rediscovered the Prophets as presenting another perspective on society – more resonant for them than the details of the rabbinic code developed for a world out of which they'd gladly moved.

There is, as you'd expect, substantial overlap between Rabbinic and Prophetic ethics – after all, the Prophets were no less heirs to Torah than the Rabbis. But we can pick out, as with Rabbinic ethics, key Prophetic values. Here are five.

1. The Maintenance of Faithfulness – Fidelity
The theme of fidelity, widespread in Prophetic Literature, is central to the book of Hosea. Hosea marries a woman called Gomer who bears him three children, but is unfaithful; he uses his bitter, personal experience as a metaphor for all that's wrong with the Israel of his day. Its behaviour, as with Gomer's behaviour, constitutes adultery; Israel has betrayed God just as Gomer has betrayed Hosea; God, like Hosea, feels aggrieved and rejected.

Hosea prophesied during a century that saw the decline and fall of the Northern Kingdom. Through his extended metaphor, he accused Israel of political adultery and predicted catastrophic downfall.

What's so striking is Hosea's insistence that in acting out of political expediency, Israel has betrayed God's love. He places such personal, sadly haunting words in God's mouth: 'I am the Eternal Your God [Who brought you out] from the land of

Egypt … It was I who knew you in the wilderness, in the land of drought.'[26] The use of 'knew' is telling; it's the same word as in 'Adam knew Eve, his wife' – intercourse as the most intimate form of knowledge. Israel entered into an intimate, loving relationship with God; Israel – like Gomer – has betrayed it. Today, says Hosea: 'There's no truthfulness, no compassion and no knowledge of God in the Land.'[27] How those words contrast with Hosea's poignant description of Israel's wedding in the wilderness, a betrothal in righteousness and justice, kindness and compassion, and faithfulness.[28]

Though Hosea's metaphor of marriage to God is his own, it echoes something familiar – covenant, the promissory model. In its youth, Israel was faithful to that covenant of mutual love; now, Israel has betrayed it. For the sake of short-term expediency, Israel has broken its marriage vow of faithful love and entered into promiscuous, adulterous relationships with other nations and faith-cultures. The underlying perception is characteristic of Prophetic Literature: faithfulness, fidelity, loyalty to the commitments we've made, is a quintessential value.

2. Social and Economic Justice

One of my earliest memories is of sitting in the front room of the house in Ilford that served as my parents' first Reform synagogue. Even before the arrival of Dow Marmur, the community had a rabbi, Oxford University and Jews' College graduate Alan Miller. A small group of us sat on dusty upholstery while he introduced us to the Prophets and their message of social and economic justice. It provided a formative inspiration, enduring to this day.

This passage is from the first prophet to be called Isaiah and dates to the eighth century BCE. It begins with what American biblical studies professor Joseph Blenkinsopp calls a 'series of woes':

Woe to those who add house to house,
Who join one plot of land to another,
Until there is no space left
For any but you to be settled on the land!
God has sworn in my hearing:
many houses will be turned into ruins,

houses splendid and spacious left without occupants;
A vineyard of ten hectares will yield but one barrel of wine,
A homer of seed will produce but one bushel.[29]

As a teenager, I realized 'those' were people who evict smallholders in order to seize sole ownership of the land. Isaiah was denouncing economic policies that led to extremes of landedness and landlessness, wealth and poverty. More nuanced and precise, Professor Blenkinsopp describes Isaiah as exposing the manipulation of the legal system by royal officialdom to sequester property and enclose peasant holdings. He explains:

> From the prophetic perspective legality is not the same as justice, and the legal transfer of property can be tantamount to robbery ... Prophetic protest in the eighth century [BCE] was on behalf of the poor, not the destitute so much as members of peasant households eking out a precarious subsistence on the ancestral plot of land. In a society organized along patrilineal lines the lot of any woman or child deprived of male protection could be hard, and in Israel the situation was not improved by the relative absence of *legal* protection for these charter members of the disadvantaged ... [What took place was] officially and legally sanctioned robbery of the poor.[30]

Social and economic injustice are separate but each reflects an abuse of power and the one leads to the other.

I've retained an ambivalent attitude towards Abraham Joshua Heschel's *The Prophets*. I'm disturbed by Heschel's unquestioning endorsement of the Prophetic view of God as acting in history, but his portrait of the Prophets themselves is unsurpassed. Here he introduces Amos:

> When Amos appeared in the North there was pride (6.13–14), plenty, and splendor in the land, elegance in the cities, and might in the palaces. The rich had their summer and winter palaces adorned with costly ivory (3.15), gorgeous couches with damask pillows (3.12), on which they reclined at their sumptuous feasts ... At the same time there was no justice in the land (3.10), the poor

were afflicted, exploited, even sold into slavery (2.6–8; 5.11), and the judges were corrupt (5.12).[31]

What Amos, a shepherd, saw with irresistible clarity was injustice, in the face of which, Amos insists, a society cannot stand; meticulous performance of prescribed rites and rituals is a useless, hypocritical façade:

> I detest, I loathe your festivals,
> I derive no satisfaction from your solemn gatherings.
> Whatever you sacrifice to Me – your burnt offerings and gifts –
> I cannot accept – your peace offerings and fat cattle –
> I cannot approve
> Take your loud songs away from Me!
> I won't listen to your instrumental music.
> But let justice roll down like a flood of water
> and righteousness like a perennial stream.[32]

Although a memorable last couplet, the translation 'perennial stream' is inadequate; the image is of a wadi, a dry riverbed in the wilderness that has become a torrent when the rains fall. Righteousness is a flood of water bringing life; justice a perpetual torrent in the arid wilderness of social oppression. But even here there's ambiguity: 'If a wadi fills suddenly … it can become a violent, even lethal, torrent.'[33]

Justice – *mishpat* – and righteousness – *ts'dakah* – are frequently used in parallel. Attempts have been made at assigning different meanings – *mishpat* is one of several terms for law, *ts'dakah*, as we've seen, has to do with enabling others to vindicate their rights. But usages aren't consistent and, for me, the telling point is that in the succession of words God, holiness, justice, righteousness, good and truth, the first leads to the last, indicating a sequential identity rather than hierarchy.

The Prophetic analysis is incisive and painful: the ruling classes have detached law from justice, using it to increase their own wealth – principally by acquiring land at the expense of the ruled; the consequence of that abuse of power has been to dispossess, uproot and consign many to the margins. Thanks to the Prophets,

Judaism uninvolved with society and indifferent to abuse of power is inconceivable.

3. The Maintenance of Hope

Prophetic Literature has a reputation for being downbeat – Jeremiah has become synonymous with doom and gloom, perhaps from dictionary definitions of a Jeremiad as a lamentation in grief, a doleful complaint. But this is a distortion. Whether Isaiah and Micah, Amos and Hosea, writing in the eighth century BCE as Israel vacillated in the shadow of an impending Assyrian attack, or Jeremiah and Ezekiel, writing later as the cauldron of Babylon to the north bubbled over – all were filled with fear of the inevitable. Which they then witnessed, fear turning to anger at what they saw as self-inflicted, betrayal. But the special religious quality of the Prophets is that they were never without hope.

Isaiah famously promised rebirth:

> A branch will grow from Jesse's stock,
> a shoot will spring from its roots.
> God's spirit will rest on him,
> a spirit of wisdom and understanding,
> a spirit of counsel and strength,
> a spirit of knowledge and the fear of God.
> He will not judge by appearances,
> he will not decide by hearsay,
> but with righteous judgement he will judge the poor,
> and with equity defend the lowly of the earth . . .
> Justice will be the belt around his waist,
> truth will be the band around his middle.[34]

Many Jews are tentative about these and the verses that follow because of their predictive interpretation by Christianity. But it's a characteristic Prophetic metaphor of hope, of renewal after destruction and of a time when injustice will no longer prevail.

Jeremiah expresses a different kind of hope in the wake of the destruction of the First Temple by the Babylonians and the beginning of exile. His famous letter to the exiles, as we've seen, begins by telling them to make the best of it: 'Build houses and live in them; and plant gardens and eat their fruit'. He ends:

> When Babylon has completed seventy years before Me, I will attend to you and confirm upon you my good word to bring you back to this place. For I, I know the plans that I am planning concerning you – declares God – plans for your welfare, not for evil, to give to you *akharit v'tikvah*, future and hope.[35]

That's not the message of a doom and gloom merchant, emphatically not a Jeremiad. Challenging injustice never compromises the maintenance of hope; rather the former is indispensable to the latter.

4. The Goal of Peace

Micah offers this defining vision of *akharit hayamim*, the End of Days *in this world* – a time when 'the mountain of God's house will be set firm on the top of the mountains and raised up above the hills'. The vision continues:

> All nations shall flow towards it
> and many peoples shall go there, saying:
> 'Come, let us go up to the mountain of the Eternal,
> To the house of the God of Jacob,
> so that God may teach us about God's ways
> and we may walk in the paths of the Eternal,
> for Torah shall come out of Zion,
> and the word of God from Jerusalem.'

God will finally intervene, judging between the 'many nations', the 'great powers'. As a result:

> They will hammer their swords into ploughshares
> and their spears into pruning-hooks.
> Nation will not lift up sword against nation,
> never again shall they train for war.

Which leads to one of the most compelling of all Prophetic metaphors:

Each person will sit under their vine and their fig tree
and no-one will threaten them.
For the mouth of the God of creation has spoken.[36]

Justice, declares Micah, is the necessary precondition for peace. But peace is the final goal – when each person and people have their own place and space that no one threatens. While such peace is beyond human definition, the metaphor enables us to taste the fruit of the vine and fig tree.

5. The Impartiality of God

It's clear from Micah that God is not merely a Jewish talisman. God is the Teacher of all humanity, the Arbitrator for all nations, and the End of Days is one of enduring peace in which every human being will sit undisturbed in their chosen place. However, *our* mountain still tops the others; from there the teaching goes forth. But then there's the book of Jonah.

It takes the form of a brief 'biography' – of Jonah son of Amittai. About the author we know nothing; scholars even struggle to date the writing of the book – probably fifth century BCE or even slightly later. Jonah contains many timeless lessons – not least in its portrayal of a person trying to run away from who they are. But here let's focus on Jonah's relationship with God. The mission is to Nineveh, capital of the Assyrian Empire, symbol *par excellence* of oppression and destruction; Jonah is ordered to the bastion of evil and promptly sets off in the opposite direction. He takes a boat to Tarshish – somewhere remote, where a person can lose their identity. But God persists and summons up a storm, which Jonah recognises as intended for him. Jonah has the sailors throw him out of the boat, is swallowed by a big fish and compelled to go to Nineveh: though the lion has roared,[37] the reluctant prophet is forced to enter the den. Jonah is instructed to demand repentance – which he does perfunctorily, relaying God's message in the anonymity of the suburbs rather than proclaiming it in the limelight of the city centre. When, nevertheless, Nineveh repents Jonah continues to complain to God about the mission, failing to grasp the revelation of his own life and of the book: God is the God of all humanity – as concerned about the brutal, all-conquering Assyrians as God's people Israel.

How little progress so much of religion has made since then.

SECTION THREE
CATASTROPHE AND CRISIS

Three Jews – Emmanuel Levinas, Hans Jonas and Hannah Arendt – experienced the Abyss first-hand, survived and recognized the challenge of the future, the need to respond urgently with a paradigm shift in Jewish ethics.

Emmanuel Levinas

It's arguable that the five Hebrew words that end Leviticus 19.18 are the best known in the Torah. Usually translated 'You shall love your neighbour as yourself [because] I am God', my preference is for 'You shall perform loving acts towards your neighbour who is like you [because] I am God.' In either case, the key is the often omitted 'I am God' as the force behind the ethical imperative. Jewish ethics – Rabbinic and Prophetic – flows from the Jewish understanding of God; the 'because' is the unequivocal response to 'why should I?'

Highly regarded by both Jewish and Christian scholars, Emmanuel Levinas was born in Kovno (Kaunas) in 1905, and steeped in the Lithuanian tradition of rabbinic scholarship. Settling in France, he survived the war in a German Stalag and found a place in the loftiest corridors of Parisian intellectual life. His philosophical and ethical work is dazzling but difficult, not least because it often presumes an understanding of classical Jewish textual references. It's as an ethicist without parallel that he's pivotal to this chapter.

Levinas's ethics are addressed to a gentile audience but celebrate Jewish particularity. He rejects ethics based on the charismatic or numinous ('on a particular day in a particular place I experienced God'), distancing himself from Christianity. As a phenomenologist, he also rejects the ethics of analytic philosophy based on intellectual ideas and constructs. In essence Levinas implies that the Shoah has discredited the ethics of the culture in which it was perpetrated.

He pushes the Hegelian pendulum to the opposite extreme and advances an ethic focused solely on the individual, routed not rooted in Jewish texts.

Levinas takes the concept of the Other (upper case) – as used by Buber in relationship to God – and applies it to the relationship between each of us and all other (lower case) human beings. He cannot be understood without reference to the Hebrew word *hineni*, here I am, particularly as used in the first verse of the story of the binding of Isaac: God addresses Abraham and Abraham responds *hineni*. American Jewish philosopher Hilary Putnam explains:

> When Levinas speaks of saying *me voici!* what he means is virtually unintelligible if one is not aware of the biblical resonance. *The fundamental obligation we have, Levinas is telling us, is the obligation to make ourselves available to the neediness (and especially the suffering) of the other person.* I am commanded to say *hineni!* to the other (and to do so without reservation, just as Abraham's *hineni* to God was without reservation) and this does *not* presuppose that I sympathize with the other ...[38] [Putnam's italics]

Levinas insists that one's responsibility for the other is an 'infinite responsibility', again and again stressing that the relationship is 'asymmetrical'. He takes the Rabbinic principle *kol yisrael areivim zeh bazeh* – every Jew stands surety for every other Jew[39] – and universalizes it: each human being is responsible for the other.

He stresses the theme of asymmetry:

> I always have, myself, one responsibility more than the other, for I am still responsible for his responsibility. And, if he is responsible for my responsibility, I am still responsible for the responsibility that he has for my responsibility: *en ladavar soph*, 'it is never-ending' ... It is an ideal, but an ideal that implies the humanity of mankind ...[40]

As Putnam says, this is a self-punishing, utopian stance – what the American Jewish philosopher Stanley Cavell calls 'moral perfectionism'. It's at odds with the 'balance' characteristic of mainstream Jewish ethical thought. But, for Levinas, the Abyss has changed everything; universal mutual responsibility is, today, the be all and end all.

Where then is God for Levinas? Think of a painting of you, me or Emmanuel Levinas looking up into the face of an/the other; it's a framed painting and that's all it contains: two faces. Ethics is everything. Levinas acknowledges fragments, traces outside the frame, intimations of the Infinite, but the Infinite has no content other than ethics. What's special about Levinas is the importance he places on ethics and the force with which he emphasizes our responsibility for the other. What's original is his refusal to ground his ethics in anything other than the command – no Commander/commander, no 'because' – to say *hineni*, here I am, to be attentive to the other and always respond. That's what it means to be a human being.

Hans Jonas

An early midrash:

> When the Holy One, blessed be God, created the first man, God took him and led him round all the trees of the Garden of Eden. God said to Adam, 'Behold My works, how beautiful and commendable they are! All that I've created, I've created for your sake. Be very careful you don't corrupt and destroy My world; for if you corrupt it there's no one to repair it after you.'[41]

Hans Jonas was a German-born scholar of Gnosticism who fought in Israel's War of Independence, wrote his magnum opus in New York and became Hannah Arendt's most loyal friend and supporter. For me, he's a reminder of my *Kulturschock* at Leo Baeck College, of my family name Mann, and of the German *Liberale* tradition of engagement, defiance and hope with which I've come to identify.

Jonas immigrated to Jerusalem in 1933 and taught at the Hebrew University. Unlike most of his contemporaries, he enlisted and fought with the British army throughout the Second World War. When he returned, he was confronted by what he'd long feared – among the six million Jews who'd been murdered was his own mother. In the following years he came to the stark realization that these events had brought about an irreparable rupture with the ethics of the past; an entirely new ethics was required for the post-modern world.

Technology, observed Jonas, has enabled us to perform acts, shielded by their remoteness, which nonetheless threaten the very existence of humanity. The twentieth century has also exposed the causal connection between our economic activity, often at vast distance from ourselves, and the potential destruction of the entire biosphere. Up to now, such total annihilation was inconceivable, but we've demonstrated conclusively that we're arrogant, selfish and short-sighted enough to bring it on ourselves and the globe – or stand by and allow it to happen. The ethics of Torah that follow from human beings as neighbours, Jonas argued, is no longer sufficient for these mortal challenges. What is therefore required is a new ethics to address the new and critical situation.

In 1979, Hans Jonas published – first in German – *The Imperative of Responsibility*.[42] He starts with the premise of human mortality, unavoidable in due season and intrinsic not just to humanity but to every living thing. He then asks what, in addition to mortality, is characteristic of all forms of life and answers in biological terms. As far back as 1966 he'd written *The Phenomenon of Life: Towards a Philosophical Biology*[43] and identified metabolism, the set of life-sustaining chemical transformations within the cells of living organisms, as key. The reactions that allow organisms to grow and reproduce are shared by all life and what Jonas's 'ethics of responsibility' demands must be respected in every manifestation. We have an absolute responsibility to guard all forms of life, protect them and ensure they're passed on to the future. This isn't a statement of equality between human life and the simplest organism; it's a recognition of what they share and what must be handed on.

The crux of Jonas's argument is both fascinating and characteristic. He asks us to examine our responsibilities towards our children: they have no *right* to be born, he says; you can't construct a right to be born for future generations who've yet to be conceived. What, says Jonas, an ethics of responsibility asserts is our *duty* towards the not yet conceived that extends to seeking to protect them even from remote, environmental sins we've not yet committed. We have an absolute duty to ensure metabolism – cells reproducing and growing, the common feature of all life – continues.

Jonas strove for an ethics that is self-validating. Whether he's successful or whether his thesis is dependent on an underlying metaphysic isn't entirely clear, but it's very much in keeping with my metaphysics. Jonas spells out the consequences of the midrash with which I began: God says, take care of the world because there's no one to put it right after you; global warming is your responsibility.

Hannah Arendt

I hadn't anticipated drawing on Hannah Arendt at this point in the book but such is the pace of change and the difficulty of reading the present that the threat to democracy by a plague of populism has only become widely apparent in the last few years.

Arendt is another pariah within the Jewish community. Born in 1906 in Hanover, she fell under the spell of Martin Heidegger at the University of Marburg, where he was the *Wunderkind* of Western philosophy and she his student. In 1932, he declared himself to be a supporter of National Socialism. The following year Arendt left Germany, only after much wandering finding a place at the New School for Social Research in New York, where her contemporary at Marburg, Hans Jonas, was also teaching.

Hannah Arendt came to public attention in America when she reported on the Eichmann trial, using the term 'banality of evil' to describe the behaviour of the rank and file, the small cogs in the extermination machinery. In her reports from Jerusalem she also made an ill-judged critique of the *Judenraten* – Jewish councils set up by the Nazis to implement their rule in the ghettos. Her past relationship with Heidegger and the furore at her coverage of the Eichmann trial rendered Arendt *persona non grata* and she's remained a pariah ever since.

She was, in fact, a brilliant and original political philosopher who made her name with an immense study of totalitarianism,[44] virtually defining the term herself. Throughout her career she insisted that the Abyss and subsequent post-modern world required new forms of political association to avoid the corruption and abuse of power of the past.

Today, it's clear that totalitarianism hasn't been eradicated and, throughout the post-modern Western world, democracy is in danger – very often from people who achieve power by democratic means and then, protesting their innocence all the while, undertake the process of dismantling the prerequisites of democracy – unfettered opposition parties, a free press and independent judiciary.[45] Democracy is the political context in which Jews and Judaism flourish best – regardless of whether it's a capitalist democracy or a socialist one. Jews are ill-served by those among us who declare democracy is of Athens and therefore has nothing to do with Jerusalem. Churchill's famous statement underlines its universal importance: 'No one pretends that democracy is perfect or all-wise. Indeed, it has been said that democracy is the worst form of Government except all those other forms that have been tried from time to time.'[46]

What do Levinas, Jonas and Arendt tell us? That the post-modern world has placed humanity in a new situation; that we're on the edge of global catastrophe (through rogue use of nuclear weapons and climate change); that our only hope is an ethics widely compelling in itself and universally applicable. Judaism has an absolute duty to contribute to that ethics but cannot determine it alone. Cooperation in all things is the imperative of today.

SECTION FOUR
A POST-MODERN JEWISH ETHICS

The debates, discussions and disagreements are already well and truly under way – though not, in the main, in the synagogue. They're led by individuals with great expertise but not, primarily, in rabbinics. And, because it's necessarily conducted out in the world and reflective of the environment, the discussion is dominated by economics and national politics. That doesn't mean the two traditional sources of Jewish ethics, Rabbinic and Prophetic, are no longer of any use – far from it. Each speaks to the Jewish condition today – to Israel and to the Diaspora, wherever our journey continues. Both are relevant to the societies in and among which Jews live but, as Levinas, Jonas and Arendt all imply, 'the new' is also required.

There are many Jewish voices engaged in debating ethics for the post-modern world. But I'll sketch the main themes from six figures in the fields of Government, Public Ethics, Sociology, Public Health, Sustainable Development and Global Migration, all of whom are forced to grapple in different ways with the contemporary dominance of economic and nationalistic considerations.

Michael Sandel, Professor of Government at Harvard; Peter Singer, Professor of Public Ethics at Princeton and Melbourne

Michael Sandel has become a well-known figure in Britain; his ethics are familiar to his fellow Jews in their practical, case-by-case style applied to contemporary public issues. In *Justice: What's the Right Thing to Do?*[47] Sandel confronts the dominant view of the American moral and political philosopher John Rawls[48] that justice demands putting on a veil of neutrality and assuming a strict secular 'objectivity' – to which those committed to different cultural traditions cannot usefully contribute. Like both the Israeli Avishai Margalit and the great Indian thinker Amartya Sen,[49] Sandel rejects this stifling theory, insisting on a rational, pragmatic approach that must acknowledge and utilize the various traditions of ethical thinking.

In 2012 Sandel went on to write *What Money Can't Buy*,[50] questioning the penetration of economics into every facet of life and the application of the market to all situations. Sandel traces the expansion of the application of the market to the early 1980s, the Reagan–Thatcher revolution and 'their conviction that markets, not Government, held the key to prosperity and freedom'.[51] He's not an opponent of capitalism and free market economics, only of the unfettered operation of the markets, the belief that wealth will automatically trickle down and prevent extremes.

The contrary view was advanced by Harvard philosopher Robert Nozick in his 1974 book *Anarchy, State, and Utopia* in which the ideal is characterized by the inalienable right to economic advancement – government exists with the limited role of protecting that right.[52] Sandel disagrees, arguing that government can't opt out of its responsibility to correct imbalance and obviate the affront of extremes of wealth and poverty.

He also points out: 'The most fateful change that unfolded during the past three decades was not an increase in greed. It was the expansion of markets, and of market values, into spheres of life where they don't belong.'[53] He highlights a large number of situations in which selling rights for money distorts or even destroys the ethical fabric of society, concluding:

> When we decide that certain goods may be bought and sold, we decide, at least implicitly, that it is appropriate to treat them as commodities, as instruments of profit and use. But not all goods are properly valued in this way. The most obvious example is human beings.[54]

For Sandel, what is just is of supreme importance. In an interview he gave to the *Guardian*, Sandel said that Judaism provided him and his children with a 'framework for moral enquiry' and 'points to questions beyond the material'.[55] The value of a person cannot be assessed simply in economic terms; a values-driven approach is required to building a just and compassionate society. Sandel's pragmatic, case-by-case method, teasing out the ethics in complex situations, is fully in tune with the Rabbinic approach: whatever aspects of life, be it the operation of the legal system, the decisions of government necessitated by economics, or the implications of technological advance, we must never surrender the authority of values, or allow the ethical to be pushed aside.

Similarly pragmatic is the Australian philosopher Peter Singer. The son of Viennese Jewish refugees, Singer is drawn to Buddhism rather than Judaism but his pragmatic approach, insistence on the value of each human life and the need for direct action demand our attention. In *Practical Ethics*, he highlights equality, taking life (in all forms), extremes of wealth and poverty, climate change and the environment, and civil disobedience as the central issues for contemporary ethical debate.[56] Those are the key areas that all faiths, humanists and secularists must address cooperatively and with respect.

Zigmunt Bauman, Professor of Sociology

Zigmunt Bauman was born in Poznan in 1925. His family escaped the Nazi invasion by fleeing to the Soviet Union, where he studied sociology and philosophy. Because his father was an unrepentant Zionist, Bauman was purged and returned to Warsaw – where he taught at Warsaw University until 1968, but then lost his Chair during anti-Semitic purges. He tried to make a life in Israel but later accepted a Chair in sociology at Leeds University – almost from the outset publishing in English, his third language.

Bauman has always been a controversial figure, not least because past experiences didn't disabuse him of his socialist, collectivist instincts, which shine through in his critique – far more radical than Sandel's – of unbridled free market economics. But in his later years he still has much to say, his views being prophetic as well as Marxist.

He developed the thesis of 'liquid modernity', arguing that modern Western society has turned a 'society of producers' into a 'society of consumers'. In *Consuming Life*,[57] Bauman takes the argument further, suggesting that consumerism has prompted people, loathing their treatment as faceless commodities, to try to get one step ahead of the herd and reinvent themselves as a more desirable commodity, which the herd will seek to consume. Bauman writes:

> Beneath the dream of fame, another dream, a dream of no longer dissolving and staying dissolved in the grey, faceless and insipid mass of commodities, a dream of turning into a notable, noticed and coveted commodity, a talked-about commodity, a commodity standing out from the mass of commodities, a commodity impossible to overlook, to deride, to be dismissed. In a society of consumers, turning into a desirable and desired commodity is the stuff of which dreams, and fairy tales, are made.[58]

Bauman's very different approach to ethics from Sandel's reflects not only the difference between Europe and America but also the difference between the Prophetic and Rabbinic.

Michael Marmot, Professor of Public Health

Michael Marmot is one of the world's leading experts on the social determinants of health – the consequences of social policy for the health of the individual. Professor Marmot's many publications reveal how social policies impact on health and life expectancy – unconscionable differences of life expectancy in different London boroughs or parts of Glasgow, and between the wealthy enclaves and appalling slums of Indian cities. Differentials in access to education in Africa affect not only life opportunities and livelihood but healthy lives themselves. It's deprivation that shortens the lives of those with learning disabilities, not the medical condition itself. 'Social Injustice is Killing on a Grand Scale' says the cover of a major World Health Organization report.[59] Marmot's compelling arguments are brought together in *The Health Gap: The Challenge of an Unequal World*.[60] Economic policy determines health as well as wealth.

Professor Marmot challenged his fellow Jewish thinker Garry Becker, Nobel Laureate and driving force behind the Chicago School of economists. Here's Marmot, in a book review, writing of an encounter with a Chicago School colleague of Becker's:

'If you want to know how much people value a television set see how much they are willing to pay for it. So it is with human life. See how much people are willing to pay for another year of life and, ergo, you have the value of human life.' Thus spake an economist of the ultra-rationalist Chicago school, at a recent meeting … I wondered about the incommensurability of human life and televisions. Provoked, he said: 'What's the difference between a life and a television set? You can't answer that, can you!' I mulled over this telling point. Of course our students are motivated to go off to Africa to improve the dire situation of suffering televisions. The continued violence to female televisions is unacceptable. We could have Millennium Television Goals. Easier to meet than

MDGs … I was mused to ask: If a poor person were willing to pay less for another year of life than a rich person, does that mean that a poor person's life is worth less than a rich person's. Absolutely, was the answer. Bangladeshi lives all worthless? Pretty much. Well, at least that's clear.[61]

Marmot posed the case of a wealthy American in need of a kidney transplant who bought a kidney for a relatively small amount from a man in a Rio favela, desperate for money to survive. Professor Marmot pointed out that the Brazilian's chances of survival long-term were small and the transaction, even if acceptable in any form, didn't provide enough to buy adequate healthcare in proportion to the increased risk. The response of the Becker school was to apply 'instrumental rationality' and assess the life of a productive American as higher in economic terms than that of a vulnerable Brazilian.

Michael Marmot is a member of a synagogue in north-west London and a personal friend. He's a scientist and humanist; I'm a rabbi – it's becoming clear, with a grudging commitment to metaphysics. Despite that, we've regularly studied together on Shabbat – Jews with a shared commitment to help build the good, decent society of compassionate justice.

Jeffrey Sachs, Professor of Sustainable Development and UN Advisor

One of the world's most articulate advocates of ending poverty now is an American Jew, Jeffrey Sachs. Sachs writes explicitly that, for the first time in history, we have the technology and the global reach to end extreme poverty – defined as lack of basic nutrition, healthcare and education. In *The End of Poverty*,[62] published in 2005, he argued that 2025 was a realizable date. I'm reminded of the midrash that concludes 'Today, if you would only listen to God's voice.'[63] Sachs, a renowned economist and UN special advisor, says not only that it's in our self-interest but also that it's ethically imperative: 'Will we have the good judgement to use our wealth wisely, to heal a divided planet, to end the suffering of those trapped by poverty, and to forge a common bond of humanity, security, and shared purpose across cultures and regions?'[64]

In a later, post-banking crisis book, *The Price of Civilization*,[65] Sachs argues that, despite the economic earthquake and prevailing cynical view of human beings as 'hard-wired' to act out of self-interest, countries like America and Britain still have the ability to play a determinative role in a global economy and society. We are, he says, 'stewards of the future'[66] and that future lies 'in a healthy, productive balance of competition and cooperation in an interconnected society'.[67] What I find so uplifting is that Sachs continues to argue the case in terms of ethics as well as economics and security. Indeed, he pointedly subtitles the book *Reawakening Virtue and Prosperity After the Economic Fall*.

Sachs is not just committed to humanity; he's also concerned about sustainable development and the crisis faced by the planet – the twin issues identified by Hans Jonas.[68] A response to the environmental crisis has been pioneered within the Jewish world both in continental Europe and Britain by two graduates of the Leo Baeck College – Rabbi Awraham Soetendorp from The Hague and Rabbi Jeffrey Newman from London, indefatigably advancing the cause of the Earth Charter.

Building on verses in Torah, Rabbinic Judaism revealed early signs of awareness of the environment. A midrashic source declares: 'When a tree that bears fruit is cut down its moan goes from one end of the world to the other, yet no sound is heard.'[69] Maimonides famously offered the following perspective:

> The quality of urban air compared to the air in the deserts and forests is like thick and turbulent water compared to pure and light water. And this is because in the cities with their tall buildings and narrow roads, the pollution that comes from their residents, their waste, their corpses, and offal from their cattle, and the stench of their adulterated food, make their entire air malodorous, turbulent, reeking and thick, and the winds become accordingly so, although no one is aware of it. And since there is no way out, because we grow up in cities and become used to them, we can at least choose a city with an open horizon.[70]

One can claim that pre-modern Judaism exhibits, if not a green tradition, green shoots: much more importantly, a major shift in perspective is taking place. Tradition focused on the interests of human beings – with the environment demanding our conscientious stewardship. Today, we realize we have to adopt a different perspective, understand the obligation as sharing and not dominating the environment, accept the world does not exist for us alone. Such a view is implicit in Jonas and cogently expressed by Rabbi Dr Charles Middleburgh:

> We should contemplate the Natural World not as disconnected observers but as active participants. We are part of Nature, but unlike the rest of the animal kingdom we alone have the ability to save it, or to do it irreparable damage ... Those who share creation with us should be counted as precious to us as ourselves, for without their presence our own existence would be immeasurably the poorer ... it is high time we knew our place.[71]

We may function in multi-purpose utilitarian synagogues built to a budget, but that budget now has to stretch to buildings that take their sustainability and carbon footprints seriously. As must their members. Not just for our own sakes but for the sake of all life.

David Miliband, President and CEO, International Rescue Committee

The experience of fleeing famine in Canaan only to be enslaved in Egypt imprinted itself on Jewish consciousness. '*Va'ahavtem et ha'ger* – you shall love the stranger, the foreigner, the immigrant, for that's what you were in the land of Egypt' – is a refrain voiced, according to Rabbi Eliezer, 36 times in the Torah.[72] As early as the 1940s, Hannah Arendt reminded Jewry of the need to understand refugees in the light of their own contemporary experience.'[73] Rabbi Hugo Gryn called the twentieth century the century of the refugee but couldn't have imagined the global refugee crisis of the early twenty-first. Whether Jews perceive themselves as part of the establishment in Britain today or identify with those at the margins, the Jewish narrative reinforces the *mitzvah*, obligation to perform loving deeds towards the refugee – adding to the preceding challenges at the core of Jewish ethical responsibility today. The challenge is not just paying lip service to the responsibility but agreeing how to fulfil it and collaborating in effective action.

David Miliband was one of the ablest ministers in the Blair government. His grandparents were Bundists, socialists from Warsaw who migrated to Belgium after the First World War. His father, Ralph, fled Brussels in 1940 and established himself as the leading Marxist theoretician in post-war Britain. Political fratricide forced David Miliband to leave Britain in 2013 to head the International Rescue Committee in New York.

In *Rescue: Refugees and the Political Crisis of Our Time*[74] Miliband reflects on his family's story before setting out the full extent of the global crisis. He details the widespread suffering and death, attributing it to globalization, the collapse of the international order and the subversion of responsibility in the name of populism. He argues that our security and humanity both demand a response – by acting in the place from which refugees are fleeing and in our own countries:

> This is a fight for international cooperation over unilateral grandstanding, for the benefits of pluralism over the tyranny of groupthink, and for the enduring importance of universal values over the slicing and dicing of populations and religions in a fake and faulty clash of civilizations. It is a fight for values, insights, and institutions that imperfectly uphold the best of human nature in the face of impulses and arguments that humor the worst.[75]

The distinction between refugee/asylum seeker and refugee/economic migrant has always been blurred. I'll never know for sure the motives that prompted my great-grandfather Mordechai Mann to leave Eastern Europe. I suspect he was driven by the need to find a place where he could be more fully himself – socially, culturally as well as economically. Isn't that a human right derived directly from the duty to love the stranger?

The Public Square

A familiar term concerning how democracy functions with regard to public policy is the Public Square,[76] the place or places where ethical problems can be debated by informed representatives of all parts of society. The dysfunctionality of the Public Square in Britain is widely and loudly articulated, for which there are numbers of reasons. First, underlying the concept is the assumption that government listens to public discussion of issues of social policy and then responds. Indeed, the great twentieth-century political philosopher Isaiah Berlin – a Jewish refugee from Imperial Russia – saw a principal role of government as recognizing incompatible views and containing them within a functioning liberal democracy.

Today, government leads and orchestrates the response from its own particular ideological position; the Public Square appears to independent voices to be occupied by government, the media and powerful vested interests. Our Digital Age provides democracy with every opportunity to revitalize the Public Square, but its efficacy is dependent on the very powers who dominate the Public Square resisting the temptation to strengthen their hold.

Secularists have been strongly bent on excluding religion by insisting only 'secular reasoning' should be used in debates on social policy. It seems to me extraordinary that reasoning should be qualified by the word secular, but it's clear that what secularists object to is the religious veto – revealed religion dictating that its adherents adopt a particular position which is not open to reasoned debate and discussion. The obverse of the secularist position is equally objectionable: self-styled 'pro-life' groups who ignore the confines of debate and engage in direct action. We're in the midst of a major new development whereby medicine can keep people alive long beyond the traditional four-score years. It can also maintain quality of life for many elderly people – but not all. There's an urgent debate that must be had – crossing the religious and secular divide – about the maintenance of life that has ceased to have meaning. Such a debate needs an unfettered Public Square, with no bars to participation but in which reason prevails; in which declared 'vested interests' can take part but individuals aren't undermined by the cynical abuse of social media.

But where am I in all of this – if at all?

PART FOUR

Jewish Faith Today: God, Suffering and Silence

An Alte Kashe	*An old question*
Fregt di velt an alte kasha	The world asks an old question
Tra-la tra-di-ri-di rom?	Tra-la tra-di-ri-di rom?
Entfert men:	Comes the reply
Tra di ri-di-rei-lom! Oy Oy!	Tra-di ri-di rei-lom! Oy Oy!
Un az men vil, kon men oikh zugen:	And if you wish you may say
Tray dim!	Tray dim!
Blabt dokh vater di alte kashe:	But still the old question remains
Tra-la tra-di-ri-di-rom.	Tra-la tra-di-ri-di-rom.[1]
	(Yiddish Folk Song)

God. Where are you? I wish you would talk to me. God. It isn't just me. There's a general feeling. This is what people are saying ... They want to know where you are. The joke wears thin. You must see that. You never say anything. All right, people expect that, it's understood. But people also think, I didn't realize when he said nothing, he really did mean absolutely nothing at all. You see, I tell you, it's this perpetual absence – yes? – this not being here – it's that – I mean, let's be honest – it's just beginning to get some of us down. You know? Is that unreasonable? There are an awful lot of people in a very bad way. And they need something beside silence. God. Do you understand?[2]

(REV. LIONEL ESPY IN DAVID HARE'S *Racing Demon*)

8

Fragments after the devastation

It's difficult to pinpoint when precisely this book became an attempt to discover whether I could write a systematic account of Jewish theology and whether my belief in God would stand up to my own scrutiny. Faith has been integral to the Jewish journey – but it's not immutable. Whatever drove Abraham to smash his father Terah's idols and leave Haran,[1] it wasn't another artefact to be curated in a museum. Faith changes with the environment, not just for a given group but for each individual. This chapter and the next hold my personal faith up for inspection – the most unnerving experience.

I need to begin by reflecting on my journey – what ideas and experiences have formed my present convictions? This isn't straightforward; my recall of events is frustratingly patchy and I'm adept at blotting out what's too hurtful to remember. I was a precious, vulnerable child and teenager, much bullied; past pain and embarrassment have been buried. The more I try to recall, the less sure I am of its authenticity: how much has it been embellished or diminished by previous attempts at recall and retelling? But I need to try.

That last observation is reinforced by reading the Four Horsemen of the New Atheism. A noticeable aspect of their assault is how little they have to say about the personal experiences that may have brought them to their collective faith in the evils of faith. Such matters aren't 'determinative', but where we've come from and what/who we've been exposed to – the lives we've lived and are living – can't be divorced from how we frame our belief (or non-belief). While probing past experience is vital, our personal responses are often unpredictable. Belief and unbelief are reflections of who we are and, as we journey on, they change.

And Me?

Oh, You never change, You've been nagging and kicking me for as long as I can't remember.

Which brings me to a final introductory observation. It's not only life experience that has an impact on how we see – or don't see – God; the language of the tradition in which we're brought up also plays a part. I once said of a Christian dialogue partner Rev Alan Race and me that we'd been brought up on the same side of the same street – but in different houses. They spoke different languages in our respective houses, and that influenced not just how we think about but how we *experience* God.

SECTION ONE
BEFORE DECIDING

Thinking about God and experiencing God are not the same. As a child and teenager, small of stature, physically timid but bright, I was always more comfortable with the intellectual. It's no coincidence that my teachers during those teenage years, Alan Miller and Dow Marmur, both appealed. Although very different – the former an opera-loving Oxford graduate, the latter a self-educated Shoah survivor – both read voraciously, giving sermons of the highest intellectual quality. Would I have become a rabbi without them? I doubt it.

It's tempting to say God didn't feature at all in my childhood – certainly the word and maybe more. It hadn't always been like that. The film *Fiddler on the Roof*, hardly a masterpiece of historical research, is relatively authentic in its portrayal of Tevye the milkman and his relationship with God.[2] At the end of the nineteenth century, as Tsarist persecution gathered pace, God was alive, well and part of the conversation of ordinary Jews, including milkmen. Leaving Anatevka for America or Britain brought about overwhelming theological as well as geographical dislocation.

For my grandparents growing up in the East End of London, as for many of their generation, God had changed dramatically on the journey from Anatevka to Cannon Street Road, London E1. Take my great-grandfather, Mordechai Mann, for example. Born in the town of Przemysl, in a remote province of the Austro-Hungarian Empire, he moved to a neighbouring village, Hussakov, then emigrated with his wife and two children to London in 1894. Frustratingly, he's out of reach, having died before his granddaughter – my mother – was born; all who knew of him are long gone.

My mother's parents, Perel (Pearl) and Nisan (Nathan) Mann, were faithful Jews – synagogue *makhers* who kept a kosher home and lit candles on Friday night. Curiously, I don't remember Friday nights with them but do recall the brick store behind the Edwardian terraced house in Seven Kings[3] where my grandfather kept his jars of pickled onions, red cabbage and *reitakh*, Polish black radish. He'd acquired both the taste and skills from his parents, who'd brought him to the East End from Hussakov – but I don't remember any God-talk.

Several processes were afoot. My grandparents' Jewish life consisted of their family, *shul*, some traditional ritual and an anthology of values. The easy conversations with God had evaporated – even if the desire expressed by Tevye for a prominent seat in the synagogue hadn't! This disappearance had much to do with exposure to the modern world – the Haskalah had already made inroads in their part of the *Heim*. It also reflected the events of the First World War, its aftermath and the new environment in which Pearl and Nat had been brought up: 'the melancholy, long, withdrawing roar' from 'Dover Beach' could be heard un-muffled in pre-Second World War Whitechapel.

It will also have had to do with the Shoah. Only now, writing that sentence, do I realize that my grandparents never said anything to me about the Shoah, even though they must have had some idea of how many of their family had been murdered. My father knew of the atrocities committed against Amsterdam Jewry but not the extent of the incineration of well over a hundred Dutch Goudekets (his mother's family) until, much later, when I researched our family tree. This widespread, well-documented and familiar silence of the 1950s and 60s extended to silence about God: *Eli, Eli, lama azavtani*[4] – where were You when we needed You?

Alan Miller's introduction to the Prophets in my early teens left a lasting conviction in ethics commanded from outside ourselves. Was God the source of Amos and Isaiah's searing pronouncements? Yes, God was. But I don't remember thinking very much about the metaphysics. On coming down from university, it was embarrassing letting people know my chosen career. My discomfort had little or nothing to do with belief in God and everything to do with the unappealing, 'foreign' image of rabbis and the effete, *über*-English caricature of Christian clergy – I wasn't going to be either!

I began decades of unconscious packing, unpacking and rearranging my backpack for the theological journey ahead. What follows is an acknowledgement of the source of the *ideas* that contribute to my present statement of belief. And, of equal importance, the *experiences* that help balance and explain why those ideas have chosen me. Fragments. They are what I carry in the backpack today. They may not all resonate for you but they will raise questions – of reason and intuition, of thought and feeling, of a metaphysic beyond humanism – that cry out to be confronted.

SECTION TWO
AT LEO BAECK COLLEGE

Ignaz Maybaum: Theology Is Not Only Still Possible but Indispensable

At Leo Baeck College – with its German Jewish refugee teachers and sense of obligation to the Berlin Hochschule – God wasn't top of the agenda. At least, that was my perception. It was 1969. Many students in the years above me had been affected by the June War of 1967: soon-to-become-close friend Colin Eimer had volunteered and spent several months in Israel covering for those who'd been mobilized. By contrast, I remember Rabbi Lionel Blue writing in the Jewish press that a single human life was worth infinitely more than any stone from the Holy Places – and student outrage on his behalf as a tidal wave of public disapproval struck him. God did crop up, but only in that difficult, contentious context, which most people quickly realized was far too raw to grapple with if any semblance of harmony was to be maintained.

In my second year we were packed off to Edgware for theology classes with Ignaz Maybaum, one of 35 German and Czech rabbis who'd been rescued and brought to this country.[5] Maybaum's theology was idiosyncratic, out of tune with the times, but his was the only class where what I wanted most appeared to be on offer. I went to those sessions with questions formed over previous years – most obviously about God's place at Auschwitz; more fundamentally about what Maybaum meant by God; and the ultimate question about God's existence.

Reading Maybaum's latest book *The Face of God after Auschwitz*,[6] I was immediately taken with his account of the binding of Isaac and the return of father and son to the blessings of peaceful family life with their flocks in the fields of Beersheba, and its equation with 'the good life'. For Maybaum, Judaism's founding father Abraham was, above all else, a *mensch*. The book contained many of Maybaum's characteristic themes. He condemned as medieval all Judaisms that hadn't embraced reason and the highest of modern Western values. He praised Leo Baeck, who 'in the hour of the barbarisation of Europe was not prepared to dismiss its Greek heritage which the pharisaic [sic] rabbinate had declared incapable of a synthesis with Judaism'.[7] Maybaum held Christianity responsible for what he called the third Hurban – he saw the Jew as the recurring victim of Golgotha, the place of Jesus' crucifixion – and abhorred mysticism, particularly as expressed by Islam. The book's title struck me as misleading – I couldn't find anything about the face of the God in Whom Maybaum so evidently still believed. It was only much later that I realized something my Bible teacher Ellen Littmann taught applied to both of them. Genesis says of Abraham, '*he'emin b'Adonai*' – he had faith in, trusted God;[8] Maybaum was able to teach theology because of his extraordinary trust.

Dr Maybaum was a major influence on me because he spoke about theological subjects using reason and in language I could sometimes understand. I realized how politically incorrect he was, how distorted were his pictures of Christianity and Islam, but felt he was entitled to hold such views. Above all, he asked theological questions without fear or favour – even though they weren't my questions. With hindsight, how could they have been?

Leo Baeck: Reason and Ethics

Leo Baeck gained *s'mikhah* from the Lehranstalt (later Hochschule) in Berlin, served as a congregational rabbi and, early in his career, wrote *The Essence of Judaism*,[9] an influential book responding to Adolf von Harnack's stripped-back Lutheranism. In 1933, Baeck was elected leader of German Jewry and, though given opportunities to leave, refused to abandon the community. He was taken to Terezin, which, by a quirk of fate (another rabbi, whose surname was 'Beck', was mistakenly sent to Auschwitz), he survived and spent his time teaching – both Greek and Jewish philosophy. He exemplified the German Jewish determination not to be written out of modern Western culture, to demonstrate that it was the Nazis who were betraying the religious and ethical culture of Beethoven and Goethe, not Jewry. After the war he came to London and his magnificent book *This People Israel*,[10] begun on scraps of paper in Terezin, reaffirmed the paradoxical complexity of the Jewish spirit – mystery *and* commandment, poetry *and* law, individual *and* community, desert *and* settled land, particularity *and* universality. There's no wavering in his faith, only affirmation. Evil – even the ultimate evil that Baeck endured and to which he bore such close witness – was a misuse of human freedom.

Baeck reflected the German Jewish respect for reason and the Western philosophical tradition. He also stressed ethical monotheism – one God who demands just behaviour. As early as 1922, in the final version of *The Essence of Judaism*, he added a third component: that of religious consciousness, awareness.

In my early sermons, ethical monotheism became the cliché that we worship God at least as much in our behaviour towards our fellow human beings as through prayer. But I had no feeling whatsoever for the experiential dimension to Baeck's faith. Baeck was part of a tradition of never using 'I' during sermons, yet a member of his synagogue board of trustees recalled his sermons were like listening to 'private conversations with God'. I'd give a great deal to hear one of those conversations.

Harlow: an Indelible Experience

Harlow is not a theologian in the conventional sense! All LBC students were expected to take on a small, rabbi-less community for a year, lead Friday evening and Saturday morning services, and organize the Sunday morning *heder*, school for children. True, Harlow was, geographically, on the road back to Cambridge, but the proximity was deceptive. Harlow was then a New Town, rehousing families from the blitzed slums of East London with a small, displaced Jewish community, some of whom had formed a Reform synagogue and acquired a modest, prefabricated building. My immediate challenge was to hide the graduate arrogance and communicate in plain English; thanks to Linda's love of people and smiling interpersonal skills, I did fine. Until Pesach and my first communal *Seder*.

I remember the shock and terror. One of the synagogue families was hurrying to the *Seder*. Their little boy of three or four wriggled out of his grandmother's hand crossing the road to the *shul*, was hit by a car and taken to hospital. I was told. In fear and trembling, I made the decision, probably wrong – and, if right, for the wrong reasons – to carry on with the *Seder*. I then went to the hospital with no clue about what to do. The father told me his child had died and asked if I'd go with him to see the body, which I did. I can still recall my horror, reluctance – and inadequacy. I also remember a tiny, blond-haired boy lying there.

I must have coped, because the parents didn't complain, nor did the Harlow community ask for me to be replaced. Indeed, the community and I – Linda and I – formed a lasting bond of friendship and affection. But something surprising happened to me. An immediate, unprocessed response proved sustaining, quickly intellectualized but never erased. That beautiful but lifeless body wasn't just a sophisticated machine irreparably broken by a car; what had been there – that which had animated, given individuality, personality – had gone; we come from God and we return to God. I could say no more but I could say that – and mean it. I experienced the same conviction 35 years later when Linda died. It could be wishful thinking, a psychological defence mechanism against the intrusion of reality into the pretences of my career. But ambiguity and uncertainty are of the essence of this book – others may decide.

Martin Buber: the Miraculous Doesn't Fit Reality; the Revelation of 'I and You' Does

Like Freud, Popper and Wittgenstein, Martin Buber was born in Vienna. His father was an Austrian Jew, traditional in practice but integrated into wider society. When Martin was aged seven, his mother walked out on the family. Buber never knew why or saw her again and was brought up largely by his grandparents in Poland, the product of two worlds, both integral to his thought.

My first acquaintance with Martin Buber was as the author of a collection of Hasidic stories.[11] Hasidism began as a populist movement, soon at odds with the Orthodox establishment of the day: it's not surprising that Buber's extensive collection of the stories by which the Hasidic masters connected with ordinary Jews and rekindled Jewish passion should appeal to enthusiastic young Progressive rabbis going out into communities of Jews who were alienated from the Orthodoxy of their day. The material was ripe for creative services and sermons.

Though I was at first enthusiastic, dissatisfaction soon took over; some stories rang true but others appeared simplistic, even trite. I could relate to one entitled 'The Story Teller',[12] in which the Baal Shem – on the advice of a peasant – counselled an opponent to 'slacken the reins on his horses' and they would once more neigh. But I rejected 'The Wheel',[13] in which an old wagon wheel becomes 'a wheel of the Chariot of Heaven' providing warmth on a freezing night for a saintly rabbi, persuading a tax collector to change his ways. Many of the tales embodied a valuable observation but were set in the *shtetlakh* of Eastern Europe, a world so different from mine as to be largely inaccessible. I could even cope with those differences – except when they didn't correspond to any *religious* reality with which I could identify.

Thankfully, there's much more to Buber than his love of Hasidic stories. I read *I and Thou* with considerable interest but only gradually came to appreciate Buber's major contribution to twentieth-century theology.[14]

I was helped by German-born American philosopher Walter Kaufmann's observation that the title *Ich und Du* should be translated *I and You* because *Du* is the pronoun one uses in talking to someone familiar, the archaic 'Thou' giving a false impression of distance.[15] Buber asks us to address God just as we'd address the people closest to us, rather than introducing a distancing solemnity. He invites us to speak directly to God, the antithesis of theorizing or speculating about God – for Buber a fatal mistake. These I–You relationships would only be of short duration but they transform the I–It world. It sounded enticing intellectually, but what it meant experientially had to wait decades.

Lionel Blue: Engaging with God Can Be a Normal, Everyday Experience

Present as an indigenous British voice among all the Berlin and Viennese accents was one of the first graduates of the College, Lionel Blue. Lionel couldn't have been more different from the continental refugees if he'd tried. Despite being from the Jewish East End, he appeared very English – an Oxford graduate. At the time, he was a reluctant congregational rabbi, responsible for one of my favourite coalface remarks. Told by his Synagogue Council that they were setting up a Ritual Committee (to curb Lionel's idiosyncratic way of leading services and preaching), Lionel smiled his Buddha-like smile and 'hoped they'd enjoy their meetings'. He talked about God in an accessible, intimate way that was to make him the voice of Judaism – religion, even – on Radio 4 in the pre-Jonathan Sacks era.[16]

Lionel was very keen on retreats and meditation. While other students couldn't get enough of this, I was wary. It wasn't so much his use of monastic retreat centres as his techniques, bereft of Maybaum-style reason. I remember going with Lionel and other Leo Baeck students to a monastery nestling in the shadow of Rugeley A and B power stations in Staffordshire. Male retreat centres were grubby (but you could sneak into the kitchen late at night and make a raw-onion sandwich). It was at this monastic centre that Lionel introduced me to meditation. I spent a great deal of time sitting with the group in a circle, staring at the flame of a candle and trying to allow my mind to clear itself of the 'rubbish' (Lionel's word) that kept coming into my head. Although extremely suspicious, I astonished myself by finding it a worthwhile experience, yet was left puzzled by the insistence that I needed to vacate the space in my head that opens up in meditation. About this time, I'd learned from another of my teachers, Rabbi Louis Jacobs, about the Hasidic pursuit of *bittul ha-yesh*, abnegation of the self.[17] I acknowledged the aphorism 'there's no room for God in a person who's full of themselves' but couldn't let go of my insistence on the rational and my admittedly hubristic determination to challenge. There's a theme in Jewish thought, rooted in Prophetic texts, that if we go towards God, God will meet us halfway. But I didn't want just to meet God; I wanted to sit God down and conduct an interview Jeremy Paxman or John Humphrys[18] style. I couldn't, didn't.

Michael Goulston: Holy Future

An early role-model, Rabbi Michael Goulston died tragically young, aged 40, just after I received *s'mikhah*. The year before his death, Goulston gave the most compelling sermon I've ever heard.[19] He described the present as a 'holy whirlwind' blowing through all religious attempts to resurrect the pre-Shoah world and identified God as 'pure and holy future' Who 'has become Present and says to us, "Accept Me and live."' He concluded:

> Our *zekhut*, our merit as a people covenanted to the future, the merit of our identity as Jews is now tested by whether we will open the doors of affirmation and let God, as holy future, come in. For the crisis is not in society, that we should respond to it, but in ourselves, the crisis of whether to go forward or opt for stasis. It is a lonely decision. But the 'Age of Gold' exerts its awesome attraction … 'We cannot choose the dreams of unknowing … We are hunters after reality, wherever it may lead.'[20] We will not fail the test, for to be a Jew is to live with God, which means to live the future – to serve the ONE whom we cannot really have in us, or over us or behind us, but always and only before us.

That is our hope and our homecoming, our time, our light and our joy.

Michael Goulston was constantly frustrated by the post-Shoah British Jewish community, Orthodox and Reform – with its 'ersatz piety' (Colin Eimer's pots-and-pans Judaism), and misuse of the Shoah to 'rot livers with guilt'. He raged against a community desperate to crawl 'between dry ribs to keep our metaphysics warm',[21] failing to engage with the God of the post-modern world. I turn and return to that sermon but have come gradually to realize I don't see God as holy future to be uncritically embraced but as the One Who urges us to journey on: *Lekh l'kha* – leave; *Vayisa'u* – go forward into the future.

Goulston was an outstanding, innovative Jewish educator and, after his death, I helped continue his work – religious education became the focus of my non-congregational activities for the next decade.

Being Rather than Having or Doing[22]

Away from the coalface of Jewish life, I did have my moments:

> The cottage was at Alnmouth, which I remember for its wonderful expanse of sand, a beach we had entirely to ourselves and our anoraks. I also remember that holiday for a particular piece of serendipity.
>
> I was not a particularly generous father and insisted as soon as I decently could that Lucy, Daniel and Miriam must have had enough of the kind of things children actually enjoy doing on holiday and, instead, we should go for drives and explore. Much to the children's disgust, one drive took us to yet another old ruin (they insist it was always either old ruins or National Trust houses): Brinkburn Priory beside the River Coquet. From my perspective, it was the perfect spot – the beautiful, austere shell, a flowing river and utter peace. Linda took the children down to the river to have a picnic; I wandered back into the church. Standing there, the prayers that had been prayed in that place became tangible. I was overwhelmed with the conviction that

those prayers were good prayers, true prayers, laid before the same Ultimate Reality addressed by prayers in the synagogue.[23]

Life in the *shul* was too crowded for such an experience.

SECTION THREE
THROUGH DIALOGUE TO THE HEART OF DARKNESS

My first Jewish–Christian dialogue group – established in the 1980s with Reverend Dr Marcus Braybrooke, who was to become the leading Christian figure in interfaith dialogue in Britain and a lifelong dialogue partner – was both pivotal to my theological journey and added in unexpected ways to the backpack. One of the Jewish members of the group was Rabbi Albert Friedlander.

Albert Friedlander: Holding to Account, Tempered Hope and a Suffering God

Albert Friedlander, LBC's first part-time Dean, was a small, round, cuddly man – extremely short-sighted and prone to double if not treble booking. His narrowest of escapes – first on Kristallnacht in Berlin and then on the last boat out of Germany – were formative events in his life and theology. He trained at Hebrew Union College in Cincinnati but came to Britain, where he frustrated successive congregations by maintaining interests other than those of the parish. I loved him deeply and owe him more than I can express.

A survivor, Albert was driven with particular intensity by his own autobiography. It led neither to bitterness nor to despair but to – his words – 'tempered hope'.[24] Central to his life was the pursuit of a theology of reconciliation with the Church in his native Germany. He was unflinching in his condemnation of the German churches – both for their active complicity and for their role as bystanders – determined to hold them to account. He was equally determined that out of recognition of what cannot be forgiven (except, perhaps, by God) should come reconciliation and moving on together. There were only fragments, broken shards to build with; ones he knew to be ambiguous and fragile.

His final book, *Riders Towards the Dawn*,[25] brings together those he'd met who'd found the courage to join him in continuing the journey, riding on. I'm in awe of Friedlander's personal and theological courage but bothered by the limitations of his metaphors. Friedlander wrote of 'horizon' and 'dawn' but horizon is an illusion – ever receding and never reached. Dawn always comes from the same direction but direction is the issue. Friedlander's life made Kafka's 'away from here; away from here' an imperative for every generation to grapple with. But where to? That question became an important fragment enabling me to begin moving on.

I remember the day, occasion and room: a meeting of that first Jewish–Christian dialogue group in 1985. Albert gave a paper to the group on 'The Suffering God in Rabbinic Tradition'. In a collection of *midrashim*, Exodus Rabbah, God is portrayed as participating in the captivity and suffering of Israel in Egypt. One rabbi uses the analogy of twins: 'If one has a pain in their head, the other feels it also.'[26] The twins, astonishingly, are Israel and God. Another rabbi quotes Isaiah: 'In all their troubles, God was troubled.' He goes on: 'God said to Moses: "Don't you realise I live in trouble just as Israel lives in trouble … I am, as it were, partner in their troubles."'[27] Lamentations Rabbah – as we've already seen – uses the destruction of the First Temple to talk about the destruction of the Second. In a particularly moving passage, God weeps both at what God has permitted to happen – at God's own sense of guilt – and also at the suffering of God's people. When an angel tries to intervene, God insists on being allowed to weep alone.[28] The midrash continues:

> In that hour [when God saw the Temple] the Holy One, blessed be God, wept and said: 'Woe is Me for My House. My children, where are you? My priests, where are you? . . .
> 'What shall I do with you? I warned you, but you didn't repent.'

It goes on:

> The Holy One, blessed be God, said to Jeremiah: 'I am now like a person who had an only child and prepared the bridal canopy for

them – but the child died under the bridal canopy! Don't you feel anguish for Me and My children? Go! Call Abraham, Isaac, Jacob and Moses out of their graves – they know how to weep!'

Classical Rabbinic Judaism, I discovered from Rabbi Friedlander, includes the experience of God weeping inconsolably at our suffering, at the suffering we inflict on others and – most remarkably – at suffering caused in some way by God's own actions.

Albert Friedlander's work in Germany was an uncompromising response to the Shoah, revealing a view of the nature of God that Judaism and Christianity share. His defining teaching – that no theology is valid unless it can be written or spoken in the presence of a million murdered children – is a terrifyingly honest challenge to all faiths.

Richard L. Rubenstein: Rejecting God as Omnipotent, Understanding God as Holy Nothingness

Richard Rubenstein was born in New York in 1924, to parents already estranged from Jewish life. They'd been impoverished by the Depression and Rubenstein grew up – as Spinoza three hundred years earlier – a Jew on the margins, an outsider. He first turned to Unitarianism, then enrolled at Hebrew Union College, but soon moved to the Jewish Theological Seminary, attracted by its emphasis on greater observance. His infant son died the day before Yom Kippur in 1950. Rubenstein's personal biography alone would prompt a radical challenge to a just and powerful God, but it's coupled with a particular perspective – looking in on a community just beginning to break its post-Shoah silence.

Categorized as Judaism's only 'Death of God' theologian, Rubenstein was the first major Jewish thinker to argue that the Shoah demanded a far-reaching rethinking of God and a rejection of traditional faith. In *After Auschwitz*,[29] Rubenstein declared that no traditional theodicy could be defended; the idea that God could in any way be held responsible for the Shoah was untenable. He wrote:

Traditional Jewish theology maintains that God is the ultimate, omnipotent actor in the historical drama. It has interpreted every major catastrophe in Jewish history as God's punishment of a sinful Israel. I fail to see how this position can be maintained without regarding Hitler and the SS as instruments of God's will. The agony of European Jewry cannot be likened to the testing of Job ... The idea is simply too obscene for me to accept.[30]

In *Morality & Eros*, published in 1970, Rubenstein redefined God:

[In Western and Oriental mysticism] God is spoken of as the *Holy Nothingness*. When God is thus designated, he is conceived of as the ground and source of all existence. To speak of God as the *Holy Nothingness* is not to suggest that he is a void. On the contrary ... Perhaps the best available metaphor for the conception of God as the Holy Nothingness is that God is the ocean and we are the waves. In some sense each wave has its moment in which it is distinguishable as a somewhat separate entity. Nevertheless, no wave is entirely distinct from the ocean which is its substantial ground.[31]

Rubenstein's dismissal of an interventionist God is fundamental to a theology vindicating both reason and ethics. Once again, the outsider saw what so many declined – and still decline – to acknowledge. But I don't find the idea of the Holy Nothingness attractive. It may be reasonable but it has long been at odds with obstinate experience. I can't let go of this God Who won't let go of me, Who's anything but Nothingness, holy or otherwise.

Eliezer Berkovits: the Turning Away of God's Face

Romanian-born American Orthodox Rabbi Eliezer Berkovits was one of the first to attempt to reconcile the God of Abraham with the obscenity of Auschwitz. He'd studied at a traditional yeshivah, received *s'mikhah* from the Orthodox Hildesheimer rabbinical seminary in Berlin, and served Orthodox communities in Berlin, Leeds, Sydney and Boston. Then, aged 50, he accepted an academic post and set about addressing contemporary theological problems from an orthodox stance. Berkovits reaffirmed free will in the starkest of ways:

> We never seem to realize that while God is long-suffering, the wicked are going about their dark business on earth and the result is ample suffering for the innocent. While God waits for the sinner to turn to him, there is oppression and persecution and violence among men. Yet, there seems to be no alternative. If man is to be, God must be long-suffering with him; he must suffer man. This is the inescapable paradox of divine providence. While God tolerates the sinner, he must abandon the victim; while he shows forbearance with the wicked, he must turn a deaf ear to the anguished cries of the violated … It is the tragic paradox of faith that God's direct concern for the wrongdoer should be directly responsible for so much pain and sorrow on earth.[32]

Though patently honest, that highlights the problem rather than providing an answer. Why would the God of compassionate justice place God's Self in such an unethical position? In the context of the Shoah it fails the Friedlander test for authentic post-Shoah theology. It's true the Holocaust didn't pose – formally – any new theological questions; but the old ones bear down with such an irresistible force they're changed into something new. What kind of God values the experiment of creating human beings with free will to such an extent that the same God can stand by and watch a million children murdered? How can God be good if God can witness children consigned to the flames and say: 'This hurts me as much as it hurts you; I could intervene but I won't.'

Berkovits then draws on a Rabbinic teaching, derived from Job – Hester Panim, God's hiding of the divine face. He argues there were those who found God in the camps through God's Erekh Apayim, God's 'patiently waiting countenance',[33] which, he says, is of necessity identical with God's Hester Panim, the face hidden from others. God, he concludes, was both present and hidden, accessible and inaccessible at the same time. That, it seems to me, fails the test of reason; more importantly, for God to withdraw, make God's Self inaccessible, avert God's face from some of suffering humanity, challenges the very ethicality of God. But no one identified the core issue and confronted it out of Jewish tradition more fearlessly than Berkovits.

Emil Fackenheim: the 614th Commandment; Returning to the Theology of Job

In Leo Baeck College circles the name Emil Fackenheim was frequently invoked. If you want to do theology, read Fackenheim, they said. Born in Halle in Germany in 1916, he studied at the Hochschule in Berlin. After a brief spell in Scotland, Fackenheim went to Canada and taught at the University of Toronto. He later made aliyah and died in Jerusalem in 2000. Yet again, biography tells the story.

My first acquaintance with Fackenheim's thought came through a contribution to a 1960s symposium on 'Jewish Values in the Post-Holocaust Future.'[34] It's an assertion that faith in God *is* still possible after Auschwitz and has been read by some as a direct reply to Rubenstein. Fackenheim also wrote:

> In the present situation, this question becomes: can we confront the Holocaust, and yet not despair? ... We have lived in this contradiction for twenty years without being able to face it. Unless I am mistaken, we are now beginning to face it, however fragmentarily and inconclusively. And from this beginning confrontation there emerges what I will boldly term a 614th commandment: *the authentic Jew of today is forbidden to hand Hitler yet another, posthumous victory.*[35]

Fackenheim was arguably the finest philosopher of Judaism in the second half of the twentieth century. Yet his 614th commandment is what he's most widely remembered for, dominating his legacy. It's been doubly criticized – first, for suggesting that light can come out of darkness, and second, because not granting Hitler a posthumous victory is a wholly/holy inadequate reason for continuing to live as a Jew. Both challenges miss the point. Fackenheim's magnum opus, *To Mend the World*, published in 1982, is subtitled *Foundations of Future Jewish Thought*;[36] it acknowledges the extreme difficulties for those not wedded, like Berkovits, to traditional theology but doesn't retreat into impersonal concepts such as the Holy Nothingness, like Rubenstein. Fackenheim insists the Jewish God and Jewish theology were never more important than after the greatest assault ever perpetrated by humanity. He doesn't offer a glib answer to Rubenstein's question, my question, many people's question – where was God and what was God up to? He adopts Job's stance of silence, accepting what is unknowable.

Which leads me to a pressing conclusion. What we've been looking at over the last pages is widely termed Holocaust theology – often placed by academics on a shelf of its own. But there's no such thing: what's labelled Holocaust theology is Jewish theology confronting the issues that press down on us with unbearable force after the Shoah. Friedlander was right: no theology today – Jewish or any other – is authentic unless it can be voiced against the background of a million murdered children. Shelving Holocaust theology doesn't make other theology any more authentic; it makes it far less.

Theodicy, Job and Linda: The Unfairness of Life

The thirteenth-century philosopher and commentator Nachmanides wrote that evil is 'the most difficult matter which is at the root both of faith and of apostasy, with which scholars of all ages, peoples and tongues have struggled'.[37] He says something of the utmost importance in identifying evil as *the* challenge to faith: we're not dealing with a philosophical conundrum, an exclusively intellectual matter, but with the place where our deepest feelings are engaged. For me, the nub of the problem was holding together what appeared non-negotiable – the reality of evil with a good, just and all-powerful God. I got very tied up in definitions of evil and whether human wickedness – drivers speeding, genocide – was the same thing as natural 'evil' – cancers and tsunamis. Wrestling both intellectually and emotionally has finally made clear I wasn't starting in the right place – which is with all human suffering, regardless of its cause. Suffering is shocking and appalling, indefensible and inexcusable.

In July 2003, my wife Linda died of cancer at the age of 55. Linda and I met when she was 14 and I was 16; for over forty years we were inseparable. She shared 'my' work as a congregational rabbi and our home was the centre of the community; our three children were born into Jewish communal life and grew up in an environment to which Linda made an incalculable contribution. Ours wasn't an unreal, idyllic relationship – there were always differences of priority and need – but we were essential to each other; everything I know about love I learned and experienced in that relationship.

By the summer of 2000, Linda had been increasingly unwell for the best part of two years. A routine ultrasound eventually revealed a large soft tissue sarcoma wrapped round a kidney and her aorta; it was removed in a lengthy operation. But too late. The sarcoma had spread and chemotherapy, rarely effective in such cases, prolonged her life for less than three years.

We both went through the inevitable range of emotions – among them, anger that the diagnosis had come too late for effective treatment. Linda insisted it was worse for her than for me – which, with hindsight, it was. That was a clue to her most frequently vocalized emotion: at the enforced retirement party from her beloved Akiva School (where she was a much loved as well as a much respected head teacher), she said there'd only been three things she wanted from life: to marry, have children and teach. Now she realized there was a fourth: to grow old. She desperately wanted to see her children marry and have grandchildren; she wanted to enjoy the fruits of what she'd worked at so hard and that had been the passion of her life: the nurturing of her family. What for her was so angrily painful was the unfairness of it all; I shared that profound sense of unfairness, still do. Watching her suffering was excruciating but, to the very end – and beyond – her sense of injustice, of being robbed of the opportunity to grow old, became my emotional response as well. I stress emotional because the intellectual was never seriously challenged.

Byron Sherwin's essay on 'Theodicy'[38] is characteristically clear and incisive. He offers no apologia in asserting that whether we're dealing with an individual afflicted by human evil or illness, whether it's people who suffer as a result of a natural catastrophe or a collective, national disaster, the dominant Jewish response has been to see the affliction, the suffering, as punishment for sin. He says divine punishment is 'the most representative and the most prevalent response throughout the history of Jewish theological speculation to the problem of evil and human suffering'.[39] But, applying the Friedlander test, such a response is no longer tenable – either for humanity or God. Neither is the fall-back claim that suffering is *yissurim shel ahavah*, trials imposed out of love. Judaism does, however, have a timeless resource, curiously under-used by the Rabbinic and medieval philosophic traditions – the book of Job.

Job is a wealthy man with a wife, three sons, seven daughters, many possessions – widely respected by his neighbours for his uprightness and integrity. God's pretty smug about him – Job, after all, provides God's model of piety. Enter the figure who in Christian literature becomes Satan but in Jewish literature is simply *Satan*, not the devil but the cunning, relentless, prosecuting counsel. *Satan* says to God: Job may be pious now but just watch what happens when things start to go wrong in his life. Whereupon every imaginable tragedy is inflicted on Job; he loses everyone and everything.

Three friends, Eliphaz, Bildad and Tsophar, come to see him and tell him he's got what he deserved – he must have been sinful, what's happened is God's punishment for wickedness. 'Job's comforters' has become the term for the bereavement counsellors from hell; Job refuses to accept their verdict. He doesn't have an unrealistic view of himself – he knows he's not a saint but he's damned . . .

Nice choice of word, rabbi.

. . . if he's going to accept their verdict. Nothing he'd ever done could possibly merit what had happened to him and his family.

Finally, God confronts Job, points to all the wonders of the world and says: 'Could you have made the world and all the glory of the cosmos? No, well you're not Me, can't do what I can do, so don't expect to understand Me.' Job is silenced by the argument; he never doubts God's existence, doesn't challenge the impenetrability of God's ways, but there the conversation ends. The book closes with Job remaking his fortune and being blessed with a second, even larger family.

Job seemed to me to be a promising tradition leading nowhere. Then New York State University Professor of Philosophy Kenneth Seeskin offered a way forward.[40] He points out that the book of Job wasn't written by one person from start to finish; it's a complex literary composition with components from different times, eventually knitted together, taking its final form in the Bible. Seeskin then compares the Greek translation of Job with the Hebrew original and observes that, in the Greek, Job is milder, humbler, more accepting. In the original Hebrew, Job is tougher on God, more challenging and less easily satisfied. The Job of the Hebrew original accepts God is infinitely greater than he, God's ways are not our ways, the reasons for why life is as it is are inscrutable. But he doesn't, in one vital respect, back down; he doesn't let go of the fact that what's happened to him is grossly unfair.

And God doesn't argue the point any further. Yes, God rebukes Job for speaking about things he doesn't understand, but God doesn't refute or reprove him for protesting his innocence. Job says: 'This can't be a punishment for sin. I'm not a great sinner, I'm innocent of anything that could possibly have warranted this degree of punishment,' and adds, 'I accept my intellectual limits; I accept You're infinitely greater than I am – but I insist on my moral integrity and worth as a human being. I'm innocent.'

God doesn't argue.

God turns the divine face away and withdraws God's presence from Job. God departs to the silent distance of the Eternal's own awesome incomprehensibility. And Job, being respectful, continues to affirm his innocence and integrity but doesn't call after God. As I insist on doing:

Wait a moment, God, don't go away and hide Your face. Let's accept the marvel of Your creation. You still haven't answered Job's question – and mine – as to why he, an innocent man, should suffer such grievous blows. And please don't give us the old bubbe-meisse (grandmother's fable) tacked on to the end of his book about renewed health, wealth and family. This is real life, not redactor's embroidery.

Silence.

Let me put it to You, God, You're not the all-powerful, super-magician You've allowed us to suppose. Isn't

it a fact that even Your power doesn't extend to the impossible or the incredible?

Silence.

Isn't it true, God, that ... the world You created, the real world in space and time, is governed by laws both of certainty and uncertainty, predictability and chance. And Your world, God, couldn't be any different from how it is. It is as it is: terrible things happen to innocent people, which are not directly Your doing and which even You are powerless to stop. Isn't that right, God? Yes or no.

Silence.

Answer me, yes or no.

Still silence.

Or was that a still, small voice reluctantly whispering 'yes'?

Arthur A. Cohen: the *Tremendum* as Abyss; God as the Filament within the Historical

In 1983, I moved on from Weybridge to take charge of the development of a new Jewish religious educational and cultural centre in Finchley, but felt the sting of the charge that I'd left the rabbinate for administration. The idea of writing flickered. I discovered Arthur A. Cohen, a New York-born Jewish intellectual, writer and publisher, and his book *The Tremendum*.[41] Cohen had established his reputation with *The Natural and the Supernatural Jew*,[42] published in 1962 when he was in his mid-thirties. It's a direct, uncompromising critique of mid-century American Jewish theology – of both the religious left and right. He argued that much of American Jewish thought was obsessed with Jewish peoplehood and survival, evading the central post-modern, post-Shoah questions about God. A prime target was Mordecai Kaplan, author of both the book and the project *Judaism as a Civilization*,[43] the reconstruction of Judaism in 'natural', non-metaphysical terms.

For Arthur A. Cohen, the role of the Jew is not to preserve a culture like other cultures and reduce God to a form of words – be it Rubenstein's sea on which we're waves or Kaplan's power in the cosmos that gives human life direction – but to pursue a supernatural vocation. 'Supernatural' has been rendered theologically useless by the secularization of language – ghosts and Ouija boards are not at all what Cohen means by the word; Cohen sees the Jewish vocation in metaphysical terms. He said more clearly than most of his contemporaries that God's relationship to the Shoah had to be addressed because it's the root cause of so much unbelief; God's role with regard to the Death Camps is an aspect of God's contentious role in history as a whole.

In 1981 Cohen followed the logic of his own philosophy and faith with *The Tremendum: A Theological Interpretation of the Holocaust,*[44] alluding to the *mysterium tremendum,* the dimension of terror invoked by the Divine.

Cohen urges us to see God 'less as the interferer'[45] and offers this theological breakthrough:

> God is neither a function nor a cause of the historical nor wholly other and indifferent to the historical. I understand divine life to be rather a filament within the historical, but never the filament that we can identify and ignite according to our requirements, for in this and all other respects God remains God. As filament, the divine element of the historical is a precarious conductor always intimately linked to the historical … and always separate from it, since the historical is the domain of human freedom. [It means] that man – not God – renders the filament of the divine incandescent or burns it out.[46]

The Tremendum remains where it has long been – near the top of my backpack. The metaphor of God as a filament – shedding light, not intervening, present but vulnerable to human behaviour – is decisive. Cohen affirms the 'supernatural', the metaphysical and doesn't reduce God to Holy Nothingness. God is present, accessible, available, yet not the Director of History Who uses rulers and nations as instruments of His will. God, says Cohen, did not decline to intervene in the Shoah; God is not that kind of God.

Amen. Ehyeh asher Ehyeh, I am Who I am.[47]

Tel Aviv's Rubbish Dump: Today's Thorn-bush?

From the beginning of my post-congregation career, I flew to Israel annually on working trips. In 2009, I went to another World Union Conference. One afternoon the programme offered a number of visits ranging from Progressive synagogues to social action projects and I nobly joined the least well-subscribed. They told me they'd received a grant towards the Conference from the Tel Aviv municipality and, in return, had agreed to send a group to visit the city's rubbish dump. Since Tel Aviv's rubbish dump had not proved a widespread attraction, it was suggested I'd be most welcome on that coach trip and, being a generous and supportive person, I agreed to go.

The Hiriya landfill site had developed into a 200-foot mountain of rubbish, which spread smell, pollution and disease to the poorer – Mizrahi, Middle Eastern – suburbs of Tel Aviv. From this had come a plan to create a 'green lung' for Israel's coastal towns. The rubbish mountain had been earthed over and seeded; work on creating an ecology park, vast by the scale of Israel – it would both benefit local people and show Israel at its best – was already well under way. We stood on top of the heap-become-green-mountain and surveyed the 2,000-acre site extending to the distant suburbs of Tel Aviv, now largely rid of smell, pollution and rubbish-generated disease.

The head of the project pointed to the far corner of the park. One could just make out, in the distance, some ruins that he identified as those of an Arab village called Hiriya, from which the inhabitants had fled in 1948. I was shaken by instant, painful, conflicted feelings. He then added that the Arab village itself had been built on the ruins of an ancient Jewish site – B'nei Brak – where, according to the *Haggadah*, five leading Rabbis of Roman-occupied Judea in the early second century CE were so struck by the relevance of the journey from slavery to freedom that they stayed up all night discussing their own situation under Hadrianic rule and persecution. The greatest of the five, Rabbi Akiva, supported the third and final revolt against Roman rule, was tortured to death, and *galut* – exile – began. Completely oblivious of others, I sat looking out into the distance, in conversation with myself . . .

Why is today's journey so difficult and fraught with ethical challenges? Why is Israel always at the centre of world attention?

Where does the future of the Jewish people lie? What kind of nation should Israel be? What purpose does Diaspora have? Why do I always have to live on the horns of a dilemma, with paradox? At that point, I remembered a midrash in which a Rabbi is asked why God chose to speak to Moses out of a thorn-bush. The question appears to take Rabbinic insistence on the significance of every word in the Torah beyond the boundaries of absurdity – but back came the response: 'To teach that there's no place where God isn't present, not even a thorn-bush.'[48]

Even a rubbish heap?

The poet Elizabeth Barrett Browning wrote in *Aurora Leigh*:

> Earth's crammed with heaven,
> And every common bush afire with God:
> But only he who sees, takes off his shoes;
> The rest sit round it, and pluck blackberries . . .[49]

The reference is to Moses' thorn-bush – and, Who knows, to Tel Aviv's rubbish heap. Did I take off my shoes for a moment? Am I able, despite the never-ending scream of the Shoah, the cacophony of conflicting opinions inside and outside Eretz Yisrael, the impossible conflict of triumph and tragedy, to affirm God in the agonies and commonplaces of the Jewish world? Was that a religious experience on Tel Aviv's tip?

Did I encounter God? It did provoke a whole range of interesting intellectual responses and ideas.

If that's how it works for you, Tony, don't knock it.

SECTION FOUR
THE GERMAN TRADITION

In the course of drafting this book, I, at long last, grasped my connection to the German *Liberale* tradition. Ironically, it was clarified through a large tome by a French Jewish intellectual, Pierre Bouretz, the title of which – *Witnesses for the Future: Philosophy and Messianism*[50] – speaks for itself. Bouretz assesses nine figures, almost all of whom appear somewhere in this book. He begins with Hermann Cohen, a fascinating, even contradictory person. The son of a cantor, he intended to study for the rabbinate and went to the Jewish Theological Seminary in Breslau, where he flourished but was drawn to philosophy – becoming the first Jew permitted to teach the subject in Germany as a full professor (at Marburg in 1876). He taught Kant, then developed his own philosophical system, adopting Kant's approach but radicalizing the logic of pure reason. Cohen was revered as the most important Jewish philosopher since Moses Mendelssohn and the outstanding German philosopher of his time.

In 1912, seemingly at the end of his career, Cohen moved to Berlin and started teaching at the Hochschule. Based on his lectures there, he wrote *Religion of Reason: Out of the Sources of Judaism*,[51] published in 1919. It's considered such an inaccessible book that the modern English-language edition requires two introductory essays. It's problematic in its identification of Jewish suffering as necessary to salvation, a theology made – if it ever was tenable – untenable by the Shoah.

What makes Cohen so important? He was the first Jew permitted to teach philosophy in a German university – less than 150 years ago (modern Western culture has a long tradition of exclusion). Changing career at 70, Cohen acknowledged that Judaism and faith cannot be encompassed by the intellectual – by reason – alone. By moving to the Hochschule, he indicated the possibilities presented by two worlds engaging: Judaism and Western Culture could both develop through critical dialogue.

Cohen stressed that religious authenticity is only achieved when the relationship between God and humanity determines that the relationship binding human to human is fully ethical. What characterized the Literary Prophets, Cohen argued, is their vision of human history, a future in opposition to the present actuality in which power and amorality predominate. Others look back to a Golden Age for their people; Jewish messianism looks forward to a future for all humanity. Through his life and thought, Hermann Cohen laid the foundation stone for the *Liberale* tradition.

We now move forward – far further than mere years would suggest – to the edge of the Abyss and beyond.

Ludwig Wittgenstein encapsulates the triumph and tragedy of Viennese Jewry, distant yet familiar. He came from an affluent family that had embraced Christianity out of expediency but embodied to a painful extent Jewish neurosis. American philosopher Hilary Putnam stresses Wittgenstein's lack of Jewish intellectual background but compares him to Rosenzweig – who, he writes, Wittgenstein most resembled![52]

In his twenties, in the trenches, Wittgenstein kept a diary that makes clear he's far from being an opponent of religion – understood by him as a way of living life meaningfully.[53] That, says Putnam, lies at the heart of his challenging philosophy, rigorous in its quest for clarity: not clarity as an end in itself but as the necessary medium for seeking meaning. I'm surprised how many ignore the fact that Wittgenstein called the only book he published during his lifetime *Tractatus Logico-Philosophicus*. The title, of course, echoes the *Tractatus Theologico-Politicus* of Spinoza.

Wittgenstein played down his Jewish identity at Cambridge – until the outbreak of war, when he became raucously a Jew.[54] In 1941, already in his fifties, he volunteered for manual work as a hospital porter. Of faith he would say: '*Ich glaube manchmal*', I believe sometimes. He died of cancer in 1951 and was given a Catholic burial – but those responsible subsequently doubted whether they'd done the right thing!

Wittgenstein's is a run-of-the-mill story of a conflicted Jewish intellectual in modern Western society and culture. It's also the story of a champagne Jew, of his contribution and the price paid.

Walter Benjamin was born in Berlin in 1892, described best as literary critic followed by essayist and philosopher. One of his most important essays was devoted to a novel by Goethe but he was equally interested in the French Jewish writer Marcel Proust. His areas of expertise are language, translation and aesthetics, representative of German scholarship and thought in the first half of the twentieth century. But he was also a Jew, unwilling to join the assimilationist tide, and his Jewish consciousness is as present when discussing Goethe as when discussing Proust. He's an exemplar of what Michael Löwy called 'elective affinity'[55] – choosing to engage with wider culture, expecting both parties to that dialogue to be changed and enriched. He is, for me, a most important representative of *Liberale Judentum*, committed to Jewish identity as faith, as metaphysic, a mystery existing beyond the world of literary theory and philosophy of language.

In the 1930s Benjamin became heavily influenced by Marxism, associated with the early days of the Frankfurt School of Marxist Jewish intellectuals (which included such influential Jewish thinkers as the psychoanalyst and social philosopher Erich Fromm), but was determined to go beyond materialism to a more humanist political philosophy. The rise of National Socialism forced him to leave Germany; he moved around Europe, coming to an uneasy rest in Paris, agonizingly aware of the gathering storm. Bouretz explains Benjamin's attitude to history and catastrophe by using a haunting image he found in Benjamin's correspondence:

> An angel with its face turned toward the past, looking wide-eyed, with open mouth and wings spread – uncovering a heap of ruins where we thought we saw a chain of events. Benjamin had acquired one of the multiple variants of this *Angelus Novus*, conceived by Paul Klee, in Munich, on or before 1921, in the form of a little watercolour, which he would always keep. It gives birth to the following allegory. 'The angel would like to stay, awaken the dead, and make whole what had been smashed. But a storm is blowing from Paradise and has got caught in his wings; it is so strong that the angel can no longer close them. The storm drives him irresistibly into the future, to which his back is turned, while the pile of debris before him grows toward the sky. What we call progress is *this* storm.'[56]

It's a harrowing intimation of the unimaginable and inexorable. But, says Bouretz, don't think of it as 'a melancholic concession to Nietzsche's nihilism' but as 'enjoining the thinker to tirelessly assume hopes and hardships, past and future'.[57]

In 1940, Benjamin fled before the advancing Nazis to the Spanish border; a day earlier and he'd have escaped but the regulations had changed and he was turned back. On 26 September 1940, at Portbou, he committed suicide. This final act was, it's widely believed, neither one of cowardice nor despair but recognition that he'd done all he could to keep alive the Jewish metaphysic that had become so closely aligned with German culture. The Jewish future – and there was to be one – was already in the hands of others in other places.

The Leo Baeck College saw itself as heir to the German *Liberale* tradition. I fought that inheritance and responsibility with every fibre of my Anglo-Saxon intellectual upbringing – and, thank God, lost.

Elie Wiesel: Faith Murdered; Ambiguity, Anger and Accusation Remain

I've repacked my backpack, yet again. I think I can now make out the road immediately in front, despite the gloom – but I need to take one final influence with me.

Elie Wiesel was present in the Death Camps and became spokesperson *par excellence* for all survivors. He wrote no formal theology but expressed his experience in a brief but incomparable testimony, *Night*,[58] through a series of mystical and allusive novels; and through a lifetime of work dedicated to trying to make 'never again' a reality for all humanity – it was for that work he was awarded the Nobel Peace Prize in 1986. Like Berkovits, Wiesel was born in Transylvania. Aged just 16, he found himself in Auschwitz, walking towards the flames in which he expected to die, reciting the *Kaddish*:

> For the first time, I felt revolt rise up in me. Why should I bless His name? The Eternal, Lord of the Universe, the All-Powerful and Terrible, was silent. What had I to thank Him for? . . .
>
> Never shall I forget that night, the first night in camp, which has turned my life into one long night, seven times cursed and seven times sealed. Never shall I forget that smoke. Never shall I forget the little faces of the children, whose bodies I saw turned into wreaths of smoke beneath a silent blue sky.
>
> Never shall I forget those flames which consumed my faith forever.
>
> Never shall I forget the nocturnal silence which deprived me, for all eternity, of the desire to live. Never shall I forget those moments which murdered my God and my soul and turned my

dreams to dust. Never shall I forget these things, even if I am condemned to live as long as God Himself. Never.[59]

God is no longer the Conductor of History, the 'Great, Mighty and Awesome' of the liturgy. God isn't All-Powerful, doesn't rescue and save — that God has been murdered and the dreams that went with Him have been turned to dust. And yet ... .

Auschwitz renders the issue of human evil and a silent, non-intervening God inescapable: 'Never shall I forget these things, even if I am condemned to live as long as God Himself. Never.' Honest anger and necessary ambiguity are essential to a resumption of the dialogue.

Honest, Tony? What about that 'painful' childhood you acknowledge but about which you've remained tight-lipped? If you're really honest, isn't that your problem, not Me?

I think I did choose the rabbinate over the law to prove the bullies wrong — more impressive, more reassuring to be a big fish in a small pond. That's still relevant to my personality but no longer, I think, my theology. I'm a product of my past — but You're not.

Then, Rabbi Professor Bayfield, do we resume our dialogue? If I'm not what you say I'm not, Who am I? Are you — with all your characteristic humility — finally going to tell Me?

Yes [uttered quietly and apprehensively]. I'm going to try.

9

My God, my God – what kind of God are you?

SECTION ONE
A CHALLENGING TRADITION

Challenging God

Judaism has a long tradition of protest – protests directed at God. During the early stages of writing this book, I mentioned the *marmite passages* (conversations with God) to a much-respected, senior colleague. He was horrified – at my temerity, my arrogance. Yet arguing with God, challenging God, is quintessentially Jewish.

It begins in Genesis with a debate between Abraham and God over the fate of the inhabitants of Sodom and Gomorrah.[1] Punishing the righteous – even ten – along with the wicked would be wrong, he tells God. In his overriding concern for divine justice, Abraham establishes not only form but content: how can the God of compassionate justice allow the innocent to suffer?

Prophetic Literature takes up the challenge, with Jeremiah saying defiantly: 'You will be vindicated, God, if I make an accusation against You, yet I shall present charges against You nevertheless: Why does the way of the wicked prosper? Why are the faithless at ease?'[2] The prophet Habakkuk begins more directly still: 'How long, God, shall I cry out and you not listen? I shout "violence" but You don't save!'

A number of Psalms, notably Psalm 22, are filled with pain and questioning:

> My God, my God, why have You forsaken me?
> dismissing my plea,
> the roar of my words?
> My God, I call out by day,
> but You don't answer.

Then, of course, there's Job. He begins with a general statement:

> Calamity is surely for the iniquitous;
> Misfortune, for the workers of mischief.

Then moves to the personal:

> Surely God observes my ways,
> Takes account of my every step.
> Have I walked with worthless men,
> Or my feet hurried to deceit?

He reiterates his own innocence:

> Let God weigh me on the scale of righteousness;
> Let God ascertain my integrity.
> If my feet have strayed from their course,
> My heart followed after my eyes,
> And a stain sullied my hands,
> May I sow, but another reap,
> May the growth of my field be uprooted.

But concludes with resignation:

> Would that I had someone to give me a hearing; Would that God
> Almighty reply to my writ.[3]

In *Arguing with God: A Jewish Tradition*[4] American Rabbi Anson Laytner makes two cogent points. First, the tradition is invariably expressed as a legal challenge, with the Jew as complainant and

God as both prosecutor and judge. Second, the stress is always on questioning the suffering of the innocent. The Talmud refers to such protest as *hutzpah k'lapei shemaya*, bare-faced defiance of God.[5]

Each example of protest in Torah is taken up by Rabbinic Literature and reframed. Laytner points to the echoes of slavery in Egypt for Jews under Roman rule. 'When Moses protests against God's inactivity (or ineffectuality) early in his mission,' Laytner writes, 'the Rabbis found a ready hook on which to hang their own generation's complaints':[6]

> Moses exchanged words with God: I have taken the Book of Genesis and read in it the doings of [previous generations] and how they were punished ... But what has this people done that they are more abjectly enslaved than all earlier generations?[7]

Laytner continues with a debate between Rabbis Ishmael and Akiva over the meaning of the words: 'And still You have not delivered Your people' (Exod. 5.23). 'Ishmael insists the words be interpreted literally, that is, that God in truth had not saved and would not save his people.'[8] Akiva is less resigned, more daring. According to Akiva, Moses insisted: 'I know that You will save them in the future, but what do You care about those entombed under the buildings [now]?'[9]

The most extended and painful challenges are to be found in Lamentations Rabbah[10] — we've already looked at the passage in which Israel, in the guise of the rejected consort, accuses the king of betrayal by permitting the destruction of the Temple and the agonies of expulsion. Laytner concludes: 'Israel demands nothing less than total vindication by God before all the Nations for the suffering she has endured since the destruction of the Temple.'[11] Confronted by suffering out of all proportion to sinful behaviour, Israel challenges God. As in Torah, so in Rabbinic Literature the theme is not marginal but central, definitive; not for nothing does the name Israel mean one who struggles with God.

The tradition resurfaces in seventeenth-century Eastern Europe in the face of the massacres by Bogdan Khmelnitsky's Cossacks:

> Dear people, let us weep and wail
> Over the dread events occurring in our days ...

With scythes the evil ones ran about, cutting us down like sheaves;
Rather had we been taken prisoner by the Tartars.
They chased and killed everyone alike,
Many were drowned in the deep river;
Those who swam out were slain without mercy;
No one was spared, young or old, poor or rich . . .
Dear God, why do you withhold your mercy? Witness our
helplessness![12]

The author is unknown but the words are those of all faithful Jews from
that horrifying time who couldn't understand why so many innocent
women and men had been slaughtered – and they challenged God.

Hasidic rebbe Levi Yitzhak of Berditchev is famed for his *Din
Toyre mit Got*, his lawsuit against God. It's also known as his *Kaddish*,
since he wove it into the declaration made in the face of death:

I, Levi Yitzhak, son of Sarah of Berditchev, say,
'From my stand I will not waver,
And from my place I shall not move
Until there be an end to all this.
Yisgadal v'yiskadash shmei raboh –
Magnified and sanctified is your Name.'[13]

The culturally rich yet persistently suffering world of Eastern
European Jewry gave rise to folk music, which included theological
protest songs:

Eyli Eyli	**My God my God**
Eyli Eyli lomo azavtoni	My God, my God why have you forsaken me?
In fayer un flam hot men undz gebrent	In fire and flames they burned us
Iberal hot men undz gemakht	Everywhere they shamed and
Tsu shand un shpot	mocked us
Dokh optsuvendn hot undz keyner gekent	But no one could turn us away
Fun dir mayn Got,	From You my God
Un fun dayn heliker toyre	Nor from your holy Torah
Fun dayn gebot	From Your commandment

Eyli Eyli lomo azavtoni	My God, my God why have you forsaken me?
Eyli Eyli lomo azavtoni	My God, my God why have you forsaken me?[14]

At the beginning of the twentieth century, Russian-born Alter Brody took the tradition of challenge and protest with him to New York and expressed it with anguished precision in a poem, 'The Holy Ledger':

The Jew
Like a mad accountant
Trying to make sense out of a senseless ledger
Balancing the Holy Scriptures of his life
With double entry bookkeeping.
With good and with evil.
With reward and with punishment.
Juggling the accounts
To make debit and credit meet.
To cover up
The latest overdraft on his agony.
But sometimes
In a moment of revulsion
In a moment of insidious sanity
He flings down his pen,
Calling God Himself to account.
For the terrible, impossible, inexcusable
Entries in his book.[15]

Hebrew poet Hayyim Nahman Bialik straddles two worlds – those of Eastern Europe and the Yishuv. Following the Kishinev pogrom of 1903, he wrote two poems 'On the Slaughter' and 'City of the Killing'. In the second and longer poem, Bialik cries out against both the horror of the pogrom and the attitude of the victims, putting the following revealing words in God's mouth:

And see, O see: while they fester in their pain
all succumb to weeping, raise a dirge with their wails

and already they're drumming on their breasts and telling of
their guilt
saying: 'We're guilty, we're traitors' – and their hearts don't
believe their mouths.
Can a shattered vessel sin and shards of clay be accused?
And why do they plead with me? – Speak to them and they'll
thunder!
They'll raise a fist against me and protest their insult
the insult to all the generations from the first to the last.[16]

Professor of Liturgy Jacob Petuchowski argued that the protest
literature of Eastern Europe had been blunted by passive submission
to the recurring catastrophes of Jewish life. Bialik's poems, he wrote,
are 'a call to rebellion against the exile mentality and against God
Himself'.[17]

The tradition of Eastern European protest is still evident – in
the United States it was taken up by the grandson of a Hasidic
rebbe, composer Leonard Bernstein, in his Third Symphony, *Kaddish*.
Adopting the model of Levi Yitzhak's *Din Toyre mit Got* set in the
Kaddish prayer, Bernstein agonized over words to express his own
struggle with faith, revising the text again and again, recalling the
'alte kashe' – 'old question' – of the past in the fog of the present.[18]

Challenging Belief

The destruction of that past world and our immersion in a new
environment has led to an even more far-reaching rebellion – against
belief itself. Who is this God, Rabbi, whose voice you claim – like
Joan of Arc – to hear? You're delusional. What is it that you're trying
to sell us like a mountebank which makes no material difference to
your life or anyone else's? Where's the proof? Where's the cash value?
You're a fraud.

I've a fantasy in which my mobile phone goes off just before the
sermon on Yom Kippur morning and I conduct my own conversation
with God, allowing the congregation to eavesdrop. It's the product
of anxiety tethered to an ironic sense of humour, the point at which
irrepressible hope and personal theology collide. Why am I so sure

God won't phone and allow me to vindicate my faith in front of all those who'd welcome assurance and those who cry fraud? Because such a demonstration is inconsistent with Who God Is. If I could welcome God to the synagogue even long-distance, hold God up in a test-tube or encompass God's mind in a formula; if God were the author of a book dispatched long ago across time and space – such a god wouldn't be God.

There's a revealing conversation between Moses and God near the beginning of Exodus.[19] Moses has been instructed to go back to Egypt, confront Pharaoh and liberate his people. He's reluctant – who wouldn't be – and searches around for something to make the task do-able. 'Tell me Your name,' he says, desperate to be able to say to the Israelites, 'I know Who God is. I can control Him, conjure Him up by uttering His name and then you'll all believe in Him – and in me.' But what does God reply? '*Ehyeh*[20] *asher Ehyeh* – I am Who I am', 'I will be Who I will be.' That's Who I am, that's Who God is. God can't be conjured up like a genie in a bottle or called on a mobile. God can't be possessed, controlled, owned. God can't be proved because to prove God is to diminish to human categories, subordinate to a Stephen Hawking Theory of Everything, define out of divinity.

SECTION TWO
WHAT CAN WE SAY ABOUT GOD?

Both reason and experience coerce me down a road I now tread with a measure of relief and hope – whatever angels may fear.

God Is Not Omnipotent

Abraham Joshua Heschel, the Polish-born American theologian, completed his magnum opus at the very end of his life. *Heavenly Torah: As Refracted through the Generations*[21] is a voluminous work, begun in the late 1950s, published posthumously in Hebrew. The *Heavenly Torah* of the title is *Torah min ha-Shamayim*; *As Refracted through the Generations* acknowledges that Rabbinic interpretation is key. Heschel's great lesson is the extent to which classical Rabbinic thought follows one of two interpretive schools: those of Rabbi Ishmael and of his contemporary, Rabbi Akiva.

Both men lived in the first half of the second century. Writing this, I'm conscious of Ignaz Maybaum's insistence on connecting the Shoah to the destruction of the Second Temple by using the term 'Hurban', destruction, for both. Less than 75 years after the liberation of Auschwitz, the trauma of the survivors and their descendants is all too self-evident; the destruction of the Second Temple had the same shattering effect on the survivors of that calamity, one of whom was Ishmael ben Elisha.

As a child, Ishmael was taken captive to Rome and, some years later, ransomed by Rabbi Joshua, whose student he became. When Ishmael, in turn, became a teacher, his *raison d'être* was re-establishing order in Jewish life. Heschel shows that Ishmael – and, later, his school – understood God as wholly transcendent: God had provided Israel with Torah and Israel's task was to live in accordance with the Divine will discernible in Torah. Ishmael is famed for formulating hermeneutic rules to govern the development of halakhic midrash; he was the linchpin of the Rabbinic enterprise of developing a code of practice, an all-embracing way of life that would assure Jewish continuity. Concentration on restoring order to Jewish life, creative obedience to the Torah text, is, in reality, a gritting of teeth, an unflinching response to disaster. Heschel goes to the heart of the matter:

> The Rabbis in the generation we are considering experienced things that others have not seen: the sacking of Jerusalem, the humiliation of the House of Israel, and the profanation of the Holy Name [*hillul haShem*] in the sight of the whole world ... a nation that has been belittled by the nations of the world is likely to verge on belittling the great presumptions: that God is merciful and compassionate and that God is the great and the powerful.
>
> Now in the school of Rabbi Ishmael they expounded 'Who is like You, God, among the mighty [*ba-'elim*]' (Exod. 15.11) – 'Who is like You, God, among the *mute* [*ba-'ilemim*], who is like You in how you see the humiliation of Your children and remain silent?'[22]

Confronted only by the Face turned away, shaken to the core by divine silence, Ishmael grits his teeth and prescribes obedience to divine law. Thus and only thus is omnipotence in the face of suffering and humiliation maintained.

Ishmael's illustrious contemporary Akiva saw the same world but differently and, says Heschel, was captivated by what lay beneath the surface of the biblical text, finding an immanent God disclosed in the world and in the events that unfold here. Akiva is filled with awe, experiencing the Sh'khinah, God's immanent face, even amid the suffering and humiliation. Akiva taught:

> Wherever Israel was exiled, the Sh'khinah went into exile with them. They were exiled to Egypt, and the Sh'khinah went with them … They were exiled to Babylon, and the Sh'khinah went with them … They were exiled to Edom [Roman Empire], and the Sh'khinah went with them … And in the future, when they will return from exile, the Sh'khinah will, as it were,[23] return with them as well.[24]

Israel has been expelled from its Holy Land; the Divine Presence goes into exile with Her people. Israel has been humiliated and weeps; so too the Divine Presence, God is revealed in the thorn-bush and says: 'Do you now realise that I live in sorrow just as my people Israel lives in sorrow. You should know that in speaking to you here in the midst of the thorns, I am a partner in their suffering.'[25]

Israel suffers; but God doesn't intervene to prevent that suffering. More than that: there's a direct connection between worldly and heavenly pain. As Heschel says: 'The Holy and Blessed One is a partner in the suffering of His creatures, He is involved in the lot of His people, wounded by their sufferings and redeemed by their liberation.'[26]

There's a verse in Jeremiah: 'Because my people is shattered, I am shattered; I am dejected, seized by desolation.'[27] Some Rabbis understood those words as applying to God and not the Prophet:

> This is like a young prince who tried to lift a heavy rock. As he lifted it, it fell and crushed him. When the king heard his son had been crushed, he began to cry: 'I've been crushed.' The palace

guard, not understanding, said to him: 'Your son has been crushed. Why do you say *you've* been crushed?' But this was the reaction of the Holy and Blessed One, as it were: 'Because My people are shattered, I'm shattered; I'm dejected, seized by desolation.'[28]

The bond between God and Israel is intimate, one of parent and child: the former suffers when the latter suffers.

A renowned disciple of Akiva, Rabbi Shimon bar Yohai, takes a verse from the Prophet Amos:

Rabbi Shimon bar Yohai formulated a parable concerning God's bond, as it were, to His people Israel: 'Who built His chambers in heaven and founded His vault on earth' (Amos 9.6). It's like to a person who tied two ships together with anchor chains and iron moorings, put them out to sea, and built a palace on them. The palace endures so long as the ships are tied to one another; were the ships to float apart, the palace couldn't endure. So it is here: When Israel fulfils God's will, the chambers of heaven are built up, but when Israel does not, God's vault, as it were, founders on earth.[29]

Likewise: '"For the name of God I proclaim; Give glory to our God!" (Deut. 32.3). If I proclaim God's name, God is great, but if not, God is – as it were – not great.'[30] And climactically: 'When you are My witnesses, I am God, but when you are not My witnesses, I – as it were – am not God.'[31]

The dependence of God on Israel as well as of Israel on God, the mutuality of need, is the arresting feature of the theology we owe Akiva and his followers.

I've already referred to Byron Sherwin's essay on theodicy. In it he overturns conventional Jewish wisdom about omnipotence:

While most of the medieval Jewish philosophers stressed divine omnipotence as a crucial feature of a self-sufficient perfect God, the notion of divine omnipotence seems either unknown or irrelevant to biblical and to rabbinic theology. Certainly, biblical and rabbinic sources discussed the 'power' of God, but omnipotence, as it was understood by many of the Jewish philosophers, does not seem to have been a characteristic of Jewish thought until the Middle Ages, when it was probably introduced through Islamic philosophical influence.[32]

How right Sherwin is — as Heschel demonstrates so conclusively. While Ishmael gritted his teeth to maintain omnipotence, Akiva offers a different understanding, startling but perhaps better suited to the survivors of the Third Hurban. *Elu va'elu*, these and these are both the words of the living God.

God Can Be Experienced

As a very British rationalist, I'd long been sceptical of Kabbalism, Jewish mysticism, and am appalled by those 'Kabbalists' of today both in in the United States and Britain who peddle magic in the guise of religion and fund themselves by appealing to credulous, vulnerable 'celebrities'. Eventually I overcame my prejudices sufficiently to read Gershom Scholem's universally respected study *Major Trends in Jewish Mysticism*.[33] Scholem was born in Berlin, made aliyah in 1923 and became one of the seminal academics of the Hebrew University.

Scholem doesn't see mysticism as a separate category cutting across religions but as a stage in the development of each independent faith: for him it represents the point at which some within a religious tradition wish to experience the God whom their particular tradition discloses. Mysticism 'seeks to transform the God whom it encounters in the peculiar religious consciousness of its own social environment from an object of dogmatic knowledge into a novel and living experience and intuition'.[34]

Although intellectually interested I still couldn't engage — until Scholem's narrative moved to Safed in Galilee and encountered the creative genius of Isaac Luria. Luria was born in Jerusalem in 1534 and died in Safed aged only 38. The Kabbalists of Safed embodied the agony of expulsion from Spain in 1492, predicted by them with horrible irony as the year of messianic arrival. Their thinking, says Scholem, reflects the terrible reality of exile and yearning for redemption. Scholem studied and lectured among German Jews: though Zionists for idealistic reasons, they'd also been exiled and lived through the inexplicable, devastating destruction of German Jewry and German Jewish culture. Even though the Final Solution had yet to unfold, Scholem and his fellow German Jewish intellectuals at the Hebrew University in Jerusalem were already anguished witnesses. When they asked questions about the presence of evil in the world – about God, creation and human suffering – it was no theoretical issue, but as immediate as it had been for Luria and the Kabbalists of Safed four hundred years earlier.

Lurianic Kabbalah is founded on a complex creation myth. It refers to God (as God is in God's Self) as *Ein Sof*, Without End. If God is Everything and Everywhere, how can the universe exist? How can we human beings not be consumed, overwhelmed by God? The Lurianic creation myth describes how God felt compelled to make room for the world by, as it were, abandoning a region within God's Self, 'a kind of mystical primordial space from which He withdrew in order to return to it in the act of creation and revelation', explains Scholem.[35] *Tsimtsum* is how the Kabbalists termed this divine contraction.

That may well sound like religious mumbo-jumbo. But reflect: this world is self-evidently not God but many people sense that God is present – not manipulating the weather, not zapping the wicked and rewarding the good, but in a way different from the God Who would overwhelm us if we came into the presence of the Without End. Lurianic Kabbalah 'solved' what may seem a remote religious conundrum but passed on, at least, to me, an intuition, *tsimtsum*, to which I can relate.

Two further teachings also speak to me: a doctrine called *sh'virat ha'keilim* (breaking of the vessels) and *tikkun* (mending or repairing defects). The details of *sh'virat ha'keilim* are so complicated and obscure that even Scholem is forced to simplify them. In essence, the Lurianic metaphor for what emanates from God is light. It streamed forth, filled *S'firot* – emanations or vessels of descending strength, the first five being strong enough to contain that light. But the last five were shattered and the light scattered; sparks of light – *nitsotsot* – adhered to *k'lipot* – husks or shells – that do not derive from God and represent the evil forces in the world.

Once again, apparent hocus pocus. But this is myth, metaphor – intuitions searching for words. God is present in the world, not as the overpowering *Ein Sof* but as the lowest of the emanations and as the imprisoned sparks of light awaiting release. Equally important, evil doesn't come from God; it exists in the world but isn't divine punishment either for national failings or for individual sins.

Finally to *tikkun*, repair. The term may be familiar from the phrase *tikkun olam*, widely used by Progressive Jews to mean social justice, mending the world. Whenever I become over-enthusiastic in invoking Lurianic Kabbalah and the doctrine of *tikkun*, my colleague Rabbi Professor Marc Saperstein cautions about a major shift in the meaning of the word. He's absolutely right, and to understand his point, let's clarify further. Scholem tells us 'the process in which God conceives, brings forth and develops Himself does not reach its final conclusion in God. Certain parts of the process of restitution [*tikkun*], are allotted to man':

Not all the lights which are held in captivity by the powers of darkness are set free by their own efforts; it is man who adds the final touch to the divine countenance; it is he who completes the enthronement of God, the King and the mystical Creator of all things, in His own Kingdom of Heaven; it is he who perfects the Maker of all things![36]

That's eye-opening: Lurianic Kabbalah underscores God's need for human beings. The process of creation has brought about a world in which restitution, rectification, repair is required; the remaining Holy Sparks, embedded in the broken fragments – trapped by the forces of evil – demand release. Only human beings can do that.

The last of the *S'firot*, the Holy Vessels, is also the Sh'khinah, the immanent Divine Presence. Scholem emphasizes the exile of the Sh'khinah as a genuine symbol of the 'broken' state of things in God's realm – and the human role in the repair:

The Shekhinah fell, as the last Sefirah, when the vessels were broken ... To lead the Shekhinah back to her Master, to unite her with Him, is in one way or other the true purpose of the Torah. It is this mystical function of human action which lends it a special dignity. The fulfilment of each and every commandment was to be accompanied by a formula declaring that this was done 'for the sake of uniting the Holy One, praised be He, and his Shekhinah, out of fear and love.'[37]

Here we meet the difference in usage of *tikkun* that Marc Saperstein warns about. How is rectification or repair to be effected in the Lurianic system? Scholem explains that it's dependent on 'acts of religion, on the fulfilment of the commandments and meritorious deeds ... on spiritual actions, of which the most important is prayer'.[38] In Lurianic Kabbalah, the *tikkunim*, the repair-actions, are spiritual, mystical – prayers and rituals that strive to unify God's Name; they're also messianic, seeking to bring an end to the exile of the Sh'khinah, the Face of God Who accompanied us when the Temple fell. The result is not to make the world in which we live a better place, but to remove everything of value from this world and restore it to God.

The world is as it is – God's creation but not God. Evil is real but not a divine instrument of punishment or affliction. God and humanity are partners in setting right the imperfections, necessarily part of the creation process. These are powerful theological insights indicating that even in remote Safed 450 years ago, Jews were desperately concerned for an understanding of life in tune with their experience of how life actually is.

God and Humanity Need Each Other

In Jerusalem, both before and after the Second World War, Scholem was friend and mentor to Hans Jonas. Jonas's failure to gain a Chair at the Hebrew University prompted his leaving – but not before Scholem and Lurianic Kabbalah had left their mark.

In 1968, Albert Friedlander published an anthology *Out of the Whirlwind*.[39] Shamefully, my copy is stamped 'Library, Leo Baeck College' – which tells you how early in my rabbinate I thought the book worth stealing! It contains an article entitled 'The Concept of God After Auschwitz' by Hans Jonas, which begins with a creation myth that Jonas formulated in 1967 or 68 – with issues of human mortality at the forefront of his mind. Over the next 20 years, he wrote several glosses to his myth, responding to criticism. The myth has always attracted me; its essence grapples with Who God is and what God wants of humanity.

Jonas begins the myth with God 'for unknowable reasons' giving God's Self over 'to the chance and risk and endless variety of becoming'.[40] God renounces something of God's Self to make space for the world. 'For aeons God's cause is safe in the slow hands of cosmic chance and probability' — God cannot lose in the great evolutionary game. But then comes humanity and the game changes entirely because it brings about the 'awesome impact of [humanity's] deeds [for good or evil] on God's destiny, on the very complexion of eternal being':

> With the appearance of man, transcendence awakened to itself and henceforth accompanies his doings with the bated breath of suspense, hoping and beckoning, rejoicing and grieving, approving and frowning ... making itself felt to him even while not intervening in the dynamics of his worldly scene.

The debt to Scholem and Luria is obvious. God's renunciation of something of God's Self is *tsimtsum*. The evolution of human beings with a sense of good and evil and the ability to do both is crucial to God. Henceforth, what we do impacts on God; our deeds, as it were, affect the Divine Countenance 'approving and frowning'. In the original gloss, Jonas explains: 'the image of God is in danger as never before ... We literally hold in our faltering hands the future of the divine adventure and must not fail Him, even if we would fail ourselves.' He ends: 'We can have immortality at heart when in our brief span we serve our threatened mortal affairs and help the suffering immortal God.'

God is not the Deist God, the divine watchmaker who sets the world ticking and goes away. God is present but unable, because of the intrinsic nature of the universe, to suspend the laws of nature — to intervene in that sense. The insistence that what we do matters to the outcome of the divine *tsimtsum*, the adventure of being; that our deeds, as it were, mark the Divine countenance — is provocative and challenging. But it draws on the most ancient of traditions: the parity covenant. The intuition that God and humanity are in partnership and need each other takes us back to the Torah itself.

SECTION THREE
REASONING ABOUT GOD

My core conviction is that faith demands justification both by reason and by experience. To rephrase Heschel: belief without reason is wild and dangerous; belief without experience is arid and ritualistic. Let me start with reasoning and offer three propositions.

One: the World Exists Independently of God, In Its Own Space

At some point, outside or beyond time and space, God committed God's Self to the universe, the world of being. It began with time and unfolded in space according to laws of both certainty and probability; it led inexorably from then until now. The 'beginning' can be regarded as compatible with what today's cosmologists call the Big Bang. The most remarkable characteristic of the unfolding process is evolution – with its astounding leaps from inert matter to living organisms and genetically programmed brain to human consciousness. All this accords with today's physics and biology but I would make one addition. With the emergence of human consciousness, a new dimension was added – our awareness of uncertainty, unpredictability, chance as a consequence of how life is – its 'is-ness' – and their reality in the domain of human freedom.

The *tsimtsum* myth that God contracted into God's Self to make space for the world has an intellectual persuasiveness that makes me smile ruefully in recognition. Jonas's myth – in which God decides to commit to existence and then watches our universe, our world, our lives evolve according to the laws of contemporary cosmology and biology in time-space that is not God – makes sense and feels right. The space is by definition inviolable. It's not that God has chosen not to manipulate it – it's not open to manipulation: the laws of nature are the laws of nature – 'is-ness' once again. The change of pace and tone in Jonas's myth once human life emerges is understandable: human beings can't alter those universal laws but can intervene in the process of all life – for ill as well as for good.

Linda's death shook me to the core. My place on the happiness–misery axis changed; but not my theology, my rational understanding and intuitive sense of the relationship between God and a world in which countless people die before their time and even more are scarred by loss. The world is as it is: it came into being and has evolved in the only way it could – if the world as we know it is to exist. It's not 'the best of all possible worlds';[41] it's the only way the world could be.

A decade or more ago, the Western world appeared to discover tsunamis. Like everyone else, I was appalled as television pictures revealed mile after mile of land flattened and lifeless, littered with wrecked boats, uprooted trees and the debris of homes. It was heart-breaking; nothing could diminish my sorrow and anger at such loss and suffering. But my theology remained the same: this is how life is. The world exists and behaves according to laws cosmologists, geologists, volcanologists, seismologists and biologists observe and measure. I wasn't being heartless, didn't query the need for aid and action to relieve suffering when tsunamis, inevitably, occur; I wasn't denying God. I was putting in prose what Luria and Jonas had expressed through myth.

Human beings have free will and often choose to do what causes suffering to others; similarly, we often find reasons for abstaining from doing what would alleviate suffering in others. That's what I believe the word evil refers to. I've readily acknowledged the qualifications to free will – real choice is often restricted by social circumstances or individual psychology; nevertheless, evil is human action or inaction, the result of which is the suffering of others. Evil and sin are synonymous. Cancers and tsunamis cause suffering – as much and of the same nature – but they aren't evil.[42] The source of cancers and tsunamis is the reality of existence, the unfolding of the universe since its creation: how life is. Cancer and tsunamis are part of the 'is-ness' of life. I don't say, 'It's just how life is.' I say, 'It's how life is. And it isn't just at all.'

Two: God Doesn't Intervene in the World

The New Atheism claims all religions rely on miracles; what was once an ignorant interpretation of something natural or a conjuring trick has been cynically used to exploit the credulous; there's no miraculous abrogation of the laws of nature for healing, rescue or any other purpose. Religions, they insist, rest their case for God on miracles; therefore the case for God is lost.

Interference with the laws of nature is the accepted meaning of the word miracle in modern Western society, defined by the *Shorter Oxford English Dictionary* as: 'A marvellous event, exceeding the known powers of nature, and therefore supposed to be due to the special intervention of the Deity or of some supernatural agency.' I've no argument with that; however the Torah – and the Tanakh as a whole – isn't nearly as reliant on miracles as this definition might be read to imply.

Many passages in the Torah and Tanakh describe divine intervention but have different contexts and tone. Sometimes they're narrative embellishments to match the cultural trappings of others – Jewish magic competes with Egyptian magic in the court of Pharaoh;[43] sometimes they're ways of expressing the idea that 'our God' is not only different from 'your God' but also better at doing the things your gods do.[44] At other times, notably in the case of Elijah, they're the attributes of a holy man.[45] There are also disturbing passages like 2 Samuel 6.1–7 in which Uzza seeks to steady the Ark and dies. But none are central to the theological narrative; little if anything is lost by ignoring them.

The 'miracle' of the oil that lasted for eight days at Hanukkah is particularly apposite. The historical account of Hanukkah is found in the book of Maccabees in the Apocrypha;[46] the 'miracle' first appears several centuries later, in the Talmud.[47] It's a later addition – perhaps absorbing a winter festival of lights – which has come to obscure the core teaching, resistance to cultural imperialism and nothing to do with magical intervention. But even in this instance, the Hebrew word used is *nes*. At a much later time, in Eastern Europe, Jews began playing a game with a *dreydl*, a spinning top that proclaimed '*nes gadol hayah shum*', a great 'miracle' happened there. But nowhere in the entire Hebrew Bible does the word *nes* mean miracle in the sense of an abrogation of the laws of nature; it means a sign. To say we can find signs of God, even in thorn-bushes, is very different from saying God intervenes by suspending the laws of physics.

Neither the Torah nor the rest of the Hebrew Bible depends on miracles for their authority — religious or ethical; miracles are, I believe, marginal. With one glaring exception: only the crossing of the Reed Sea has embedded itself in Jewish consciousness — through liturgy and the *Haggadah* — literally, not metaphorically. There, at the Reed Sea, God intervened, rescued and saved. Which is why Emil Fackenheim, in his study of God in history,[48] wrestles with the presence of a saving God at the Reed Sea and the absence of a saving God in the Death Camps. For me, there's no other conclusion: those who experienced the escape from their Egyptian pursuers and passed the story down the generations to the biblical redactors saw in their liberation and survival the hand of God. Literalism diminishes rather than enlarges the awe of this foundational event.

Another aspect of the same challenge is presented by the Prophets and their conviction that the leaders of the Great Powers — Babylon and Egypt — are the instruments of God's will. If God literally interfered with the laws of nature at the Reed Sea, then it's both religiously and ethically inexplicable that God didn't intervene on behalf of the million murdered children. If God manipulates Assyrians and Babylonians to bring punishment for faithlessness on Israel and Judah, it must today be legitimate to ask, as Rubenstein did, about God's role with regard to Hitler, Stalin, Mao, Pol Pot and the other monsters of recent history — and today. The inference is obscene, blasphemous, nonsensical.

A third dimension to the question of divine intervention further reinforces the need for theological change. The doctrine of reward and punishment is present in Torah — notably in the second paragraph of the *Sh'ma*[49] read twice daily and written on the parchment contained in every *mezuzzah* case on each Jewish doorpost. Curiously, while the doctrine of suffering as divine punishment persisted long after Job had challenged it, Rabbinic Judaism acknowledged that reward would not be experienced by the righteous in this life but in the world to come.[50] If reward is clearly postponed, so too is punishment.

I can't resist referring to episodes witnessed from time to time on television. There's a devastating natural disaster, an earthquake, for instance; many people are killed; a group of survivors walks into shot, expressing their thanks to God for having been saved when others were not. Such theology truly passeth all understanding, spiritual and ethical.

Three: God Needs Us; We're Locked In a State of Interdependence and Partnership

I readily acknowledge that using the metaphor of person for God is, these days, idiosyncratic, quirky even. Secular fundamentalists are not alone in pouring scorn on the anthropomorphic, caricaturing it as an old man with a white beard sitting on a cloud. Depicting God owes a great deal to the Christian artistic tradition: the authors of the Torah and their successors strongly disapproved of any representation of God in human form no matter how magnificent and inspirational the Sistine Chapel. Judaism is a tradition that prohibits representations of God, whether in sculpture or painting, however the artist might intend them to be perceived. Instead, biblical and Rabbinic Judaism use word-portraits – different from paintings even though both are intended as metaphors. It's true the Jewish philosophic tradition became increasingly troubled even by word-portraits, but that represents only one strand of Judaism.

Today, I'm strongly attracted to Rabbinic God-talk and can only express my experience of God in such language. Without word-portraits, metaphors and myths, I'd be unable to reason about God. I recognize the scepticism many may feel but is it possible that, as so often when addressing the past, we're dominated by the sophistication of our own thought processes? This leads us to attribute unwarranted naïveté to our forebears: we can find their mode of expression uncomfortable and fail to recognize the intuitive substance underlying the form they adopted. When the Torah depicts God's relationship with us as one of parity or partnership, it isn't telling us that God is an inadequate human being; when Hans Jonas speaks of God as having a countenance that frowns, he's not suggesting God has a face of flesh and blood, still less that God is perpetually grinning or grimacing like an actor in a pantomime. In both cases word-portraits best convey the nature of the divine commitment to creation. It's at this point that the parity model of covenant becomes illuminating. God and human beings can have a relationship which, if not between equals, is nevertheless one in which debate and recrimination can take place. Covenant implies a mutual commitment; parity a responsibility to engage on both sides.

The Akiva tradition deepens the insight further. The word Heschel uses is pathos: God is affected by, touched by human suffering. Let's go back to Albert Friedlander's paper given to the Manor House Dialogue Group on the suffering God in Jewish tradition. God weeps. After the Second Hurban, the Rabbis said: 'When the Holy and Blessed One calls to mind His children and their suffering among the nations of the world, two of His tears fall into the ocean and the sound is heard from one end of the earth to the other.'[51]

The Akiva tradition pushes parity and pathos further: God, as it were, participates physically in Israel's suffering. Consider this challenging passage in the Talmud, in Tractate Hagigah:

> Rabbah ben Shela met Elijah. He asked him: 'What is the Holy One, blessed be God, doing?' Elijah answered: 'God utters traditions in the name of all the Rabbis, but in the name of Rabbi Meir God does not utter.' Rabbah asked him, 'Why?' 'Because he learnt traditions at the mouth of Akher [Elisha ben Abuyah].' [Rabbah] said to him: 'So what? Rabbi Meir [is like a person who] found a pomegranate; he ate [the fruit] within it, and the peel he threw away!' Accepting this, Elijah answered: 'Now God says: Meir my son says: When a man suffers, to what expression does the Sh'khinah give utterance? "My head is heavy, my arm is heavy." If the Holy One, blessed be God, is thus grieved over the shedding of the blood of the wicked, how much more so over the blood of the righteous.'[52]

Leave aside the harsh treatment of Rabbi Meir, God — says this early-fourth-century Babylonian teacher — is, as it were, *physically* affected by the suffering even of the wicked, let alone the righteous.

A passage in the Talmud, in Tractate Shabbat, discusses the balance between the Rabbinic role of judging in disputes and the need to study. In the Torah it says Moses judged 'from the morning to the evening' (Exod. 18.13). If the phrase is taken literally, it prompts the question 'then when did Moses find time to study?' The Talmud responds that the phrase 'from morning to evening' is not there to suggest Moses was so busy judging he had no time for anything else. Instead: 'It is to teach you, every judge who judges with objective truthfulness even for a single hour, Scripture gives him credit as though he had become a partner with the Holy One, blessed be God, in the work of creation.'[53] The Hebrew word used for partner is *shutaf* – the same root is used by the halakhah in commercial partnership law. But here it's making a daring theological statement: human beings and God are partners in *ma'aseh v'reishit*, the ongoing work of creation. It's characteristically Jewish that the fulcrum of the partnership is the dispensing of justice.

What at first looks new is, in fact, rooted in the logic of Torah and indeed of the Creation narrative itself. In an article entitled 'The Concept of Power in the Jewish Tradition',[54] Louis Jacobs reiterated Rabbinic insistence that human beings are stewards of creation, not owners with unconditional power: 'In later Judaism, the Sabbath, on which "work" is forbidden, was interpreted as a weekly reminder to man that God alone has absolute control of His universe, man enjoying his privileges as a permission, not as a right.' But he added:

> We read in the Babylonian Talmud (Shabbat 119b): 'Rabbi Hamnuna said: "He who prays on the eve of the Sabbath and recites 'and the heaven and earth were finished' (Gen. 2.1), Scripture treats of him as though he had become a partner [*shotef*] with the Holy One, blessed be God, in the work of creation."'

In the Jonas myth, God committed God's Self to creation; the world came into being and is how it is. It's of the nature of creation that God cannot intervene or, as Jacobs puts it, power has been given, delegated. The partnership is a necessary consequence of the nature of the world. A midrash in the name of both Akiva and Ishmael makes clear that just as the farmer prunes and waters fruit trees, so the doctor provides medication for the body – both are partners with God in the furtherance of life.[55]

Like all true partnerships, it exists to fulfil mutual needs. What is that need? Rabbi Eleazar Ha-Kappar, who lived at the time of the compilation of the Mishnah, offers the following answer:

My Torah is in your hands; the time of Redemption is in Mine. We therefore need each other. Just as you need Me to bring about the Redemption, so I need you to fulfil the Torah and thus bring near the rebuilding of My House and of Jerusalem.[56]

The daring is both daunting and exciting. God and the Jewish people are partners in redemption. Let the aforementioned Rabbi Meir, a student of Akiva's, have the last word on this:

'Thus God saved [*va'yosha*] Israel that day' (Exod. 14.30) – [the Hebrew consonants can be read as if it were] written, 'Thus God was saved [*va'yiv'asha* – and God was saved]' – when Israel is redeemed, God, as it were, is redeemed.[57]

By re-vocalizing one word, revelation takes place: God – not just humanity but God – is waiting to be redeemed.

Redemption

In Rabbinic theology redemption became an extensive, almost all-embracing concept, the defence or justification of last resort for God's lack of intervention and delay. Only when all are faithful to Torah, when all live according to the *mitzvot*, when Israel returns to its Land, when the Temple is rebuilt, when the Sh'khinah is restored to Her place, will the End of Days have been reached. Only then will suffering cease and will Israel – and God – have been redeemed. Or any combination of those justifications of divinity in relation to our present ills.

Such a notion of redemption doesn't speak to me; my sense of redemption is more closely tied to the present. The Hebrew for redeemer is *go'el*, the term used of Boaz in relation to Ruth, the kinsman obliged to redeem Ruth from her lowly position as a childless widow and restore her to the status of a married woman.[58] God is my Redeemer because only God can rescue my existence from its apparently trivial and meaningless state. I've no sense that my unimportant and inconsequential life has any enduring significance; such acts of righteousness and repair that I perform may or may not endure. I'm with the Psalmist: 'A human being is like a wild flower – the wind passes over it, it's gone and its place no longer knows it.'[59]

Our descendants and their memories, our genes and the *mitzvah* of passing on teaching '*b'shem omro*', in the name of the teacher, only delay the inevitable. Sooner or later, it will be as if we'd never existed: only God can give enduring significance to ordinary lives. The Jonas myth offers the sole hope of redemption from pointlessness: we leave marks on the face of God, even though we leave no enduring marks on this life. As Jonas wrote, 'We can have immortality at heart when in our brief span we serve our threatened mortal affairs and help the suffering immortal God.'[60] The 'death of God' wounds God but obliterates humanity.

SECTION FOUR
EXPERIENCING GOD

How do you feel about what you've said so far?

How do You feel about it?

You're not going to answer that are You. It's not been me talking to You but me talking about You. Reason clarifies, tests experience but doesn't replace it.

Liturgy

For the greater part of the last two thousand years, rabbis have been scholars, commentators and teachers, not service leaders – that task is performed by the *sh'liakh tsibbur*, the delegate of the congregation. In the Progressive tradition rabbis did and do lead services – which has as much to do with competencies as with the influence of the church model. As a congregational rabbi in north-west Surrey, I led services in the approved British Reform manner, reading rather than chanting.

Leading services brought me enormous satisfaction: Orthodox services are chanted rapidly, exclusively in Hebrew and consequently not understood by many; Progressive services, with their mix of Hebrew and English, are more readily comprehensible. All I had to work from was the thin and dated British Reform Prayer Book of the 1930s — belonging to a different age. But I could at least choose which passages to read in Hebrew or English, enabling me to emphasize what I thought was meaningful. Where the text was inaccessible — which usually meant incomprehensible — I could innovate to my heart's content by using alternative readings. As Prayer Book revision got under way in the 1970s,[61] I was invigorated by the step change Rabbis Lionel Blue and Jonathan Magonet made and enjoyed service leading all the more. Was this purely an ego trip, an opportunity to be on stage and bask in my own performance? A factor perhaps, but it wasn't everything. I was young enough not to have internalized the difference between life as I'd grown up to expect it and life as it really is.

My attitude to services changed when I ceased being a congregational rabbi and began spending *Shabbatot* in synagogue as an 'ordinary congregant'. Sitting there, no longer responsible for leading the community and disaffected by my non-role, I began to think about the words themselves. The painful process of learning the difference between liturgy and prayer was under way.

Twenty years later, as Head of the Movement when the Assembly of Reform Rabbis embarked on their latest revision of the Sabbath and Daily Prayer Book,[62] my new role was to support colleagues in that task. But I was also a member of the Assembly and had my own views, trenchantly — others would use a different term — advanced during the process. We were rightly concerned about meeting different needs — today no one form of service will suit everyone — but, even more important to me were the words themselves, the theology they expressed.

Earlier, I voiced doubts at the God conveyed by the public reading of Torah: from my seat in the congregation, I'd now become aware that the words of the liturgy bore no relation to the God of anyone likely to be there. The God of the new *Siddur*, thankfully, would no longer be male but was still Great, Mighty and Awesome; God would still part the waters of the Reed Sea, save and heal. We'd continue to elevate the Torah, proclaiming it to be the self-same Torah that

God gave to Moses; we'd continue to pray to an omnipotent, interventionist deity. I pointed this out, becoming increasingly strident, and in the end – you'll recognize the strategy – was asked by the Chair of the Assembly to set up a working party to produce material reflecting both our wish to engage with God and a new understanding of Who God might Be.

Four colleagues joined me and, to an extent, we succeeded – thanks largely to Rabbi Howard Cooper, Leo Baeck College graduate, a pioneer of the engagement between Judaism and psychotherapy and specialist in reflective services.

However, I'd misjudged what our communities wanted, mistaking my needs for those of others. The misjudgement went further: the trend nowadays – irrespective of *Siddur* revision – is towards less English, more Hebrew, particularly more chanted Hebrew – enabling those who so wish to sidestep or distance themselves from the liturgy's more challenging assertions and, at the same time, sound more 'authentic'. More importantly, I hadn't recognized just how much music trumps words and can be determinative in creating the mood most responsive to a given need.

I was irritable, discontented, but continued attending Shabbat morning services, more or less religiously, usually with bad grace. Returning with renewed conviction to a practice from some years earlier, I sat on my own. At first the starting point was the writing I was now engaged in: I'd find a relevant passage in the innovative Blue and Magonet Study Anthology at the back of the *Siddur* and withdraw from the service to wrestle with the difficult questions raised for me. But they were silent conversations with myself about my current intellectual agenda. Then, from time to time, I permitted the conversations to be *lishmah*, for their own sake, gradually allowing what went on to be more open, more intuitive. On such occasions my distance from the service, the liturgy – and, today, even from the people I'm sitting with – is considerable.

Prayer

I surface aware the Other has been involved. At first the recognition came reluctantly; I dismissed it as wish-fulfilment, analysing the experience repeatedly and rejecting it again and again as self-deluding. But now, I don't feel the need to push it away – the awareness is of Something, no, Some One other than me, more enduring than me, Who permits me to engage and challenge. And Who invariably challenges me back, hard.

Uncertainty, I maintain, is preferable to certainty – people with doubts are far less likely to abuse others than those convinced of their own rightness. I've said that God – *Ehyeh asher Ehyeh*, I am Who I am – by definition can't be proved. Does ending with my personal experience betray this observation; is it a case of having my rocky road and eating it, dealing myself the winning hand? I hope not: I stand by my personal experience while doubting and questioning it with painful regularity.

You think you're pretty smart don't you, rabbi?

I sit in the synagogue. Despite all the muffling, desensitizing layers of biological inheritance, subconscious drives, intellectual scepticism and egotism, W/we sometimes engage. I doubt it, dismiss it, analyse it repeatedly to death. But You won't leave me alone.

I can't prove it. I'm hoist by my own petard. But You won't go away.

Reason helps – to a point. You contracted into Yourself and, in so doing, made space for a world moving remorselessly on according to the laws of nature – mathematics and physics, chemistry and biology. The world is impervious to physical intervention; that's how You created it and that's how life is.

You created it. Why? Because You were compelled to? Because You need us to partner You in bringing about redemption? Why?

I acknowledge You against my will; I'm angry. The suffering of humanity is appalling, unfathomable and meaningless. Levi Yitzhak of Berditchev said: 'I do not wish to know why I suffer, only that I suffer for Your sake.'

That's not good enough – what about the suffering of others? It's not just, not fair – it's an impossible sacrifice You ask of us in return for the lives You say You need us to live.

Why do we need You? Most people think we don't. Life goes on without You. You make no difference – You don't punish the wicked or reward the righteous; You don't heal the sick or rescue those in mortal danger. You've no 'cash value'; You're as ineffectual as the Blind Watchmaker – in fact, You're completely irrelevant to the majority in today's world.

But You won't go away. I sit in the synagogue and You irritate me, annoy me, kick me in uncomfortable places. You don't allow me to be content or satisfied; You needle me, push me, expose me to myself. You're the Itch which defies scratching, the Maggot[63] in my brain, the Supreme Source of dissatisfaction. You're a constant challenge to me – which is why this book is framed as a challenge to You. What is this need You have of us that we must endure the unfairness of indiscriminate suffering? Why must we be Your partner in the endlessly demanding work of redemption?

Suddenly, I'm stopped short. God's need for redemption is a proposition I'm forced to accept; my own need for redemption depends on it. Without God, deeds of compassionate justice don't endure; without God, life has no meaning. The post-modern world stares meaninglessness in the face; some have the courage of their convictions and accept it, either trying to impose a meaning on the absurd or acknowledging despair. But I can't. Because God won't go away, won't leave me alone, won't let me be.

I'm thrown back on one of God's innumerable paradoxes – the two paragraphs before the *Sh'ma*. In the first, God is the distant, inscrutable Power behind the universe; in the second, God is Personal, the One Who cares, no, loves an insignificant little people, Israel. I'm compelled to acknowledge that in our mutually challenging engagement lies the same paradox. God cares enough to urge me / us to perform redemptive acts of justice and compassion, goodness and love – for my / our sake, for the sake of the world, as well as for God.

I maintain my challenge. The suffering of humanity is inexplicable and indefensible; my anger – and that of so many in this generation, as well as in the past – is undiminished. It's endemic in Your world, the ineradicable challenge to humanity, demanding impossible acts of rectification and repair. You didn't will it but it's characteristic of how life, which You created, is; the ultimate paradox which I have no alternative but to accept.

So there it is. Say something.

What do you want Me to say?

Life beyond death: Individual survival and messianic hope

SECTION ONE
INDIVIDUAL SURVIVAL

Bodily Resurrection

Towards the end of the twelfth century, Maimonides formulated – in his Commentary on the Mishnah – 'Thirteen Principles of Faith',[1] representing the high point of the encounter, mediated by Islam, between Judaism and the Greek philosophical tradition. He shoehorned Judaism into 13 principles, providing an authoritative commentary on each. The Thirteenth Principle is the only one to deal with what follows death and is expressed through the assertion of belief in the resurrection of the dead. What's odd about what one might expect to be the climax of a characteristically ambitious venture is that Maimonides' explanation of the thirteenth principle is the shortest: 'Resurrection of the dead. We've already explained it.' That's it – so terse as to make one question what Maimonides really believed – which, when the Thirteen Principles first appeared, people most certainly did.

To understand just how shocked Maimonides' contemporaries were, we need to explore the background.

Not just the Torah but the entire Hebrew Bible is sparse in references to resurrection: there are only two obvious ones – in Isaiah[2] and Daniel,[3] the latter being a particularly late book. In fact, detail of what happens after death is conspicuous by its absence from Tanakh. Genesis says of the Patriarchs simply that they were 'gathered to their ancestors'.[4] Deuteronomy 18.9–12 recognizes that the Canaanites practised necromancy and believed in ghosts – and is explicit such practices are incompatible with Judaism. We find the term *Gehinnom* in the book of Joshua,[5] meaning valley of gratuitous destruction and referring to a place, south of Jerusalem, associated with a cult that sacrificed children to the Canaanite god Moloch. It became the metaphor for a place of torment. There's little else.

This is what Louis Jacobs has to say on the subject in his analytical study *Principles of the Jewish Faith*:

> It is generally assumed that the Hebrew Bible is silent on the whole question of the Hereafter, with the exception of some few references in the later books. However, it is extremely unlikely that there was no belief in some kind of immortality during the earlier period. All ancient peoples shared a belief in a life after death. The Hebrews must have been aware of the beliefs of their neighbours and it is hard to see how they kept themselves from adopting the idea of an existence of some kind even after the death of the body … It is hard to believe that an Isaiah or a Jeremiah, for instance, had no hope of further communion after their death with the God they worshipped in their lifetime.[6]

Jacobs's argument is plausible but may tell us more about his faith than that of our biblical ancestors. Unusually, he seems to miss an obvious inference: two issues were more important to Isaiah and Jeremiah. First, the behaviour of the living, their commitment to righteousness and integrity; second, the fidelity of the group to God and the survival of the Jewish people. These mattered much, much more.

Jacobs goes on:

> Scholars are generally inclined to the view that a full belief in immortality came into Judaism at the time of the Maccabees when young men were dying in defence of their faith. It was no longer possible at that time to account for human death and suffering solely in terms of divine retribution and reward in this life, and the complete belief in an after-life was felt to be necessary for theodicy.[7]

That's very telling, highlighting the need to account for the suffering of the innocent as the reason for the development of a theology of afterlife.

Classical Rabbinic Literature is full of vivid and imaginative ideas about what form life after death might take. I say 'might take' because no single, definitive system emerged – which is why it's difficult to summarize. Some painted colourful pictures of a demonstrably corporeal afterlife – with eating, drinking, marrying and even procreating; Rabbis, however, would continue to debate, discuss and disagree, only now in the presence of the Holy One (God forbid!). Others were more tentative and ethereal. Today, textbook summaries attempt systemizations but invariably serve up a mishmash misrepresenting their individual, speculative nature.

These pictures variously included a place of bliss, *Gan Eden*,[8] one of torment, *Gehinnom* – and belief in the bodily resurrection of the dead. Resurrection – which some scholars believe is of Babylonian origin – plays a large part in early Rabbinic Judaism and also, of course, Christianity. As with the doctrine of Messiah, resurrection underlines both the common background of the siblings and the different theological directions in which they took a hitherto shared tradition (itself composed of several concepts with different origins).

So *ideologically* important was resurrection to the Pharisees, they insisted bodily resurrection of the dead was a principle of the Torah itself,[9] deploying it as a belief distinguishing them from the literalist Sadducean 'party'. The doctrine also found a prominent place in the earliest stratum of the liturgy, with the second paragraph of the *Amidah* proclaiming a belief in *t'khiyat ha'meitim*, the bringing back to life of the dead. Rabbinic Literature includes many eschatological references to resurrection – what will happen to all Jews at the End of Days on earth. The process is worked out in enthusiastic detail – even to the extent of insisting the dead will travel from their graves, via tunnels, to Jerusalem.[10] The resurrection of the dead was as important to the Rabbis as it was unimportant in Tanakh.

If we move forward into the Middle Ages, we arrive at the codification and systematization process of which Maimonides was the philosophical pinnacle. Returning to his decision not to provide further explanation of his own thirteenth principle is fascinating. Rival scholars suggested he was personally uncommitted and applied pressure – to which, after some years, he finally succumbed. His defence took the form of an essay, *Treatise on Resurrection*.[11] Here he says those who'd concluded he didn't believe in the bodily resurrection of the dead were wrong. He *did* believe in the resurrection of the body; it would take place after the coming of the Messiah, part of a three-stage process. The individual dies but the soul survives incorporeally, independently of its body. At the End of Days here on earth, the bodies will be resurrected; the souls return to their bodies and people will eat, drink, marry and procreate. Then, after enjoying a long span of renewed life ushered in by the Messianic Age, they'll die for a second time. Maimonides cites a saying of Rav that in the world to come there are no bodies and no pleasures of the body but the righteous sit with crowns on their heads and bask in the radiance of the Sh'khinah.[12] That, he says, is the third and final stage, lasting for all eternity. Maimonides was therefore able to demonstrate his views weren't heretical – he believed in bodily resurrection but for the limited period of the Messianic Era. Only the soul survives for all time.

Whether you think Maimonides' explanation should be taken at face value or is a fig leaf for his belief in incorporeality (my view) probably says as much about us as about Maimonides. There was, however, an underlying problem implicit in the codifying process itself: resolving differing biblical and Rabbinic sources and integrating three separate concepts – bodily resurrection, the Messianic Age and the world to come. In any event, Maimonides' views were far from normative: resurrection had been painted in vivid verbal colours by many of the Rabbis and belief in the bodily resurrection of the dead, officially at least, continued until challenged by post-Enlightenment Reformers.[13]

The Impact of the Modern World

It was indeed these early Reformers – with their Platforms in Germany and America – who articulated the change brought about by modernity.

Here's a contemporary tale. Morrie dies. Sadie is distraught and, in defiance of Deuteronomy 18.9–14, goes to a medium. In no time at all she's talking to her late husband: 'Morrie darling, how are you?' 'I'm fine Sadie.' 'What's it like up there? What do you do all day?' 'It's nice here. I wake up in the morning and have a swim. Then I have some breakfast and a *shloof* [nap]. Then I have another swim and lunch and another *shloof*. Then a swim, light supper and bed.' 'That sounds lovely darling but, by me, you didn't do all that swimming when you were down here.' Says Morrie: 'By me, when I was down there, I wasn't a duck.'

I ask myself why I find that joke so funny; it's a gentle way of saying that the very idea of Heaven – and Hell – teeters on the edge of the ridiculous. Even though I'm convinced that, for classical Rabbinic Judaism, resurrection was more important ideologically than theologically and the interest was primarily eschatological (what happens at the end of our collective existence in this world), modern Western culture has still had an impact on Jewish belief or disbelief – Louis Jacobs called it ruefully 'the modern mind' – in continued personal existence after death. It's both a paradigm shift and a return to a much earlier paradigm.

Reflecting on my own childhood, death was greeted with a full panoply of traditional practices and Eastern European superstitions but not by assurance that the deceased had gone to a better place and we'd be reunited with them in due course – still less by a celebratory gathering. What was clear, undisguised and acknowledged was the pain and loss suffered by those left behind. I can identify with the timeless longing to be physically reunited with loved ones – in my case, with Linda; I can tolerate liturgical circumlocutions such as 'united in eternal blessedness', but more than that I just don't know and don't feel the need to go there.

Try going where you don't 'need' to go, rabbi.

Still there, nagging away. [Sighs]

Let me take you back to my experience of seeing the body of that little boy killed crossing the road on his way to the *Seder* service in Harlow. What struck me so sharply was that the beautiful body was not the child; it wasn't just a case of irredeemably damaged machinery – something had gone, departed. The Hebrew word for soul is *nefesh*. In Brown, Driver and Briggs's *Lexicon of the Hebrew Bible*, *nefesh* is defined as soul, living being, life, self, person, and its primary meaning is given as 'that which breathes, the breathing substance or being'.[14] I find that helpful: the soul is that which animates the human being, enters at some stage in the procreative process and departs around the point of death – I'm necessarily vague about the timing because birth and death are processes. I'm convinced we have souls and follow the lead given by the etymology of *nefesh* – the soul is what makes the difference between being and not being, defines us as humans and makes each of us who we are. The soul can't be observed by fMRI scanners any more than can consciousness. If you push me, I'll affirm our souls come from God and return to God. That's it. Not, as in Maimonides' case, because I don't want to be drawn but because I can't say any more.

Can't say or don't want to go there?

Why won't You ever, ever leave me alone?

Some years ago, I made my first foray into systematic theology by compiling a 'Platform' covering much the same ground as this book but in a fraction of the space.[15] It was my initiative but far from all my own work, with substantial input from my colleagues Rabbis Eimer, Gryn and Magonet.

We circulated the *MANNA* Platform to a wide range of Jewish thinkers and elicited encouraging feedback. One response that has stayed with me over the intervening quarter of a century came from an American-trained Reform Rabbi, Dan Cohn-Sherbok, who'd earned a reputation in the non-Jewish world as Professor of Judaism at the University of Wales. He was critical of what he regarded as the major weakness of the Platform, arguing it said too little about life after death. Professor Cohn-Sherbok spent most of his academic career on the margins of the Jewish community and I'm far from sure how typically Jewish his challenge was, but it's an important, relevant observation. 'Afterlife' occupied only one of forty-five sections and it said:

> We believe there is a part of each human being – personality, spirit, soul – which is unique and indestructible. *It comes from*

God and returns to God. Our tradition uses the term 'the world to come' to speak of existence beyond death. There is a wide range of imagery reflecting the very personal and individual nature of such speculation. We believe that, after our deaths, *judgement is passed upon our lives.*

Death, which is the natural end to human life, has an unavoidable finality and is a source of pain and anguish for the bereaved. Nevertheless, we face death with trust and hope, not least in the knowledge that love and goodness are mightier than the grave and *leave an indelible mark on the face of God.*[16]

I can't avoid taking personal responsibility for this section of the Platform – so many of the phrases are mine. It's interesting how little my intellectual position has changed over the last 25 years, Linda's death notwithstanding. But it isn't simply my idiosyncratic view – my colleagues must have agreed the final draft, not being people to give their name to statements with which they disagreed!

It's evident we wanted to say something affirmative about afterlife and were prepared to make three assertions. Twenty-five years later I stand by them and clarification serves only to underline the claim of this chapter.

I remain convinced there's an indestructible dimension to each human being: that which made them who they were, their soul, returns to God whence it came. And again, I can't say more.

I feel equally strongly about judgement. A passage from Franz Rosenzweig clarifies exactly what I now mean:

The horn blown on the New Year's Day at the peak of the festival stamps the day as a 'day of judgment'. The judgment usually thought of as the end of time is here placed in the immediate present ... The year becomes representative of eternity, in complete representation. In the annual return of this judgment, eternity is stripped of every trace of the beyond, of every vestige of remoteness; it is actually there, within the grasp of every individual ...[17]

We are judged not on a distant day of judgement but in the here and now.

I explored what I mean by the endurance of the good in the previous chapter: good vanishes in the vagaries of history and extinction of memory as far as the life of humanity is concerned but survives in eternity, on the Face of God.

Isn't some of that unusually twee for you, Rabbi Bayfield? It's not like you to be sentimental.

It's my way of saying that life has a meaning which You, my Partner, compel me to accept.

Personal Survival and 'the Modern Mind'

A few years ago I came across – and much enjoyed – a book which, at first glance, has nothing to do with Jewish theology. In _The Ends of Life: Roads to Fulfilment in Early Modern England_,[18] Oxford historian Sir Keith Thomas examines the obscure, neglected records of ordinary people in sixteenth- to eighteenth-century Britain, in order to understand what drove and motivated them, how – in Thomas's words – they sought and found fulfilment.

Thomas is clear that in the stratified, authoritarian world of the Middle Ages, the Church's teachings on Heaven and Hell were widely believed and effective – both in directing behaviour and in offering meaning and hope, particularly to the majority of the population for whom life was all too often mean, cruel and repetitive. The onset of modernity precipitated noticeable change:

> One eighteenth-century game-keeper, living in Fernditch Lodge on Cranborne Chase, Dorset, said that he had heard the parson talk about 'a place called Paradise'. 'By the account he gave of it, it seemed to be a desperate pleasant place … but when I had considered everything, I made up my mind to believe, and I do now believe, notwithstanding what the parson said, that if there was but a good trout-stream running down Chicken Grove Bottom, Fernditch Lodge would beat it out and out.'
>
> Others found the prospect of future bliss intimidating. An Elizabethan preacher promised the inhabitants of Wilton, near

Salisbury, that 'to live in Heaven together is better than to live in Wilton together'. But an old lady on her sickbed, near Lewes, Sussex, was not so sure; when a well-intentioned neighbour informed her that she would shortly go to heaven to be with God, Jesus Christ, angels, and saints, she answered that 'she had no acquaintance there, she knew nobody there, and therefore she had rather live with her and her other neighbours here than to go thither to live amongst strangers'.[19]

The scepticism is characteristic of the modern world; religion has to add something to this life. The Church was compelled to persuade its followers of the intrinsic merits of living according to its teachings. But, argues Thomas, many people sought fulfilment, satisfaction and meaning to life elsewhere.

Fulfilment was gained through work and vocation. Sir Keith identifies men in particular as finding satisfaction in work and the bonding offered by their workplace. In the period before the industrialization and brutalization of labour, they found meaning and dignity in 'humble' occupations, in jobs well done. People also found satisfaction in wealth and possessions: goods were prized – for themselves, for the esteem they brought with them, for the social relationships they made possible. Families attached importance to the front parlour, the room only used on special occasions, where the furniture and ornaments on display attested to a life of achievement.

Thomas moves on to honour and reputation. 'In early modern England, the desire to secure the favourable opinion of other people was a primary determinant of human behaviour.'[20] The biblical maxim 'tov shem mi'shemen tov, a good name is more valuable than fragrant ointment'[21] springs to mind. Thomas stresses the development of the idea of fulfilment through friendship and the importance attached to 'friends in the modern sense, that is intimate companions, freely chosen, without regard to an ulterior end'.[22] He links this with marriage and children, where children were becoming more than just a means of 'perpetuating the lineage' or an 'investment for old age' but also 'sources of delight and appropriate objects for deep emotional investment'.[23]

Progressive rabbis like me attach considerable importance to the hesped, funeral sermon, and what's said about the deceased at their home in the prayers during the seven days of mourning (*shiva*). We talk to relatives and reflect back how they describe the person who's died. Work, achievements, reputation, family life and friendships are almost invariably central. As too are their acts of compassionate justice and repair – what they did for others to make community, society and the world a better place. Living on through others – children if, by good fortune, there are children – is frequently implied, often expressed. But thoughts of an afterlife are seldom present.

Thomas makes a further point: 'After the Reformation, funeral monuments no longer sought prayers for the soul of the deceased. Their purpose now was not intercession but commemoration.'[24] He identifies the rapid expansion among wealthy families of the seventeenth and eighteenth century in commissioning family portraits and books recording family achievements as an indication of the desire for enduring fame. As Thomas explains, people increasingly wanted, above all else, to be remembered. Immortality may or may not be granted through an afterlife; being remembered was a more assured guarantee of perpetuity. I'm reminded of a trip to Worms in Germany and a visit to one of the few surviving Jewish cemeteries – row after row of small gravestones, humble and modest. One could immediately spot the transition from the medieval to the modern – being Jews, this happened at the beginning of the nineteenth century – for suddenly the gravestones became larger, louder, competitive, each calling out for recognition and remembrance.

Today, the vast majority live their lives as if this life is all we have. Some are driven to get as much pleasure out of it as possible; some to make a difference to the lives of others. Many make the most of satisfying work, family, friends and leisure; many long to be significant, leave a mark, be remembered. Few are motivated by what meriting life after death might demand. Such is the 'modern mind'. It isn't as alien to Judaism as some might claim.

Sitting in synagogue thinking about this, I turned to the Reform Movement's Sabbath and Daily Prayer Book 'Study Anthology' with its extensive section headed 'Life's Journey'.[25] There are several passages on loss and bereavement, a wry poem on ageing and several passages on dying. But nothing on life after death.

The liturgical passage that characterizes the rites of death across the Jewish denominations is *El Malei Rakhamim*, chanted to a plaintive melody. It reads as follows (with a parallel passage for 'her'):

> God full of compassion whose presence is over us, grant perfect rest beneath the shelter of Your presence with the holy and pure on high who shine as the lights of heaven, to _____ who has gone to his everlasting home. Source of mercy, cover him in the shelter of Your wings forever, and bind his soul into the gathering of life.[26] It is God who is his heritage. May he be at peace in his place of rest. Amen.[27]

That's as explicit about the nature of life after death as we get. More we don't know and aren't troubled by our not-knowing. In that respect we resemble Isaiah and Jeremiah – we have other priorities; how we live this life is much, much more important. Which explains why this chapter is the shortest in the book.

SECTION TWO
JEWISH SURVIVAL, MESSIANISM AND THE GOAL OF THE JOURNEY

Where Does the Road Lead?

I began this book by establishing the physicality and metaphor of journey. Judaism begins with Abram and Sarai responding to the call to go, leave; in the face of mortal danger God instructed the Children of Israel *vayisa'u*, go forward. Joshua discovered that the Promised Land wasn't an endpoint but the next stage of the journey. But what is the endpoint? Where are we heading?

From time to time we've thought the end was close, only to be proved disturbingly wrong: 2,700 years on from Micah, it seems further away than ever. As a people, we've experienced just how thankless the journey can be and trudge on, defiantly or wearily concentrating on survival – both in Israel and Diaspora. I try to live in the present, committed to *tikkun* as worldly repair, hoping to patch and mend – if you have no great expectations, you're less likely to be disappointed. When I once said this to Michael Marmot, he pulled me up sharply. 'To what end? What outcome are you working towards? It's important,' he argued, 'to pay attention to process but equally necessary to be clear about outcomes. My goal,' he said, 'is universal equity in health provision. What's yours?'

The Ashkenazi morning service includes the following affirmation:

> *Ani ma'amin b'emunah sh'leimah b'viat ha'mashiakh*
> *V''af al pi she'yitmamei'ah im kol zeh akhakeh lo.*
> I believe with complete faith in the coming of the Messiah
> And even though he tarries, I'll wait for him.[28]

Those familiar words were sung to a new tune by Hasidic Jews, a melody said to echo the rhythm of the cattle trucks on the railway lines taking them to the gas chambers.[29] Reform Jews sing those words, me included. But what do I mean by them? Michael Marmot rightly insists that for me to retreat into despair at the world or, alternatively, into a mystical agnosticism would be a betrayal of the nine preceding chapters. Where does the road lead? What's the end of the journey and the end of life?

The Outrider of the Destination – Elijah

A pregnant moment has fallen victim to paediatric evasions: towards the end of the *Seder*, the children are sent to open the door and Elijah's absence is greeted with self-conscious, deflecting cries about whether they can see him. In fact, there are few customs that better express sharp religious ambiguity than this moment. Elijah is the outrider of the Messiah; we don't expect to greet him in our lifetime but hold the door open to the hope that, one day, the tarrying will finally end.

Judaism is a story with as many ways of telling as there are Jews, populated by innumerable characters. Though some are figures of towering importance, others vivid and memorable, none merits the epithet 'unique' in quite the same way as Elijah. He enters near the beginning of our story, makes periodic appearances and, according to Rabbinic tradition, will announce the final chapter.

His story starts abruptly, in Chapter 17 of the book of Kings: 'Elijah the Tishbite, an inhabitant of Gilead, said to Ahab, "As God lives – the God of Israel whom I serve – there shall be neither dew nor rain these years except at my order."'[30] The drama of Elijah's appearance from nowhere is deliberate, the opening scene electing to characterize him in a particular way – Elijah confronts the king, issuing a fierce and peremptory challenge. The narrator tells us King Ahab was an appalling man, 'worse than all his predecessors',[31] who'd married Jezebel, daughter of the King of Sidon, and proceeded to worship Baal. This first Elijah is a prophet in the mould of the future Literary Prophets, a fearless challenger of political power and corruption.

To demonstrate Ahab's gullibility and infidelity, Elijah then becomes a cultic champion, taking on and defeating the priests of Baal. Here, the prophet has more than just the words of an Isaiah or Jeremiah as weapons at his disposal and is portrayed a man able to play the same game as the exponents of the rival Canaanite cult and beat them. Several chapters later, in 1 Kings 21, the clash between Elijah and Ahab resumes as the prophet confronts the king again, this time with Ahab's murder of vineyard-owner Naboth.

In the midst of these political and cultic battles, we meet a quite different Elijah. In 1 Kings 19, forced to flee from Ahab and Jezebel, he goes into the wilderness and journeys – for 40 days and 40 nights – to Horeb, synonymous with Sinai. There he experiences God in a way that continues to echo Moses. Go out, he is told, and stand on the mountain before God:

> Then God went by. There was a mighty wind, so strong it split the mountains and shattered the rocks before God. But God was not in the wind. After the wind, an earthquake but God was not in the earthquake. After the earthquake – fire. But God was not in the fire. And after the fire – *kol d'mama daka*.[32]

I've left the last three words untranslated because their precise meaning is open to debate. What, in all probability, they don't mean is 'a still small voice', the familiar translation. Instead, they suggest a faint, whispering sound, a breeze, something elusive, something suggestive of religious experience, of Divine Presence: the sound of silence.

In 2 Kings 2 comes a fourth characterization of Elijah. The cycle ends unexpectedly, complementing his sudden appearance, confirming his uniqueness. Elijah hands on the mantle of prophecy to his disciple Elisha and disappears as abruptly as he came: 'Now as they walked, talking as they went, a chariot of fire appeared and horses of fire, coming between the two of them; and Elijah went up to heaven in the whirlwind.'[33] Elijah vanishes, leaving Elisha with his cloak and memories of episodes he will go on to re-enact. Elijah appears mysteriously, challenges power, unmasks the surrounding cult, experiences God not as – in Moses' case – the author of words but as an elusive presence, and is the only person in the entire Tanakh not to die.

Elijah is changed yet again in the book of Malachi, the positioning intentional. Malachi – the name means Messenger – contains a series of 'oracles'. Its author lived around 500 BCE, at a time of great anxiety and reassessment of what it meant to be a Jew. Malachi, who calls for repentance, is placed last in *N'vi'im*, the Prophetic section of the Tanakh. Elijah reappears at the very end of this final Prophetic book. The closing verses read:

> Remember the Torah of Moses my servant, whom I commanded at Horeb on behalf of all Israel [to impart the] statutes and [the] ordinances. See! I am sending Elijah the prophet to you before the coming of the great and terrible day of God. He will reconcile forebears with their descendants and descendants with their forebears. Or else, when I come, I will strike the land with a curse for destruction.[34]

Two things stand out. First, the parallel between Moses and Elijah – their overwhelming experiences of God at Sinai/Horeb – is brought into sharp relief. But, second, the equally important differences. Moses was born in Egypt and died on the brink of the Promised Land; Elijah appeared suddenly, mysteriously and didn't die. Now he's become the last-ditch figure of reconciliation; should he fail, God's judgement will be visited on the People. Here the two seals (verse 22 and verse 23) that close the book of Malachi place the authority of the Torah of Moses and the authority of Prophetic Literature side by side – with Elijah providing the link between the Literary Prophets and their earlier history. Such is the significance of Elijah in this, his second coming.[35]

We meet Elijah, in yet another manifestation, in classical Rabbinic Literature, under the shadow of a destruction that felt ominously like the awesome, fearful day of God and some thought was. Here's an illustrative passage from Tractate Sanhedrin about second-century Rabbi Joshua ben Levi:

> Rabbi Joshua ben Levi met Elijah standing by the entrance to the cave of Rabbi Simeon bar Yohai … Joshua asked Elijah: 'When will the Messiah come?' He said: 'Go and ask him.' 'And where is he to be found?' 'At the gates of the town.' 'And what are his signs?' 'He's sitting among the poor suffering from sores. They remove and remake all their bandages at once, but he removes and remakes his one at a time, thinking: Should I be required, I shall not be delayed.' Rabbi Joshua went there. He said to the Messiah: 'Peace be upon you, my master and teacher.' He said to him: 'Peace be upon you, son of Levi.' He said: 'When will the master come?' He said: 'Today.' Rabbi Joshua went back to Elijah and said to him: 'He lied to me, for he said he would come today, but he hasn't come.' Elijah said to him: 'This is what he said to you: "Today – if you would only listen to His voice!"' (Ps. 95.7).[36]

There's a sense of urgency here; it may suggest the influence of the Christian Messianic tradition: Elijah tells us that the Messiah can be found right now among the most deprived and shunned, outside the walls of the city. Rome – as the Vilna Gaon insisted? Any city? The city *you* live in? What's striking is the sense of imminence – the Kingdom is very close at hand. Yet it's a Rabbinic, qualified imminence: the Messiah will come today – but only if *you* do what is necessary, only if there's reconciliation between generations past and present, only if the ethical and ritual imperatives of Rabbinic Judaism are heard and observed.

The imminence of Elijah's mission then receded. Rabbinic interrogation of the Torah, debate, discussion – and disagreement – continued. Many different interpretations of Torah were accepted and further attempts at reconciling conflicting positions were postponed − *teyku*, let it stand, appears more than three hundred times in the Babylonian Talmud.[37] In time *teyku* came to be read as an acrostic for *tishbi y'taretz kushyot u'va'ayot*, the Tishbite will solve all problems and difficulties; leave it to Elijah to settle, at the onset of the End of Days.

That was probably how Elijah found his place at the *Seder* meal on the first evening of Pesach. Disputes arose over whether to drink four cups of wine or five, settled for practical purposes at four. The fifth was acknowledged − *teyku* − and became known as the cup of Elijah, poured but not drunk. As a result, Elijah became a presence to be welcomed at the *Seder*. The door was opened to show the innocence of the ceremony to the outside world; and also as a sign of longing for the restoration of our freedom − freedom from the terrible reality of prejudice and oppression, freedom from both outer and inner enslavement for us and all peoples. Elijah embodies the hope for a time that's radically different at the end of history, insisting that, despite all evidence to the contrary, human existence can be transformed.

Elijah promises a future for the Jewish people − and for all peoples − *ba'olam hazeh*, in this world, *b'akharit ha'yamim*, at the End of (this life's) Days. Whereas there's diversity and unknowing about individual survival after death, collective survival and renewal at the end of this life is and remains an undying hope and article of faith. We will maintain that hope; we will endure because we have a part to play in the eventual transformation of humanity and the globe. There is a goal, and though its realization is delayed, we must continue the journey towards it; if not us, a future generation will encounter Elijah − in his guise as outrider.

Midwife of the Destination − The Messiah

Messianism is, perhaps, the most distinctive features of Prophetic Literature. Its impact on Rabbinic Judaism and Christianity couldn't possibly be overestimated − nor could the difference in direction in which the two faiths took the vision, with its implications for their relationship.

Messiah is a translation of the Hebrew word *mashiakh*, anointed one. The word itself is rarely used in Prophetic Literature but the concept is clear: a descendant of King David – whose coronation was marked by anointing with oil[38] – will appear; the restoration of the Davidic line will usher in an age in which Israel is restored to its former independence, taking its rightful place among the nations of the world. That's particularistic but the Prophetic vision is anything but.

Almost all the Prophetic books, both major and minor, contain 'messianic' texts. They're not always consistent or even compatible – and some are disturbing – but they provide the different elements from which subsequent theology is derived. I want to work with three texts, personally meaningful and vital to a contemporary messianism.

Transformation

My starting point is the opening of Isaiah 11, quoted in Chapter 7. The concept of Messiah – which began as the anointed descendant of King David – has developed much further. Here the Messiah will embody the values understood by the Prophets as God's values and, vindicating the rights of the poor, lead the world to justice. The Messiah has become midwife to the End of Days.

Now comes an inspiring yet sobering dimension:

> The wolf will live with the lamb,
> the leopard lie down with the kid;
> the calf, the beast of prey, and the fatling together,
> with a little boy to herd them.
> The cow and the bear will graze,
> their young will lie down together;
> and the lion, like the ox, will eat straw.
> A baby will play
> over a viper's hole,
> and an infant wave his hand
> over an adder's den.
> In all My holy land
> nothing evil or vile will be done;
> for the land will be filled with devotion to God

as water covers the sea.[39]

Total change. It's a vision of a far different time, one that demands the most far-reaching of transformations – to the very nature of Nature. For me, this sudden realization stops me in my tracks: I can see the road at my feet and immediately ahead but then it disappears into uncertainty long before the ultimate goal.

The End of Days

A second passage, equally characteristic, comes from Micah[40] and is repeated in Isaiah.[41] It's that spell-binding glimpse of the End of Days quoted in full in Chapter 7 when swords will be turned into ploughshares and each person will sit unthreatened under their vine and fig tree.

Micah lived at the end of the eighth century BCE, during the reign of King Hezekiah, witnessing at first hand the disastrous attacks made by the Assyrians. He was a contemporary of both Amos and the first of the authors known as Isaiah[42] – this was a period rich in religious genius as well as existential threat. The passage was composed under the spectre of national annihilation but, crucial to Judaism, offers a vision of hope. The journey of the Jewish people wasn't seen as leading directly to glory, nor even as indicative of inexorable progress; but it has an end point, a destination, a goal – for us and all people. It's compelling that, from its very beginnings, both in the face of impending disaster and in the midst of actual catastrophe, Judaism offered a vision of hope, to be realized, at the End of Days, in this world, not in a world to come.

Micah continues:

> Though all the peoples walk
> Each in the names of its gods,
> We will walk
> In the name of *Yud-Heh-Vav-Heh*, our God
> Forever and ever.

Perhaps Micah was of the view, implied by one translator's omission of a capital letter at the end of the second line,[43] that only our God is the true God. But that's not how I read the text and, whatever the reservations, the verse is a major advance on obtusely insisting that everyone must accept our God as the only God. It also prefigures the great step forward taken by the book of Jonah in revealing God as the God of all humanity. From there, it isn't so far to the realization that people experience God through their particular narrative, the Face they encounter – each providing an intimation of the Unnameable, the Without End, the One Who wills us all to build the world of justice, peace and mutual respect envisaged by Micah.

There's something else equally noteworthy about the text – it doesn't focus on a Messiah, a person, but on what we've come to call the Messianic Age. That time will come about, we're assured, but whether there will be a midwife is left open. The Prophets – not just Micah and First Isaiah but the body of literature known as the Literary Prophets – provide us with a 'motley',[44] a colourful patchwork of visions of the End of Days, of a world that is finally mended, a life and environment no longer unjust, fractured, filled with pain and suffering. Jewish messianism, though far from uniform, is characterized by unquenchable hope for this world.

National restoration
The third Prophetic Text will be familiar (not least from American spirituals) but is different again and comes from Ezekiel:

> Thus said God to these bones … I will put breath into you, and you shall live again … these bones are the whole House of Israel. They say, 'Our bones are dried up, our hope is gone; we are doomed' … I will put my breath into you … and I will set you upon your own soil.[45]

This isn't a prophecy of posthumous resurrection; it's a vision of the revival of the Jewish People, the assurance a remnant will experience national restoration at the end of history. Individual survival has rarely been uppermost in the Jewish theological mind but group survival – that's different both traditionally and personally. What stitches together so many of the vivid and colourful Prophetic texts is an abiding concern for the survival of the Jewish people: so many have been or will be lost, but a remnant will remain.

There have long been those ready to dismiss such 'particularism' as flawed, a primitive stage before a mature universalism – but they miss the point: the vision is not of survival at the expense of others or of self-serving national triumph. It's a statement that, whatever the fate of the individual and the cruel vicissitudes of Jewish history, the Jewish people – with its particular experience of God – can play a role (not exclusively but indispensably) in the transformation of this world into what its Creator hoped it would become for all peoples.

Prophetic Literature offers us both a personal Messiah and a Messianic Age. Rabbinic tradition favoured the personal Messiah, filled with wisdom and respect for God but not himself God, not the Christian Messiah.

That text in which Elijah declares the Messiah is waiting at the gates of our city is characteristically Rabbinic but of the same mind-set as the early Church. I'm drawn to a more wary approach, later becoming the norm but one that may well pre-date Joshua ben Levi as well. It's expressed in a story about Yokhanan ben Zakkai, a one-off figure from the time of the Roman assault on Jerusalem, who was in favour of suing for peace. In a laconic text, ben Zakkai says that if you're planting a sapling in your garden (for future generations) and hear shouts that the Messiah has come, finish off planting before you go out to see what all the fuss is about.[46] Between the ben Levi and ben Zakkai texts there's a clear difference regarding the timing of the coming of the Messiah and the Messianic Age, but it's a difference only of timing – between imminence and tarrying. A millennium later, Maimonides' twelfth principle affirmed the doctrine of the Messiah; a thousand years further on, the *Havdalah* ritual – across all Jewish denominations – still ends by invoking Elijah.[47] Although the Messiah is self-evidently delayed, we continue to wait.

The overwhelming weight of Progressive Jewish Theology in the nineteenth, twentieth and twenty-first centuries has favoured Messianic Age over Messiah. That's also my personal inclination; as so often, Lionel Blue offered a twinkle-eyed caveat. 'Which', he asked, 'do you think is more probable – human beings transforming the world themselves or needing divine help to do it?' Since I believe in a God who needs humanity and our shared goal depends on a partnership in which we are the actors in this world, I take Rabbi Blue's point about the enormity of the task but not his rhetorical inference. Whatever your view, the road forward disappears into uncertainty long before each person can finally sit un-terrorized under his or her vine and leopards live happily with kids rather than devouring them. But the immediate way forward is visible; daunting but visible.

Immature Enthusiasm

Remarkably, the length of the journey and the extent of the transformation required have seldom deterred Jews, whatever the emphasis of their theology. But it has made us impatient, particularly at times when the world has been at its darkest and our suffering at its most intense. German-born Hebrew University Professor Zvi Werblowski called it 'theological immaturity'.[48]

There's a Rabbinic term, *dekhikat ha-keitz*, which means forcing the End.[49] When Linda and I were first in Jerusalem, we came across a short story by New York Jewish novelist Hugh Nissenson 'In the Reign of Peace'.[50] It's about a simple Jew from Morocco who shows the narrator what he means by the reign of peace – when the Messiah comes – by pointing to a field mouse trapped between two flagstones, eaten alive by black ants: '"Not then." The finger wagged, and I understood. On the flagstone path, under the eucalyptus trees, he had shown me what he expected to be redeemed.'[51]

Nissenson knew his Isaiah, his motley texts and his prophetic vision. Another story, 'Forcing the End', is set in the near-future but this time echoes Rabbi Yokhanan ben Zakkai, his pursuit of peace with the Romans and his messianic scepticism. In Nissenson's story a patient, peace-seeking reincarnation of Yokhanan ben Zakkai is murdered in a battle for Jerusalem which seeks to 'force the end'. Misjudged messianic enthusiasm can have dire consequences.

We've already considered the story in the *Haggadah* of the five Rabbis of the early second century CE whose *Seder* lasted through the night. At that time, Simon bar Koziba, known as Bar Kokhba, Son of a Star, was prepared to take arms against Hadrianic oppression. Some, including Rabbi Akiva, hailed him as Messiah; Bar Kokhba's rebellion was brutally put down. Over subsequent centuries

Jews – like their Christian counterparts – looked for signs of the Messiah and speculated over the date of his coming. More than once this enthusiasm led to hopes raised and dashed, each episode leaving its scars on the People Israel.

As recently as the early 1990s, a rash of car stickers appeared in Jewish areas of New York and London declaring: 'We want Moshiach now.' This time those anticipating the End were Lubavitch Hasidim – with their leader, Rabbi Menachem Mendel Schneerson, as candidate for the position. According to Orthodox Rabbi David Berger in a book *The Rebbe, the Messiah and the Scandal of Orthodox Indifference*,[52] when the Rebbe suffered a severe stroke, many of his followers were convinced he wouldn't die. On his death, not long later, claims were made he was the Messiah and would return. This 'naïve enthusiasm' persists, which, if not scandalous, is far from mainstream.

The more characteristic response of Jews in modern times has been to recognize, implicitly or explicitly, that we are the partner with responsibility for transforming this life. Let me conclude with a passage from Elie Wiesel, from his novel *The Gates of the Forest*,[53] relating the story of Gregor, who survives the Shoah but is deeply affected by the experience. Gregor says to his wife Clara:

> The struggle to survive will begin here, in this room, where we are sitting. Whether or not the Messiah comes doesn't matter; we'll manage without him. It is because it is too late that we are commanded to hope. We shall be honest and humble and strong, and then he will come, he will come every day, thousands of times every day. He will have no face, because he will have a thousand faces. The Messiah isn't one man, Clara, he's all men. As long as there are men there will be a Messiah. One day you'll sing, and he will sing in you.[54]

Such is the affirmation of the great spokesperson for the survivors: it's down to us. We have to manage without the intervention of a personal Messiah because we've misunderstood who the Messiah will be; we've been too literal in the reading of our tradition – an easy mistake to make when you're desperate.

Messianic Not Utopian

Prophetic Literature is dramatic and committed; it's also subtle, sophisticated and metaphorical. Hitherto, I've used the word 'visionary' – which isn't inaccurate but is open to misunderstanding. What characterizes the Literary Prophets is their use both of specific examples to vocalize overarching ethical values and metaphor to go where the literal would betray the vision. Prophetic metaphor takes us as far as we can go in pursuit of that which can't be named or captured – be it the End of Days or God.

Jews have clung to the messianic metaphor. At times we've become frustrated by the delay and tried to force the end; at other times, we've despaired of ever seeing its realization. Some – like Karl Marx – have secularized the vision and, in so doing, highlighted a clear distinction. John Gray's dystopian portrayal of *homo rapiens* rather than *Homo sapiens* directs his wrath against (Christian and Humanist) utopianism.[55] Although the English term was first coined by Sir Thomas More in the early sixteenth century, the universally acknowledged source of the concept is Plato. Both in *The Republic* and *The Laws*, Plato describes in detail the ideal city – its governance, laws, political structure, make-up of its population – as well as discussing pros and cons for each component of the ideal. All utopian visions – those of Plato, More, Hegel, Marx and the many others who've attempted to describe the ideal world – share a common feature. Utopianism is defined by concrete plans, detailed blueprints of what constitutes the perfect society, accompanied by strategies for their achievement and even necessary tactics for the campaign. Its hubris restricts the values it proclaims. Such planning, argued Karl Popper, is the enemy of freedom, the pursuit of which takes us back to the paradigmatic beginning of the Jewish journey.[56]

Prophetic messianism is different. Its End can only be approached through metaphor, evoked in images, suggested by but not spelled out in words, which recognize our limitations. The End of Days defies blueprints and architects' plans. It will be a space at the end of time where each human being can sit, as it were, under their vine and fig tree unthreatened; where no one feels humiliated or oppressed, where mutual respect and tolerance hold sway, compassionate justice reigns, each person is treated as equally precious in non-monetary terms – and everyone has equal access to health provision.

The End is too vulnerable to human pride to be definable, rendered a Tower of Babel constructed by political philosophy. But there are metaphors and hints enough to keep us walking, limping along the road – visible beneath our feet, disappearing in the distance – that leads to the End of Days. Whether or not we get there as individuals is unimportant. What matters is the survival of the People Israel, since the tradition we bear is integral to the human vision. Can we be sure of its realization? No. Are we compelled to hope – and act on that hope? Yes.

Glossary

This glossary is a guide to Hebrew and Yiddish terms used. It isn't comprehensive – terms appearing only once are usually translated or explained in the body of the text.

My starting point for transliteration is the system adopted by the *Encyclopaedia Judaica* but I often depart to give precedence to aiding pronunciation over reflecting Hebrew grammar. I have avoided italicizing Hebrew (and other foreign words) if the word appears in the English dictionary un–italicized. However, there will be inconsistencies – for instance as some festivals are already 'English' words, I've left all festivals un–italicized. I've struggled with which words to capitalize since Hebrew doesn't have capital letters, but I've followed my sense of English usage.

Some terms below are grouped thematically rather than in strict alphabetical order.

Aggadah: The dimension of classical Rabbinic Literature that deals with homiletics, ethics, theology.

Aggadic: Relating to homiletic, ethical, theological literature.

Aliyah: Literally 'going up'. Specifically: two 'waves' of resettlement of Palestine before the First World War. Generally: 'making aliyah', going to live in Israel.

Apocrypha: Books from the late biblical period not included in the canon.

Bar/bat mitzvah (pl. *b'nei/b'not mitzvah*): Literally son/daughter of obligation/command. Reaching the legal age of majority (and the accompanying celebration) and assuming full responsibility for Jewish living.

CALENDAR: Occasions referred to in the text of this book, here given in sequence:

Shabbat (pl. *Shabbatot*)★ (Sabbath): Weekly. All days in the Jewish calendar begin in the evening, so Shabbat begins at sunset on Friday night (Erev Shabbat, eve of the Sabbath) with the ceremony of **Kiddush** and ends, 25 hours later, at nightfall on Saturday, with the ceremony of **Havdalah**.

Rosh Hashanah★ (Literally 'Head of the Year'): Judaism's New Year, marking the beginning of the annual cycle of the religious year. It begins ten days of prayer, introspection and self-evaluation. Early autumn.

Yom Kippur★ (Day of Atonement): Ten days after Rosh Hashanah. A 25-hour fast, much of which is spent in synagogue. The evening service is called **Kol Nidrei** (literally 'all vows') from the opening words of a petition asking for forgiveness for undertakings given in vain.

Sukkot★ (Tabernacles): Seven-day festival beginning five days after Yom Kippur.

Simkhat Torah★ (Rejoicing the Torah): Day after end of Sukkot, marking the end and beginning of the annual cycle of Torah readings.

Hanukkah (Dedication): Mid-winter. Recalls the re-dedication of the Temple by the Maccabees after Greek desecration.

Tu BiSh'vat: Fifteenth of the month of Sh'vat, the New Year for trees, marking the annual renewal of the natural world. January/ February.

Purim (Lots): Late winter. Story of Esther.

Pesach★ (Passover): Spring. Liberation from Egyptian slavery. *Seder*: narration of the Exodus story from the **Haggadah** with an integral meal on the first evening of Pesach.

Shavuot★ (Pentecost): Late spring. Revelation at Sinai.

Tisha b'Av: Fast on the ninth of the month of Av, recalling the major catastrophes of Jewish history. July/August.

Yom Ha'atzmaut (Israel Independence Day): April/May.

★ Days on which Jewish tradition prescribes rest from work/school.

Calendar Years: This book follows Christian usage but replaces BC with BCE (before the Common Era) and CE (Common Era).

DENOMINATIONS (British):

Liberal Judaism Formerly Jewish Religious Union, then Union of Liberal and Progressive Synagogues. Founding synagogue: Liberal Jewish Synagogue (St John's Wood, 1911).

Masorti (Traditional) Founding synagogue: New London Synagogue (St John's Wood, 1964).

Movement for Reform Judaism Formerly, Reform Synagogues of Great Britain. Founding synagogue: West London Synagogue (Marble Arch, 1840).

Sephardi (Spanish and Portuguese) **Community** Founding synagogue: Bevis Marks (built 1701).

United Synagogue (mainstream Orthodox) Founded London 1870, bringing together three Ashkenazi synagogues.

Eretz Yisrael: Land of Israel.

Genizah: Storeroom in Ben Ezra Synagogue, Cairo, where a vast number of Hebrew documents from centuries of Jewish life were found

Halakhah: Jewish law.

Halakhic: That dimension of classical Rabbinic Literature relating to Jewish law, practice, observance.

Hanukkiah (pl. *Hanukkiot*): The eight-branched candelabrum lit at Hanukkah.

Haredi: Literally 'trembling'. Term for the Ultra-Orthodox community.

Haskalah: Enlightenment. Often used to refer to its spread to Eastern Europe.

Hebrew Bible (Tanakh): Largely what Christianity terms Old Testament – there are minor discrepancies, particularly over the order of the books. Called in Hebrew *Tanakh*, the acronym for its three parts: *Torah* (the five books of Moses, Genesis to Deuteronomy), *N'vi'im* (Prophets); *K'tuvim* (Writings).

Heim: Eastern Europe, described with affection and nostalgia as in *heimishe*, homely, home-style.

Hurban: That which has been put to the sword; destruction.

Hutzpah: Bare-faced cheek, nerve.

LITURGY

Amidah: Standing Prayer consisting of 19 blessings.

Sh'ma: Three paragraphs from the Torah: Deut. 6.4–9; 11.13–21; Num. 15.37–41.

Kaddish: Doxology (praise of God) recited in memory of the dead.

Siddur: Sabbath and daily prayer book.

Makher: Yiddish from the German 'a doer': important person in the community, often used ironically.

Mizrahi: Jews from Arab lands.

Mensch: German for man but, in Yiddish, a person of kindness and integrity.

Mitzvah (pl. **mitzvot**): Commandment, obligation (used in Yiddish as both an honour in the service and a kind act).

Pharisees: Political party/school of thought out of which Rabbinic Judaism emerged. Vied with the **Saducees**, considered the party of the priestly class and its supporters.

RABBINIC COLLEGES:

Jews' College (United Synagogue), now closed.

Leo Baeck College (Reform, Liberal and Masorti), London.

Hebrew Union College (HUC), American Reform, four campuses in Cincinnati, New York, Los Angeles and Jerusalem.

Jewish Theological Seminary (JTS), American Conservative, New York.

RABBINIC LITERATURE (used in the book and cited):

Mishnah: Oral teachings codified under the supervision of Judah HaNasi, Judea c.200 CE.

Talmud: There are two – **Babylonian**, **Bavli** (BT in endnotes) and **Jerusalem**, **Yerushalmi**. During the years 200 CE to c.450 CE the **Mishnah** was analysed and discussed passage by passage. A process of redaction then began in which these oral debates, called **G'mara**, were assembled in carefully selected and constructed literary form, resulting in the many tractates of the **Talmud**.

Tosefta: Texts from the Mishnaic period not included in the Mishnah.

Midrash: Rabbinic commentary and analysis of the Torah.

Midrashim (pl.) appear widely in the Talmud and also in independent collections – some predominantly for the purpose of formulating practice (halakhic midrash), some predominantly for ethical and theological purposes (aggadic midrash). The various compilations contain earlier material.

First and second century:

Sifra: Halakhic midrash on Leviticus.

Sifre: Halakhic midrash on Deuteronomy.

Mekhilta de-Rabbi Ishmael: Halakhic midrash on Exodus.

Fifth to mid-seventh century:

Genesis and **Lamentations Rabbah:** Aggadic midrash.

Tankhuma: Aggadic midrash.

Pesikta de-Rav Kahana: Aggadic midrash.

Mid-seventh to ninth century:

Ecclesiastes Rabbah: Aggadic midrash.

Pesikta Rabbati: Aggadic midrash.

Tanna Devei Eliyahu (Seder Eliyahu Rabbah and **Zuta)**: Two books: narrative and theological account of history.

Avot de-Rabbi Natan: Aggadic commentary on **Pirkei Avot**, a tractate of the Mishnah.

Pirkei de-Rabbi Eliezer: Aggadic midrash.

Tenth century or later:

Exodus and **Numbers Rabbah**: Aggadic midrash.

Lamentations Zuta: Aggadic midrash.

Midrash on Psalms: Aggadic midrash.

Sefer Torah (pl. *Sifrei Torah*): The Scroll (literally book/books of the Torah).

Shoah: Destruction. Preferred Jewish term for the Holocaust (a Holocaust was a burnt offering and carries theologically problematic sacrificial overtones).

Shtetl (pl. *shtetlakh*): A (predominantly) Jewish village in Eastern Europe.

Shulkhan Arukh: Literally a 'Table Prepared'. Sixteenth-century codification of Jewish law – the first printed – by Sephardi Rabbi Joseph Caro in Safed. It always appears with an Ashkenazi corrective, *Mappah* meaning tablecloth supplied by Rabbi Moses Isserles of Krakow, recognizing where Ashkenazi practice differed.

Sitzfleisch: Literally the ability to 'sit on one's bottom' and therefore to stay in one place for any length of time.

S'mikhah: Rabbinic ordination, the term deriving from Moses' laying on of hands to pass on leadership to Joshua. Earned after a considerable period of study, the contents of which vary according to denomination.

Synagogue: Greek-derived word for buildings used for study, prayer and meeting. Possible origins in BCE Babylon; key to the development of Rabbinic Judaism in Judea. Hebrew terms: ***bet midrash*** (study), ***bet t'fillah*** (prayer), ***bet k'nesset*** (assembly). The Yiddish term ***shul*** is widely used.

Tetragrammaton: Four-letter Hebrew word (***Yud-Heh-Vav-Heh***) for God, which Jews do not pronounce – replacing it with ***Adonai*** (Lord). It gave rise to Jehovah in the past and, among Bible scholars today, Yahweh. All are agreed it has to do with 'being'.

T'fillin: Small leather boxes containing the *Sh'ma*, strapped to the forehead and arm during morning prayers (phylacteries).

Torah: Literally 'teaching' and not 'law', as the word is frequently but erroneously translated. The scroll containing the first five books of the Bible. Heb: ***Sefer Torah*** (pl. ***Sifrei Torah***). In services it is often chanted, **leyned**, hence **leyning**, with tropes for different occasions.

Ulpan: Israeli educational network of schools/classes for teaching immigrants Hebrew.

Yeshivah (pl. ***Yeshivot***): Place of higher rabbinic learning, originating in Eastern Europe.

Yishuv: Term for the returning Jewish community before 1948.

Zohar: Kabbalistic commentary on Torah by Moses de Leon, Spain, late thirteenth century.

Jewish thinkers contributing to this book

Rachel Adler	Feminist Theologian b. Chicago, IL 1943
Ahad Ha'am (Asher Ginsberg)	Zionist Theoretician b. Skvyra, Russian Empire 1856, d. Tel Aviv 1927
Hannah Arendt	Philosopher, Political Theorist b. Hannover 1906, d. New York 1975
Leo Baeck	Rabbinic Leader, Theologian b. Lissa, Germany 1873, d. London 1956
Zigmunt Bauman	Sociologist b. Poznan, Poland 1925, d. Leeds, UK 2017
Gary Becker	Economist b. Pennsylvania, 1930, d. Chicago 2014
David Ben-Gurion (David Grün)	First Prime Minister of Israel b. Plonsk, Russian Empire 1886, d. Ramat Gan, Israel 1973
Walter Benjamin	Literary Critic, Philosopher b. Berlin 1892, d. Portbou, Spain 1940
Miriam Berger	Rabbi, Innovator, Compassionate Justice Activist b. Chertsey, Surrey 1979
Eliezer Berkovits	Rabbi, Theologian b. Oradea, Romania 1908, d. Jerusalem 1992
Isaiah Berlin	Political Philosopher b. Riga, Russian Empire 1909, d. Oxford 1997
Leonard Bernstein	Composer b. Lawrence, MA, 1918, d. New York 1990
David Biale	Historian b. Los Angeles 1949

Hayim Nahman Bialik — Poet b. Zhitomir, Russian Empire 1873, d. Vienna 1934

Lionel Blue — Rabbi, Liturgist, Writer, Broadcaster b. Hackney, London 1930, d. Finchley, London 2016

Eugene Borowitz — Rabbinic Scholar, Theologian b. Columbus, OH 1924, d. Stamford, CT 2016

Martin Buber — Existentialist Philosopher b. Vienna 1878, d. Jerusalem 1965

Judith Butler — Philosopher b. Cleveland, OH 1956

René Cassin — Human Rights Jurist b. Bayonne, France 1887, d. Paris 1976

Stanley Cavell — Philosopher b. Atlanta, GA 1926, d. Boston, MA 2018

Arthur A. Cohen — Writer, Publisher and Theologian b. New York 1928, d. New York 1986

Hermann Cohen — Philosopher b. Coswig, Germany 1842, d. Berlin 1918

Shaye J. D. Cohen — Professor of Hebrew Literature and Philosophy b. USA 1958

Dan Cohn-Sherbok — Rabbi, Professor of Judaism b. Denver, CO 1945

Howard Cooper — Rabbinic Scholar, Psychotherapist b. Manchester 1953

Ned Curthoys — Literary Critic and Intellectual Historian b. Sydney 1974

Jacques Derrida — Philosopher b. El Biar, Algeria 1930, d. Paris 2004

Colin Eimer — Rabbinic Scholar, Grammarian b. London 1945

Albert Einstein — Theoretical Physicist b. Ulm, Germany 1879, d. Princeton, NJ 1955

Arnold Eisen — Chancellor, Jewish Theological Seminary b. Philadelphia 1951

David Ellenson	Rabbi, Professor of Jewish Religious Thought, Chancellor Emeritus of Hebrew Union College b. Brookline, MA 1947
Emil Fackenheim	Philosopher b. Halle, Germany 1916, d. Jerusalem 2003
Sigmund Freud	Founder of Psychoanalysis b. Moravia, Austro-Hungarian Empire 1856, d. Hampstead, London 1939
Albert Friedlander	Rabbinic Scholar, Theologian b. Berlin 1927, d. Knightsbridge, London 2004
Erich Fromm	Psychoanalyst, Humanistic Philosopher b. Frankfurt 1900, d. Locarno, Switzerland 1980
Martin Gilbert	Historian b. London 1936, d. London 2015
Andrew Goldstein	Rabbi, Historian, Liturgist b. Warwick 1943
Martin Goodman	Historian, b. London 1953
Michael Goulston	Rabbi, Theologian, Educator b. London 1931, d. London 1972
Irving (Yitz) Greenberg	Modern Orthodox Rabbi and Scholar b. Brooklyn, New York 1933
Wendy Greengross	Physician, Counsellor b. Golders Green, London 1925, d. Finchley, London 2012
Hugo Gryn	Rabbinic Leader, Broadcaster b. Carpathian Ruthenia (now Czech Republic) 1930, d. Marble Arch, London 1996
Judah Halevi	Poet, Philosopher b. Tudela, Spain c.1075, d. Egypt 1141
Yuval Noah Harari	Historian, b. Kiryat Ata, Israel 1976
David Hartman	Rabbi, Theologian b. Brooklyn, New York 1931, d. Jerusalem 2013

Will Herberg	Rabbi, Theologian b. Lyakhavichy nr Minsk, Russian Empire 1901, d. New Jersey 1977
Theodore Herzl	Journalist, Zionist Theoretician b. Pest, Austro-Hungarian Empire 1860, d. Lower Austria 1904
Abraham Joshua Heschel	Rabbinic Scholar, Theologian b. Warsaw 1907, d. New York 1972
Susannah Heschel	Jewish Scholar b. USA 1956
Moses Hess	Zionist Theoretician b. Bonn 1812, d. Paris 1875
Samson Raphael Hirsch	Rabbinic Scholar b. Hamburg 1808, d. Frankfurt 1888
Abraham ibn Ezra	Philosopher, Exegete and Wandering Rabbinic Scholar b. Tudela, Navarre (then under Muslim rule), 1089, d. (place unknown) 1164
Moses Isserles	Ashkenazi Rabbinic Authority b. Kracow 1530, d. Kracow 1572
Louis Jacobs	Rabbinic Scholar b. Manchester 1920, d. St. John's Wood, London 2006
Hans Jonas	Philosopher b. Mönchengladbach 1903, d. New Rochelle, NY 1993
Franz Kafka	Writer b. Prague 1883, d. Kierling, Lower Austria 1924
Daniel Kahneman	Psychologist, Economist b. Tel Aviv 1934
Deborah Kahn-Harris	Rabbinic Scholar, Principal, Leo Baeck College b. Tulsa, OK 1968
Mordecai Kaplan	Rabbinic Scholar b. Lithuania, Russian Empire 1881, d. New York 1983
Abraham Isaac Kook	Rabbinic Scholar b. Greva, Latvia, Russian Empire 1865, d. Jerusalem 1935
Thomas Kuhn	Philosopher of Science b. Cincinnati, OH 1922, d. Cambridge, MA, 1996
Emma Lazarus	Author, Poet and Activist b. New York 1849, d. New York 1887

Michael Leigh	Rabbinic Scholar b. London 1928, d. London 2000
Levi Yitzhak of Berditchev	Founder of Hasidic Dynasty b. Hussakov, Polish-Lithuanian Commonwealth c.1740, d. Berditchev, Russian Empire 1809
Emmanuel Levinas	Philosopher b. Kovno, Lithuania, Russian Empire 1905, d. Paris 1995
Ellen Littmann	Bible Teacher b. Danzig 1900, d. London 1975
Isaac Luria	Kabbalist b. Jerusalem 1534, d. Safed 1572
Jonathan Magonet	Former Principal Leo Baeck College, Bible Scholar, Liturgist b. London 1942
Moses ben Maimon (Rambam, Maimonides)	Philosopher b. Cordova, Almoravid Empire 1135, d. Fustat, Egypt 1204
Jacob Mann	Rabbinic Scholar, Genizah Authority b. Przemysl, Austro-Hungarian Empire 1885, d. Cincinnati, OH 1940
Michael Marmot	Professor of Public Health, Authority on Social Determinants of Health b. London 1945
Dow Marmur	Rabbinic Scholar, Theologian, Zionist Theoretician b. Sosnowiec, Poland 1935
Karl Marx	Philosopher b. Trier, Germany 1818, d. London 1883
Ignaz Maybaum	Rabbinic Scholar, Theologian b. Vienna 1897, d. Edgware, London 1976
Moses Mendelssohn	Philosopher b. Dessau, Germany 1729, d. Berlin 1786
Charles H. Middleburgh	Rabbinic Scholar, Dean, Leo Baeck College b. Hove 1956
David Miliband	Politician b. London 1965
Alan Miller	Reconstructionist Rabbinic Leader, Psychoanalyst b. Hull 1926, d. New York 2016
Edwin Montagu	Politician b. London 1879, d. London 1924

Moses ben Nachman (Nachmanides)	Philosopher b. Gerona, Aragon 1194, d. Acre, Kingdom of Jerusalem 1270
Thomas Nagel	Philosopher b. Belgrade 1937
Jeffrey Newman	Rabbinic Scholar, Campaigner for Environmental Issues b. Reading, Berks. 1941
Robert Nozick	Philosopher b. Brooklyn 1938, d. Cambridge, MA 2002
Amos Oz	Writer b. Jerusalem 1939, d. Tel Aviv 2018
Jacob Petuchowski	Liturgist b. Berlin 1925, d. Cincinnati, OH 1991
Philo	Philosopher c.20 BCE to c.50 CE Alexandria
Steven Pinker	Psychologist b. Montreal 1954
Leon Pinsker	Zionist Theoretician b. Tomaszow Lubelski, Russian Poland 1821, d. Odessa, Russian Empire 1891
Diana Pinto	Intellectual Historian b. USA 1949
Judith Plaskow	Feminist scholar b. Brooklyn, New York 1947
Karl Popper	Philosopher of Science b. Vienna 1902, d. Croydon, South London 1994
Marcel Proust	Writer b. Paris 1871, d. Paris 1922
Leon Radzinowicz	Criminologist b. Lodz, Russian Empire 1906, d. USA (buried Cambridge, UK) 1999
Rashi (Rabbi Shlomo ben Yitzahak)	Rabbinic Commentator b. Troyes, France 1040, d. Troyes, France 1105
John Rayner	Rabbinic Scholar, Liturgist b. Berlin 1924, d. London 2005
Franz Rosenzweig	Philosopher b. Kassel, Germany 1886, d. Frankfurt 1929
Mark Rothko (Markus Rothkowitz)	Abstract Expressionist painter of the human condition b. Dvinsk, Latvia 1903, d. New York 1970
Walter Lionel Rothschild	Zionist Leader, Politician b. London 1868, d. Tring Park, Bucks. 1937

Richard Rubenstein	Theologian b. New York 1924
Jeffrey Sachs	Economist, International Development Authority b. Detroit, MI 1954
Jonathan Sacks	Former Chief Rabbi, Rabbinic Scholar and Writer b. Lambeth, London 1948
Herbert Samuel	Politician b. Toxteth, Liverpool 1870, d. London 1963
Michael Sandel	Political Philosopher b. Minneapolis, MN 1953
Marc Saperstein	Rabbinic Scholar, Homiletics Historian, b. Brooklyn, New York 1944
Elli Tikvah Sarah	Rabbinic Scholar, Feminist Theoretician b. South Shields, Co. Durham 1955
Simon Schama	Historian b. Marylebone, London 1945
Gershon Scholem	Scholar of Kabbalah b. Berlin 1897, d. Jerusalem 1982
Harold Schulweiss	Rabbinic Scholar b. Bronx 1925, d. Encino, CA 2014
Ari Shavit	Political Commentator, Writer b. Rehovot, Israel 1957
Byron Sherwin	Rabbinic Scholar b. New York 1946, d. Chicago, IL 2015
Sheila Shulman	Rabbinic Scholar, Feminist Theoretician b. Brooklyn, New York 1936, d. Kensington, London 2014
Awraham Soetendorp	Rabbinic Scholar, Campaigner for the Environment b. Amsterdam 1943
Baruch Spinoza	Philosopher b. Amsterdam 1632, d. The Hague 1677
George Steiner	Essayist, Literary Critic b. Neuilly-sur-Seine 1929
Sigmund Sternberg	Community Leader, b. Budapest 1921, d. Kenwood, London 2016
Vilna Gaon (Elijah ben Solomon)	Talmudist, Mitnagdic Leader b. Sialiec, Polish-Lithuanian Commonwealth 1720, d. Vilna 1798

Michael Walzer

Rabbinic Scholar, Political Theorist
b. New York 1935

Chaim Weizmann

Chemist, First President of Israel
b. Motel, nr Pinsk, Russian Empire
1874, d. Rehovot, Israel 1952

Elie Wiesel

Writer, Peace Activist b. Sighet,
Transylvania 1928, d. New York 2016

Zvi Werblowski

Scholar of Comparative Religion
b. Frankfurt 1924, d. Jerusalem 2015

Jonathan Wittenberg

Rabbinic Scholar, Theologian
b. Glasgow 1957

Ludwig Wittgenstein

Philosopher, b. Vienna 1887,
d. Cambridge, UK 1951

Notes

PREFACE

1   I refer to 'Jew, Christian, Muslim' because, as we'll see in Chapter 2, the three Abrahamic Faiths are integral to the formation of modern Western culture. The presence of religions from the Indian sub-continent and the Far East today enriches the contemporary dialogue. Hopefully, what this book has to say will be of interest to their adherents living in post-modern Western society.

2   These terms are defined in Ch. 2, pp. 46-7.

PART I

1   Lionel Blue (1975), *To Heaven with Scribes and Pharisees*. London: Darton, Longman and Todd, p. 23.

CHAPTER ONE

1   Simon Schama (2013), *The Story of the Jews: Finding the Words 1000 BCE–1492 CE*. London: The Bodley Head.

2   Amos Oz (2005), *A Tale of Love and Darkness*. London: Vintage Books.

3   UK (not US) pronunciation for routed – as in routes, roads, journeys.

4   Gen. 12.1–5. Abraham and Sarah are Abram and Sarai until the covenant, symbolized by circumcision, in Gen. 17.

5   Genesis Rabbah 39.2.

6   Exod. 14.15.

7   Rashi on Exod. 40.38.

8   Gen. 19.26.

9   Thomas S. Kuhn (1962), *The Structure of Scientific Revolutions*. Chicago: University of Chicago Press (4th edn. 2012). See 'The Nature and Necessity of Scientific Revolutions', pp. 92–110.

10   The importance of the Land in Judaism is explored in Ch. 4, especially pp. 129-33.

11 Byron, *The Destruction of Sennacherib* (1815), st.1.

12 Ps. 137.1.

13 Ps. 137.4.

14 Jer. 29.5–7.

15 Exod. 12.24–28 and 23.14–17.

16 Franz Kafka (1961), *Parables and Paradoxes*. New York: Schocken Books, p. 189.

17 The Hebrew is *Yam Suf*, Sea of *Reeds*, not Sea of *Red*.

18 *Vayisa'u*, go forward, Exod. 14.15. I have combined Mekhilta de-Rabbi Ishmael B'Shalakh 4 and 6 with BT Sotah 37a.

19 Revered second-century Rabbi.

20 Contemporary of Rabbi Meir.

21 Referred to in Exod. 6.23 as Aaron's brother-in-law.

22 Mekhilta de-Rabbi Ishmael B'Shalakh 6.34.

23 See Ch. 7, pp. 205-12 for Prophetic Ethics.

24 2 Sam. 7.

25 1 Kings 17ff.

26 The point at which 'Israelite/Hebrew religion' becomes 'Judaism' is debatable; this may be an anachronism but I think it is excusable in a book of theology.

27 See Ch. 7, pp. 206-9.

28 Jer. 29.4ff.

29 See Ch. 5, pp. 142–55 for the Dual Torah. Term taken from Jacob Neusner (1990), *Torah Through the Ages*. London: SCM.

30 See Ch. 4, p. 107.

31 For the interrelatedness of the three Abrahamic faiths see Tom Holland (2012), *In the Shadow of the Sword*. London: Little Brown.

32 Avigdor Levy (ed.) (2002), *Jews, Turks, Ottomans: A Shared History, Fifteenth Through the Twentieth Century*. New York: Syracuse University Press, part 1, pp. 3–74.

33 For the important exception of Amsterdam and the Dutch Republic – but also its limitations – see Jonathan I. Israel (1995), *The Dutch Republic: Its Rise, Greatness, and Fall 1477–1806*. Oxford: Clarendon Press.

34 Amos Elon (2003), *The Pity of it All: A Portrait of Jews in Germany 1743–1933*. London: Allen Lane.

35 Ned Curthoys (2013), *The Legacy of Liberal Judaism: Ernst Cassirer and Hannah Arendt's Hidden Conversation*. New York: Berghahn, p. 1.

36 See Charles Taylor (2007), *A Secular Age*. Cambridge, MA: Belknap Press, p. 449.

37 Dow Marmur (1991), *The Star of Return: Judaism after the Holocaust*. West Point, CT: Greenwood Press.

38 Steven Gimbel (2015), *Einstein: His Space and Times*. New Haven: Yale University Press, p. 152.

39 Hawking cited by Hans Küng (2007), *The Beginning of All Things*. Grand Rapids, MI: William B. Eerdmans Publishing, p. 22.

40 Gen. 32.32.

41 Exod. 33.20–23.

42 Lawrence A. Hoffman (1989), *Beyond the Text: A Holistic Approach to Liturgy*. Bloomington: Indiana University Press, pp. 20–45.

43 Explored further in Ch. 4, particularly p. 132.

44 Reference to the mass shooting of Jews in a Pittsburgh synagogue in 2018.

45 Zech. 4.6.

46 Gen. 22.17.

47 Explored further in Ch. 3, pp. 81–5.

48 Explored further in Ch. 3, pp. 98–100.

49 Mekhilta de-Rabbi Ishmael Bakhodesh 5.92–8.

50 See Ch. 9, p. 278.

51 The subject of Chs 8 and 9.

52 The subject of Chs 8 and 9.

53 Deut. 30.19.

54 Rabbi Akiva in Pirkei Avot 3.19.

55 See the conclusion of Ch. 9.

56 Franz Kafka (1973), *Shorter Works*. Vol. 1, London: Secker & Warburg, p. 84.

57 Ezek. 37.

58 Daniel Kahneman (2011), *Thinking, Fast and Slow*. London: Penguin.

59 Janan Ganesh, *Financial Times*, 31 October 2018.

60 BT Eruvin 13b.

61 Tosefta Sotah 7.12.

62 Yerushalmi Sanhedrin 4.2 (22a).

CHAPTER TWO

1 Norman Solomon, 'The Third Presence: Reflections on the Dialogue', in Tony Bayfield and Marcus Braybrooke (eds) (1992), *Dialogue With a Difference: The Manor House Group Experience*. SCM Press, pp. 147–8.

2 Hans Küng (2007), *The Beginning of All Things: Science and Religion*. Grand Rapids, MI: William B. Eerdmans, pp. 5–6.

3 Niall Ferguson (2011), *Civilization: The West and the Rest*, London: Allen Lane.

4 Ibid., pp. 12–13.

5 Charles Taylor (2007), *A Secular Age*. Cambridge, MA: Belknap, Harvard University Press.

6 Ibid., pp. 25–43.

7 Ibid., p. 73.

8 Ezra Pound (1920), *Hugh Selwyn Mauberley*.

9 Taylor, *A Secular Age*, op. cit., p. 524.

10 Isa. 6.3.

11 Melvyn Bragg (2011), *The Book of Books: The Radical Impact of the King James Bible 1611–2011*. London: Sceptre.

12 Lev. 19.18.

13 Ferguson, *Civilization*, op. cit., p. 235.

14 Harry Ostrer (2012), *Legacy: A Genetic History of the Jewish People*, New York: Oxford University Press.

15 A rare autosomal, recessive gene disorder particularly prevalent among Ashkenazi Jews.

16 Michael Marmot, private conversation 2015.

17 Echoing Isa. 53.3.

18 Adam Phillips (2014), *Becoming Freud: The Making of a Psychoanalyst*. New Haven: Yale University Press, p. 20.

19 See Steven T. Katz (1983), *Post-Holocaust Dialogues: Critical Studies in Modern Jewish Thought*. New York: New York University Press, pp. 248–67.

20 Alvin Toffler (1970), *Future Shock*. London: The Bodley Head.

21 Tom Stonier (1983), *The Wealth of Information: A Profile of the Post-Industrial Economy*. London: Methuen.

22 Yuval Noah Harari (2014), *Sapiens: A Brief History of Humankind*. London: Vintage, pp. 445–64.

23 Stephen Hawking (1988), *A Brief History of Time*. London: Bantam, p. 175.

24 Raymond Tallis (2011), *Aping Mankind: Neuromania, Darwinitis and the Misrepresentation of Humanity*. Durham: Acumen Publishing.

25 Stephen Pinker (2018), *Enlightenment Now: The Case for Reason, Science, Humanism and Progress*. London: Allen Lane.

26 In the twelve months after 9/11, four men – two Brits (Richard Dawkins and Christopher Hitchens) and two Americans (Daniel Dennett and Sam Harris) – published books that not only express their atheist convictions but angrily attack religion as the major force for evil and conflict in the world.

27 See Ch. 7, pp. 214-6.

28 John Gray (2003), *Straw Dogs: Thoughts on Humans and Other Animals*. London: Granta Books.

29 Ibid., p. 30.

30 Ibid., p. 7.

31 Ibid., p. 5.

32 Ibid., p. 3.

33 Ibid., p. 12.

34 Ibid., p. 28.

35 Ibid., p. 116.

36 Ibid., p. 90.

37 Ibid., p. 81.

38 Harari, *Sapiens*, op. cit.

39 Ibid., p. 23.

40 Ibid., p. 27.

41 Yuval Noah Harari (2017), *Homo Deus: A Brief History of Tomorrow*. London: Vintage.

42 Yuval Noah Harari (2018), *21 Lessons for the 21st Century*. London: Jonathan Cape.

43 Harari, *Sapiens*, op. cit., p. 458.

44 *Forms of Prayer for Jewish Worship* (1985), Vol. III, *Prayers for the High Holydays*, Eighth Edition, London: Reform Synagogues of Great Britain, p. 500.

45 Bryan Magee (2010), *The Story of Philosophy*. London: Dorling Kindersley, p. 193.

46 Keith Ward (2008), *Why There Almost Certainly Is a God: Doubting Dawkins*. Oxford: Lion, pp. 6–8.

47 Christopher Butler (2002), *Postmodernism: A Very Short Introduction*. Oxford: Oxford University Press, p. 21.

48 See Ch. 5, pp. 138-42.

49 But not religious minorities such as Jews.

50 Bernard-Henri Lévy (2017), *The Genius of Judaism*. New York: Random House, p. 193.

51 See *Jewish Chronicle*, *Jewish News* and *Jewish Telegraph*, 25 July 2018.

52 Bernard-Henri Lévy, op. cit., p. 4.

53 Zohar III 73a.

PART 2

1 Isaiah Berlin (2002), *Liberty*, ed. Henry Hardy. Oxford: Oxford University Press, p. 345.

CHAPTER THREE

1   Jewish communities are self-funded from annual subscriptions paid by each member/family.

2   According to Jonathan Boyd (2003), in *The Sovereign and the Situated Self: Jewish Identity and Community in the 21st Century*. London: Profile Books: 'to the best of my knowledge, it was the British Chief Rabbi, Professor Jonathan Sacks, who coined this phrase in his impassioned attempt to challenge the sociologists' description and the possible policies it implies', pp. 1–2.

3   BT Hagigah 15a.

4   Yerushalmi, Hagigah 77b.

5   Milton Steinberg (1939), *As a Driven Leaf* (1996 edn). New York: Behrman House, p. 250.

6   BT Hagigah 15b.

7   Mishnah Yadayim 4.4.

8   Exod. 12.38.

9   Arthur Koestler (1976), *The Thirteenth Tribe*. London: Hutchinson.

10 Avishai Margalit (2017), *On Betrayal*. Cambridge, MA: Harvard University Press.

11 Ibid., p. 13.

12 Ruth 1.16–17.

13 Leo Baeck (1964), *This People Israel: The Meaning of Jewish Existence*. New York: Holt, Rinehart and Winston.

14 Shaye Cohen, 'The Origins of the Matrilineal Principle in Jewish Law', in *Association for Jewish Studies Review*, Vol. 10, No. 1, spring 1985, pp. 19–53.

15 Louis H. Feldman, 'Palestinian and Diaspora Judaism in the First Century', in Herschel Shanks (ed.) (1993), *Christianity and Rabbinic Judaism: A Parallel History of Their Origins and Early Development*. London: SPCK.

16 Martin Goodman (1994), *Mission and Conversion: Proselytizing in the Religious History of the Roman Empire*. Oxford: Clarendon Press.

17 BT Shabbat 31a.

18 Midrash Tankhuma, Lekh Lekha 6, f.32a.

19 BT Yevamot 47a–47b.

20 BT Ketubot 11a.

21 Shulkhan Arukh, Yoreh Deah 268.7.

22 J. Simcha Cohen (1987), *Intermarriage and Conversion: A Halakhic Solution*. Hoboken, NJ: Ktav, pp. 3–24.

23 Michael Walzer (1983), *Spheres of Justice: A Defense of Pluralism and Equality*. New York: Basic Books, p. xiii.

24 Seder Eliyahu Rabbah IX, cited by Max Kadushin (1972, 3rd edn), *The Rabbinic Mind*. New York: Bloch, p. 52.

25 Judith Plaskow (1991), *Standing Again At Sinai: Judaism from a Feminist Perspective*. New York: HarperSanFrancisco, p. 25.

26 Ibid., p. 89. The emphasis in the phrase is Plaskow's.

27 Susannah Heschel, 'Feminism', in Steven T. Katz (ed.) (1992), *Frontiers of Jewish Thought*. Washington, DC: B'nai B'rith Books, p. 65.

28 Anne J. Kershen and Jonathan A. Romain (1995), *Tradition and Change: A History of Reform Judaism in Britain 1840–1995*. London: Vallentine Mitchell, p. 65. (Manchester Congregation of British Jews, Park Place, 1938).

29 Sally Priesand (1975), *Judaism and the New Woman*, New York: Behrman House, is an important early text.

30 Sybil Sheridan (ed.) (1994), *Hear Our Voice: Women Rabbis Tell Their Stories*. London: SCM Press.

31 Elli Tikvah Sarah (2012), *Trouble-Making Judaism*. London: David Paul.

32 Sheila Shulman (2007), *Waiting for the Morning: Selected Sermons*. London: Peter Daniels.

33 Rachel Adler (1998), *Engendering Judaism: An Inclusive Theology and Ethics*. Philadelphia: Jewish Publication Society.

34 Deborah Kahn-Harris, 'The Inheritance of *Gehinnom*: Feminist Midrash as a Vehicle for Contemporary Bible Criticism', in Yvonne Sherwood (ed.) (2017), *The Bible and Feminism: Remapping the Field*. Oxford: Oxford University Press, p. 207.

35 Ibid., p. 209.

36 Danya Ruttenberg (2001) (ed.), *Yentl's Revenge: The Next Wave of Jewish Feminism*. New York: Seal Press.

37 BT Sanhedrin 109b.

38 Tony Bayfield, 'Introduction', in Wendy Greengross (1982), *Jewish and Homosexual*. London: RSGB.

39 Judith Butler, 'Ethical Ambivalence', in Marjorie Garber, Beatrice Hanssen and Rebecca Walkovitz (eds) (2000), *The Turn to Ethics*. New York: Routledge, p. 17.

40 Sara Salih with Judith Butler (ed.) (2004), *The Judith Butler Reader*. Malden, MA: Blackwell Publishing, p. 3.

41 Mishnah Sanhedrin 10.1.

42 I gladly acknowledge my debt to Finchley Reform Synagogue and Rabbi Miriam Berger for opening my eyes to this ethical imperative.

43 Avishai Margalit (1998), *The Decent Society*. Cambridge, MA: Harvard University Press, p. 1.

44 BT Baba Metzia 58b.

45 Born Halifax 1935, d. Highgate, London 2010.

46 This characterizes his writing on the subject but the precise formulation reflects several private 'tutorials'.

47 Deut. 7.7–8.

48 Amos 3.2.

49 Framed as a discussion with the King of the Khazar Empire over which faith to adopt: Judaism, Christianity or Islam.

50 Harold M. Schulweis in Editors of Commentary Magazine (1988), *The Condition of Jewish Belief*. New Jersey: Jason Aronson, p. 218.

51 Ibid., p. 219.

52 Contra the late Chief Rabbi Lord Jakobovits, ibid., p. 112.

53 Bernard-Henri Lévy (2017), *The Genius of Judaism*. New York: Random House, p. 131.

54 Ignaz Maybaum (1969), *Creation and Guilt*. London: Vallentine Mitchell, pp. 178–9.

55 Shmuel Feiner (2011), *The Origins of Jewish Secularization in Eighteenth-Century Europe*. Philadelphia: University of Pennsylvania Press, prefatory quotation.

56 David Biale (2011), *Not In the Heavens: The Tradition of Jewish Secular Thought*. Princeton, NJ: Princeton University Press, p. 176.

57 Ibid.

CHAPTER FOUR

1 Ari Shavit (2014), *My Promised Land: The Triumph and Tragedy of Israel*. Melbourne: Scribe Publications.

2 BT Megillah 10b.

3 Tony Bayfield (compiler and ed.) (2017), *Deep Calls to Deep: Transforming Conversations Between Jews and Christians*. London: SCM Press.

4 Simon Sebag Montefiore (2011), *Jerusalem: The Biography*. London: Weidenfeld & Nicolson.

5 Ibid., pp. 162–3.

6 The second Caliph.

7 Sebag Montefiore, *Jerusalem*, op. cit., pp. 176–7.

8 Ibid., p. 186.

9 Shia Dynasty 909–1171.

10 Sebag Montefiore, *Jerusalem*, op. cit., pp. 240–1.

11 Ibid., p. 325.

12 Mic. 4.2; Isa. 2.3.

13 Translation by Leo Baeck College lecturer David Goldstein (1971), *The Jewish Poets of Spain*. London: Penguin Classics, p. 128.

14 Lawrence Fine (ed.) (2001), *Judaism in Practice: From the Middle Ages Through the Early Modern Period.* Princeton: Princeton University Press, p. 237.

15 Bernard-Henri Lévy (2017), *The Genius of Judaism.* New York: Random House, p. 62.

16 Explored further in Ch. 10, p. 311.

17 William J. Fishman (1975), *East End Jewish Radicals 1875–1914.* London: Duckworth.

18 Moses Hess, *Rome and Jerusalem*, first published in Leipzig in 1862.

19 Herzl, 'The Jewish State', quoted in Arthur Hertzberg (ed.) (1977), *The Zionist Idea: A Historical Analysis and Reader.* New York: Atheneum, p. 209.

20 Shavit, *My Promised Land*, op. cit., pp. 25–47.

21 Ibid., pp. 99–132.

22 Kook's reference is to B.T. Eruvin 13b as in Ch. 1.

23 Abraham Isaac Kook (1983), *Commentary to the Prayer Book, Olat R'iyah, Vol. I.* Jerusalem: Mossad HaRav Kook, pp. 330–1.

24 Ahad Ha-am (1946), *Essays, Letters, Memoirs.* Oxford: East and West Library, p. 97.

25 Herbert Samuel b. Liverpool 1870, d. London 1963. A British Jew who became the first High Commissioner for Palestine and, later, leader of the Liberal Party.

26 See Martin Gilbert (1978), *Exile and Return: The Emergence of Jewish Statehood.* London: Weidenfeld & Nicolson, p. 83.

27 Lionel Walter Rothschild b. London 1868, d. Tring Park, Herts 1937. Zoologist and banker; Conservative MP for Aylesbury, 1899–1910.

28 Martin Gilbert, *Exile and Return*, op. cit., pp. 79–108.

29 Ibid., p. 109.

30 Ibid., p. 125.

31 Martin Gilbert (2007), *Churchill and the Jews.* London: Pocket Books, p. 38.

32 Quotations from Churchill's article are taken from Gilbert, *Churchill and the Jews*, ibid., pp. 38–42.

33 Martin Gilbert (2010), *In Ishmael's House: A History of Jews in Muslim Lands.* New Haven: Yale University Press.

34 Ibid., p. 116.

35 Ibid., p. 120.

36 I have taken the English translation of the original Hebrew from *Forms of Prayer*, Vol. I, *Daily, Sabbath and Occasional Prayers* (8th edn, 2008). London: Movement for Reform Judaism, op. cit., p. 395. It is noteworthy that this is included in a current prayer book.

37 Gilbert, *Exile & Return*, op. cit., p. 174.

38 Michael Walzer, Menachim Lorberbaum, Noam Zohar (eds) (2000), *The Jewish Political Tradition: Volume 1 Authority*. New Haven: Yale University Press, p. 491.

39 Shavit, *My Promised Land*, op. cit., pp. 201–25.

40 Deut. 16.20.

41 This insight originates with Rav Ashi in B.T. Sanhedrin 32b.

42 Will Herberg (1959), *Judaism and Modern Man: An Interpretation of Jewish Religion*. New York: Meridian Books.

43 Judith Butler (2012), *Parting Ways: Jewishness and the Critique of Zionism*. New York: Columbia University Press.

44 Dow Marmur (1991), *The Star of Return: Judaism after the Holocaust*. New York: Greenwood Press.

45 Abraham Joshua Heschel (1951), *The Sabbath*. New York: Farrar, Straus and Giroux.

46 Marmur, *The Star of Return,* op. cit., p. 41.

47 Franz Rosenzweig (1971), *The Star of Redemption*. London: Routledge & Kegan Paul.

48 *The Times,* Wednesday 25th July 2018, p. 21.

49 Diana Pinto, 'Are there Jewish Answers to Europe's Questions?', in *European Judaism,* Vol. 39, No. 2, pp. 55–7.

50 Shavit, *My Promised Land*, op. cit., p. 419.

PART 3

1 Elie Wiesel, acceptance speech, Nobel Peace Prize, Oslo, 1986,

CHAPTER FIVE

1 Simon Schama (2013), *The Story of the Jews: Finding the Words, 1000 BCE to 1492 CE,* London: The Bodley Head.

2 Ibid., p. 32.

3 Ibid., p. 37.

4 *The Diary of Samuel Pepys* for Wednesday 16 October 1663.

5 Jonathan Wittenberg (1996), *The Three Pillars of Judaism: A Search for Faith and Values*. London: SCM Press, pp. 35–6.

6 Schama, *The Story of the Jews,* op. cit., p. 34.

7 BT Yomah 35b.

8 Pirkei Avot 1.1.

9 An assembly of 120 sages from the end of the Biblical/early Hellenistic period.

10 High Priest c.300 BCE.

11 Gen. 1.1.

12 Deut. 34.12.

13 Seder Eliyahu Zuta, Ch. 2, beginning.

14 Abraham ibn Ezra, *Sefer Ha-yashar* on Deut. 1.1.

15 Louis Jacobs (1973), *Jewish Biblical Exegesis*. New York: Behrman House, p. 21.

16 Jonathan Sacks (1992), *Crisis and Covenant: Jewish Thought After the Holocaust*. Manchester: Manchester University Press, p. 146.

17 Eugene B. Borowitz (1991), *Renewing the Covenant: A Theology for the Postmodern Jew*. Philadelphia: Jewish Publication Society, p. 100.

18 Louis Jacobs (1995), *The Jewish Religion: A Companion*. Oxford: Oxford University Press, pp. 480–2.

19 Brian Magee (1998), *The Story of Philosophy*. London: Dorling Kindersley, p. 91, and in conversation.

20 David Ellenson (2004), *After Emancipation: Jewish Religious Responses to Modernity*. Cincinnati: Hebrew Union College Press, p.175.

21 From *Judaism Eternal: Selected Essays from the Writings of Samson Raphael Hirsch*, cited by Robert M. Seltzer (1980), *Jewish People, Jewish Thought: The Jewish Experience in History*. New York: Macmillan, p. 589.

22 Louis Jacobs (1957), *We Have Reason to Believe*. London: Vallentine Mitchell.

23 Ibid., pp. 80–1.

24 Jonathan Sacks (1992), *Crisis and Covenant: Jewish Thought After the Holocaust*. Manchester: Manchester University Press, Chs 7 and 8, pp. 176–246.

25 Jonathan Sacks, 'Torah Min Hashamayim', in *Le'ela*. London: Jews' College, No. 40, September 1995, p. 10. Subsequent quotations are from this source.

26 Ibid., p. 12.

27 Ibid., p. 15.

28 Sam Harris (2005), *The End of Faith: Religion, Terror and the Future of Reason*. London: The Free Press, p. 13.

29 Exodus Rabbah 29.9.

30 Exodus Rabbah 5.9.

31 Gabriel Josipovici (1988), *The Book of God: A Response to the Bible*. New Haven: Yale University Press, p. 87.

32 See Tony Bayfield, 'Theological Space, Partnership, and Self-criticism: The Old Agenda', in Dan Cohn-Sherbok (ed.) (1999), *The Future of Jewish–Christian Dialogue*, Lampeter: The Edwin Mellen

Press, pp. 58–62, for more detailed examination of the commentaries to the Pinchas narrative.

33 Gen. 22.1–19.

34 Søren Kierkegaard 1813–55. Danish founder of religious existentialism for whom the command of God could – as in Abraham's case – override the ethical and demand its suspension.

35 Woody Allen (1972), *Without Feathers*. New York: Random House, pp. 26–7.

36 'Retrojection': first used in Christian biblical criticism to suggest the Gospel writers read back the experience of the early Church into the life of Jesus – e.g. in shifting blame for his death from the Romans to 'the Jews'. It is used in the context of Deuteronomy by Gunther Plaut (2006), *The Torah: A Modern Commentary* (rev. edn). New York: URJ, p. 213.

CHAPTER SIX

1 Arnold Eisen, 'Covenant', in Arthur A. Cohen and Paul Mendes-Flohr (1988), *Contemporary Jewish Religious Thought: Original Essays on Critical Concepts, Movements, and Beliefs*. New York: The Free Press, pp. 107–12.

2 Ibid., p. 107.

3 Gen. 9.8–9.

4 Gen. 17.1–10.

5 Eisen, 'Covenant', op. cit., p. 108.

6 Ibid.

7 David Hartman (1985), *A Living Covenant: The Innovative Spirit in Traditional Judaism*. New York: The Free Press.

8 Ibid., p. 149.

9 Infra, Ch. 9.

10 Eisen, 'Covenant', op. cit., p. 108.

11 BT Shabbat 88a.

12 Rabbah bar Nahmani: distinguished third-/fourth-century figure, Head of the Rabbinic Academy in Pumbedita (near Fallujah, modern-day Iraq).

13 Traditional Festival Musaf.

14 BT Yoma 9b.

15 BT B'rakhot 5a.

16 Lamentations Rabbah III.1.

17 Irving Greenberg (1982), *Voluntary Covenant*. New York: National Jewish Resource Center, p. 14.

18 A. Roy Eckardt, 'The Recantation of the Covenant', in Alvin Rosenfeld and Irving Greenberg (1980), *Confronting the Holocaust: The Work of Elie Wiesel*. Indianapolis: Indiana University Press, p. 163.

19 Greenberg, *Voluntary Covenant*, op. cit., p. 15.

20 Elie Wiesel, 'Jewish Values in the Post-Holocaust Future', in *Judaism* 16, No. 3 (summer 1967), p. 281.

21 Jacob Glatstein, 'Dead Men Don't Praise God', in *Selected Poems of Jacob Glatstein* (1972). New York: October House, pp. 68–70.

22 Greenberg, *Voluntary Covenant*, op. cit., p. 17.

23 Eugene B. Borowitz (1991), *Renewing the Covenant: A Theology for the Postmodern Jew*. Philadelphia: Jewish Publication Society.

24 Ibid., pp. 284–9.

25 BT Makkot 23b–24a.

26 *Encyclopaedia Judaica* (1972), Jerusalem: Keter, Vol. 5, Commandments, columns 763–82.

27 BT Eruvin 13b.

28 Abraham Joshua Heschel (1955), *God in Search of Man – A Philosophy of Judaism*. New York: Farrar, Straus & Cudahy, pp. 336–7.

29 Mt. 26.57–68.

30 Mishnah Sanhedrin 7.1.

31 Jacobs (1995), *The Jewish Religion: A Companion*. Oxford: Oxford University Press, p. 68, citing BT Sanhedrin 41a and 52b.

32 Mishnah Makkot 1.10.

33 Mishnah Shevi't 10.1, 2 and 4.

34 BT Gittin 36b.

35 BT Shabbat 150a.

36 BT Shabbat 112b.

37 By sixteenth-century Moses Isserles of Cracow.

38 Shneur Zalman of Lyady, *Shulkhan Arukh HaRav*, 1814.

39 Yechiel Michael Epstein, *Arukh HaShulkhan*, Orach Chayyim, 62.4.

40 This is the approach taken by Arnold Eisen (1998), *Rethinking Modern Judaism: Ritual, Commandment, Community*. Chicago: Chicago University Press.

41 Tony Bayfield (1993), *Sinai, Law and Responsible Autonomy: Reform Judaism and the Halakhic Tradition*. London: RSGB.

42 K. W. M. Fulford (2012), *Essential Values-Based Practice: Clinical Stories Linking Science with People*. Cambridge: Cambridge University Press.

CHAPTER SEVEN

1   Genesis Rabbah XII.15.
2   Gen. 18.23–32.
3   Genesis Rabbah XXXIX.6.
4   BT B'rakhot 7a.
5   Mishnah Sanhedrin 4.5.
6   Byron L. Sherwin (2000), *Jewish Ethics for the Twenty-First Century: Living in the Image of God*. Syracuse: Syracuse University Press.
7   Yerushalmi, Rosh Hashanah 1:3 57b.
8   Sherwin, *Jewish Ethics* op. cit., p. 1, citing Deuteronomy Rabbah IV.4.
9   Ibid., citing Pirkei Avot 3.18.
10 BT Sota 14a.
11 Haim Cohen (1984), *Human Rights in Jewish Law*. New York: Ktav.
12 Amitai Etzioni (1995), *The Spirit of the Community: Rights, Responsibilities and the Communitarian Agenda*. London: Fontana.
13 Judah Halevi, *Kuzari* 2:50. Translation taken from *Forms of Prayer*, Vol. I: *Daily, Sabbath and Occasional Prayers* (8th edn, 2008). London: Movement for Reform Judaism, p. 520.
14 Popper's highly influential opposition to totalitarianism and its embodiment in centrally imposed utopian doctrines is found in: Karl Popper (1946), *The Open Society and Its Enemies*. London: Routledge.
15 Pirkei Avot 2.21.
16 Genesis Rabbah IX.9.
17 BT Yoma 69b.
18 BT Niddah 16b.
19 Hans Küng (2007), *The Beginning of All Things: Science and Religion*, Grand Rapids, MI: William B. Eerdmans, pp. 179–84. Küng documents 'Das Manifest', a 2004 statement by German neuroscientists pushing back at the 'Fundamentalists' and identifying areas lying outside the sphere of competence of neuroscience.
20 Steven Pinker (2003), *The Blank Slate: The Modern Denial of Human Nature*. London: Penguin.
21 Thomas Nagel (2012), *Mind & Cosmos: Why the Materialist Neo-Darwinian Conception of Nature Is Almost Certainly False*. Oxford: Oxford University Press, p. 68
22 Ibid., p. 72.
23 Professor of Epidemiology and Public Health and Director of the International Centre for Health and Society, University College London.
24 Private conversation.

25 Mal. 3.22–24: translation follows Andrew E. Hill (1998), Malachi, Vol. 25D, *The Anchor Bible*. New York: Doubleday, op. cit., p. 390.

26 Hos. 13.4–5.

27 Hos. 4.1.

28 Hos. 2.21–22.

29 Isa. 5.8–10. I've largely followed the translation of Professor Joseph Blenkinsopp (2000), *Isaiah 1–39: A New Translation with Introduction and Commentary*. New Haven: Yale University Press.

30 Ibid., pp. 212–13.

31 Abraham J. Heschel (1962), *The Prophets*. New York: Harper & Row, p. 33.

32 Amos 5.21–24.

33 Tim Franks, private correspondence.

34 Isaiah 11:1–5.

35 Jeremiah 29.10–11.

36 Mic. 4.1–4.

37 Amos 3.8.

38 Hilary Putnam (2008), *Jewish Philosophy as a Guide to Life: Rosenzweig, Buber, Levinas, Wittgenstein*. Bloomington, IN: Indiana University Press, p. 74.

39 Sifra, Parashat B'khukotai, Perek 7 interpreting Lev. 26.37.

40 Emmanuel Levinas (1994), *Beyond the Verse: Talmudic Readings and Lectures*. London: Athlone Press, p. 85.

41 Ecclesiastes Rabbah, VII.12.1.

42 Hans Jonas (1979), *Das Prinzip Verantwortung. Versuch einer Ethik für die technologische Zivilisation*. Frankfurt am Main: Insel Verlag. Hans Jonas (1984), *The Imperative of Responsibility: In Search of an Ethics for the Technological Age*. Chicago: University of Chicago Press.

43 Hans Jonas (1966), *The Phenomenon of Life: Towards a Philosophical Biology*. New York: Harper and Row.

44 Hannah Arendt (1951), *The Origins of Totalitarianism*. London: Penguin Modern Classics.

45 For views of the threat to democracy in Europe and the United States see David Runciman (2018), *How Democracy Ends*. London: Profile Books, and Steven Levitsky and Daniel Ziblatt (2018), *How Democracies Die: What History Reveals About Our Future*. London: Viking.

46 Speech, *Hansard*, 11 November 1947, col. 206.

47 Michael Sandel (2009), *Justice: What's the Right Thing to Do?* London: Allen Lane.

48 Born Baltimore 1921, d. Lexington, MA 2002.

49   Amartya Sen (2009), *The Idea of Justice*, London: Allen Lane. Preface, p. xiii, makes clear how important it is that different voices from different parts of the community be heard.

50   Michael Sandel (2012), *What Money Can't Buy: The Moral Limits of Markets*. London: Allen Lane, 2012.

51   Ibid., p. 6.

52   Robert Nozick (1974), *Anarchy, State, and Utopia*. Malden, MA: Blackwell Publishing.

53   Sandel, *What Money Can't Buy*, op. cit., p. 7.

54   Ibid., p. 9.

55   The *Guardian*, 27 April 2013.

56   Peter Singer (2011), *Practical Ethics* (3rd edn). Cambridge: Cambridge University Press.

57   Zygmunt Bauman (2007), *Consuming Life*. Cambridge: Polity Press.

58   Ibid., p. 13

59   Cover of the report of the Commission on Social Determinants of Health, ('Marmot Report') World Health Organization, 2008.

60   Michael Marmot (2015), *The Health Gap: The Challenge of an Unequal World*. London: Bloomsbury.

61   *The Lancet*, Vol. 368, 16 December 2006, p. 2117.

62   Jeffrey Sachs (2005), *The End of Poverty: How We Can Make It Happen in Our Lifetime*. London: Penguin.

63   BT Sanhedrin 98a.

64   Ibid., p. 3.

65   Jeffrey Sachs (2012), *The Price of Civilization: Reawakening Virtue and Prosperity After the Economic Fall*. London: Vintage Books.

66   Ibid., p. 263.

67   Ibid.

68   Professor Sally Wheeler underlines Jonas' importance to the current climate change debate and provides an excellent guide to navigating the politics with regard to his arguments in: Sally Wheeler, 'Climate change, Hans Jonas and indirect investors', in *Journal of Human Rights and the Environment*, Vol. 3 No. 1, March 2012, pp.92–115.

69   Pirkei de-Rabbi Eliezer 34 commenting on Deut. 20.19–20, *bal tashkhit*, do not destroy.

70   Taken from Maimonides, *The Preservation of Youth: Essays on Health*, written in Arabic in 1198. Cited in Ronald H. Isaacs (1998), *The Jewish Sourcebook on the Environment and Ecology*. Northvale, NJ: Jason Aronson, pp. 9–10.

71 From *Forms of Prayer*, Vol. 1 (8th edn), op. cit., p. 558 and Charles H. Middleburgh, 'High Time to Know our Place', in *MANNA*, No. 110 (winter 2011), p. 33.

72 BT Baba Metzia 59b.

73 Hannah Arendt in 'We Refugees', in Jerome Kohn and Ron H. Feldman (eds) (2007), *The Jewish Writings*. New York: Schocken Books, pp. 264–274.

74 David Miliband (2017), *Rescue: Refugees and the Political Crisis of Our Time*. London: Simon & Schuster.

75 Ibid., p. 119.

76 See Tony Bayfield, 'Religion, Secularism and the Public Square', in Noake and Buxton (eds) (2013), *Religion, Society and God*. London: SCM.

PART 4

1 Yiddish folk song used by Maurice Ravel in 'L'énigme éternelle, no. 2' of *Deux Mélodies Hébraiques*

2 David Hare (1990), *Racing Demon*. London: Faber & Faber, p. 1.

CHAPTER EIGHT

1 Genesis Rabbah 38.13.

2 A 1971 film adaptation of a Broadway Musical set in 1905 Tsarist Russia. based on *Tevye and his Daughters and Other Tales*, a book of short stories in Yiddish, published about 1895 by Jewish writer Sholem Aleichem.

3 Part of Ilford, now in the East London Borough of Redbridge.

4 Ps. 22.1.

5 Anne J. Kershen and Jonathan A. Romain (1995), *Tradition and Change: A History of Reform Judaism in Britain 1840–1995*. London: Vallentine Mitchell, p. 166.

6 Ignaz Maybaum (1965), *The Face of God after Auschwitz*. Amsterdam: Polak & Van Gennep.

7 Ibid., p. 126.

8 Gen. 15.6.

9 Leo Baeck (1948), *The Essence of Judaism*. New York: Schocken Books.

10 Leo Baeck (1964), *This People Israel: The Meaning of Jewish Existence*, translated by Albert H. Friedlander, New York: Holt, Rinehart and Winston.

11 Martin Buber (1948), *Tales of the Hasidim: Early Masters*. New York: Schocken Books. (Also 1948), *Later Masters*. New York: Schocken Books.

12 *Early Masters*, ibid., pp. 56–9.

13 *Early Masters*, ibid., p. 248.

14 Martin Buber (1937), *I and Thou*. Edinburgh: T&T Clark.

15 Hilary Putnam (2008), *Jewish Philosophy as a Guide to Life: Rosenzweig, Buber, Levinas, Wittgenstein*. Bloomington: Indiana University Press, p. 61.

16 His essence is expressed in Lionel Blue (1975), *To Heaven with Scribes and Pharisees: The Jewish Path to God*. London: Darton, Longman and Todd.

17 See Louis Jacobs (1972), *Hasidic Prayer*. London: Routledge & Kegan Paul.

18 Jeremy Paxman and John Humphrys: British television interviewers renowned for their inquisitorial style. Humphrys wrote (2007) *In God We Doubt: Confessions of a Failed Atheist*. London: Hodder & Stoughton.

19 Privately printed, entitled *The Age of Gold in Judaism is Yet to Come*, London, 1972.

20 He was quoting George Steiner, *In Bluebeard's Castle*.

21 T. S. Eliot (1918/19), *Whispers of Immortality*, last stanza.

22 Allusion to Erich Fromm (1997), *To Have or to Be?* London: Bloomsbury Academic.

23 Tony Bayfield and Marcus Braybrooke (eds) (1982), *Dialogue with a Difference: The Manor House Group Experience*. London: SCM, p. 4.

24 From the subtitle of Albert Friedlander (1993), *Riders Towards the Dawn: From Ultimate Suffering to Tempered Hope*. London: Constable.

25 Ibid.

26 Exodus Rabbah II.5.

27 Ibid.

28 Lamentations Rabbah, Proem 24.

29 Rubenstein revised *After Auschwitz*, greatly strengthening it. Richard L. Rubenstein (1966), *After Auschwitz: Radical Theology and Contemporary Judaism* (1st edn). Indianapolis, IN: Bobbs-Merrill. (Also 1992), *After Auschwitz: History, Theology and Contemporary Judaism* (2nd edn). Baltimore: The Johns Hopkins University Press.

30 Ibid. (1st edn), p. 153.

31 Richard L. Rubenstein (1970), *Morality & Eros*. New York: McGraw-Hill, pp. 185–6.

32 Eliezer Berkovits (1973), *Faith after the Holocaust*. New York: Ktav Publishing House, p. 106.

33 Ibid., p. 107.

34 Emil Fackenheim (1967), 'Jewish Values in the Post-Holocaust Future: A Symposium', in *Judaism* 16 (summer 1967).

35 Ibid.

36 Emil Fackenheim (1982), *To Mend the World: Foundations of Future Jewish Thought*. New York: Schocken Books.

37 Quoted by Byron L. Sherwin in 'Theodicy', in Arthur A. Cohen and Paul Mendes-Flohr (1988), *Contemporary Jewish Religious Thought: Original Essays on Critical Concepts, Movements, and Beliefs*. New York: The Free Press, p. 960. Citing C. Chavel (1963) (ed.), *Perush le-Sefer Kohelet* in *Kitvei Rabbenu Moshe ben Nahman*, p. 193.

38 Sherwin, 'Theodicy', in *Contemporary Jewish Religious Thought*, ibid.

39 Ibid., p. 961.

40 Kenneth Seeskin (1990), *Jewish Philosophy in a Secular Age*. New York: State University of New York, Ch. 7.

41 Arthur A. Cohen (1981), *The Tremendum: A Theological Interpretation of the Holocaust*. New York: Crossroad.

42 Arthur A. Cohen (1967), *The Natural and the Supernatural Jew*. London: Vallentine Mitchell.

43 Mordecai Kaplan (1981), *Judaism as a Civilization: Toward a Reconstruction of American-Jewish Life*. Philadelphia: Jewish Publication Society.

44 Arthur A. Cohen, *The Tremendum*, op. cit.

45 Ibid., p. 97.

46 Ibid., pp. 97–8.

47 Exod. 3.14.

48 Exodus Rabbah II:5.

49 Elizabeth Barrett Browning, *Aurora Leigh* (1857), bk. 7, l.821.

50 Pierre Bouretz (2010), *Witnesses for the Future: Philosophy and Messianism*. Baltimore: The Johns Hopkins University Press.

51 Hermann Cohen (1995), *Religion of Reason: Out of the Sources of Judaism*. Atlanta, GA: Scholars Press.

52 Putnam, *Jewish Philosophy as a Guide to Life*, op. cit., pp. 9–16.

53 Jeffrey Newman, 'Ludwig's Quest for Clarity', in MANNA 96 (summer 2007), pp. 28–9.

54 Ibid.

55 Michael Löwy (1992), *Redemption & Utopia: Jewish Libertarian Thought in Central Europe – A Study in Elective Affinity*. London: Athlone Press. You may wish to refer back to Ch. 1, p. 24.

56 Bouretz, *Witnesses for the Future*, op. cit., pp. 214–15.
57 Ibid.
58 Elie Wiesel (1972), *Night*. London: Fontana Books.
59 Ibid., pp. 44–5.

CHAPTER NINE

1   Gen. 18.23–33.
2   Jer. 12.1.
3   Job, 31.3–8 and 35.
4   Anson Laytner (2004), *Arguing with God: A Jewish Tradition*, Lanham, MD: Rowman & Littlefield.
5   In BT Sanhedrin 105a Rabbi Nachman justifies the use of this Aramaic phrase.
6   Laytner, *Arguing with God*, op. cit., p. 49.
7   Exodus Rabbah 5.22.
8   Laytner, *Arguing with God*, op. cit., p. 50.
9   Exodus Rabbah 5.22.
10 Particularly in Proem 24.
11 Laytner, *Arguing with God,* op. cit., p. 82.
12 Taken from a 78-stanza lament written in the wake of the massacres of 1656.
13 Samuel H. Dresner (1986), *The World of a Hasidic Master: Levi Yitzhak of Berditchev*. New York: Shapolsky, p. 86.
14 Attributed to Jacob K. Sendler, 1860–1931.
15 Alter Brody, *Lamentations: 4 One-Act Plays*. Unpublished.
16 Atar Hadari (2000), *Songs from Bialik: Selected Poems*. Syracuse, NY: Syracuse University Press, pp. 6–7.
17 Jacob J. Petuchowski (1978), *Theology and Poetry: Studies in the Medieval Piyyut*. Cincinnati: Hebrew Union College.
18 Malcom Singer (2018), 'A Crisis of Faith – the Concert Music of Leonard Bernstein', in *The Friends Quarterly.* Vol. 46, no. 4, November 2018, pp. 32–8.
19 Exod. 3.13–14.
20 The word is derived from the Hebrew root to be – and can be understood both as 'I am' and 'I will be'.
21 Abraham Joshua Heschel (2005), *Heavenly Torah: As Refracted through the Generations*, New York: Continuum.
22 Heschel, *Heavenly Torah*, op. cit., p. 118. The text at the end is from Mekhilta de-Rabbi Ishmael, Shirata 8.

23 The 'as it were' is often inserted by the Rabbis to remind readers this is metaphor.

24 Mekhilta de-Rabbi Ishmael, Piskha 14, 99–107.

25 Exodus Rabbah 2.5.

26 Heschel, *Heavenly Torah*, op. cit., p. 120.

27 Jer. 8.21.

28 Lamentations Zuta 1:18.

29 Sifre, Piskha 346.

30 Ibid.

31 Midrash Psalms Ps. 123.2, commenting on Isaiah 43.12.

32 Byron L. Sherwin in 'Theodicy', in Arthur A. Cohen and Paul Mendes-Flohr (1988), *Contemporary Jewish Religious Thought: Original Essays on Critical Concepts, Movements, and Beliefs*. New York: The Free Press, pp. 966–7.

33 Gershom G. Scholem (1941), *Major Trends in Jewish Mysticism*, Jerusalem: Schocken. Quotations from the 1961 paperback edition.

34 Ibid., p. 10.

35 Ibid., p. 261.

36 Ibid., pp. 273–4.

37 Ibid., pp. 275–6.

38 Ibid., p. 274.

39 Albert H. Friedlander (1968), *Out of the Whirlwind: A Reader of Holocaust Literature*. New York: Doubleday.

40 All the following quotations are from 'The Concept of God after Auschwitz', in Friedlander, *Out of the Whirlwind*, op. cit., pp. 465–76.

41 Phrase coined by Gottfried Leibniz in an essay of 1710.

42 I acknowledge both cancer and environmental catastrophes can be caused by human action – moving them into the category of 'evil'. However, I don't want to obscure the argument.

43 Exod. 7.8–12.

44 Elijah and the prophets of Baal in 1 Kings 18.

45 1 Kings 17.

46 1 Macc. 4.42–49.

47 BT Shabbat 21b.

48 Emil Fackenheim (1972), *God's Presence in History: Jewish Affirmations and Philosophical Reflections*, New York: Harper Torchbooks.

49 Deut. 11.13–21.

50 Pirkei Avot 2.21. BT Hullin 142a.

51 BT Berakhot 59a.

52 BT Hagigah 15b.

53 BT Shabbat 10a.

54 Louis Jacobs, 'The Concept of Power in the Jewish Tradition', in *Conservative Judaism* 33/2 (winter 1980), pp. 18–28.

55 Midrash Shmuel, Parashah 4.5, cited by Miriam Bayfield (2006), Leo Baeck College Rabbinic Dissertation, p. 5.

56 Pesikta Rabbati 31.5.

57 Numbers Rabbah 2:2.

58 Ruth, Ch. 2.

59 Ps. 103.15–16.

60 Jonas, 'The Concept of God after Auschwitz', op. cit., p. 476.

61 Resulting in the seventh edition of *Forms of Prayer for Jewish Worship*, Vol. I: *Daily, Sabbath and Occasional Prayers* (1977). London: Reform Synagogues of Great Britain.

62 Resulting in the eighth edition of *Forms of Prayer*, Vol. I: *Daily, Sabbath and Occasional Prayers* (2008). London: Movement for Reform Judaism.

63 As in John Fowles (1996), *A Maggot*, London: Vintage Classics – an insidious idea, a quirk, an obsession.

CHAPTER TEN

1 *Mishnah with Rambam's Commentary* (1962), Jerusalem: Mossad HaRav Kook. Statement of principles and commentary found at Mishnah Sanhedrin 10 in Vol. 2, pp. 141–4.

2 Isa. 26.19.

3 Dan. 12.2.

4 Abraham, Gen. 25.8; Isaac, 35.29; Jacob, 49.29, 33.

5 Josh. 15.8.

6 Louis Jacobs (1964), *Principles of the Jewish Faith: An Analytical Study*, London: Vallentine Mitchell, p. 411.

7 Ibid.

8 Garden of Eden. Rabbinic Literature suggests two Gardens: one earthly, one heavenly. But there isn't a clear differentiation between them.

9 See the considerable discussion which begins in BT Sanhedrin 90a.

10 See Naftali Silberberg, *The Resurrection Process*, at www.chabad.org.

11 Joshua Finkel (trans.) (1939), *Tehiyyat ha-Metim [Treatise on Resurrection]*. New York: AAJR, Vol. IX.

12 BT B'rakhot 17a.

13 For example in the 1885 Pittsburgh Platform: W. Gunther Plaut (1965), *The Growth of Reform Judaism*. New York: WUPJ, p. 34.

14 F. Brown, S. R. Driver and C. A. Briggs (1966 printing), *Hebrew and English Lexicon of the Old Testament*, Oxford: Clarendon, p. 659.

15 *MANNA* Platform, *MANNA* 27 (spring 1990). Responses in *MANNA* 29, 30 and 31.

16 'Progressive Judaism: A Collective Theological Essay and Discussion Paper', *MANNA* 27, spring 1990 (emphasis added).

17 Franz Rosenzweig (1971), *The Star of Redemption*, London: Routledge & Kegan Paul, p. 324.

18 Keith Thomas (2009), *The Ends of Life: Roads to Fulfilment in Early Modern England*, Oxford: Oxford University Press.

19 Ibid., p. 229.

20 Ibid., p. 147.

21 Eccl. 7.1.

22 Thomas, *The Ends of Life*, op. cit., p. 193.

23 Ibid., p. 218.

24 Ibid., p. 245.

25 *Forms of Prayer* (2008), Vol. 1: *Daily, Sabbath and Occasional Prayers* (8th edn). London: Movement for Reform Judaism, pp. 518–47.

26 The phrase is adapted from 1 Sam. 25.29: *V'hai'y'ta nefesh adoni tsrurah bitsror ha'khayim*: My Lord's soul will be bound up in the bundle / gathering of life (with God). It is found on most gravestones and is how Judaism succinctly articulates life after death.

27 *Forms of Prayer* (8th edn), op. cit., p. 427.

28 Based on Maimonides' Twelfth Principle, probably formulated as early as the fourteenth century.

29 Attributed to Azriel Fastag, a Modzitzer Hasid, on his way to Treblinka.

30 1 Kings 17.1. Bible scholars believe there was an 'Elijah document', which the compiler of the First Book of Kings chose to include at this point. The Elijah cycle opens with the first verse of Ch. 17 and occupies five chapters to the end of 1 Kings, continuing into 2 Kings.

31 1 Kings 16.30–33.

32 1 Kings 19.11–12.

33 2 Kings 2.11–12.

34 Malachi 3.22–24. The translation largely follows Andrew E. Hill (1998), *Malachi*, Vol. 25D, *The Anchor Bible*, New York: Doubleday, p. xliii.

35 See Hill, *Anchor Bible*, op. cit., pp. 382–90.

36 BT Sanhedrin 98a.

37 Louis Jacobs (1981), *Teyku: The Unsolved Problem in the Babylonian Talmud*. London: Cornwall Books.

38 2 Sam. 5.3.

39 Isa. 11.6–9.

40 Mic. 4.1–4.

41 Isa. 2.2–4.

42 Isaiah was, until recently, seen as the work of three authors – First Isaiah, Chs 1–39; Deutero-Isaiah, Chs 40–55; and Trito-Isaiah, Chs 56–66. The latest scholarship sees the dividing lines as less clear cut and prefers to view Isaiah as a literary whole in two parts.

43 The 1978 Jewish Publication Society of America translation.

44 Zvi Werblowski, 'Messianism', in Arthur A. Cohen and Paul Mendes-Flohr (eds) (1988), *Contemporary Jewish Religious Thought: Original Essays on Critical Concepts, Movements and Beliefs*. New York: The Free Press, p. 597.

45 From Ezek. 37.5–14.

46 Avot de-Rabbi Natan 31b.

47 *Forms of Prayer*, Vol. I (8th edn), op. cit., p. 461. 'Elijah the prophet / Elijah the Tishbite / Elijah the man of Gilead / may he come to us soon / with the Messiah, son of David.'

48 Zvi Werblowski, 'Messianism', op. cit., p. 602 – referring to the hailing of the rebirth of the State of Israel as the 'beginning of the sprouting of our redemption' by Israel's two Chief Rabbinates.

49 It comes from a variant reading of a passage about three oaths in B.T. Ketubot 111a.

50 One of a number of short stories later published as a book. Hugh Nissenson (1972), *In the Reign of Peace*, London: Secker & Warburg.

51 Ibid., p. 104.

52 David Berger (2001), *The Rebbe, the Messiah and the Scandal of Orthodox Indifference*, London: Littman Library of Jewish Civilization.

53 Elie Wiesel (1967), *The Gates of the Forest*, New York: Avon Books.

54 Ibid., p. 223.

55 John Gray (2003), *Straw Dogs: Thoughts on Humans and Other Animals*. London: Granta Books, pp. 168–70, 183–4.

56 Karl Popper (1945), *The Open Society and Its Enemies*. London: Routledge.

Acknowledgements

My boundless gratitude to Jacqueline Fisher, my partner, who persuaded me to return to the project after I'd abandoned it and insisted it shouldn't be hidden under a blanket of academic pretence. She went through the text with me countless times, clarifying meaning, refining language but avoiding the impoverishment of contemporary speech. Jacqui also prepared the manuscript! Were it not for her, there would be no book.

To my father who, at the age of 94, read the entire manuscript and objected only to my self-deprecation.

To my rabbinic role-model Rabbi Dow Marmur.

My debt to the Leo Baeck College is considerable. Primarily to the eight who gave me *s'mikhah*: Albert Friedlander, Ignaz Maybaum, Hugo Gryn, Louis Jacobs, Lionel Blue, Ellen Littmann, John Rayner and Georg Nador. Also to today's leadership – particularly the Principal, Rabbi Dr Deborah Kahn-Harris, who transformed my long professional association with the College into the ideal base from which to write this book. And to the enthusiastic and insightful students in my 2015, 2016, 2017 and 2018 classes, who have contributed much more than they will realise.

My thanks to my long-standing dialogue partners: Revd Dr Marcus Braybrooke, Regius Professor David Ford, Lord Richard Harries, Sister Margaret Shepherd, Revd Dr Alan Race, Imam Abduljalil Sajid, and Dr Ataullah Siddiqui.

To my mentors: Philip Boxer, Professor Bill Fulford and Professor Sir Michael Marmot.

To those who supported and encouraged the project from the beginning; Professor Ludwik Finkelstein *z'l*, Rabbi Dr Charles Middleburgh, Rabbi Jeffrey Newman, Simon Rocker, David Walsh.

ACKNOWLEDGEMENTS

To those who read the manuscript so thoroughly and commented so thoughtfully: Student Rabbi Deborah Blausten, Mike Frankl, Tim Franks, Rabbi Dr Andrew Goldstein, Professor Marc Saperstein, Student Rabbi Igor Zinkov.

To Rabbi Neil Janes who helped me locate some of the more obscure texts and stopped me straying unnecessarily into contentious academic areas.

To supportive and encouraging friends: Corrine and Donald Brydon, Jane and Mike Grabiner, Barbara and Professor Chris Hamnett, Jennifer Jankel, Janet and Leo Liebster and Professor Graham Zellick.

To those who are not referred to by name but will recognise themselves as cherished players in my life when reading this book.

To those guiding me to the right publisher: Vivienne Shuster and Andrew Franklin.

To my thoughtful and gracious copy-editor and fellow theologian Nick Fawcett, who shares a similar perception of the real issues.

To my editor, Jamie Birkett – a model of supportive efficiency, and Kealey Rigden who opened my eyes to the importance of social media.

Last but by no means least, to my wise and sympathetic publisher, Robin Baird-Smith, who knew much better than me the book I should write.

Index

Abraham (Abram) 9, 11, 20, 160–1, 166,
    167, 196, 213, 233, 259
Adam, the Creation narrative, first
    human 197–8, 214
Adler, Rabbi Rachel 92
Aelia Capitolina 19
afterlife 289–99
aggadah 178–80, 184, 189–90, 198
Ahab, King 301
Ahad Ha'am 117–18
Akedah (Binding of Isaac) 160–1, 213,
    233
Akher, the Other 74–5
Akiva, Rabbi 181, 198–9, 252, 261, 266,
    267–8, 269, 279, 280, 309
al-Husseini, Amin 124
Aliyah, First and Second 115
Alkabetz, Solomon 109
Allen, Woody 67, 160–1
Allenby, General 120
Almohads and Almoravids 21
American Jewry 26–7, 50–1, 86, 134,
    137, 187
American Reconstructionist
    Movement 187
American Reform Movement 86, 134
Amidah 110, 186, 291
Amos 99, 175, 207–8, 268
Amsterdam, Dutch Republic 147
anti-Semitism 31, 50–1, 67, 102, 106,
    112, 113–14, 123, 132–3, 220
    see also Nazis; Shoah (Holocaust)

Apocrypha 17, 276
Arendt, Hannah 216–17, 224
Ark of the Covenant 13, 14, 276
Arnold, Matthew – 'Dover Beach' 2
aron hakodesh – the ark 138
Artaxerxes 138
Artificial Intelligence 60
Ashkenazi Jews 21, 26, 52, 78, 117, 128,
    129, 185, 300
Asquith, H.H. 119
Assembly of Reform Rabbis 39, 283–4
Assyrian Empire 11, 209, 211, 306
Auschwitz 49, 172–3, 233, 234, 243,
    257–8
Avdimi, Rabbi, Sinai as inverted cask
    170–1

Babel, Tower of 135
Babylon 11, 16, 20, 107, 138, 209, 277
Babylonian Talmud 20, 35–7, 170–1,
    183–4, 280, 304
Baeck, Rabbi Leo 56, 233, 234
balance and Rabbinic ethics 200–1,
    214
Balfour, Arthur 119
Balfour Declaration 120–2
Bar Kokhba 128, 309–10
Bauman, Zigmunt 220–1
Bayfield, Linda 34, 235, 247, 275
Bayfield, Rabbi Tony 229–30, 284–7
    a child's death in Harlow 235–6,
    293–4

family background 25, 102, 112,
    230–1
German *Liberale* tradition 253–7
influence of Albert Friedlander
    240–2
influence of Arthur A. Cohen 250–1
influence of Elie Wiesel 257–8
influence of Eliezer Berkovits 243–4
influence of Emil Fackenheim
    245–6
influence of Ignaz Maybaum 232–4
influence of Leo Baeck 234
influence of Lionel Blue 237–8
influence of Martin Buber 236–7
influence of Michael Goulston 238–9
influence of Richard L. Rubenstein
    242–3
Jewish-Christian dialogue groups
    39–40, 240
Leo Baeck College 54–5, 56–7
liturgy 282–4
ruins of Brinkburn Priory 240–1
Tel Aviv's rubbish dump 252–3
the unfairness of life 246–50
Becker, Garry 221, 222
Ben-Gurion, David 125–6
Benjamin, Walter 255–7
Bentwich, Herbert 115
Berger, Rabbi David 310
Berger, Rabbi Miriam 155, 239
Berkovits, Rabbi Eliezer 243–4
Berlin, Isaiah 71, 226
Bernstein, Leonard 264
Biale, David 101
Bialik, Hayyim Nahman 263–4
biritu 166–8
bittul ha-yesh 238
Blausten, Deborah 58–9
Blenkinsopp, Joseph 206
Bloomfield, Irene 94
Blue, Rabbi Lionel 5, 232, 237–8, 283,
    308
Borowitz, Rabbi Eugene 31, 148, 173,
    177

Bouretz, Pierre 254, 256
Bowden, Rev John 97
Boxer, Philip 31–2
Bragg, Melvyn 47–8
Braybrooke, Rev Marcus 240
brit, covenant 166–8, 170
b'rit milah, circumcision 166
Britain 27, 31, 46, 54, 133
British Empire 109, 115, 118–21,
    123–4
British Jewish community 49, 50, 53,
    66–9, 75–7
Brittain, Sister Teresa 106, 132
Brody, Alter 263
Browne, Cecil 98
Browning, Elizabeth Barrett 253
Brunner, Emil 151
Buber, Martin 118, 213, 236–7
Butler, Judith 66, 94–6, 131
Butler, Christopher 65
Byzantine Empire 107

Cain and Abel 197
Canaan/Canaanites 11, 12, 13, 14,
    29–30, 160, 162, 290, 301
capital punishment 180–1, 196–7
Caro, Rabbi Joseph 109, 185
Cassin, René 200
Catherine the Great 23
Catholic Church 21, 114
Cavell, Stanley 213–14
Central Conference of American
    Rabbis 86
champagne Jews, uncorking 48, 50–3,
    255
Children of Israel 12–14, 105, 156, 162
Chinese Jews 77–8
Chmielnicki Massacres 22–3
'chosen people' 98–100
Christian harvest festival 14
Christian Zionists 21
Christianity/Christians 18, 20, 21, 25,
    32, 39–40, 42–4, 47–8, 79, 97,
    105–6, 122–3, 129, 132, 133,

139–40, 147, 209, 233, 240–1,
291, 311
the Church 41, 46, 296–7, 308
  see also Christianity/Christians
Churchill, Winston 121–2, 217
circumcision 83, 166, 167
civil law, Jewish 181–2
'Cognitive Revolution' 63–4
Cohen, Arthur A. 250–1
Cohen, Harry 81
Cohen, Hermann 56, 148, 254
Cohen, Leonard 161
Cohen, Shaye, J.D. 80
Cohn-Sherbok, Rabbi Dan
  294–5
Cohn, Supreme Court Justice Haim
  199
Colonialism 41, 115
commentary 19, 82, 139, 142, 157, 178,
  195
  see also midrash
Common Era 12
communications, Digital Age 58–9
community 68–9, 73–7, 192, 199
compassionate justice 192, 195–6, 222,
  244, 259, 286, 298, 311
consumerism 220–1
conversion to Judaism 81–5
Cooper, Rabbi Howard 284
Copernicus 40–1
Corbyn, Jeremy 106, 132
Cordovero, Moses 109
Cosmologists 40, 274–5
cosmology 60, 274
Cossack revolt 22
covenant theology
  compelled and free paradox 170–1
  halakhah 178–93
  mitzvah 174–8
  parity model of covenant 166, 168,
    169–70, 177, 278–81
  promissory model of covenant
    166–7, 168, 176, 206
  Prophetic ethics 205–12

Rabbinic ethics 195–204
Shoah - covenant broken 171–4
suzerainty model of covenant 166,
  167, 169, 171, 176
three models of covenant 165–70,
  176–7
criminal law, Jewish 180–1
Crusades 21, 108
Curthoys, Ned 24–5
Cyrus of Persia 16, 138

Daily Prayer Book 283–4
Damascus 17
Damascus Affair (1840) 122–3
Daniel, book of 289–90
dati 165
David, King 11, 167, 175, 305
Day of Atonement 16
death penalty 180–1, 197
Declaration of the Establishment of
  the State of Israel 124–6
Degania kibbutz 115
democracy 34, 67, 126–8, 201, 216–7,
  225–6
Derrida, Jacques 65, 95, 159
Deuteronomy 14, 29, 35, 97, 98–9,
  128–9, 146, 161–3, 168, 181–2,
  199, 268, 290
dhimmi 20–1
Diaspora - golah 11, 16, 17, 19, 20–3,
  130–1, 132
dietary laws (kashrut) 165
Digital Age 57–9
Disraeli, Benjamin 109
dreydl 276
Dreyfus, Alfred 113
Dual Torah 18, 142–55
Duties precede rights 199–200
Dylan, Bob 161

Earp, Wyatt 26
Earth Charter 223
Eastern Europe 22–3, 25–6, 78, 111,
  113, 114, 261–4

economics 59–60, 200–1, 207–8,
    218–23
Egypt 7, 9, 12, 15, 17, 105, 108, 124, 261,
    265, 277
Eichmann, Adolph 216
Eimer, Rabbi Colin 179, 232, 294
Ein Harod kibbutz 116, 118
Einstein, Albert 28, 118
Eisen, Arnold 166–8, 169
El Malei Rakhamim 299
elective affinity 24, 133, 255
Elephantine Jewish community 7, 16
Elijah 14, 276, 300–4, 308
Elisha ben Abuya 74–5
Ellenson, David 149
Elon, Amos 24, 41
elu va'elu, conflicting arguments both
    God's word 35–7, 269
End of Days 15–16, 132, 210–11, 281,
    291, 292, 304, 306–7, 311–12
Enlightenment, Age of 24, 84, 111, 149,
    150, 152, 185–7, 189
environmental crisis, global 223–4
eruv 68, 189
Esther 16–17, 89, 171
ethics
    David Miliband 224–5
    Emmanuel Levinas 212–14
    Hannah Arendt 216–17
    Hans Jonas 214–16
    Jeffrey Sachs 222–3
    Michael Marmot 221–2
    Michael Sandel and Peter Singer
        218–20
    post-modern Jewish 217–25
    in Prophetic Literature 205–12, 218
    in Rabbinic Literature 195–204, 218
    Zigmunt Bauman 220–1
Etzioni, Amitai 199
evolutionary biologists 61, 203
evolutionary theory 61, 204, 274
Ewer, William 98
exegesis 19, 143, 188
    see also midrash

exile - *galut* 11, 16, 19–22, 29–30, 107,
    108, 138, 171, 209–10, 252, 267,
    269–70
Exodus 9, 12, 35, 78, 89, 156–7, 167,
    168, 170, 174, 176, 189, 265,
    266, 279
expulsion *see* exile
Ezekiel 14–15, 307–8
Ezra 138–9

Fackenheim, Rabbi Emil 245–6, 277
Fatimids 108
Feiner, Shmuel 101
Feldman, Louis 81–2
Ferguson, Niall 41–2, 45–6, 50
fertility cults, Canaanite 11
fidelity in Prophetic Literature 205–6
Fine, Lawrence 110–11
Finkel, Irving 158
Finkelstein, Daniel 132
Finnart House School 81
First World War 44, 54, 115, 118, 119,
    231
Fishman, Bill 112
Foucault, Michel 65–6, 94, 95, 96
Four Horsemen secular
        fundamentalists 154
Fourth Lateran Council 21
France 24, 67, 113, 118, 119, 122, 133
Frank, Jacob 23
free will 201–4, 244
Freud, Sigmund 55–6, 118
Friedlander, Rabbi Albert 240–2, 272,
    279
Fulford, Bill (KWM) 56, 190–1
fundamentalism 9, 66, 107, 128, 154,
    204
funeral sermons 297–8
Futurologists 57–8, 60, 64

Galilee 19, 107, 115
Galileo 40–1, 45, 149
Ganesh, Janan 34
Gehinnom 290

gender equality 85–7, 190
gender neutral language 2
Genesis 8–9, 88, 159, 160, 166, 195,
    198–9, 201, 233, 259, 290
genetics 50, 51
Ge'onim 20
German Jewry 55, 56, 65, 149, 205, 234,
    269–70
German Liberale tradition 133, 214,
    253–7
Germany 21, 22, 24–5, 112, 186–7
Gilbert, Sir Martin 121, 122
Gilgamesh 158
Ginsberg (aka Ahad Ha'am), Asher
    117–18
Glatstein, Jacob 173
Glemp, Cardinal 49
global warming 216
    see also Jonas, Hans (214–16);
        post-modern Jewish ethics
        (environmental)
G'mara 35, 171, 183, 186
God 33, 35, 37, 43–4, 55–6, 61, 78–9,
    83, 90, 98–100, 105, 132, 141–2,
    148–9, 151, 153, 154, 155–63
  of Abraham and Sarah 192
  in dark texts 159–63
  experience of 156–8, 242, 278, 308
  hidden face of 244–5
  and Job 248–9, 260
  in Lurianic Kabbalah 269–72
  Prophetic ethics 205–12
  question of divine intervention 274–7
  question of omnipotence 242–3,
      265–9
  Rabbinic ethics 195–204
  reasoning about 274–82
  redemption 281–2, 286–7
  the Shoah 242–6, 251–2 (see also
      post-modern Jewish ethics)
  tradition of challenging 259–64
  Voice of God 156–8
  what can we say about God?
      265–73

see also covenant theology
Golden Calf, Exodus 156
Goldstein, Rabbi Andrew 86
Goodman, Martin 82
Goulston, Rabbi Michael 238–9
Gray, John 62–3, 311
Greece 17, 21
Greenberg, Rabbi Irving 172–3, 177
Greengross, Wendy 93
Gross, Rita M. 89
Gryn, Rabbi Hugo 47, 64, 224, 294

Habakkuk 175, 259
Hadrian, Emperor 19, 107, 128
Haganah 124
Hagigah, Tractate 279
Hakim, Caliph 108
halakhah (Jewish law) 35–6, 68, 93–4,
    110, 138, 280
  and aggadah 178–80, 198
  application specific to circumstance
      190–1
  authoritarianism and elitism 189–90
  civil law: the Prosbol 181–3
  criminal law: capital punishment
      180–1
  decline of serving overarching
      vision 184–5
  difficulty of hermeneutics 188–9
  impact of the Enlightenment 185–7
  post-enlightenment choices 187–8
  post-halakhic Judaism 191–3
  responsible autonomy 188–93
  the Shabbat 183–4
Halevi, Rabbi Judah 99, 110–11, 116,
    200–1
Haman 17
HaNasi, Rabbi Judah 107
Hanukkah 17, 276
Harari, Yuval Noah 60, 63–4, 204
Haredi Jews 133, 176
Harris, Sam 154
Hartman, Rabbi David 168–9, 176, 178
Hasidism 23, 236, 238, 300

Haskalah 25–6, 113, 231
Hasmonean dynasty 17
Havdalah 30, 308
Hawking, Stephen 61
health and life-expectancy, issue of
    221–2, 226
Hebrew Bible 16, 17, 47–8, 78, 159,
    276–7, 290–1
    see also Torah; individual books by
    name
Hebrew language 139
Hebrew Union College, Cincinnati
    90–1
Hebrew University, Jerusalem 118, 269,
    270, 272
Heidegger, Martin 216
Hellenistic Culture 17, 18
Herberg, Rabbi Will 130
hermeneutics and the Torah 188–9,
    266
Herzl, Theodor 113–14, 115
Heschel, Rabbi Abraham Joshua 131,
    179–80, 207–8, 265–7, 279
Heschel, Susannah 90
hesped 297–8
Hess, Moses 111, 112–13
Hezekiah, King 306
Hildesheimer, Rabbi Azriel 84–5
Hill, Andrew E. 205
Hillel 36–7, 82, 142, 182–3
Hillel, Bet (House/School of) 35–7,
    82–3, 177
hineni 213–14
Hirsch, Rabbi Samson Raphael 149–
    50, 189
Hitler, Adolph 27, 44, 49, 54, 124, 245
Hochschule für die Wissenschaft des
    Judentums 55, 102, 106, 232,
    245, 254
Hoffman, Rabbi Lawrence 30
Hoffman, Rabbi David Zvi 152–3
Hollywood 50–1
Holocaust (Shoah) *see* Shoah
    (Holocaust)

homosexuality 93–4, 95–6
hope in Prophetic Literature 209–10
Hosea, book of 205–6
Hov'vei Tzion 113
Hughes, Bethany 158
human rights 199–200
human sacrifice 160
human (individual) uniqueness 196–7
Humanism 148, 204, 311

Ibn Ezra, Rabbi Abraham 146–7
identity, Jewish
    being a Jew: by birth 79–80
    being a Jew: by choice 81–5
    children of survivors 102
    chosenness 98–100
    gender equality 85–91
    inner definition 75–9
    Jewish education 83–4
    leaving the people 87–8
    mistake of the *mamzer* 97–8
    secularity 101–2
    sexual orientation 93–4
Illustrated Sunday Herald 121
image of God 198–9, 278
imitatio dei 198–9
impartiality of God 211–12
inequality in Israel and Judah 15
Inquisition 21
intellectual leadership and Judaism 52–3
International Rescue Committee, NY
    225
Interpretation in Judaism 97–8, 140–4,
    153–64, 176, 181–8, 209, 265–6,
    303
    see also midrash
intersectionality 96–7
Iraq 118, 122, 124
Isaac, binding of 160–1, 213, 233
Isaiah 14–15, 99, 175, 206–7, 209, 289,
    305–6
Islam 19–21, 32, 39–40, 107–8, 109, 122,
    132, 289
Ishmael, Rabbi 261, 266–7, 269, 280

Israel (as Land) 10–11, 15, 27–8, 31, 46, 69, 88
  the Balfour Declaration 120–2
  the five rights 128–34
  Judaism and the Land 106–11, 128–32
  Mizrahi Jews 122–3, 128
  recognition of the State of Israel 124–6
  triumph and tragedy 126–8
  Zionism 111–17
    and Britain 118–20, 123–4
  see also exile – galut
Israel (as People) 73–8
  acquisition of Jewish identity 79–85
  definition 78–9
  uniqueness of Jewish identity 75–9
  'who is a Jew?' 69, 75–7

Jacobs, Rabbi Louis 97–8, 146–7, 148, 150–1, 238, 280, 290–1, 293
jaliya 20
Jeremiah 14–15, 16, 162, 209–10, 259, 267
Jerusalem 11, 12, 16, 18, 19, 106–8, 109, 110, 118, 120, 123, 131, 138
Jerusalem Talmud 37, 74, 110
Jesus 48, 132, 140, 180, 233, 291
Jewish and Homosexual (W. Greengross) 93–4
Jewish Community Secondary School (JCoSS) 76, 77
Jewish Enlightenment 41
Jewish Religious Union 90
Jewish year 12–14, 16, 17
Jews' Free School (JFS) 75, 76–7
Job 33, 244, 246, 248–9, 260
Jonah 211, 307
Jonas, Hans 62, 214–16, 223, 224, 272–3, 274, 280, 282
Jonas, Rabbi Regina 91
Jordan 124
Jordan, crossing the 10
Joshua ben Levi, Rabbi 198, 303, 308

Joshua, book of 290
Josiah, King 161
Josipovici, Gabriel 158–9
journeying 7, 8
  the first stage 8–9
  the second stage 10–17
  the third stage 18–23
  the fourth stage 24–7
  the fifth stage 27–8
  after the Shoah 27–8
  Babylon 20–3
  Eastern Europe 22–3
  Imperial Russia 23
  liminality 29–32
  North America 23, 26–7
  paradigm shifts 10, 18–19, 28
  paradox 32–3
  pluralism 35–6
  provisionality 28–9
  the Shoah 27–8
  Spain 20–2
  three pilgrim festivals 12–14
  uncertainty 33–4
Jubilee Year 200
Judah 11, 15, 16, 17, 138
Judaism USP 65, 138–43
Judea 19, 128
Judeo-phobia 21
Judges, book of 89
June War (1967) 232
justice, social and economic 15–16, 206–9, 219–22
JW3 community centre 101–2

Kabbalah 109, 269–72
Kafka, Franz 12, 33
Kahn-Harris, Rabbi Deborah 92
Kahneman, Daniel 34
Kalischer, Rabbi Zvi Hirsch 84
Kant, Immanuel 254
Kaplan, Rabbi Mordecai 250
Karaites 145
Kaufman, Walter 237
Kepler 40–1

Khazars 78
Khmelnitsky, Bogdan 261–2
kibbutzniks 115, 116
Kierkegaard, Søren 160
King James Bible 47–8
Kingdom of Himyar 19
Kings, book of 161, 301–2
Kishinev pogrom (1903) 263–4
Koestler, Arthur 78
kol yisrael areivim zeh bazeh 213
Kook, Rav 116, 117, 130
K'tuvim 16
Kuhn, Thomas 10, 40
Kulturschock, 54–7, 214
Küng, Hans 41
Kuzari 99

Labour Brigade 115–16
Labour Party 67, 68, 106, 132–3
Lamentations Rabbah 172, 241, 261
Law of Return 88
Laytner, Rabbi Anson 260–1
Lazarus, Emma 27
League of Nations (1923) 122
Lebanon 118, 122, 124
Leigh, Rabbi Michael 169
Leo Baeck College 54–5, 56–7, 90–1,
        94, 102, 133, 169, 232–3
lesbians 91, 93–4, 95–6
Levinas, Emmanuel 212–14
Leviticus 14, 176, 199, 200, 212
Lévy, Bernard-Henri 67, 100
leyning 140–1
LGBTQ+ community 93–6
Liberal Judaism 25, 86, 87, 90–1, 179
Liberal Movement, British 86,
        87, 179
life after death 289–98
liminality and Judaism 29–32
Lithuania 22, 23
Littmann, Dr Ellen 55, 233
Lithuanian Orthodoxy 116–17
liturgy 140–2, 282–4, 299
L'kha Dodi 109

Lloyd George, David 119
Lot's wife 10
'love your neighbour' (Leviticus 19.18)
        212
Löwy, Michael 255
Lubavitch Hasidim 310
Luria, Isaac 109, 269
Lurianic Kabbalah 270–2
Lydda, Israel 116

Maccabees 17, 290
Magee, Bryan 64, 148
Magen David 131
Magonet, Rabbi Jonathan 283, 294
Maimonides (Rabbi Moses ben
        Maimon) 99, 108, 116, 175–6,
        185, 223, 289, 291–2, 308
Malachi 205, 302
mamzer 97–8
MANNA Platform 294–5
Mappah 185
Marcus, Josephine 'Sadie' 26
Margalit, Avishai 78, 97, 218
Marmot, Michael 52, 204, 221–2, 300
Marmur, Rabbi Dow 27–8, 131–2, 206,
        230
Marx, Karl 111, 311
Marxism 111–12, 256
Masoretes 139
Masorti Movement 97–8, 150, 187
matrilineal principle 80
Matthew's Gospel 49, 81–2, 180
Matthew's Passion 49, 67
Maybaum, Rabbi Ignaz 56–7, 100, 102,
        233, 266
Mecca 19
meditation 237–8
Mediterranean Diaspora 19
Meir, Rabbi 12, 279, 281
Mendelssohn, Moses 41, 48–9, 101
Mendenhall, George 166–7, 168
merchants, Jewish 20
Mesopotamia 15
Mesopotamian Gilgamesh 158

Messiah 292, 300, 303, 304–6, 307, 308–10

Messianic Age 292, 307, 308–10, 311–12

metaphystory 155

mezuzah 139

Micah 175, 210–11, 306–7

Middleburgh, Rabbi Charles 224

midrash, *midrashim* 19, 139, 160, 178–9, 241, 266

  see also interpretation

Miliband, David 224–5

Miller, Rabbi Alan 206, 230, 232

miracles 276–7

mishkan 189

Mishnah 77, 80, 107, 110, 143, 144, 184–5, 186

  Sanhedrin 96, 180–1, 196–8

Mishneh Torah 185

Mitnagdim 23

mitzvah/mitzvot 174–8, 187, 199, 281

Mizrahi Jews 122–3, 128, 252

Modern Orthodox Judaism 176, 187

modernity, definitions

  modern 45

  western 45

  civilization 45–7

  culture 45–7

  environment 46–7

  terrain 46–7

modernity, Judaism and 40 53, 57

Montagu, Edwin 119–20

Montagu, Lily 90

Montefiore, Simon Sebag 107, 109

Moses 9, 10, 12, 89, 105, 143–4, 146–7, 149, 156, 174, 176, 205, 253, 261, 265, 279–80

Muhammad 19, 122

Muslims 108, 122–3, 129, 133

Mussolini, Benito 44

mysticism, Jewish 269–72

Nachmanides (Rabbi Moses ben Nachman) 246

Nagel, Thomas 203–4

Nakhshon son of Amminadav 12

Nathan (Prophet) 14

Nation State Act (2018) 125

Nazis 27, 124, 216, 234, 256

nefesh 293–4

Nehemiah 138–9

neuroscientists 203

New Atheism (Four Horsemen of) 62, 162, 229, 275–6

New Testament 17, 47–8, 123

New Year, Jewish 16

Newman, Rabbi Jeffrey 223

Nissenson, Hugh 309

Noah 166–7

North West Surrey Synagogue 81

Northern Kingdom of Israel 11

Nozick, Robert 219

Numbers 9, 14

Office of Chief Rabbi 76

Omar, Caliph 107–8

Omar II, Caliph 108

omnipotence of God 242–3, 265–9

oppression in Western society 94–7

Oral Torah 36, 144–6, 188–9

Orthodox Jewry 25, 40, 41, 75–7, 81, 84–5, 87, 91, 116–17, 149–51, 176, 179, 187, 189, 236, 283

Ostrer, Harry 52

Ottoman Empire 21–2, 108–9, 118, 120, 122–3

Owen, Wilfred 160

Oz, Amos 8

Pale of Settlement 23, 51, 113

Palestine 106, 110, 112, 114, 115, 116, 117, 119–20, 123, 128

  Arab State of 124, 127–8, 132

paradigm shift (Thomas Kuhn) 10

paradox and Judaism 32–3

pariah 147–9, 216

parity model of covenant 166, 168, 169–70, 177, 278–81

partners/partnership, God and
　　humanity as 278–81
patriarchy, questioning Jewish 89–93
patrilineality 86
peace, the goal of 210–11
Peoplehood 2, 32, 79–83, 96, 250
Pepys, Samuel 140
Persian Diaspora 16
Persian Empire 16, 107, 138
Pesach/Passover 12–13, 16,
　　110, 304
Petuchowski, Rabbi Jacob 264
the Pharisees 291
Phillips, Adam 55–6
Philo 17, 82
philosophy 64–6
Pilgrim Festivals 12–14
Pinchas 159
Pinker, Stephen 61, 203
Pinkser, Leon 113
Pinto, Diana 133
Pirkei Avot 5, 71, 143–4
Pittsburgh Synagogue shooting 34
Plaskow, Judith 89–90
Plato 311
pluralism and Judaism 35–7
Polish-Lithuanian Commonwealth
　　22–3
politics, ancient Great Power 10–11,
　　15, 17
Popper, Karl 201, 311
Portugal 45, 46, 108, 147
post-halakhic Judaism 191–3
post-modern Jewish ethics 217–18
　　addressing poverty 222–3
　　consumerism 220–1
　　David Miliband 224–5
　　environmental, 223–4
　　health and life-expectancy 221–2,
　　　226
　　Jeffrey Sachs 222–3
　　Michael Marmot 221–2
　　Michael Sandel and Peter Singer
　　　218–20

refugees 224–5
social and economic injustice
　　218–23
Zigmunt Bauman 220–1
post-modern world 57–8
　　communications 58–9
　　economics 59–60
　　philosophy 64–6
　　science and technology 60–4
Postmodernism 65–6, 94–7
Pound, Ezra 44
poverty, addressing 222–3
power, abuse of 94–7
prayer 18–19, 110, 169, 196, 239–40,
　　283
Priests 18–19, 144, 161
Priesand, Rabbi Sally 91
printing press, invention of the 185
Progressive Jewish day schools 75, 77
Progressive Judaism 77, 85–6, 91, 133–4,
　　147, 236, 271, 282–3, 308
Promised Land 10, 15–16, 29, 161–2
　　see also Israel
promissory model covenant 166–7,
　　168, 176, 206
Prophetic Literature 14–16, 48, 205–12,
　　254, 259–60, 277, 302–8, 311–12
　　see also individual books by name
Prosbol 181–3
provisionality and Judaism 28–9
Przemysl, Austro-Hungarian Empire
　　25–6, 102, 231
Psalms 260
Ptolemy 17
Public Square function 225–6
Pumbedita, Babylon 20
Purim 17
Putnam, Hilary 213–14, 255

Rabbinic Academies, Lithuania 23, 116,
　　184, 212
Rabbinic Academies of Babylon 20
Rabbinic Judaism 18–9, 52–3, 80, 83,
　　89, 97, 107, 110, 143–5, 149,

151–2, 157–8, 176, 178–9, 184–5, 223, 242, 277, 291, 293, 303–4
Rabbinic Literature 12–13, 74, 83, 143–4, 179, 261, 266, 291
  classical Rabbinic ethics 195–204
  see also Torah; individual books by name
Race Relations Act (1976) 76–7
Race, Rev Alan 230
Rashi 9, 32
Rawls, John 218
Rayner, Rabbi John 179, 186, 188
Reagan-Thatcher governments 218
redemption 281–2, 286–7
reductionism, scientific 61–4
Reed Sea 12–13, 105, 277
Reform Bet Din 81
Reform Jewry 25, 41, 56, 76, 81, 86–7, 90–1, 93–4, 137, 141, 148, 149, 169, 179–80, 186–7, 205, 206, 282–4, 294–5
Reform Movement, British 86–7, 93–4, 282–4
Reformation of the Church 43–4, 45
refugees 224–5
resurrection 289–92
retrojection 162
revelation *see* Torah
Revisionist Zionists 124
Ricoeur, Paul 65
ritual and conversion 83–4
Roman Empire 17, 18, 19, 80, 252, 261, 266, 308
Rosenzweig, Franz 64–5, 131, 169
Rosh Hashanah 16, 138–9, 160
Rothko, Mark 53
Rothschild, Lionel Walter 119, 120
Rubenstein, Richard L. 242–3
Rufeisen, Oswald 88
Russia 23, 115, 118, 120, 121
Ruth, book of 78–9, 80, 83, 281
Ruth the Moabite 32, 78–9, 89, 110
Ruttenberg, Rabbi Danya 92

Sabbatical Year 181–3
Sachs, Jeffrey 222–3
Sacks, Chief Rabbi Jonathan 73, 148, 151–4, 157
sacrificial system 18, 19, 160
Safed 108, 269, 272
Salih, Sarah 95
Samuel, book of 167, 276
Samuel, Herbert 119
Sandel, Michael 218–19
Saperstein, Rabbi Marc 271
Sapiens (Y. N. Harari) 63
Sarah (Sarai) 9, 11, 20, 88, 159
Sarah, Rabbi Elli Tikvah 89, 91
Schama, Simon 7, 16, 138–9, 157
Schneerson, Rabbi Menachem Mendel 310
Scholem, Gershom 118, 269–70, 271–2
schools, Jewish 75–7
Schulweis, Rabbi Harold 99–100
science and religion 61–4
science and technology 60–4
Second Coming 21
  see also Messiah; Messianic Age
Second World War 88, 124, 215, 255
  see also Shoah (Holocaust)
Secular Judaism 101–2
secularism 42–4, 204, 226, 278
Seder 110, 122, 235, 300, 304
Seeskin, Kenneth 248–9
Seleucus 17
Sen, Amartya 218
Sennacherib King of Assyria 77
Sephardi Jews 21, 26, 129
Septimus Severus 107
Septuagint 17
services, Jewish 68, 81, 110, 140–2, 282–4
sexual orientation 93–4
Shabbat 30, 68, 109, 110, 140, 141, 183–4, 189, 280
Shabbetai Zvi 23, 109
Shalosh R'galim 12–14

shalshelet hakabbalah 8
Shammai 82
Shammai, Bet 35–7, 177, 82
Shavit, Ari 92–3, 105, 115, 127, 129, 134
Shavuot/Pentecost 13–14, 16
Sherwin, Rabbi Byron 198, 247–8,
    268–9
Sh'khinah, Divine presence, emanation
    267, 271–2, 279, 281, 292
Sh'ma 186, 277, 286
Sh'mitah 181–3
Shoah (Holocaust) 26, 27–8, 31, 44,
    102–3, 124, 129, 171–4, 212–
    14, 215–17, 231, 233, 238–9,
    242–6, 251, 254, 257–8, 266,
    277
Shulkhan Arukh 84, 109, 185, 186, 189
Shulman, Rabbi Sheila 91
Sh'virat ha'keilim 270–1
Siddur 47, 179–80, 283–4
sidrot 140
Simkhat Torah 140
Simlai, Rabbi 174–5, 179
Sinai, Mount 13, 155–9, 167–8, 171–2,
    174–6
Singer, Peter 219–20
s'mikhah 90–1, 234, 238, 243
social and economic justice 15–16,
    206–9, 218–23
social media 58–9
Sodom and Gomorrah 10, 93, 196, 259
Soetendorp, Rabbi Awraham 223
Solomon, King 11
Solomon, Rabbi Norman 40
the soul 293–4
'sovereign self' 73
Spain 20–2, 108, 269
Spinoza, Baruch 147–9, 152, 153
Stalin, Joseph 27, 54
Steinberg, Rabbi Milton 74
Steiner, George 130
Sternberg, Sigmund 49
Stonier, Tom 60
'Suffering God' 241–2, 267–8

sukkah 14
Sukkot/Tabernacles 13–14, 16, 30
Supreme Court, British 76–7
Sura, Babylon 20
suzerainty model of covenant 166, 167,
    169, 171, 176
synagogue 110, 137–8
Syria 118, 122, 124

Tabick, Rabbi Jacqueline 90–1
takkanot 184–5
Tallis, Raymond 61
Talmud 12, 23, 35–6, 74, 83, 84, 93,
    142–3, 144, 170–1, 174–5,
    178–9, 184–5, 186, 201, 202,
    261, 276, 279–80
Tanakh 16, 88, 171, 199, 276, 290,
    302
Tarfon, Rabbi 181, 201
Taylor, Charles 42–4, 46
tefillah 186
tefillin 139
Tel Aviv's rubbish dump 252–3
Temple (First), Jerusalem 11, 138, 172,
    241
Temple (Second), Jerusalem 12, 18, 19,
    102, 138, 171, 172, 242, 266
Temple Mount 107–8
Ten Commandments – *Asseret Hadibrot*
    35, 167, 174–6
Terezin death camp 49, 234
'The Holy Ledger' (A. Brody) 263
The Times 49, 132
theodicy 246–8
thick and thin relationships 78
third presence, modernity 39–40
Thirteen Principles of Faith 289,
    291–2
Thomas, Keith 296–8
Three Foot festivals 12–14
tikkun 271–2, 300
Titus, Emperor 19
Torah 10, 13, 16, 18, 19, 28–9, 33, 35, 37,
    48, 69, 82, 89, 90, 93, 97, 100,

110, 128–9, 276–7, 279, 281, 302–3
dark texts 159–63
difficulty of hermeneutics 188–9
Dual Torah 142–55
Jonathan Sacks 151–5
Louis Jacobs 150–1
min ha-Shamayim 145–59
mitzvah 174–8
Prophetic ethics 205–12
Rabbinic ethics 195–204
revelation, Sinai 155–9
Samson Raphael Hirsch 149–50
significance and interpretation 138–64
Spinoza: iconoclast and pariah 147–9
the Voice of God 156–8
see also covenant theology; halakhah; Prophetic Literature; Rabbinic Literature
totalitarianism 217
tribes of Israel 11, 14
tsimtsum 270, 273, 274
Tu BiSh'vat 110

Ukraine 22
Umayyads 107–8
uncertainty and Judaism 33–4, 158–9
Unitarianism 242
United Nations 124, 129
United States of America 23, 26–7, 31, 46, 50–1, 114, 120
see also American Jewry
United Synagogue 69, 76, 151
Utopianism 311

van der Zyl, Rabbi Werner 55
Verdi, Requiem 49
Voice of God 156–8
volcanic eruption, Santorini 155
von Harnack, Adolf 234

Walzer, Michael 85
Ward, Keith 65
Wardrop, John 120–1

Water Gate, Jerusalem 138–9
Weizmann, Chaim 119, 120
Werblowski, Zvi 309
West London Synagogue, Marble Arch 47, 55, 91
Western civilization 41–7, 50
Western culture
contribution to the modern world 50–1, 53
and Judaism (before 1500) 47–8
and Judaism (from 1800 to 1945) 48–50
post-modern world 57–66
Wiesel, Elie 135, 173, 257–8, 310
Wittenberg, Rabbi Jonathan 141
Wittgenstein, Ludwig 255
World Union for Progressive Judaism 133–4, 252
Written Torah 144, 145–6
see also Torah

Yahadut 80
Yathrib 19
Yemen 19
Yerushalmi (Jerusalem Talmud) 198
Yeshua 138
YHWH (Tetragrammaton) 15
Yitzhak, Rabbi Levi 262, 285
Yitzhaki (aka Rashi), Rabbi Shlomo 9, 32
Yokhanan ben Zakkai, Rabbi 157, 183, 308
Yom Kippur 16, 149

Zera, Rabbi 185
Zerubbabel 138
Zion 11, 110, 111, 113, 130, 210
Zionism 111–16
Balfour Declaration 120–2
and Britain 118–20
and Judaism 116–18
recognition of the State of Israel 124–6
Zohar 69

A Note on the Author

Rabbi Professor Tony Bayfield CBE, DD (Cantuar) was born in London, educated at Royal Liberty Grammar School, Romford and read Law at Cambridge. He received *s'mikhah*, rabbinic ordination at Leo Baeck College.

A pioneering contributor to Reform Judaism in Britain, he was the founding rabbi of North West Surrey Synagogue, first Director of the Sternberg Centre for Judaism in North West London and founder editor of the Journal *MANNA* from 1983 to 2011. From 1995 to 2010 he was Chief Executive, then professional Head of the Movement for Reform Judaism. He has long taught at Leo Baeck College where he is Professor of Jewish Theology and Thought.

A leading figure in the methodology and theology of dialogue between the Abrahamic Faiths, he is responsible for four books, the most recent being *Deep Calls to Deep* (2017). He is only the third Jew ever to have received a Doctorate in Divinity from the Archbishop of Canterbury.

He and his late wife Linda have three children and six grandchildren. He lives with his partner Jacqueline Fisher in London.

Cover Artwork: Mark Rothko, Untitled, c. 1950–2

The son of a militantly secularist Jewish refugee from Russian Latvia, Mark Rothko came to paint the search for meaning – grappling with the human condition, offering what his own son calls 'windows on the soul'. Yet his most famous works are housed in a chapel and he took his own life. Rothko's story is integral to the one explored in *Being Jewish Today*: the paradox of harrowing anguish and glorious artistic contribution epitomizes those whom this book refers to as 'champagne Jews'.

A Note on the Type

The text of this book is set in Bembo, which was first used in 1495 by the Venetian printer Aldus Manutius for Cardinal Bembo's *De Aetna*. The original types were cut for Manutius by Francesco Griffo. Bembo was one of the types used by Claude Garamond (1480–1561) as a model for his Romain de l'Université, and so it was a forerunner of what became the standard European type for the following two centuries. Its modern form follows the original types and was designed for Monotype in 1929.